Massachusetts Historical Society

Founded 1791

COLLECTIONS

VOLUME 77

Committee of Publication

GEORGE FOOT MOORE
CHESTER NOYES GREENOUGH
HENRY WINCHESTER CUNNINGHAM
GARDNER WELD ALLEN
WORTHINGTON CHAUNCEY FORD

IN CONGRESS

The DELEGATES of the UNITED COLONIES of *New-Hampshire*, *Massachusetts-Bay*, *Rhode-Island*, *Connecticut*, *New-York*, *New-Jersey*, *Pennsylvania*, the Counties of *New-Castle*, *Kent* and *Sussex* on *Delaware*, *Maryland*, *Virginia*, *North-Carolina*, *South-Carolina*, and *Georgia*,

TO All unto whom these Presents shall come, send GREETING: KNOW YE

THAT we have granted, and by these Presents do grant Licence and Authority to *Daniel Hathorne*, Mariner, Commander of the *Schooner called the Sturdy Beggar* of the Burthen of *Ninety* Tons, or thereabouts, belonging to *Jonas Nathan Hy____ and ____ of Salem* in the Colony of *the Massachusetts Bay*, mounting *five* Carriage Guns, and navigated by *Sixty* Men, to fit out and set forth the said *Schooner* in a warlike Manner, and by and with the said *Schooner*, and the Crew thereof, by Force of Arms, to attack, seize, and take the Ships and other Vessels belonging to the Inhabitants of Great-Britain, or any of them, with their Tackle, Apparel, Furniture and Ladings, on the High Seas, or between high-water and low-water Marks, and to bring the same to some convenient Ports in the said Colonies, in Order that the Courts, which are or shall be there appointed to hear and determine Causes civil and maritime, may proceed in due Form to condemn the said Captures, if they be adjudged lawful Prize; the said *Daniel Hathorne* having given Bond, with sufficient Sureties, that Nothing be done by the said *Schooner*, or any of the Officers, Mariners or Company thereof contrary to, or inconsistent with the Usages and Customs of Nations, and the Instructions, a Copy of which is herewith delivered to him. And we will and require all our Officers whatsoever to give Succour and Assistance to the said *Daniel Hathorne* in the Premises. This Commission shall continue in Force until the Congress shall issue Orders to the Contrary.

Dated at *Watertown* the *1st* of *August* 1776.

By Order of the Congress,

John Hancock PRESIDENT.

A Privateersman's Commission

MASSACHUSETTS PRIVATEERS of the REVOLUTION

Gardner Weld Allen

HERITAGE BOOKS
2010

HERITAGE BOOKS
AN IMPRINT OF HERITAGE BOOKS, INC.

Books, CDs, and more—Worldwide

For our listing of thousands of titles see our website
at
www.HeritageBooks.com

A Facsimile Reprint
Published 2010 by
HERITAGE BOOKS, INC.
Publishing Division
100 Railroad Ave. #104
Westminster, Maryland 21157

Originally published
Boston:
Massachusetts Historical Society
1927

— Publisher's Notice —
In reprints such as this, it is often not possible to remove blemishes from the original. Also, page 34/35 is missing from this book, as it was missing from the original edition. We feel the contents of this book warrant its reissue despite these blemishes and hope you will agree and read it with pleasure.

International Standard Book Numbers
Paperbound: 978-0-7884-0965-3
Clothbound: 978-0-7884-8379-0

ILLUSTRATIONS

A Privateersman's Commission . . . . *Frontispiece*
    State Archives, **166**, 72.

Letter urging the Need of Armed Vessels . . . . *facing page* 20
    State Archives, **193**, 277.

Petition for a Commission for a Vessel which has already taken Prizes without one 32
    State Archives, **165**, 477.

Bond of a Whaler 38
    State Archives, **139**, 65.

A State Bond 44
    State Archives, VII, 204.

Inquiry as to Disposal of Prisoners 56
    Massachusetts Historical Society, Pickering Papers, XXXIII, 138.

Bond not to recruit in any Town which has not raised its Quota for the Continental Army 66
    State Archives, **139**, 127.

The First Massachusetts Privateer Bond in the Revolution . 86
    State Archives, VII, 48.

Petition for a Letter of Marque 100
    State Archives, **167**, 17.

Petition for Liberty to sail notwithstanding Embargo . . . 126
    State Archives, **166**, 115.

Warrant for Impressment of a Vessel for the Penobscot Expedition 152
    State Archives, **145**, 8.

Bond not to enlist New Englanders other than those of Massachusetts 164
    State Archives, **139**, 141.

ILLUSTRATIONS

nd not to enlist Continental Soldiers 180
    State Archives, **139**, 158.
nd for a Voyage to Salem with Military Stores 212
    State Archives, **209**, 53.
Continental Bond in the Library of Congress 244
    Papers of the Continental Congress, **196**, XII, 23.
tition for a Letter of Marque for a Vessel of the State Navy 254
    State Archives, **166**, 195.
signment of Prize Money 264
    Massachusetts Historical Society, Nathan Dane Papers.
fidavit concerning a Vessel taken by the British. 284
    Massachusetts Historical Society, Dolbeare Papers.
Continental Bond 304
    State Archives, VII, 199.
fidavit as to the American Ownership of a Vessel 324
    Massachusetts Historical Society, Dolbeare Papers.

MASSACHUSETTS PRIVATEERS
OF THE REVOLUTION

INTRODUCTION

IT WOULD be difficult to determine when licensed privateering began in Europe, but it was probably not earlier than the thirteenth century. Private armed ships roamed the sea long before national navies were organized, but they were unregulated and irresponsible in very early times. Their crews were ready to fight against the enemies of their country when at war, or against pirates. They were perhaps not always averse to piracy themselves in time of peace, when there were no national enemies to pursue. The Royal Navy of England seems to have had its beginnings during the reign of King John; at least it is known that the king then had his own ships. It was long after John's time, however, before anything like a navy of real force existed; and national defense, therefore, continued to depend chiefly upon private enterprise. Privateering was extensively carried on by other nations as well, especially France and the Netherlands.[1]

The right of the crown to all prizes and captured goods was always unquestioned, but as a matter of justice, or for the encouragement of the sea-rovers and to stimulate their exertions in worrying the enemy, it was the part of wisdom to grant to the captor a share in his prize. What is presumably the oldest British document relating to such affairs, a grant of this sort issued in 1205, reads as follows: "The King to all to whom these presents shall come, Greeting. Know ye that we have granted to the crews of the galleys, which

---

[1]. Marsden, *Law and Custom of the Sea* (Publications of the Navy Records Society, XLIX), I, Introduction; *English Historical Review*, XXIV (Oct. 1909), 675.

Thomas of Galway has sent to us, one half of the gains which they may make in captures from our enemies; and we will, besides, recompense them for their service . . . in such sort that they shall be well satisfied." [1]

The earliest mention of letters of marque or reprisal appears in a document of 1293, though they were probably used before that.[2] Such letters were sometimes granted to individuals who had been robbed, allowing them to make reprisals against the robbers or their countrymen, until the value of the stolen property had been made good. In 1295 the vessel of Bernard Dongresilli, lying peacefully in a harbor of Portugal, was seized by "certain sons of perdition coming out from Lisbon," who

carried off the whole to the aforesaid city of Lisbon. And, of all the goods so spoiled and carried off, the King of Portugal received for his own use a tenth part; and the rest of the goods the robbers divided amongst themselves. . . . And we, considering the wickedness of the aforesaid robbers, in committing this spoil in time of peace, and having seen a letter under the seal of the council of Bayonne aforesaid, by which the mayor, jurats, and council, after having taken trustworthy proofs thereon, signify to our lord, the King,[3] the truth of the premises, yielding to the prayer of the said merchant, have given and granted and now give and grant to him, Bernard, his heirs, successors, and posterity, liberty to make reprisals upon people of the realm of Portugal, and particularly upon those of the city of Lisbon aforesaid, and upon their goods, wheresoever he may find them, whether within the dominion of our lord, the King and Duke, or without, [and] to retain and keep them for himself, until he and his heirs or successors or posterity shall be fully satisfied for [the loss of] his goods so spoiled as aforesaid, or their value as declared above, together with expenses reasonably incurred by him in that behalf. . . . We, therefore, approving and ratifying the above licence, confirm the same by virtue of these presents, so nevertheless that in case satisfaction shall be made to the said Bernard in the premises, reprisals shall thereupon cease, [and] there shall be no further keeping or appropriation [of

1. *Law and Custom of the Sea*, I, 1.   2. *Ibid.*, 19.
3. Edward I.

goods]; and if it shall happen that he shall have captured and shall keep anything beyond [the value of his loss], he shall be obliged to answer faithfully for such excess.[1]

The terms letters of marque, letters of reprisal, and letters of marque or (or *and*) reprisal were used indiscriminately for privateers' commissions and no distinction between them was made before the seventeenth century. These terms were not always used in commissions. The following, granted by Henry IV in 1404, is an example:

> The King to all and singular Admirals, captains, castellans, and to their lieutenants, and to keepers of ports of the sea and other maritime places, and to mayors, bailiffs, constables, provosts, and officers, and to masters and owners of ships, and mariners, and also to victuallers of ships, and to all other our lieges and subjects, whether on land or at sea, within liberties or without, to whom these presents shall come, Greeting. Know ye that we have granted and given leave to our well-beloved Henry Paye to sail and pass to the seas with as many ships, barges, and balingers of war, men-at-arms and bowmen properly equipped, as he may be able to provide himself with, to do all the hurt he can to our open enemies, as well for their destruction as for the safe guarding and defence of our faithful lieges, and for the safety of our realm. And therefore we command you, and each of you, that you supply the said Henry with ships, barges, and balingers, victuals, and all other things necessary and useful to him in this behalf, he paying for the same as shall be reasonably agreed between you and him; and that you be aiding, advising, and assisting to him, Henry, in the performance and execution of the premises, as beseems you. In witness, &c. These presents to endure according to our pleasure. Witness the King, &c.[2]

In the same reign letters of marque and reprisal against the inhabitants of Genoa were issued to a number of London Merchants. The document presents in detail the conditions and reasons involved and illustrates the forms used at that period:

1. *Law and Custom of the Sea*, 1, 38-41.   2. *Ibid.*, 112.

The King to all to whom these presents shall come, Greeting. Our well-beloved lieges William Waldern, Drugo Barantyn, Walter Cotton, John Reynewelle, William Flete, Thomas Brown, William Brekespere, John Glamville, John Sutton and their fellows, merchants of the city of London, have shown unto us that of late they, with our licence, despatched certain factors and attorneys of theirs with a great quantity of wools and other merchandise, to the value of 24,000 $l.$, shipped in divers ships, to be carried carefully and in safety by way of the Straits of Morocco to Western parts, there [to be sold] for the advantage and increase of our realm; and, to the end that the aforesaid ships so laden should have sure and safe passage, we caused our letters of recommendation to be sent to the Governors, worthies, and community of Genoa, which letters were, as we hear, duly presented to them by certain of the aforesaid factors; but they of Genoa, paying no regard at all to our letters aforesaid, and wickedly scheming, to the injury of the commonweal of our realm aforesaid, to hinder their passage, first of all detained the aforesaid ships, and afterwards compelled them to enter the harbour of Genoa, and, after their entry, spoiled them of the wools and merchandise aforesaid, and took them into their own hands, and sold them for their own use and profit; and, further, that the aforesaid factors were prevented from writing to their own magistrates upon the matter, and were, and now are, to the grievous hurt and injury of our said lieges, unable to get possession of any part of the aforesaid wools and merchandise, for their own support, or of any of the money arising from the sale thereof. Wherefore they have prayed us that we should think fit to issue to them our letters of marque and reprisal. And we, in compliance with their prayer, of our especial grace, and with the assent of our council, have, for ourselves and our heirs, given and granted to the aforesaid William, Drugo, Walter, John, William, Thomas, William, John, John, and their fellows aforesaid that they of themselves or by their deputies may seize, keep, and retain such and so many Genoese, or subjects or inhabitants of Genoa or the confines of Genoa, or their factors or agents, as they think fit, whether on this side of the sea or beyond it, and whether on land or sea, together with their ships, vessels, goods, and merchandise of what kind soever, until full restitution and satisfaction shall be made to them for the value of the aforesaid wools and merchandise, to the amount aforesaid, together with their costs, damages, outgoings, and expenses, which by fair estimate amount to the sum of 10,000 $l.$; and that they have liberty to put into execution or cause to be put into execution these present letters of marque and reprisal so often as they think fit, without hindrance by us or our heirs or by the Admirals of us or our heirs or by their lieutenants or other our officers or ministers whatsoever, [and that] notwithstanding any letters of safe-conduct granted or hereafter to be granted to the aforesaid Genoese, or subjects or inhabitants of Genoa or its confines, or their factors or agents, or anyone else of the country or territory of their community or confederacy. Moreover, we straitly command all and singular [our] Admirals, captains, castellans, and their lieutenants, customers, keepers of ports, keepers of the sea and sea coasts, sheriffs, mayors, bailiffs, constables, ministers and other our lieges and subjects, as well on this side of the sea as beyond it, that in the execution of the premises they be aiding, helping, and assisting to the aforesaid William, Drugo, Walter, John, William, Thomas, William, John, and John, and their fellows, as beseems them &c. In witness, &c. Witness the King at Westminster the 3rd day of February, [1413].

By the King himself and the council.[1]

The earliest bond or security for good behavior was given in 1486 by "the meyre, shiref, aldermen, and commonaltie of the town of Newcastell upon Tyne," who "covenaunted, promised, and granted to our said sovereyn lord the Kyng," that they would "take sufficient suretie of and for thowner, maister, or purcer of every ship English in the said town of Newcastell, to the double valew of the said ship, takyll, and vitayle of the same, that the mariners of the said ship shall, in the see and in the stremys of the same, kepe the peax agenst all the King's subjetts," etc.[2]

The recognizance of Captain John Hawkins, for £1000, for the good behavior of his ship, commissioned to search for contraband and to take pirates, is dated November 17, 1571:

The condicion of this recognizance is suche that, whereas Raffe Lane, Esquier, one of the Querries of her majesties stable, havinge speciall commission from her highnes to searche by hymself or his

1. *Law and Custom of the Sea*, I, 121.
2. *Ibid.*, 141. About this time the documents begin to be written in English. The earlier ones are translations from the Latin.

depute for wares prohibited to be transported withowte licence, hathe receyved from the right honorable the Lorde Clinton, Lorde highe Admirall aforesayde, commission to apprehende and take pirattes, and the same withe ther shippes, vessells, and goodes, to bringe into some harboroughe of this realme, there by perfect inventorye to be saffely kept, untill farder ordre from his Lordeshippe or this courte of Thadmiralltie shalbe prescribed therein. For whiche her highnes' service the bovesayde John Hawkyns, as depute of the saide Raffe Lane, ys to furnishe and sett furthe unto the seas one barcke. Yf, therefor, that the master, mariners, and all suche others as shalbe reteyned and serve in the sayde barcke, soe to be sett furthe by the saide John Hawkyns uppon the forsaide chardge and service, doe not transgresse, but observe, accomplishe, performe, and fulfill, the contentes of the sayde Lorde Admirall's commission for the seisinge uppon and takinge of pirattes, ther shippes and goodes, as is before expressed, according to the purporte, effect, and true meaninge thereof, and that the saide master, his mate, mariners, and companye goinge uppon the sayde service, ne anye of them, doe not robb, spoile, molest, ne evill entreate, anye of her Majestie's subjects, nor the subjectes of anye other prince withe whome her highnes ys in league and amitye, That then this recognizaunce to be voyde and of none effect; Or elles to stande in his full force strenght and vertue.

JOHN HAWKYNS.[1]

In early times the law of the sea was administered by the king in council or in the common law courts. Prize cases and the trial of pirates came before them. In the fourteenth century the admirals held local courts, but in the course of time they proved inefficient and expensive. Toward the end of the fourteenth century common law procedure had also shown itself inadequate for the administration of maritime law. The High Court of Admiralty was established at the beginning of the fifteenth century, but for the first hundred years or more was inactive as a prize tribunal. In later times, however, it became the supreme prize court; vice-admiralty courts were set up in the colonies and

---

1. *Law and Custom of the Sea*, I, 190.

plantations. In the eighteenth century, colonial governors were given commissions of vice-admiral, in time of war, with authority to hold court and condemn prizes or to appoint vice-admiralty judges for the purpose.[1]

During the seventeenth century and later, privateering continued prosperously and played an important part in naval warfare. Letters of reprisal were no longer issued to individuals for the redress of private grievances. The decline of French naval power after defeat at La Hogue in 1692 was slow and gradual and the respect of the English and Dutch for the great French admiral, Tourville, caused them to keep their fleets together instead of scattering in pursuit of hostile cruisers preying upon their commerce; and the French took advantage of their opportunity. As their naval ships were laid up in port, their crews, both officers and men, were allowed to take service in private ships. Even ships of the royal navy of France were in some cases loaned to private adventurers and cruised in squadrons. These were the days of privateering on a grand scale, the days of Jean Bart and other great French privateersmen.[2]

As time went on and the American colonists grew in numbers, they took an increasing interest in privateering. The more enterprising and adventurous American merchants and seamen engaged in this pursuit whenever England was at war with other nations. American newspapers recount the fortunes of these sea-rovers.[3]

1. *Law and Custom of the Sea*, I, Introduction, 12, 81, 124, 254, 359, 360, 408, 470; Jameson, *Privateering and Piracy in the Colonial Period*, xi–xiii, 187, 275, 285, 312, 318, 355, 517, 519, 524.
2. Mahan, *The Influence of Sea Power upon History*, 193–196.
3. *Privateering and Piracy*, 276, 473, 503, 571. The very interesting journal of Captain Norton's sloop *Revenge* is in *Ibid.*, 380; many other privateering narratives will be found, mostly in court proceedings, in this volume. Instructions for privateers at different periods are in *Law and Custom of the Sea*, I, 197, 218, 236, 252, 410, 502, II (Navy Records Society, L), 403–435; *Privateering and Piracy*, 347.

In time of war the colonial governors, along with their judicial functions, were given authority to issue letters of marque or privateer commissions. During the war of 1739 with Spain, such a commission was granted to Captain Benjamin Norton, of Newport. This long document differs little from those of the fifteenth century, in contrast with the much briefer form used a generation later, during our Revolution. It is here quoted in full:

Richard Ward Esq Governour and Commander in Chief in and over his Majesty's Colony of Rhode Island and Providence Plantations in New England.

To all Persons, to whom these Presents shall come, Greeting.

Whereas his most Sacred Majesty George the Second, by the Grace of God of Great Britain, France, and Ireland King, Defender of the Faith, etc., hath been pleased by his Declaration of the nineteenth Day of October, in the year of our Lord One Thousand seven hundred Thirty and nine, for the Reasons therein contained, to declare War against Spain, And has given Orders for the granting Commissions to any of his loving Subjects, or Others that shall be deemed fitly qualified in that Behalf, for the apprehending, seizing and taking the Ships, Vessels and Goods belonging to Spain, or the Vassals and Subjects of the King of Spain, or others inhabiting within any of his Countries, Territories, and Dominions, and such other Ships, Vessels and Goods, as are or shall be liable to Confiscation Pursuant to the respective Treaties between his Majesty and other Princes, States and Potentates, and to bring the same to Judgment in the High Court of Admiralty in England, or such other Court of Admiralty as shall be lawfully authorized for Proceedings and Adjudication, and Condemnation to be thereupon had according to the Course of Admiralty and Laws of Nations.

And Whereas Benjamin Norton, Mariner, and John Freebody, Merchant, both of Newport in the Colony aforesd. have equipped, furnished, and victualled a Sloop called the *Revenge* of the Burthen of about One hundred and Fifteen Tons, whereof the said Benjamin Norton is Commander, who hath given Bond with sufficient Sureties.

Know Ye therefore That I do by these Presents, grant Commission to, and do license and authorize the said Benjamin Norton to set forth in Hostile Manner the said Sloop called the *Revenge* under his own Command, And therewith by Force of Arms (for the Space of Twelve Months from the Date hereof, If the war shall so long continue) to apprehend, seize and take the Ships, Vessels and Goods belonging to Spain, or the Vassals and Subjects of the King of Spain, or Others inhabiting within any of his Countries, Territories or Dominions, and such other Ships, Vessels and Goods, as are or shall be liable to Confiscation Pursuant to the respective Treaties between his Majesty and other Princes, States and Potentates, and to bring the Same to such Port as shall be most convenient, In order to have them legally adjudged in such Court of Admiralty as shall be lawfully authorized within his Majesty's Dominions, which being condemned, It shall and may be lawful for the said Benjamin Norton to sell and dispose of such Ships, Vessels and Goods so adjudged and condemned in such Sort and Manner as by the Course of Admiralty hath been accustomed (Except in such Cases where it is otherwise directed by his Instructions) Provided always That the said Benjamin Norton keep an exact Journal of his Proceedings, and therein particularly take Notice of all Prizes that shall be taken by Him, the Nature of such Prizes, the Times and Places of their being taken, and the Value of Them as near as He can judge; As also of the Station, Motion and Strength of the Enemy, as well as He or his Mariners can discover or find out by Examination of, or Conference with any Mariners or Passengers in any Ship or Vessel by Him taken, Or by any other Ways or Means whatsoever, touching or concerning the Enemy, or any of their Fleets, Ships, Vessels or Parties, and of what else Material in these Cases that may come to his or their Knowledge, of All which He shall from Time to Time as He shall have an Oportunity, transmit and give an Account unto me (or such Commander of any of his Majesty's Ships of War as He shall first meet with). And further Provided that Nothing be done by the said Benjamin Norton or any of his Officers, Mariners and Company contrary to the true meaning of the aforesaid Instructions, But that the said Instructions shall be by Them, as far as They or Any of Them are therein concerned, in all Particulars well and duly observed and performed, And I do beseech and request all Kings, Princes, Potentates, Estates and Republicks being his Majesty's Friends and Allies, and All Others to whom it shall appertain to give the said Benjamin Norton all Aid, Assistance and Succour in their Ports, with his said Sloop and Company and Prizes without doing, or suffering to be done to Him any Wrong, Trouble or Hindrance, His Majesty offering to do the like, when by Any of Them thereto desired, Requesting likewise of All his Majesty's Officers whatsoever to give Him Succour and Assistance as Occasion shall require.

Given under my Hand, and the Seal of said Colony, at Newport aforesaid the Second Day of June, Anno Dm. 1741, and in the Fourteenth Year of his said Majesty's Reign.

RICHARD WARD.

Sealed with the Seal of said Colony
by Order of His Honour the Governour
JAS. MARTIN, *Secry*.[1]

The commissioning of privateers by colonial governors removed them to a certain extent from home control and sometimes caused misunderstanding. In 1746 the Lords of the Admiralty wrote:

Your Lordship will please to observe that these complaints [by the Dutch] are not made against any of His Majesty's ships of war, but against privateers in America and the West Indies, over whom we have no influence, they receiving their commission for acting hostilities from the Governors of His Majesty's colonies abroad. And therefore we would humbly propose that in these and the like cases His Majesty would be pleased to send his directions to his said Governors, who alone have power to curb the insolencies of privatiers by calling their sureties to account, by revoking the commissions of such as are refractory, and by the influence of their power with the judges of the Vice Admiralty courts to prevent their proceeding to rash and unjust condemnation. . . .[2]

Massachusetts seamen took a leading part in the Louisburg Expedition of 1745 and American privateers were active during the Seven Years' War. An agreement drawn up between the captain and crew of the New York private armed brigantine *Mars* in 1762 reveals something of the sea customs of the time and life aboard a vessel of that sort. One half the proceeds of all prizes and prize goods belonged to the owners, the other half

---

1. *Privateering and Piracy*, 378; original, with accompanying documents, in Massachusetts Historical Society collections. A MS. letter telling how the letter of marque *Bethel*, of Boston, captured a Spanish ship of greatly superior force, in 1748, and a picture of the scene, are in the possession of the Society. The letter has been printed in *U. S. Naval Institute Proc.*, no. 200 (Oct. 1919), 1695.

2. *Law and Custom of the Sea*, II, 327.

to the crew. The division of the crew's portion is minutely provided for, the captain receiving six shares, the able seaman one share, and the others in proportion according to rank and rating. Those performing meritorious service were rewarded by extra shares and those disabled by wounds received money compensation, which, in case of death, went to their heirs. Punishment seems to have taken the form of fines or loss of shares and was inflicted for theft, desertion, cowardice, disobedience of orders, drunkenness, and profanity; and particularly. "whoever of the Company shall breed a Mutiny or Disturbance, or strike his Fellow, or shall Game with Cards or Dice for Money, or any Thing of Value, or shall sell any strong Liquors on board," or whoever shall "Assault, Strike or Insult any Male Prisoner, or behave rudely or indecently to any Female Prisoner . . . shall be punished as the Captain and Officers shall direct." [1]

Having served their apprenticeship in the trade of privateering in the various wars of the colonial period, American shipowners and mariners at the outbreak of the Revolution naturally turned to this method of harassing their enemy and profiting by the operation. The number of American privateers in commission during the war was large, certainly exceeding two thousand different vessels, and very many were commissioned more than once; some, several times. Massachusetts contributed a larger number than any other state.

The word "privateer" has commonly been used with entire disregard of its true meaning. At the period with which we are now concerned, persons with an understanding of maritime affairs constantly spoke of cruisers

---

1. *Privateering and Piracy*, 581–585. See Hough, *Reports of Cases in the Vice Admiralty of the Province of New York*. In Emmons, *Statistical History of the U.S. Navy*, 124–126, is a list, doubtless incomplete, of colonial privateers.

of the Continental Navy and the state navies as privateers and the term was often wrongly employed even in official correspondence. A privateer, strictly speaking, was a private armed vessel carrying no cargo and devoted exclusively to warlike use. Letters of marque, so called from the letters or privateer commissions they bore, were private armed cargo carriers authorized to take prizes. They were generally and less improperly called privateers, and in this study no attempt has been made to separate them; in fact, to do so would be impossible, since in most cases the information necessary for that purpose is lacking.

The sea power of America would probably have been more effective if part of the effort, money, and men expended in privateering had been devoted to organizing and maintaining a larger regular naval force. The Continental Navy was too weak to fight the British Navy with any hope of a fair share of success and therefore was for the most part limited in its operations to commerce-destroying. The state navies and the privateers were also, of course, devoted almost wholly to that form of warfare.

Privateering was in greater favor with seamen than the regular naval service on account of the comparative freedom from the restraints of discipline and because the profits were larger. Closer attention was paid to the matter of profits. The entire net proceeds from the sale of prizes and captured goods went to the owners and captors, which resulted in the crews getting a larger proportion of prize money than regular naval seamen, who were obliged to share with the government; the privateersmen, moreover, had higher pay. To frustrate the allurements of privateering it was several times necessary to lay an embargo on the sailing of these vessels until recruits in sufficient number had been obtained to man the Continental Navy and to fill the quota for the army. William Vernon, of the Eastern [Continental] Navy Board at Boston, wrote to John Adams, December 17, 1778, that the Continental ships in port "may sail in Three Weeks, if it was possible to get Men, wch we shall never be able to accomplish, unless some method is taken to prevent desertion and a stopage of Private Ships Sailing, until our ships are Mann'd. The infamous practice of seducing our Men to leave the ships and taking them off at an out Port, with many other base methods, will make it impossible ever to get our ships ready to Sail in force, or perhaps otherwise than single Ships." [1]

American privateersmen in general conducted themselves in an orderly manner. They gave the usual bonds for their behavior and if excesses were committed they must have been rare. The commonly expressed opinion that privateering was little better than piracy did not apply to these men. Nevertheless, their thoughts were bent on gain and at times patriotism doubtless languished accordingly. William Whipple, writing to Josiah Bartlett from Portsmouth, New Hampshire, July 12, 1778, says:

I agree with you that the privateers have much distressed the trade of our Enemies, but had there been no privateers, is it not probable there would have been a much larger number of Public Ships than has been fitted out, which might have distressed the Enemy nearly as much and furnished these States with necessaries on much better terms than they have been supplied by Privateers? ... No kind of Business can so effectually introduce Luxury, Extravagance and every kind of Dissipation, that tend to the destruction of the morals of people. Those who are actually engaged in it soon lose every Idea of right and wrong, and for want of an opportunity of gratifying their insatiable avarice with the property

1. *Publications R. I. Historical Society*, VIII, 256.

of the Enemies of their Country, will without the least compunction seize that of her Friends. . . . There is at this time five Privateers fitting out here, which I suppose will take 400 men. These must be by far the greater part Countrymen, for the Seamen are chiefly gone, and most of them in Hallifax Gaol. Besides all this, you may depend no public ship will ever be manned while there is a privateer fitting out. The reason is plain: Those people who have the most influence with Seamen think it their interest to discourage the Public service, because by that they promote their own interest, viz., Privateering.[1]

When Whipple speaks of seizing the property of friends, he alludes to the conduct of certain American privateers in seizing neutral vessels, generally in European waters. This reprehensible practice was afterwards corrected by stringent regulations. Privateering and speculating in the stock market had much in common and were open to the same objections. After the war, that is on December 9, 1783, John Pickering wrote to his brother, Colonel Timothy Pickering, that "there were many persons in Salem dejected on the return of peace, but a greater spirit of industry arises among the inhabitants than I expected to see, after the Idleness and dissipation introduced by the business and success of privateering." [2]

John Adams had a better opinion of this institution. In 1780 he wrote that "the feats of our American frigates and privateers have not been sufficiently published in Europe. It would answer valuable purposes, both by encouraging their honest and brave hearts and by exciting emulations elsewhere, to give them a little more than they have had of the fame they have deserved. Some of the most skillful, determined, persevering and successful engagements that have ever hap-

1. *Historical Magazine*, March, 1862. See Paullin, *The Navy of the American Revolution*, 145–148.
2. Pickering Papers, XVIII, 181.

pened upon the seas have been performed by American privateers against the privateers from New York." [1]

Contemporary letters give occasional glimpses of this phase of seafaring life. A British officer, a prisoner in Boston, has this to say of conditions at that place in May, 1777, as he observed them: "Boston harbour swarms with privateers and their prizes; this is a great place of rendezvous with them. The privateersmen come on shore here full of money and enjoy themselves much after the same manner the English seamen at Portsmouth and Plymouth did in the late war; and by the best information I can get there are no less than fifteen foreign vessels lately arrived in the harbour with cargoes of various articles." [2] James Warren wrote from the same place, August 15, 1776, to Samuel Adams: "The Spirit of Privateering prevails here greatly. The Success of those that have before Engaged in that Business has been sufficient to make a whole Country privateering mad. Many kinds of West india Goods, that we used to be told we should suffer for want of, are now plentier and cheaper than I have known them for many Years." [3]

All classes of vessels were engaged in privateering: ships, brigs, schooners, sloops, and boats. The largest carried twenty to twenty-four guns and a hundred and fifty or even two hundred men; the smallest a few swivels, or only small arms, and ten men or less. Whaleboats, sometimes with crews of twenty-four, were employed in Nantucket and Vineyard Sounds, but more commonly in waters south of New England. On November 14, 1775, very soon after the fitting out of

---

1. Wharton, *The Revolutionary Diplomatic Correspondence of the United States*, III, 650.
2. *London Chronicle*, July 3, 1777.
3. *Warren-Adams Letters*, II, 438.

private armed vessels had been legalized by the General Court of Massachusetts and before the business had got fairly started, James Warren wrote to John Adams:

> As to ships and other vessels, I believe there are great numbers very suitable to arm already on hand. Almost every port of any consequence could furnish more or less, either great or small. Perhaps ships might be difficult to find that could mount twenty guns or upwards; but vessels to carry from six to sixteen guns I think we abound in, and I think they would soon furnish us with others. These vessels are of all burthens, drafts of water, and dimensions, and are many of them excellent sailors, and may be either purchased, or hired, on very reasonable terms.[1]

The larger vessels made long voyages and cruised in foreign seas. The apprehensions of the British were aroused by privateering in their home waters. According to a report from Banff, Scotland, in the summer of 1777, "times are so troublesome and our seas so full of American privateers, that nothing can be trusted upon this defenceless coast; they have taken, within these few weeks, eight ships."[2] "It is true," says a contemporary chronicler,

> that the coasts of Great Britain and Ireland were insulted by the American privateers in a manner which our hardiest enemies had never ventured in our most arduous contentions with foreigners. Thus were the inmost and most domestic recesses of our trade rendered insecure, and a convoy for the protection of the linen ships from Dublin and Newry was now for the first time seen. The Thames also presented the unusual and melancholy spectacle of numbers of foreign ships, particularly French, taking in cargoes of English commodities for various ports of Europe, the property of our own merchants, who were thus seduced to seek that protection under the colours of other nations, which the British flag used to afford to all the world.[3]

Long before privateering had become regulated by law in Massachusetts, hostilities were conducted on the water. The vessels and boats engaged in such enter-

1. *Warren-Adams Letters*, I, 182.   2. *London Chronicle*, September 2, 1777.
3. *Annual Register*, XXI (1778), 36.

prises were of course not regularly commissioned, but they were usually fitted out by or under the authority of selectmen, committees of safety, or other local officials of some sort. The first episode of the kind in Massachusetts waters, as related by some writers, though on what authority is not quite certain, was the exploit of Captain Nathan Smith of Tisbury, Martha's Vineyard, in April, 1775. Setting out in a whaleboat Smith captured the armed schooner *Volante*, tender to the British cruiser *Scarborough*, probably in Homes Hole.[1]

Early in May, 1775, "we hear that an armed Vessel [H. M. sloop of war *Falcon*] a few Days ago, on some frivolous Pretence, took Possession of two other Vessels in the Vineyard Sound; on which the People fitted out two Vessels, went in Pursuit of them, retook and brought both into a Harbour, and sent the Prisoners to Taunton Gaol."[2] In Boston harbor, during the siege of the town, there were at times clashes between the people and the British soldiers over the possession of the cattle and sheep on the islands.

The capture of the British armed schooner *Margaretta* off Machias in June is well known. The hero of this event, Jeremiah O'Brien, in the sloop *Unity*, was assisted by Benjamin Foster in a small schooner. A month later O'Brien in the same sloop, renamed the *Machias Liberty*, and Foster in another vessel took two British vessels.

Another incident took place in October, in which the vessel engaged had presumably been sent out by local authorities at Beverly. The following is the story:

> Last Tuesday one of our Privateers from Beverly, having been on a Cruize in the Bay, was followed, on her Return into Port, by the *Nautilus* Man of War. The Privateer run aground in a Cove

1. Banks, *History of Martha's Vineyard*, I, 404, 405.
2. *N. E. Chronicle*, May 18, 1775.

a little without Beverly Harbour, where the People speedily assembled, stripped her and carried her Guns, etc., ashore. The Man of War was soon within Gunshot, when she also got aground; she however let go an Anchor and bringing her Broadside to bear, began to fire upon the Privateer. The People of Salem and Beverly soon returned the Compliment from a Number of Cannon on Shore, keeping up a warm and well directed Fire on the Man of War for two or three Hours, and it is supposed did her considerable Damage and probably killed and wounded some of her Men; but before they could board her, which they were preparing to do, the Tide arose about 8 o'Clock in the Evening, when she cut her Cable and got off. Some of her Shot struck one or two Buildings in Beverly, but no Lives were lost on our Side and the Privateer damaged very little, if any.[1]

In the spring of 1775 the first halting steps were taken towards the creation of some sort of sea force in Massachusetts. Whether those who gave their attention to the matter had in mind the commissioning of privateers or a colony fleet, or both, is not apparent. Perhaps they were not at first clear in their own minds as to details. The first action taken by the Provincial Congress was on June 7, when it was

Ordered, That the Hon. Col. [James] Warren, Mr. Pitts, Mr. Gerry, the president [Joseph Warren], Col. Freeman, Mr. Pickering, Mr. Batchelder, Hon. Mr. Dexter, and Mr. Greenleaf be a committee to consider the expediency of establishing a number of small armed vessels, to cruise on our sea coasts, for the protection of our trade and the annoyance of our enemies; and that the members be enjoined, by order of Congress, to observe secrecy in this matter.[2]

It seems likely that this action of the Provincial Congress may have been stimulated by an undated letter addressed to General Joseph Warren and signed S. L. A copy of this epistle was addressed to the Committee of Safety at Cambridge. The place from whence it was sent is unknown. The letter follows:

1. *N. E. Chronicle*, October 12, 1775.
2. *The Journals of each Provincial Congress of Massachusetts in 1774 and 1775.*

To the Honble Joseph Warren, President of the Massachusetts Bay Congress, in Watertown. ——— to be communicated &c &c

Hon'd Sir It appears to me & others, that there is wanted in this Government, sum Armed Vessels, to ward of the distressing Practicall Blows, that without Doubt will be struck, by Admirall Graves's small sloops, Men a War & tenders; by taking from us our inward bound Provisions, Molasses, Soft Vessels, &c &c as they have Don. Will allmost bring on a famin in our Army, & on the Inhabitance, for this government allways was illable to support itt selfe, with Provisions &c &c, and now her in it an Army to feed; Which Will soone be felt, and be distressing to the Inhabitance & by feare Will bring on discontent & Murmorings; Which may be attended with bad consequences, to the disadvantig. of our imbarkt in: even to be som=mended Common cause: so hope that by your Wise Counsells; you will be in=abled to gaird against every Evill, that might otherwise befall us, if we Wear not under the Guideonship of Providence & your Wise Counsells. —

I heer that there is a Ship allmost, or quite ready to Lanch at Dartmouth of about three Hundred tuns; that its Probable by information, Will be a good saler, and other convenyences; by strongthning her Doth sum hanging Knees, bulding a roundhous, & a toppgallant forecastell, &c: that Would carry upward of thirty guns, and fight the Major part of her men between Decks &c. and by inquerryis, its quite Probible, that there may be founde more good saleing Vessells; now hauld up; that Would in part answer our End for our defence: &c as being Provisions from our southern Governments for our support: and sum of them might be implyd in bringing Powder and guns, from sum parts of the Spanish & French Kingedoms: and might smugell sum from other Powders: and Salt Peeter, from others: Where we could not git it maid into Powder; and Make it heer; Which would be to our Advantige to have it Manufactied here. So wishing you the smyles of Heaven in all youre undertakings, in the defence of our Invaluble Libertys, &c &c. an Remain ———

Hon: Sir Yo'r Most Humble and
Devoted
fervent
S L

Letter urging the Need of Armed Vessels

To the Hon'ble Joseph Warren, President of the Massachusetts Bay Congress, in Wartertown — to be communicated to s'd Congress.

Hon'd Sir, — It appears to me and others that there is wanted in this Goverment sum Armed Vessels, to ward of the distressing Piraticull bloos, that without doubte will be struck by Adm'll Sam'll Graves's small Menawar and Tenders, by taking from us our inward bound Provisions, Molasses, and Solt Vessells, etc. etc; as they have don. Will allmost bring on a famin in our Armey, and on the Inhabitence; for this goverment allways was illable to support it selfe with Provisions, etc. etc; and now hes in it an Armey to feede which will soone be felt, and be distressing to itt's Inhabitence; and I feere will bring on discontent and Murmorings, which may be attended with bad consequences, to the disadvantig of our imbarkt in, ever to be Commended Common cause; so hope that by your Wise Counsells you will be inabled to gard against Every Evell that might otherwise befall us, if we ware not under the Gardeenship of Providence and your wise Counsells.

I here that there is a Ship allmost or quite ready to Lanch at Danvess, of about Three Hundred Tuns; that itt's Probable by information, will be a good saler and other convenyences; by strengthing her with sum hanging Knees, bulding a roundhous and a topgallant forecastell, etc, that would carey upwards of thurty guns and fight the Majer part of her men betwene decks, etc; and by inquiery's itt's quite Probable that there may be found prou'd good saling Vessells, now hawled up, that would in part answer our End for our defence and to bring Provisions from our southern Goverments for our support; and sum of them might be imply'd in bringing Powder and Guns from sum parts of the Spanish and French Kingdoms, and might smugell sum from other Powers, and solt Peeter, from Others, where we could not gitt it maid into Powder, and Make it here, which would be to our advantige to have it Manifactrid here. So wishing you the smyles of Heaven in all youre undertakings, in the defence of our Invaluble Libertys, etc. etc. and Remain. Hon'd Sir, Youre Most Humble, and Devoted Servent

S. L.[1]

For nearly two weeks this matter was before the Provincial Congress. Changes were made in the committee, its report (in the form of a resolve) was con-

---

1. Massachusetts Archives, **193**, 277, 289.

sidered and debated from time to time, and on June 20 was finally disposed of in the following manner:

> *Resolved*, That a Number of Armed Vessels not less than six, to mount from Eight to fourteen Carriage Guns and a proportionable Number of Swivels, etc., be with all possible dispatch provided, fixed and properly man'd to Cruise as the Committee of Safety or any other Person or Persons who shall be appointed by this Congress for that purpose shall from time to time order and direct, for the protection of our Trade and Sea Coasts against the depredations and Piracies of our Enemies and for their Annoyance and Capture or destruction.
> Order'd to subside for the present.[1]

There seems to have been at this time a decided reluctance, on the part of many, to adopt radical legislation of the sort proposed. All but the more advanced still regarded themselves as loyal British subjects. In the words of a writer dealing with this period: "To grant letters of marque and reprisal is the prerogative of the sovereign and for a colony to authorize such an act against its sovereign was certainly rebellious if not treasonable." [2]

No further action was taken by the Provincial Congress, which expired a month later upon the assembling of the Great and General Court on July 19. A petition dated the same day was submitted, but no report was made on it until August 18. Being one of the few contemporary documents preserved which indicate the trend of public opinion leading up to the legislation which followed, it is here given:

> To the Honorable and Council and House of Representatives of the Colony of the Massachusetts Bay, in General Court Assembled, July 19, 1775.
>
> Humbly sheweth your Petitioner, that he with the eastern Regiment in the County of Lincoln, on hearing that a Man of War

[1]. Mass. Archives, **138**, 165.
[2]. Austin, *Life of Elbridge Gerry*, 93.

with sundry other Vessels were come to the eastern Shore of said County, in order to supply the Regulars with Wood and Provisions, went down in order to prevent their Design, and had the good Fortune to take five Vessels in that Employ, which have since been disposed of by your Honors; one of which Vessels your honors have thot fit to put into my Care, a Schooner of about 70 Tons, well found and might easily be fitted and rendered very suitable to defend the Sea Coast. Your Petitioner would further inform your Honors, that said Regiment, before they destroyed Fort Pownal, took into their Possession a Quantity of Cannon, Ball and Langrage, the Property of this Colony, which is now on board said Schooner. Your Petitioner therefore prays your Honors, that as the eastern Shore of this Colony is most exposed to the Ravages of the Enemy, he may be allowed to fix said Schooner for a Privateer, make use of said Ball and Langrage taken from Fort Pownal, enlist Thirty Men to serve on board said Vessel, and Use and improve said Vesel for the Defence of the Sea Coasts in the eastern Part of this Colony, and your Petitioner as in Duty bound shall ever pray, etc.

Your Petitioner further humbly prays he may [be] allowed 100 lb. Powder to be used on board said Vessel for the Purposes aforesaid.

EDW'D EMERSON.[1]

On September 28 it was "*Ordered*, That Col. Orne, Mr. Story, Mr. Cooper, Col. Thompson, Mr. Sullivan, Col. Grout, and Mr. Jewett be a Committee to consider the Expediency of fitting out a Number of Armed Vessels." The next day a committee was appointed "to wait on his Excellency General Washington and consult him on the Expediency of fitting out Armed Vessels and to enquire if any Powder can be spared for that Purpose."[2] On October 6 the name of Capt. Cutter was substituted for that of Mr. Sullivan on the committee.

Meanwhile, as a military measure to make more

---

1. Mass. Archives, **180**, 103. Emerson was Lieut. Colonel in Colonel William Jones' (3d. Lincoln Co.) regiment of Massachusetts Militia. He is on a list of officers chosen by the House of Representatives, January 30, 1776, but rejected by the Council, February 8, 1776.

2. *Journal of the Honorable House of Representatives.*

effective the siege of Boston, Washington had adopted the policy of fitting out armed vessels, manned by the army, to cruise in Massachusetts Bay. The first of these vessels, the schooner *Hannah*, got to sea September 2. This little fleet took many prizes and brought in military stores and other property much needed by the British army in Boston and of great value to the poorly equipped American army.

The following report of the committee appointed September 28 and October 6 was taken into consideration October 9 and accepted:

Whereas the unnatural Enemies of these Colonies have infested the Sea-Coasts with armed Vessels, and are daily endeavouring to distress the Inhabitants, by plundering Live Stock, and making Captures of Provision and other Vessels, being the Property of said Inhabitants: And whereas the Grand CONGRESS *of* America, *have resolved* "That each Colony at their own Expence, make such Provision by armed Vessels or otherwise, as their respective Assemblies, Conventions, or Committees of Safety shall judge expedient, and suitable to their Circumstances and Situations, for the Protection of their Harbours and Navigation on the Sea-Coasts, against all unlawful Invasions, Attacks and Depredations, from Cutters and Ships of War:" *And whereas it is the Duty and Interest of each Colony to exert itself as well for the Purpose of keeping Supplies from the Enemy, as for those mentioned in the Resolve just recited.*

Therefore *Resolved*, That a Committee be now appointed to prepare and bring in a Bill for the Confiscation of all armed and other Vessels, that shall be taken and brought into this Colony, together with their Cargoes, Appurtenances, &c., which shall have been found making unlawful Invasions, Attacks or Depredations on our Sea Coasts or Navigation, or improved in supplying the Enemy with Provisions, &c., or employed by them in any other Respect whatever. — And that Provision be made in said Bill for encouraging such of the Inhabitants of this Colony, as shall for this Purpose be recommended by the Committees of Correspondence and Safety of the Town in which they shall dwell, to fit out armed Vessels under such Regulations as the General Court shall order; and that all Vessels and Cargoes that shall be taken by said Inhabitants or others, properly authorized to take the same, and that shall be legally condemned in this Colony, shall be the Property of the Captors, they paying the Charges of Condemnation. Also that further Provision be made in said Bill for determining the Salvage that shall be allowed on such Vessels as shall be retaken from the Enemy before Condemnation; and for erecting a Court for the Trial and Condemnation of all Vessels, Cargoes, &c. as aforesaid, that shall be taken and brought into this Colony.

The bill was prepared by James Sullivan and Elbridge Gerry. In a letter to John Adams, written many years later, Gerry says:

This reminds me of an anecdote often told by the late governour Sullivan of an act, which was prepared by him and myself in the lobby of the Watertown meeting-house, where at that time the provincial congress [General Court] held its session, the lobby being a small apartment, with a window, under the belfry. The act was to authorize privateering. The governour agreed to draw the act on condition that I should prepare the preamble. This I grounded on the royal charter of the province, which authorized us to levy war against the common enemy of both countries. Such we considered the British nation, with the ships of war and armies employed against us; and we, accordingly, as loyal subjects, used all the power given us by the charter to capture and destroy them. The governour said the act and its preamble was printed in the *London Magazine*, as a political curiosity.[1]

This act, which was finally passed November 1, is sufficiently notable to be reproduced here without abridgment:

In the Sixteenth Year of the Reign of George the Third, King &c.

An Act for Encouraging the Fixing out of Armed Vessels to defend the Sea Coast of America, and for Erecting a Court to Try and Condemn all Vessels that shall be found infesting the same.

Whereas the Present Administration of Great Britain, being divested of Justice and Humanity and Strangers to that Magnanimity and sacred Regard for Liberty which inspired their venerable Predecessors, have been endeavouring, thro' a Series of Years, to establish a System of Despotism over the American Colonies, and by their venal and corrupt Measures have so extended their Influence over the British Parliament that by a prostituted Ma-

---

1. Austin, *Life of Gerry*, 94; *Warren-Adams*, II, 378.

jority it is now become a political Engine of Slavery: And Whereas, the Military Tools of these our unnatural Enemies, while restrained by the united Forces of the American Colonies from proceeding in their Sanguinary Career of Devastation and Slaughter, are infesting the Sea Coast with Armed Vessels and daily Endeavouring to distress the Inhabitants, by burning their Towns and destroying their Dwellings with their Substance, plundering live Stock and making Captures of Provision and other Vessels, being the Property of said Inhabitants: And whereas their Majesties, King William, and Queen Mary, by the Royal Charter of this Colony, "for themselves, their Heirs and Successors, did grant, establish, and ordain, that in the Absence of the Governor and Lieutenant Governor of the Colony, a Majority of the Council shall have full Power by themselves or by any Chief Commander, or other Officer or Officers to be appointed by them, from Time to Time, for the special Defence of their said Province or Territory to assemble in Martial array and put in Warlike posture the Inhabitants of their said Province or Territory, and to lead and Conduct them and with them to Encounter, expulse, resist and pursue by Force of Arms, as well by Sea as by Land, within or without the Limits of their said Province or Territory, and also to kill, slay, destroy and conquer, by all fitting Ways, Enterprizes, and means whatsoever, all and every such person and persons as should at any Time thereafter Attempt or enterprize the Destruction, Invasion, Detriment or Annoyance of their said Province or Territory, and to take and surprize by all Ways and Means whatsoever, all and every person and persons, with their Ships, Arms, Ammunition and other Goods, as should in a Hostile manner invade or attempt the invading, Conquering or annoying of their said Province or Territory:" And whereas it is expressly Resolved by the Grand Congress of America, "that each Colony at their own Expence make such provision, by armed Vessels or otherwise, as their respective Assemblies, Conventions or Committees of Safety shall Judge expedient and suitable to their Circumstances and Situations, for the protection of their Harbours and Navigation on the Sea Coasts, against all unlawful Invasions, attacks and Depradations, from Cutters and Ships of War," and It is the Duty and Interest of this Colony to exert itself, as well for the purpose of keeping Supplies from the Enemy, as for those mentioned in the paragraphs of the Charter and Resolve now recited: Therefore, for the more effectually carrying into Execution the purp[loses aforesai]d,

Be it Enacted by the Council and House of Representatives, in General Court Assembled, and by the Authority of the same, that all Armed and other Vessells, which shall be brought into this Colony and have been found Making unlawful invasions, Attacks or depredations on the Sea Coasts or Navigation of any part of America, or Improved in supplying the Fleet and Army, which have been or shall at any Time be Employed against the United Colonies or Employed by the said Enemy in any respect whatsoever, and also all Vessells whose Masters or Super Cargo's shall have had designs of carrying Supplies of any kind to the Enemy, or that shall be returning from the Enemy after having carried such Supplies and shall be convicted thereof, as is herein provided, such Vessell or Vessells, with their Appurtenances and Cargoes, shall be deemed forfeited, and shall be disposed of as is by this Act hereafter Ordered and directed.

And be it further Enacted by the Authority aforesaid, that the Council of this Colony or the Major part of them shall be fully Impowered to Commission, with Letters of Marque and reprisal, any person or persons within this Colony, who shall at his or their own Expence fix out and equip for the defence of America any Vessell, as also any Person who shall by the Owner of such Vessell be recommended therefor; And that all such persons, so Commissioned as aforesaid, shall have full power with such other persons as they shall engage to their Assistance, to sail on the Seas, Attack, take and bring into any port in this Colony all Vessells offending or Employed by the Enemy as aforesaid; And also to retake and bring in, as aforesaid, any Vessell or Vessells that may be taken from any person or persons by said Enemy.

Provided always, and be it further Enacted: That the Master or Owner of such Vessell shall, at the Time he receives such Commission, enter into Bond with one sufficient Surety at least, for the faithful discharge of his Office and observing the Law of this Colony relating to Armed Vessells; which Bond shall be in the form following.. viz't   Know all Men by these Presents, that We A B & C D of   &c. are holden and stand firmly bound and Obliged unto the Treasurer and Receiver General of the Colony aforesaid, in the full and just Sum of Five thousand pounds, to be paid unto the said Treasurer & Receiver General, or to his Successor in said Office; To the true payment whereof We bind ourselves, our Heirs, Executors and Administrators, jointly and severally, firmly, by these presents: Sealed with our Seals the   day of   Anno Dom'i 17   . The Condition of the aforementioned Obligation is such, that Whereas the said A B hath, on the day of the date hereof, received a Commission to Command an Armed Vessell, called the   burthen about

Tons, to make reprisals of all Armed and other Vessells, that shall be found Supplying the Enemy or Acting Counter to a Law of this Colony, entitled an Act for Encouraging the fixing out of Armed Vessels to defend the Sea Coasts of America and for erecting a Court to try and Condemn all Vessels that shall be found infesting the same. If therefore the said A B shall and do in and by all things well and truly Observe and fulfill such Instructions as he shall receive from the Council of this Colony and shall in all respects conform himself to the directions given in and by the Act aforesaid, then the aforewritten Obligation be void, otherwise to remain in full force.

And be it further Enacted, that there shall be Erected and constantly held in the Town of Plymouth, in the County of Plymouth, a Court of Justice, by such Able and discreet person as shall be Appointed and Commissioned by the Major part of the Council for that purpose, whose business it shall be to take Cognizance of and try the Justice of any Capture or Captures of any Vessell or Vessells, that may or shall be taken by any person, or persons whomsoever, and brought into either of the Counties of Plymouth, Barnstable, Bristol, Nantucket, or Dukes County; and the Judge, so Commissioned to hold said Court, as aforesaid, shall have power at all Times to Issue his Warrant or Warrants to the Constable or Constables of any Town or Towns, within the said Counties of Plymouth, Barnstable, Bristol, Dukes County, or Nantucket, or either of them, directing the said Constable or Constables to warn a Meeting of the Inhabitants of their Towns, respectively, and to draw out of the Box in such manner as is provided by the Laws of this Colony for returning Jurors to serve in the Inferior Court of Common pleas, so many good and lawful Men for Jurors as said Judge shall, in his s'd Warrant, order and direct, not Exceeding the number of twelve; and the said Constables shall immediately, as soon as may be, give Notice in Writing to such persons, so drawn, of the time and place which in the said Warrant shall be set for their appearance, and shall return said Warrant, with his doings thereon, to said Judge, at or before the time set therein for the appearance of said Jurors.

And be it further Enacted, that if any Constable, within said Counties, shall Neglect or refuse to obey the Warrant of the Judge for returning said Jurors, as aforesaid, he shall pay such fine as the Judge shall order, not exceeding the sum of Forty shillings, and if any Juror, so drawn and having Notice, as aforesaid, shall not appear at the Time and place directed in such Warrant, or shall refuse without reasonable excuse to serve on such Jury, he shall pay such Fine as the Judge shall order, not exceeding the Sum of forty shillings, but before such fine shall be awarded the said Judge shall Summon such Juryman to Appear before him, to shew forth the Reasons of his Neglect, and if such reasons shall not be satisfactory to the said Judge, then he, the said Judge, shall Issue his Warrants of distress for such fine, in manner as is directed for recovery of fines of jurors, who shall neglect or refuse to serve in the Inferior Court of Common pleas; which fines so recovered shall be paid into the Treasury of this Colony.

And be it further Enacted by the Authority aforesaid, that there shall be held in like Manner in the Town of Ipswich, in the County of Essex, one other Court of Justice, by such able and discreet person as the Major part of the Council shall appoint and Commission thereto, which Judge shall have full Cognizance of and power to Try the Justice of the Capture of any Vessel or Vessells that shall be taken as aforesaid and brought into any port in the Counties of Suffolk, Middlesex, or Essex, and shall have the like power to Issue his Warrant or Warrants for Jurors in said Counties, as is before provided for the Judge of the Counties first mentioned, and every Constable and Juror within the said Counties of Suffolk, Middlesex and Essex, who shall neglect to pay due Obedience to said Warrants, shall be Liable to the same penalties as are provided by this Act against those, in like manner offending, in the Counties of Plymouth, Barnstable, Bristol, Nantucket, and Dukes County. . . .[1]

And be it further Enacted by the Authority aforesaid, that when any person or persons shall take and bring into any Port in this Colony any Vessell or Vessells, that have been offending, or Employed by the Enemy as aforesaid, such person or persons, so taking and bringing in such Vessell, shall immediately make out a Bill in Writing, therein giving a full and Ample Account of the time and manner of the Caption of such Vessell and the Employment she was in when so taken, And of the persons who were Aiding and Assisting in taking her; and a Schedule of the Cargo on board her, to the best of his knowledge, at the Time of her Caption; And shall deliver the same to the Judge, who shall have Jurisdiction of the port where such Vessell is brought, with all the Papers that may be found on board such Vessell, to the intent that the Jury may have the Benefit of Evidence therefrom ariseing; And the Judge to whom said Bill shall be delivered, shall immediately Issue his Warrant or Warrants, as aforesaid, to any Constable or Constables within the Counties of his Jurisdiction, commanding them or either

1. The next section provides for a like court to be held at North Yarmouth.

of them, in manner aforesaid, to return Twelve good and Lawful Men to Try the Truth of any Facts alledged in such Bill, And if seven of said Jurors, so returned by said Constable or Constables, shall appear and there shall not be enough to compleat a Pannel of Twelve, or if there shall be a Legal Challenge to any of them, so that there shall be seven and not a Pannel to Try such Cause; then in such Case it shall be lawful for said Judge to order the Sherriff, or other proper Officer attending on said Court, to fill up the Jury with other good and lawful Men present, which Jury shall be sworn to return a true Verdict upon the said Bill according to Law and Evidence; And if it shall appear to said Judge by said Verdict that such Vessell had been employed or offending as aforesaid, he shall Condemn said Vessell and Cargo and Appurtenances and order them to be sold at publick Vendue and shall order the Charges of said Trial and Condemnation to be paid out of the Money such Vessell and Cargo shall sell for, unto the Treasury of this Colony and shall order the residue thereof to be delivered to the Captors, their Agents or Attorneys, for the Use and Benefit of such Captors and others Concerned therein, And if two or more Vessells, the Commanders whereof shall be properly Commissioned, shall Jointly take such Vessel, the Money She and her Cargo and Appurtenances shall Sell for, after payment of Charges as aforesaid, shall be divided between the Captors in proportion to their Men, And the said Judge, before whom any such Trial and Condemnation as is aforementioned may be, shall be Authorized to make out his Precept under his Hand and Seal, to either of the Sherriffs within his Jurisdiction, to Sell such Vessell and Appurtenances and Cargo and to pay thereout the Charges of Trial and Condemnation into the Treasury of this Colony, and to pay his own fees, and to deliver the residue to the Captors and persons concerned as aforesaid.

And be it further Enacted that there shall be paid to the Justice, Jurors and Sherriffs, out of the public Treasury, such fees as are or shall hereafter be established by Law to each and every the Officers of the said Court.

And be it further Enacted by the Authority aforesaid, that when any such Bill shall be delivered to such Judge, he shall cause Notification thereof and the Name (if known) and description of the Vessell so brought in, with the day set for the Trial thereon, to be Advertized in the several papers printed at Watertown and Cambridge, fifteen days before the time set for the Trial, that the Owner of such Vessell or any person concerned may appear and shew Cause, if any they have, why such Vessell with her Cargo and Appurtenances should not be Condemned and Sold as aforesaid.

And be it further Enacted, that the process and proceeding upon any Vessel that shall be retaken from the Enemy by any person or persons shall be in the same manner as is herein provided for other Vessels; and if by Verdict of the Jury it shall appear to the Judge that such Vessel was taken by the Enemy and was retaken by such person or persons before Condemnation by the said Enemy thereon had, the said Judge shall order such Vessel with her Cargo and Appurtenances to be sold in manner aforesaid, and shall order not more than one third nor less than one quarter of what she shall sell for (after paying Charges of Trial and Sale) to be delivered to the Captors, as is before provided for other Vessels, and the Residue to be delivered to the Owner or Owners of such Vessel: And if such Vessel so retaken shall have been Condemned by the Enemy, then the Money she and her Cargo and Appurtenances may Sell for shall be delivered to the Captors, as is above provided for Vessels belonging to the said Enemy.

And be it further Enacted by the Authority aforesaid, that each Judge of such Courts shall appoint an able Clerk, who shall keep a True and fair Record of all the proceedings of said Court and shall be duly Sworn to Act in said Office with Truth and fidelity, and his Attestations shall be received as Evidence in all Courts of Law.

In the House of Representatives, Novem'r 1st, 1775. This Bill having Had Three several Readings passed to be Enacted.

Sent up for Concurrence.

J. WARREN *Sp'kr*.

In Council Nov'r 1st, 1775, this Bill having had two several Readings passed to be enacted.

PEREZ MORTON *D't'y Sec'ry*.

We consent to the enacting of this Bill —

JAMES OTIS	MICH'L FARLEY
W. SPOONER	SAM HOLTEN
CALEB CUSHING	JABEZ FISHER
B: CHADBOURN	B: [WHITE]
JOSEPH GERRISH	MOS[ES GILL]
JOHN WHETCOMB	B: LINCOLN
JED'H FOSTER	JAMES PRESCOTT [1]
ELDAD TAYLOR	

On November 10 a resolve was adopted in the House of Representatives, supplementary to the act of Novem-

---

1. From the engrossed copy of the act in the State Archives.

ber 1, providing for the condemnation of captures made by persons not legally commissioned with letters of marque. The resolve was as follows:

Whereas by a Law of this Colony made in the present Session of the General Court, Intitled an Act for encouraging the fitting out Armed Vessels to defend the Sea-Coast of America and for erecting a Court to try and condemn all Vessels that shall be found Infesting the same — it is provided that all Vessels which shall be brought into this Colony and proved to be the Property of or any Ways employed by the Enemies of the United American Colonies or for Supplying the said Enemies, shall with their Appurtenances and Cargoes be deemed forfeited, and disposed of as by said Act is ordered and directed, and no Provision being therein made for Captors not legally commissioned therefor, who in certain Cases ought to meet with all necessary Encouragement,

Resolved, That when and so often as it shall appear to the Judge of any Court by said Act provided, that any Vessel or Vessels which shall be by such Court condemned, have been taken by any Inhabitants of the United American Colonies within thirty Leagues of the American Shore; in that Case it shall be lawful and such Judge is hereby authorized and directed to award to the Captors the amount of what such Vessel or Vessels with their Cargoes and Appurtenances shall produce, after deducting the Charges of Tryal and Condemnation; and also the Sheriff's Fees for Sale at public Auction, in the same Manner as would have been done had such Captors been commissioned with Letters of Marque and Reprisal by any of the Colonies aforesaid.[1]

It would be interesting to know how many privateersmen sailed the seas without commissions. The petition of Agreen Crabtree, dated Watertown, July 30, 1776:

Humbly shews that your Petitioner fix'd out a small Schooner called the *Hannah and Molly* as a Privateer to Distress the Enemys of the United Colonies, said Schooner Mounted Eight Swivell Guns and carried Fourteen Men and has, since she was fix'd out, taken two Sloops Employ'd in carrying Provisions to the Enemy, both which Sloops are now Libeled at the Court appointed to Try the Captures of such Vessels, and as your Petitioner has never Received any Commission, he now desires that your Honors would

1. *Journal of the House of Representatives.*

To the Honb.le the Council of the State of the Massachusetts Bay —

The Petition of Agreen Crabtree Humbly Shews —

That your Petitioner fix'd out a small Schooner called the Hannah & Molly as a Privateer to Distress the Enemeys of the United Colonies, said Schooner Mounted Eight Swivell Guns and Fourteen Men, and has since she was fix'd out, taken two Sloops Imploy'd in carrying Provisions to the Enemey, both which Sloops are now Libeled at the Court appointed to Try the Captures of such Vessels, and as your Petitioner has never Received any Commission, he now desires that your Honors would take his cause into your Consideration and grant him a Captains Commission for said Schooner and your Petitioner as in duty bound will ever pray. —

Agreen Crabtree

Watertown 30 July 1776

In Council July 31. 1776 Read & Ordered that Agreen Crabtree be commissionated also giving Bond & complying with y.e Order of this Court in such cases made —

Jn.o Avery Dp.y Sec.y

Treasurers Office 31 July 1776

I hereby Certify that Agreen Crabtree hath Given Bonds in Order to take out a Commission for the Schooner Hannah & Molly

H Gardner

take his case into your Consideration and Grant him a Captain's Commission for said Schooner. [On the following day the Council] ordered that Agreen Crabtree be commissionated after giving Bond and complying with the Order of this Court in such Cases made.[1]

Later supplementary enactments on February 14, March 19, April 13, and May 8, 1776, were the result of further consideration of the subject by the General Court. It was provided that in addition to the places named in the act of November 1 for holding prize courts, they might also be held at Barnstable or Dartmouth for the Southern District; at Boston, Salem, or Newburyport for the Middle District; and at Falmouth (Portland) or Pownalborough (Wiscasset) for the Eastern District. The judges appointed for the trial of prizes were: For the Southern District, Nathan Cushing; for the Middle District, Timothy Pickering; for the Eastern District, James Sullivan, later succeeded by Timothy Langdon. Under the authority of this legislation privateering in Massachusetts was carried on throughout the Revolution. The first Continental law for the purpose was enacted March 23, 1776. A set of general instructions, issued by the Continental Congress April 3, for the regulation of privateers, is here reproduced:

Instructions to the commanders of private ships or vessels of war, which shall have commissions or letters of marque and reprisal, authorising them to make captures of British vessels and cargoes.

I. You may, by force of arms, attack, subdue, and take all ships and other vessels, belonging to the inhabitants of Great Britain, on the high seas, or between high water and low water mark; except ships and vessels bringing persons who intend to settle and reside in the United Colonies; or bringing arms, ammunition, or war-like stores, to the said colonies, for the use of such inhabitants thereof as are friends to the American cause, which you shall suffer to pass unmolested, the commanders thereof permitting

1. Mass. Archives, **165**, 477. See below, pp. 55, 56, for schooner *Dolphin*, of Salem.

Congress of the United States, the 9th day of May, in the year of our Lord one thousand seven hundred and seventy-eight.

III. You shall permit all neutral vessels freely to navigate on the high seas, or coasts of America, except such as are employed in carrying contraband goods or soldiers to the enemies of these United States.

IV. You shall not seize or capture any effects belonging to the subjects of the belligerent powers on board neutral vessels, excepting contraband goods; and you are carefully to observe, that the term contraband is confined to those articles which are expressly declared to be such in the treaty of amity and commerce, of the sixth day of February, 1778, between these United States and his Most Christian Majesty, namely: arms, great guns, bombs, with their fuses and other things belonging to them; cannon-ball, gunpowder, matches, pikes, swords, lances, spears, halberts, mortars, petards, grenadoes, salt-petre, muskets, musket-ball, bucklers, helmets, breast-plates, coats of mail, and the like kind of arms proper for arming soldiers, musket-rests, belts, horses with their furniture, and all other warlike instruments whatever.

The proclamation of 1778, mentioned in the first of these articles, is also essential for the complete presentation of this subject:

A Proclamation

Whereas Congress have received information and complaints, "that violences have been done by American armed vessels to neutral nations, in seizing ships belonging to their subjects and under their colours, and in making captures of those of the enemy whilst under the protection of neutral coasts, contrary to the usage and custom of nations": to the end that such unjustifiable and piratical acts, which reflect dishonour upon the national character of these states, may be in future effectually prevented, the said Congress hath thought proper to direct, enjoin and command all captains, commanders and other officers and seamen belonging to any American armed vessels, to govern themselves strictly in all things agreeably to the tenor of their commissions and the instructions and resolutions of Congress; particularly that they pay a sacred regard to the rights of neutral powers and the usage and custom of civilized nations, and on no pretence whatever presume to take or seize any ships or vessels belonging to the subjects of princes or powers in alliance with these United States, except they are employed in carrying contraband goods or soldiers to our enemies, and in such case that they conform to the stipulations contained in treaties subsisting between such princes or powers and these states; and that they do not capture, seize or plunder any ships or vessels of our enemies, being under the protection of neutral coasts, nations or princes, under the penalty of being condignly punished therefor, and also of being bound to make satisfaction for all matters of damage and the interest thereof by reparation, under the pain and obligation of their persons and goods. And further, the said Congress doth hereby resolve and declare, that persons wilfully offending in any of the foregoing instances, if taken by any foreign powers in consequence thereof, will not be considered as having a right to claim protection from these states, but shall suffer such punishment as by the usage and custom of nations may be inflicted upon such offenders.[1]

In every maritime war the treatment of neutrals and questions relating to freedom of the seas and right of search have excited acute interest, acrimonious discussion and international irritation—not to say strained relations. According to Wheaton, "the right of visitation and search of neutral vessels at sea is a belligerent right, essential to the exercise of the right of capturing enemy's property, contraband of war, and vessels committing a breach of blockade. Even if the right of capturing enemy's property be ever so strictly limited, and the rule of *free ships free goods* be adopted, the right of visitation and search is essential, in order to determine whether the ships themselves are neutral, and documented as such, according to law of nations and treaties." Great Britain more than any other power has always insisted upon this right, yet not so much by the exercise as by the abuse of it and by her general arrogant practices has aroused the ire of other nations.[2]

---
[1]. Papers of Continental Congress, 24, 435.
[2]. The years preceding the War of 1812 are especially recalled, not the World War.

This is what happened in 1780 when the powers of northern Europe, led by Russia, formed the Armed Neutrality for the protection of their commerce from the interference of belligerents by enforcing the doctrine that "free ships make free goods"; they particularly claimed exemption from search of ships under the convoy of men-of-war. Circumstances made it expedient for England to avoid a breach with the members of the Armed Neutrality and the war came to an end without any settlement of the question. But afterwards and always she continued to maintain the inconsistency of the league's principles with the law of nations.[1]

For a study of Massachusetts privateering a mass of material is still accessible to the searcher, though undoubtedly much has been lost. In 1906 the Library of Congress published a calendar of *Naval Records of the American Revolution* prepared by Charles Henry Lincoln. The volume contains a list of the bonds of Continental letters of marque in the Library. There are 1697 of these bonds, of which 626 were given by Massachusetts privateersmen. With a few exceptions of earlier date (nearly all in 1777), these Massachusetts bonds begin in August, 1780. On July 27 the Continental Congress had ruled that all private armed vessels should be commissioned in the office of the Secretary of Congress. It was "the intention of Congress that all commissions and instructions in force on the 2d day of May last [1780] be cancelled as soon as possible and that commissions, bonds, and instructions of the new form be substituted in the place thereof." The bonds

---

[1]. Wheaton, *Elements of International Law*, §§ 450, 524, 526; Mahan, *Influence of Sea Power upon History*, 405. For British instructions to privateers, see Scott, *The Armed Neutralities of 1780 and 1800* (Carnegie Endowment for International Peace), 281, 328, 335, 391.

Know all men by these Presents that we Josiah Coffin & Richard Mitchell Jun.r both of Sherbourn in the county of Nantucket, are Holden, & stands firmly bound to Henry Gardner of Stow in the County of Middlesex Treasurer of the Colony of the Massachusetts Bay, or his successor in said office, in the full & just sum of Two thousand Pounds, to the which payments well & truly to be made, We bind ourselves, Our Heirs Exec.rs Administ.rs & assigns firmly by these Presents Seald with our seals dated this twenty eighth day of September in the Fifteenth year of his Majesty's Reign anno Domini 1775 —

The Condition of the above Obligation, is such, That whereas the above Named Josiah Coffin Esq.r is about to adventure to Sea on a Whaling Voyage in the Schooner Mairmaid Josiah Coffin Jun.r master, if then the s.d Josiah Coffin Jun.r or any other Person that may have the Comand of the S.d Schooner during the said Voyage shall carry no more provisions then are Necessary for said Voyage in the judgments of the selectmen of the Town of Sherbourn and shall also well & truely bring or cause to be brought into some Port, or Harbour of this Colony, other than the Port of Boston or Nantucket, all the Oil & whalbone that shall be taken by the said Vessel's Crew in the Course of the said Voyage, & shall within eighteen months from the date hereof, produce a Certifycate from the Select men of the Town adjoyning such Port, or Harbour that he has there Landed the Same — Then the above Obligation to be void & of no Effect, otherwise to abide & Remain in full force & Vertue ———

Signed Seal'd & Deliver'd
in Presence of ———
Stephen Hussey
Fre.d Jenkins

Josiah Coffin

Rich.d Mitchel jun.r

Bond of a Whaler

were to be sent out to the various states for execution and, when ready, returned to the secretary's office.[1]

In the Massachusetts Archives at the State House in Boston there is a collection of bonds representing nearly as many Massachusetts privateer commissions as those in the Library of Congress. They begin late in 1775 and end in August, 1780. In this collection there are two kinds of bonds, Continental and State, most vessels giving both. Besides these bonds there are, scattered through many volumes of the Archives, papers indicating that commissions were granted to more than a hundred and fifty additional vessels. These papers are mostly petitions, also bonds of special kinds, prize court records, and various miscellaneous documents. In such cases the original bonds have presumably been lost. That all evidence has disappeared in an unknown, but perhaps large, number is not to be doubted, and is shown by mention in contemporary newspapers and elsewhere of very many vessels of which no trace can be found in the Archives. To make a complete and correct list of Massachusetts privateers would be impossible.

The first bonds of the Revolutionary period in the Archives, about seventy in number, were given by whalers during the summer and fall of 1775 and had to do with the disposition of their cargoes of oil and whalebone. They are interesting, but the whalers, having had no letters of marque, do not come within the scope of the present study.[2] The first privateer bond issued

---

1. Mass. Archives, **202**, 403 (Charles Thomson, Secretary of Congress to the President of the Massachusetts Council, July 28, 1780). For other letters of Thomson and of John Jay on privateer commissions, etc., see *Ibid.*, **200**, 335, 404, 203, 345, 350.

2. The whalers' bonds are in Mass. Archives, **139**. See *Warren-Adams Letters*, I, 181.

under the act of November 1, 1775, was for the schooner *Boston Revenge*, Captain Stephen Mascoll, who was bound to "observe and fulfil such instructions as he shall receive from the Council of this Colony," and to "conform himself to the directions given in and by the act aforesaid." This bond and the petition of the owners for a commission are both dated December 7, 1775, and were acted on by the Council the next day. The petition for the schooner *Dolphin* is dated December 1 and was granted December 8 also; but the bond of the *Dolphin* is dated December 15. Priority, therefore, should perhaps be assigned to the *Boston Revenge*. Three other privateers were commissioned under the same authority before the end of the year. In the case of State bonds, the signers were bound to Henry Gardner, Treasurer of the Colony, or, later, the State. The signers of Continental bonds were bound to the President and members of Congress, or, after August, 1780, to the Treasurer of the United States. There were of course no Continental bonds until after the passage of the act of March 23, 1776.

After some months, printed forms came into use for the bonds. In those for the State the amount of the bond is uniformly £4000, and where a different sum is stipulated it may be assumed that the bond was written, not printed. The amount prescribed on the Continental bonds is $5000, $10,000, or $20,000, the latter sum after August, 1780. The amount of the bond seems to have borne little or no relation to the size and value of the vessel. The State, in order to facilitate the exchange of prisoners and to prevent all persons in public service going on board any private armed vessel, bound the privateer captain "to deliver to the Commissary of Prisoners in some of the United States all Prisoners by him captured," and not to "carry out with him any Person in Pay of this State, or any Officer or Soldier belonging to the Continental Army." The Continental Congress required that the commander "shall not exceed or transgress the Powers and Authorities which shall be contained in the said Commission, but shall in all Things observe and conduct himself and govern his Crew by and according to the same, and shall make Reparation for all damages sustained by any Misconduct or unwarrantable Proceedings of himself or the Officers or Crew."

The later Continental bonds went further and demanded that the commander demean himself "by and according to the said Commission, Resolutions, Acts and Instructions, and any Treaties subsisting or which may subsist between the United States of America and any Prince, Power or Potentate whatever; and shall not violate the law of Nations or the rights of neutral Powers or of any of their Subjects." These bonds, moreover, defined with greater particularity what property was subject to seizure and what was not. The commander was authorized "by force of arms to attack, subdue, seize and take all ships and other vessels, goods, wares and merchandizes, belonging to the Crown of Great Britain or any of the subjects thereof, (excepting the ships or vessels together with their cargoes, belonging to any inhabitant or inhabitants of Bermuda, and such other ships or vessels bringing persons with intent to settle within the said United States); and any other ships or vessels, goods, wares and merchandizes, to whomsoever belonging, which are or shall be declared to be subjects of capture by any Resolutions of Congress, or which are so deemed by the law of Nations." The exception in parenthesis relating to Bermuda, omitted in some bonds, was made in the hope of retaining the friendship of those islands.

To ensure a full quota for the Continental Army and Navy and the State Navy it was necessary to restrict the recruiting of privateersmen and at times to lay an embargo on the sailing of private vessels until the requirements of the public service had been met. For such purposes the owners and commanders of privateers were obliged to give additional bonds. Extracts from some of these documents will serve as illustrations. The first two are dated 1777, the third 1778.

(1) The condition of this present Obligation is such That, Whereas the Great and General Court of the State aforesaid, on the seventh of April Instant by their Resolve of that date, did allow that the Inhabitants of any Town within said State who had raised their full proportion of the Continental Army to fit out private Vessels of War, but not to Ship or receive on board any Men that are the Inhabitants of any Town in said State that have not raised their proportion of said Army. (2) The Condition of this present Obligation is such That, Whereas the Great and General Court of the State aforesaid on the nineteenth day of April last, in and by a certain Resolve allowing private persons to fit out Vessels of War, did among other things restrict them from shipping on board said Privateers any Inhabitant of any of the New England States other than the State of Massachusetts Bay. (3) The Condition of this present Obligation is Such, That if the above bounden Nathaniel Bentley, Commander, and Samuel Batchelder, the Major part of the Owners, of said Private Schooner of War shall not Inlist or take on board said Privateer any Soldier or Soldiers belonging to the Continental Army of the United States of America, then this obligation to be null and void, otherwise to remain in full force and Virtue.[1]

It would seem as if vessels of the State Navy and others belonging to the Commonwealth should have been exempt from giving bonds, but such was not the case, at least early in the war. July 26, 1776, Captain

---

1. Mass. Archives, **139**, 127, 141, 158.

Simeon Samson and James Warren, both of Plymouth, and Richard Derby, of Salem, stood

firmly bound to Henry Gardner, Esq., Treasurer and Receiver General of the State aforesaid in the Sum of two thousand Pounds. ... The Condition of this Obligation is such that if the above bounden Simeon Sampson [signed Samson] who is comander of the Brigantine *Independance*, belonging to the said State of the Massachusetts Bay and fitted out by Order of the Great and General Court to cruise on the Sea Coasts of America for the Defence of American Liberty and to make Captures of such Vessells as shall be supplying the Enemies thereof with Provisions and other Stores or otherwise infesting the Sea Coasts and for the making Captures of British Vessells and Cargoes. Now if the said Simeon Sampson, Comr. of the sd. Briga. called the *Independance* shall in all things observe and conduct himself and govern his Crew according to the Resolves of the General American Congress and according to the Acts and Orders of the Great and General Court of this State, relative to Armed Vessels fitted out for the Purpose aforesaid, and follow such Instructions as he may receive in Pursuance of his Comission, the foregoing Obligation shall be void, or Else remain in Force.[1]

Others of the sixteen vessels of the Massachusetts Navy gave similar bonds, most of them during the first year, but at least one, the *Mars*, as late as 1781. The sloop *Republic*, in 1777, gave a Continental bond.

Certain other vessels belonging to the State were bonded. The Board of War employed numerous vessels as packets, despatch boats, and cargo carriers, or for other purposes. If it was thought desirable to arm such vessels, a petition for letters of marque was addressed to the Council, as in the case of private owners, and bonds were given. Such a vessel was the sloop *Reprisal*, Captain Nathaniel Carver, bound to France in 1777.[2] The same procedure was observed in the case of Con-

[1]. Mass. Archives, **139**, 122. For forms of commission and of bond for vessels of the State Navy, adopted May 9 and 10, 1776, by order of the Council, see *Ibid.*, **164**, 345, 347.
[2]. Mass. Archives, VII, 63.

tinental vessels of a similar kind. In 1777 Colonel John Allan, "having been appointed Agent for the Eastern Indians by the Hon'ble Continental Congress," it was necessary for him, in the performance of his duties, to have in his service a vessel of force to cruise along the shore of eastern Maine. The schooner *Marisheete*, the property of "the United States of America," was bonded for this purpose in 1777 and again the next year. In 1779 the schooner *Neashquowoite*, also owned by the United States, was employed in the same service.[1]

Before a privateer could go to sea in a regular and legal way, preliminary steps were required. In the ordinary course of procedure the owner of a vessel wishing to adventure, having fitted out, manned, armed, and provisioned her, petitioned the Council that a commission be granted her commander. This petition was usually granted at once, the commission often being issued and the bond signed the same or the next day, though sometimes there was delay with the bond. The following petition is a typical example:

To the Hon'ble the Council now setting in Roxbury.

The Petition of Paul D. Sergeant, Joseph Barrel, Thos. Adams, and Daniel Martin, of Boston,

Humbly sheweth, — That your Petitioners have fitted out the Schr called the *Lee*, burthen about seventy-five Tons, mounting ten four Pound Cannon and ten Swivels, and navigated by fifty Men, having on Board as Provisions thirty Bls Beef and Pork, five thousand W. Bread; as Ammunition four hundred W. Powder, and Shot in Proportion. Officers on Board are as follows, Vizt. John Hyer, Comander, David Arnold, 1st Lieut. — Saunders, 2d Do.

Said Schr is intended to cruise against the Enemies of these united States.

Your Petitioners therefore humbly request your Honors to comission the said John Hyer as Comander of said Schr for the Purposes above mentioned and as in Duty Bound shall ever pray.

Boston, April 13, 1778.

Daniel Martin.

1. Mass. Archives, VI, 276, 335, VII, 260.

KNOW all Men by these Presents,
That we *John Conway Mariner*
as principal *Saml Pote James Laskey*
of *Barthlehem*
as Sureties are held and stand firmly bound to the Hon. HENRY
GARDNER, Esq; Treasurer of the State of Massachusetts-Bay, in the Sum
of Four Thousand Pounds, to be paid to the said HENRY GARDNER,
Esq; Treasurer and Receiver-General of the State aforesaid, or to his
Successor or Successors in the said Office, in Trust for the Use of the
said State, to which Payment well and truly to be done, we do bind ourselves, our Heirs, Executors and Administrators, jointly and severally,
firmly by these Presents. Sealed with our Seals, and dated this *Twentyth*
Day of *May* in the Year of our LORD, *1779*

The Condition of this Obligation is such, that whereas
it is necessary that all Persons taken at Sea on board of Prizes, should
be brought into this or some of the United States, to the End there may
be a Number sufficient to redeem such Subjects of the United States as
may fall into the Enemy's Hands; and also that all Persons in the Pay of
this, or any of the United States, should be effectually prevented going
on Board any Armed Vessels. Now if the said *John Conway*
or Commander of the Armed Vessel called the *Terrible*
shall well and truly put on Shore and deliver to the Commissary of Prisoners in some of the United States, all Prisoners by him captured, and shall
not carry out with him any Person in Pay of this State, or any Officer
or Soldier belonging to the Continental Army, then this Bond to be
Void, otherwise to remain in full Force and Virtue.

Signed, Sealed and Delivered,
in Presence of

H. Sibley
Jr Dall

John Conway
Samuel Pote
James Laskey

A State Bond

See pages 40, 296

In Council, April 13, 1778. Read and Ordered That a Commission be issued out to John Hyer as Commander of Schr above mentioned, he complying with the Resolves of Congress.

JNO. AVERY, *D'y Sec'y*.[1]

The first petition under the act of November 1, 1775, and dated December 1, was that of the owners of the schooner *Dolphin*, of Salem, which they had "at their own expence fixed out and equipped for the defence of America . . . and appointed Richard Masury of said Salem, mariner, to be commander thereof." The Council ordered that he "be commissionated for the purpose aforesaid on his giving Bond to the Colony Treasurer for the faithful performance of his Duty therein, agreable to the Act prescribing the Same." [2]

A petition on behalf of the State, dated January 15, 1777, represents that "the Board of War having fitted out the Sloop *Republic*, Allen Hallet, master, navigated with ten hands for the West Indies, mounting two 4 pd Cannon and ten Swivel Guns, and apprehending it may be of Service if the Master be furnish'd with a Commission for a Letter of Marque, do desire a Commission for him as such." [3] This is signed: "By Order of the Board, Sam[uel] Phi[lli]ps Savage, Prest." The *Republic* was built in 1776 for the Massachusetts Navy and in the fall of that year made a successful cruise. Soon afterwards, however, she was employed by the Board of War as a trading vessel, which accounts for the small crew and light battery mentioned in this petition.

Privateersmen frequently addressed petitions to the Council begging exemption from an embargo. These petitions seem to have been quite generally, but by no

1. Mass. Archives, 168, 238.
2. *Ibid.*, 164, 211.
3. *Ibid.*, 166, 195.

means always, granted. In 1780 Cushing & White, agents for, and part owners of, the ship *Tracy*, explained that they had "been at great panes and Expence in fitting sd. Ship for a three months Cruise against the Enemys of the United States of America. But the ship having met with and taken a Valuable Prize Ship with fifty Prisoners, the Captain thought best to convoy his prize into Port and land his Prisoners, which he has done, not Having an Idea till he came on shore of an Embargo or any thing to prevent his sailing again to finish his Cruise, which was not more than a third out, having been gone but Little more than four weeks. But as there Is an Embargo which prevents the Ship sailing Without Special leave, We therefore pray your Honours to take the matter Under your Serious consideration and that you'd be pleased to grant leave for the Ship to proceed again on her Cruise." In this case the Council "ordered that Nathl. Barber, Esq., Naval Officer for the port of Boston, be and hereby is directed to clear out the Ship *Tracy* . . . for her intended Cruise against the Enemies of these States, any Embargo to the Contrary Notwithstanding." [1]

In 1779 Richard Whellen, commander of the brigantine *Venus*, at the request of the Navy Board of the Eastern Department and after binding himself in the sum of £5000 to Henry Gardner, State Treasurer, was allowed "to sail (the Embargo notwithstanding) to Bedford in order to Convoy the Schooner *Hannah and Molley*, now laying there loaded with flour for the use of the Navy of the United States, from said Bedford to the Harbour of Boston and then to be permitted to proceed his Cruise." [2] Another petition of 1780, which

1. Mass. Archives, 176, 483, 484.
2. *Ibid.*, VII, 264.

also was granted, was that of Joseph Cutler, of Newburyport:

To THE HONORABLE THE COUNCIL OF THE STATE OF MASSACHUSETTS BAY —

Humbly shews Joseph Cutler, of Newbury Port in the County of Essex, Merchant, on behalf of himself and others concerned in the armed privateer Brigantine called the *Gates*, that said Brigantine is ready to proceed to Sea on a Cruise against the Enemies of the united States of America, but cannot proceed without the permission of your Honours; That your petitioner is induced to throw himself on the Clemency of your Honours, as his Ship is so circumstanced that the detaining of her will be exceedingly detrimental to your Petitioner and probably to the State in general. Your Petitioner conceives that the laying of the Embargo was designed for the recruiting of the Army and not to discourage the harassing the Commerce of the Enemy; that the Town of Newbury Port has already at a great expence to her Inhabitants compleated all the Levies required of her and therefore the Embargo has already had its intire Operation with respect to that Town, and as the Reason of laying it ceases so far as it respects Newbury Port, so your Petitioner conceives the Operation of it ought so far to be suspended. Your Petitioner is further induced to apply to your Honors as the Honourable Board has already granted permission to two privateers in a neighbouring Town to sail, when your Petitioner is sure that the detention of those privateers could not be more inconvenient and expensive to their owners than the detention of the *Gates* will be to your Petitioner and others concerned; and when at the same Time the Town of Salem was greatly deficient in its quota of Soldiers. Your Petitioner is conscious that your honours will not suppose the Inhabitants of Newburyport not equally intitled to favours with the Inhabitants of any other Town, as their exertions in the Common Cause are equal to those of any other Town at the least. Your Petitioner begs leave also to suggest that the public Interest requires that the American Privateers should not be confined at home at this Season and be deprived of gloriously wounding the Enemy in their tenderest part, their Commerce, and of adding their supplies to those of the united States. Your Petitioner therefore prays that your Honours would grant liberty for the Brigantine *Gates* to sail upon a Cruise and would issue the necessary Orders therefore. And as in Duty bound shall ever pray.

JOSEPH CUTLER.[1]

1. Mass. Archives, 176, 628.

No early commissions, issued by the Colony or State, have been found in the Archives or elsewhere, but the following copy is doubtless a fair sample of these documents:

Colony of the } The major part of the Council of the
Massachusetts Bay } Massachusetts Bay, in New England,

To James Tracey, Gentleman, greeting:

Whereas James Tracey, Jonathan Jackson, Nathaniel Tracey, John Tracey, and Joseph Lee, merchants, have at their own expense fitted out and equipped for the defence of America, a vessel called the *Yankee Hero*, burthen about one hundred and twenty tons, and have recommended you as a suitable person to be commander thereof, we have thought fit to commission you for the purpose aforesaid, and do accordingly by these presents give you, the said James Tracey, full power, with such other persons as you shall engage to your assistance, to sail in the said vessel on the seas, attack, take, and bring into any port in this colony all armed and other vessels which shall be found making unlawful invasions, attacks, or depredations, on the sea-coasts or navigation of any part of America; or improved in supplying the fleet and army, which have been or shall at any time be, employed against the United Colonies, or employed by the enemies of America in any respect whatsoever; and also all vessels whose masters or supercargoes shall have had designs of carrying supplies of any kind to the enemy, or that shall be returning from the enemy after having carried such supplies, that such proceedings may be had thereon as are required by a law of this colony entitled "An act for encouraging the fixing out of armed vessels to defend the sea-coast of America, and for erecting a court to try and condemn all vessels that shall be found infesting the same:" and you are hereby directed in all your proceedings to govern yourself by the said act.

Given under our hands, and the seal of the said Colony, at Watertown, the twentieth day of February, in the sixteenth year of the reign of his Majesty King George the Third [1776].

By their honor's command: PEREZ MORTON, *D. Sec.*

B. GREENLEAF,	W. SPOONER,	CALEB CUSHING,
B. WHITE,	S. HOLTON,	JOHN TAYLOR,
MOSES GILL,	JABEZ FISHER,	J. PALMER,
MICHAEL FARLEY,	ELDAD TAYLOR	B. LINCOLN,
T. CUSHING,	JOHN WHETCOMB,	JED. FORSTER.[1]

1. Force, *American Archives*, Fourth Series, VI, 748.

The Continental Congress, after the passage of the act of March 23, 1776, authorizing privateering, had forms printed and these commissions, signed by the President of Congress in blank, were sent to the various states, to be filled out and distributed. One of these forms, undated but probably printed about 1780, authorizes the commander to set forth in a warlike manner and

"by Force of Arms to attack, subdue and take all Ships and other Vessels whatsoever carrying Soldiers, Arms, Gunpowder, Ammunition, Provisions, or any other contraband Goods to any of the British Armies or Ships of War employed against these United States. And also to attack, seize and take all Ships or other Vessels belonging to the Inhabitants of Great Britain, or to any Subject or Subjects thereof, with their Tackle, Apparel, Furniture and Ladings, on the High-Seas or between high and low-water Marks (the Ships or Vessels, together with their Cargoes, belonging to any Inhabitant or Inhabitants of Bermuda, Providence and the Bahama Islands, and such other Ships and Vessels bringing Persons with Intent to settle and reside within any of the United States, or bringing Arms, Ammunition, or Warlike Stores to the said States for the Use thereof, which said Ships or Vessels you shall suffer to pass unmolested, the Commanders thereof permitting a peaceable Search and giving satisfactory Information of the Contents of the Lading and Destination of the Voyage, only excepted). And the said Ships or Vessels so apprehended as aforesaid and as Prize taken, to carry into any Port or Harbour within the Dominions of any neutral State willing to admit the same, or into any Port within the said United States, in order that the Courts there instituted to hear and determine Causes Civil and Maritime, may proceed in due Form to condemn the said Captures, if they be adjudged lawful Prize, or otherwise according to the Usage in such Cases at the Port or in the State where the same shall be carried." The commander "having given Bond with sufficient Sureties, that Nothing be done by [his vessel] or any of his Officers, Marines or Company thereof, contrary to or inconsistent with the Usage and Customs of Nations, and that he shall not exceed or transgress the Powers and Authorities contained in this Commission. And We will and require all our Officers whatsoever in the Service of the United States, to give Succour and Assistance to the said [commander] in the Premises. This Commission shall continue in Force until the Congress shall issue Orders to the contrary."[1]

Privateers were ill adapted for cruising in squadrons and failed in nearly all attempts at coöperation with regular ships or with each other. There were cases where two or three private ships were able to work together or support each other with good effect, but in larger numbers, when anything like manœuvring was required, they were incapable of concerted action. On May 21, 1777, a squadron sailed from Boston composed of the Continental frigates *Hancock* and *Boston* and nine privateers, for a cruise of twenty-five days. Great preparations were made and it was provided that the commanders were to be on the same footing as the regular officers and their vessels were to be insured by the State. Within six days of their departure the privateers, with one exception,[2] had parted from the frigates and were seen no more. The agreements drawn up between the State authorities and the privateersmen, of which the following is one, will indicate the hopes of benefit to be derived from the arrangement:

Articles of Agreement made and Concluded this Third day of May, in the Year of our Lord One Thousand Seven hundred and Seventy Seven, Between Thomas Cushing, Moses Gill, Benjamin Austin, James Warren, Tristram Dalton, William Cooper and Caleb Davis, Esq'rs, A Committee of the Great and General Court of the State of the Massachusetts Bay, for and in behalf of said State on the one part, And Thomas Davis and John Dyson of Beverly in the State of Massachusetts Bay, Merchants, for themselves and the rest of the Owners of the Brigantine *Washington* of Fourteen Carriage Guns and Manned with Seventy five Men, and Elias

---

1. Mass. Historical Society. An earlier, briefer form (Mass. Archives, 166, 72) is here reproduced as an illustration. See frontispiece.
2. Mass. Archives, XL, 129, XLIV, 438. Petition of Capt. Andrew Gardner, of the Schooner *Active*, for pay for this service, enclosing certificate of Captain John Manley of the frigate *Hancock*, to the effect that the *Active* had continued four weeks in company with the frigates.

Smith Commander of said Brigantine, a Private Vessel of War now bound on a Cruise of Twenty five days in Company with a Fleet of Continental Ships and other Vessels of War under the Command of Capt. John Manley, of the other part, Witnesseth, That the said Committee for and [on] the behalf of said State Do hereby Covenant with the said Thomas Davis and John Dyson and the said Elias Smith, Commander of the said Brigantine, in manner following, viz.: That they will Insure said Vessel at the full amount of her Costs and Outsetts from all Dangers of the Sea and the King of England's Ships and Vessels of War while under the Command of the said Capt. John Manley; That in Case of Accident during said Cruise, the Officers and Privates of said Brigantine shall be upon the same footing exactly that the Captains Manley and McNeill and their Men are as to pensions and one Month's pay; That the Ammunition expended in time of Action on this Cruise shall be made good by said State; That the Month's pay abovementioned shall be made to the Officers and Mariners of the said Brigantine, upon their producing a Certificate from the Commanding Officer of said Fleet of their having performed their part of this Agreement.

In Consideration whereof the said Thomas Davis and John Dyson for themselves and the rest of the Owners of the said Brigantine and Elias Smith, Do hereby Covenant with the said Committee, That the said Vessel shall Cruise under the Command of the said Capt. John Manly, or the Commanding Officer of the Continental Ships, for the Term of Twenty five Days from the day of Sailing, unless the Commander shall discharge her Sooner; That in Case said Vessel should by Accident be parted from the Fleet, and should take a Prize or Prizes before the Expiration of the time aforesaid, the Prizes so taken shall be equally divided among the whole Fleet, as tho' they had all been in Company. In Witness whereof the Parties aforesaid have hereunto Interchangably set their hands and Seals the day and year first within written.

And it is further Agreed, That if the said Vessel should be obliged to come into Port thro' necessity to refit in Consequence of Damage she may receive within the Twenty five Days, the Com'ttee Agree that the Owners may fit her out again without any Restrictions, And in Case she goes out short handed, she shall have liberty to return to refit and Compleat her Manning and then proceed on her Cruise at the expiration of said Twenty five days; Provided Nevertheless, if the said Brigantine is not ready to Sail by Thursday next or with the two Continental Ships, this Agreement to be void.

Signed Sealed and Deliv'd
  in the presence of   JOHN DYSON for self
MICAH HAMMON   and THOS. DAVIS
HENRY ALLINE JUN.   ELIAS SMITH.[1]

The special bond given in this case recites that "if the said Elias Smith shall accordingly with the Vessel under his Command proceed upon the Cruise aforesaid and for the Term of Twenty five days from the Fleet's sailing, and shall during this Cruise continue with and strictly Obey the Orders and follow the directions of the said John Manly or the Commanding Officer of the Fleet for the Time being, then this Obligation to be void and of none Effect, otherwise to abide and remain in full force." [2]

Twelve privateers accompanied the Penobscot Expedition in 1779 and when the time came to face the enemy they fled like stampeded cattle, but in this case the regulars, being badly led, did no better. These twelve vessels were taken into the service of the State for the occasion, being impressed when necessary. The following is a warrant for this purpose:

STATE OF MASSACHUSETTS BAY.
COUNCIL CHAMBER, BOSTON, July 2d, 1779.

Whereas it appears to this Board That it is absolutely necessary to compleat a sufficient Naval Force for the Penobscot Expedition That the Ship *General Putnam*, now in this Harbour, should be taken into that Service immediately and the Owners thereof being at a Distance, Therefore *Ordered* That the Sheriff of the County of Suffolk be and he hereby is impowered and directed to impress the Ship *General Putnam* with her Tackle and Appurtenances and deliver her . . . to the Board of War to fit her immediately for a Two Months Cruize, to Sail on an Expedition to Penobscot, to dispossess the Enemy of the United States there, and This shall be your

---

1. Mass. Archives, **139**, 93.
2. *Ibid.*, 95.

sufficient Warrant hereof; fail not and make due Return of this Warrant with your doings thereon forthwith.

In the Name and behalf of the Council

JER. POWELL, *Presid't.*

JOHN AVERY, D. *Sec'y.*[1]

The privateers made many captures and the newspapers of the day contain long lists of their prizes in their advertisements of the sessions of prize courts. The foundations of many fortunes in the seaport towns of Massachusetts were laid by these enterprising mariners. A very rough estimate based on the newspaper lists would indicate that the number of prizes taken and brought into port during the war by Massachusetts privateers and tried in the courts of the State was not far from twelve hundred. Many others must have been tried in other states and in Europe and the West Indies. The court records that have been preserved are somewhat fragmentary. The report of the trial and condemnation of the Massachusetts brigantine *Independence*, recaptured from the British, as it appears in the record of the Maritime Court of the Middle District, will show how prize cases were handled:

STATE OF THE MASSACHUSETTS BAY
Middle District Suffolk Ss.

At the maritime Court for the Middle District of the State of the Massachusetts Bay, holden at Boston in the County of Suffolk by the Honourable Nathan Cushing, Esquire, Judge of said Court, on Fryday the twenty seventh Day of June in the Year of our Lord one thousand seven hundred and seventy seven.

Be it remembered that on the twentieth Day of March in the same Year of our Lord, Mungo Mackay and Thomas Adams, both of Boston aforesaid, Merchants, in Behalf of William Brown, Commander of the private arm'd Ship called the *Boston*, the Officers, Marines and Mariners on board the same Ship, the Owners thereof and all concerned therein, came before the said Judge and filed a Libel exhibiting an Information, to wit, that the said Brown and

1. Mass. Archives, 145, 8.

his Company, in said Ship on the high Seas, on the tenth Day of February last, attacked and took and, on the same twentieth Day of March bro't into Boston in said District, the Brigantine called the *Independance* of about one hundred and twenty Tons Burthen, in Ballast, and commanded by one Harvey. Which Brigantine and Appurtenances, the said Mackay & Adams in their said Bill aver'd, were, at the Time of said Capture, the Property of and belonging to some of the Subjects of the King of Great Britain other than the Inhabitants of Bermuda, New Providence and the Bahama Islands, and was then employed by the Enemies of the united States of America. By Means whereof and by Force of the Laws of this State and the Resolves of the Continental Congress in such Case provided, the same Brigantine, her Cargo and appurtenances (the Proponents further said) are forfeit and to be distributed to and among the Captors and others concerned therein. Praying Advisement in the Premises and that, by a due Course of Proceedings, the same Brigantine and appurtenances may be decreed to be and remain forfeit and distributed as the Law directs.

And the Time and place of Trial having been duely notified, the said Proponants appear. And Richard Derby, junr., esqr., Agent within the said District for the State of Massachusetts-Bay, by William Wetmore, Esqr., his attorney comes into Court and (his Claim having been duely filed) on behalf of said State claimeth the said Brigantine, her Stores, Guns, Arms, Boat and Appurtenances, and saith "that no Condemnation of the said Brigantine, etc., hath been had by the Enemy, and the same Brigantine, etc., before the Capture thereof were and now are the Property of the Government and People of the State aforesaid and not liable to Forfeiture" and prays that the one half of what she, her Stores, Guns, Arms, Boat and Appurtenances may sell for, be restored and paid to him the said Richard, for the Use of the said Government, and People, after deducting the Charges of Trial and Sale from the Proceeds of the said Brigantine, etc.

And after a full Hearing of the Proponants and the Claimant (by their respective Counsel) the Bill aforesaid of the Proponants and the Claim of the said Richard Derby are committed to a Jury duely returned and impannelled and sworn to return a true Verdict thereon according to Law and Evidence. Which Jury are John Coburn, John Woods, Elisha Gardner, Joshua Boylston, John Hooton, David Williams, John Champney, Thomas Parker, William Bosson, Francis Archibald, John Bennet, Benaiah Perkins. Who return their Verdict to the said Judge and upon their Oath say "that the said Brigantine and her Appurtenances, Stores, Guns,

Arms and Boat were the Property of the Government and People of this State of the Massachusetts Bay and were taken by the Enemy and were in the Enemy's possession more than ninety six Hours, and then no Condemnation thereon being had, were retaken on the high Seas, to wit, the tenth Day of February last, by Capt. William Brown, Commander of the Ship *Boston*, and his Company and brought into the middle District of this State; and thereupon the Jury determine that one half of the neat Produce of said Brigt.,. Stores, Guns, Arms, Boat and Appurtenances be to the Recaptors and others concerned therein and the other half to this State of the Massachusetts Bay."

And thereupon, It is, by the said Nathan Cushing, Judge as aforesaid, considered and decreed that the said Brigantine *Independance* with her Stores, Guns, Arms, Boat and Appurtenances be sold at public Vendue; and that the Monies thence arising, after deducting the Charges of Trial and Condemnation being eight Pounds, fourteen shillings and three pence and the Charges of Sale, be delivered, to wit, one half thereof to the Recaptors aforesaid, their Agents or Attornies, for the Use and Benefit of such Recaptors and others concerned therein; and the other half thereof to the said Richard Derby for the Use of the Government and People of the Massachusetts Bay.

attest ISAAC MANSFIELD *Clerk*.[1]

Of course, it was sometimes another story. Many privateers were captured and prizes recaptured, and thousands of American seamen languished on board the *Jersey* and other British prison ships and at Mill and Forton prisons in England. Anything remotely approaching accuracy in estimating the number of Massachusetts privateers taken by the enemy would be still less attainable than in the case of captures from the British.

Knowledge concerning the disposition and exchange of prisoners is derived from various sources. November 30, 1775, the Committee of Safety, of Salem, wrote to the Council about the privateer schooner *Dolphin* of that place, which had just brought in a prize. The

1. Mass. Archives, **159**, 121.

Dolphin applied for a commission the next day and was one of perhaps a considerable number, during the early months, cruising without that important document. But this was not the subject of the letter, which related to the prisoners captured. There was no provision in the act of November 1, 1775, for the disposition of prisoners and the Committee wished to know "what ought to be their conduct respecting such cases."[1] British prisoners sometimes addressed petitions to the Council begging to be released on parole in order to seek opportunities for exchange. In 1777 the master of a vessel taken by the privateer *Warren*, Captain William Coas, represented that his "captors have generously given him half of his adventure, which has enabled him ... to bid for said Ship when put up at Vendue; they were so kind as not to bid against him." Having purchased his ship, he wished to return in her with a small crew to Jamaica. He was allowed to proceed in her to New York, giving his parole to use his best endeavors to procure in exchange the release of an equal number of Massachusetts men, detained there as prisoners.[2]

The arrivals of cartels from Nova Scotia, Newfoundland, and other places, sometimes with three or four hundred exchanged prisoners, were reported from time to time in the newspapers. The *Pliarne*, Captain Samuel Green, in the service of the State, was captured September 17, 1777. Several months later, as negotiations for the exchange of prisoners were about to be undertaken, Peter Green, of Marblehead, father of Sam-

---

1. Pickering Papers, xxxiii, 138. There is no mention of this communication in the Council Records, but on Dec. 6, 1775, the Council ordered that another captured vessel's crew should be released on giving bond that they "would not go into Boston ... nor correspond with our enemies there or elsewhere." The exchange of prisoners soon became usual.

2. Mass. Archives, 166, 287, 296, 325.

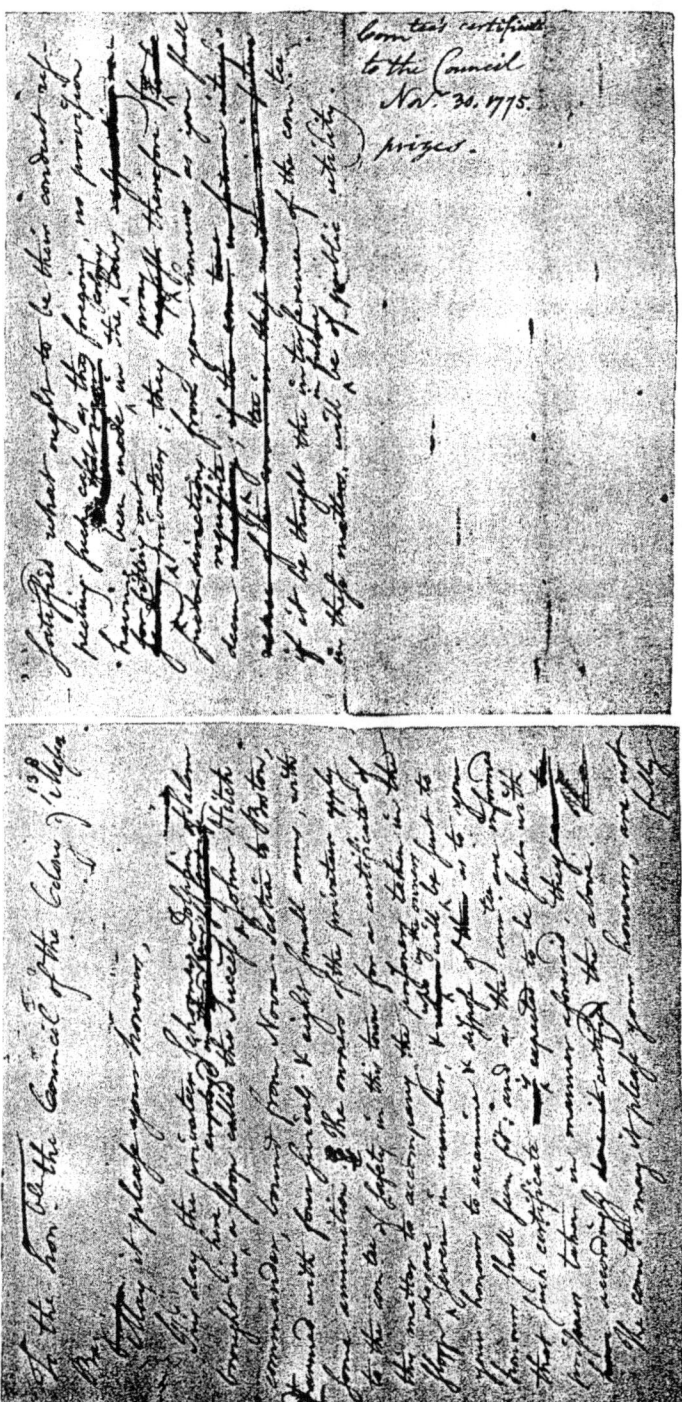

Inquiry as to Disposal of Prisoners

See pages 40, 116

uel, wished to have a British officer sent to procure the release of his son. The order on this petition was that,

Whereas Peter Green has made application to this Board to have Capt. Mark Workman sent to Rhode Island by Colonel Johonnot to be given in Exchange for Capt. Samuel Green, now Prisoner there — Therefore, Resolved that Colonel Gabriel Johonnot be and he hereby is directed to take into his Custody Captain Mark Workman and him convey to the State of Rhode Island and there cause him to be kept in safe Custody till he can be assured the Exchange can be effected and when that matter is ascertained he is hereby directed to cause the said Workman to be given in Exchange for Capt. Samuel Green.[1]

In 1781 the Massachusetts frigate *Protector*, Captain John Foster Williams, was captured by two British ships and taken into New York. Although she was not a privateer and perhaps should not concern us, a short extract from Captain Williams' letter on the subject of exchange is worth quoting, in order to put on record the peculiar status of the Massachusetts State Navy in British opinion. "I know not what we shall be Exchang'd for, as the Admeraltey here says the State of Massachetts has now Right to give a Commission, that they look on me as not a publick or privat Officer."[2]

In 1782 the petition of Edward Bacon and others was presented "To His Excellency John Hancock, Esqr., Governor, and The Hon'ble Council of the Commonwealth of Massachusetts," representing

That they are prisoners lately arrived from Halifax on Parole and must return again immediately unless they can procure a number of Prisoners to exchange for them; That there is a number of British Prisoners who have entered on board the Privateer *Grand Turk* now at Salem; That there is not Prisoners on board the prison Ship in this Harbor sufficient for your Petitioners' exchange. They therefore pray that some immediate Method may be taken that said Prisoners on board said Ship *Grand Turk* may be taken

1. Mass. Archives, 168, 186, 187.
2. Mass. Historical Society, Caleb Davis Papers.

from her in Order they may be given in Exchange for your Petitioners, otherwise they must return to Halifax agreeable to their Paroles and suffer on board the prison Ship.[1]

In October, 1781, John Moriarty, of Salem, petitioned Governor Hancock for permission to send a vessel at his own expense, with thirty British prisoners, to St. John's, Newfoundland, in order to procure the exchange of his son, Thomas Moriarty, and others of the crew of one of his privateers, probably the brigantine *Flying Fish*. The Council advised that this petition be granted.[2]

Of the many interesting miscellaneous papers in the Massachusetts Archives, the two following, in addition to the preceding, are here printed. The sloop *Swift*, whose character in the State service is clearly set forth in these instructions, was bonded as a privateer. The careers of the *General Mercer* and *Fanny* in European waters gave rise to international correspondence.

IN COUNCIL June 6th 1776.

CAPT. JOHN WIGGLESWORTH

Sir, — You being appointed Master of the Sloop *Swift* fitted out by this Colony for the gaining Intelligence Respecting the British Fleets and Armys, You are therefore, as soon as your Vessell is Ready, to Sail for some part of the Coast of Nova Scotia, or you may Cruise on the Seas between Cape Ann and Nova Scotia, and Use your utmost Endeavours for the gaining Intelligence as Aforesaid, and when you shall gain Certain Accounts of the Embarkations of the Troops at Hallifax, or the movement of any Considerable fleet of the Enemy, and the Course they have for some time Steared, you are then with all possible dispatch, to give Information to the Council of this Colony and the Committee of Safety, etc., of the Town where you may Arrive, that Such measures may be taken, as the defence and Security of this Colony may Require; and you are to use all necessary Precaution to prevent your Vessell from falling into the Hands of the Enemy, whereby

---

1. Mass. Archives, 172, 216.

2. *Ibid.*, 172, 23, 24; the next year other citizens of Salem wished to bring about the redemption of prisoners at New York in a similar manner, also at their own expense (188, 130).

the good design of fixing out your Vessell may be Frustrated. As you have received a Commission, by Force of Arms to Attack, Subdue and take all Ships and Other Vessels belonging to the Inhabitants of Great Britain on the High Seas under Certain Restrictions, you must Punctually follow the Instructions herewith delivered you for your Conduct respecting this Matter.

  Moses Gill   J. Bowdoin
  Caleb Cushing   J. Winthrop
  D. Hopkins   Rich'd Derby Junr.
    and nine other councillors.[1]

  State of Massachusetts Bay Ss.
   Council Chamber October 17th 1778.

 Be it remembered that Joseph Foster, Esqr., of Gloucester within this State, merchant, upon Petition to Us for that purpose having laid before Us the Necessary proofs, appears to be the Agent for Owners, Officers, Marines and Mariners of the Private Brigantine *Gen'l Mercer*, Jas. Babson Commander, called the *Hancock* while in France the last Year; Also Messrs. Jno. Grenell and Adam Babcock, both Boston Merchants, upon the same Petition appear to be Owners and Agents for the other Owners, Officers, marines and mariners of the Privateer Brigantine *Fanny*, Jno. Kendrick Commander, called the *Boston* while in France the last Year; which said Privateers having captured two Brittish Ships and carried them into the Port of Nantz in France the 13th August, 1777, Laden with Sugar, which they entered as Dutch Ships coming from St. Eustatia, the consequence of which occasioned the Confiscation of those two Ships by the Court of Admiralty, yet notwithstanding, His Most Christian Majesty the King of France having in his great Goodness been pleased to Order the Sum of Four Hundred Thousand Livres, French Money, to be paid to the Owners and others concurred [concerned?] in the said Two American Privateers, which order first Signified by Monsr. Le Ray de Chaumont, honorary intendant of the Royal Hotel of Invalids, and by him to Jno. Holker Esqr. Agent General of the Royal Marine and Consul of France, and by Him to the said Agents and owners of the said Privateers —

 We therefore declare that the proofs exibited appear to Us satisfactory and sufficient to authorise the said Jno. Holker Esqr. to pay the said Jos'h Foster, Esqr., and Messrs. Adam Babcock and Jno. Grenell the said Sum of Four Hundred Thousand Livres

1. Mass. Archives, **164**, 377.

French Money, according to the Order of his Most Christian Majesty the King of France.

In the Name and by Order of Council,

JER: POWELL *President*.

Boston, 17th October, 1778.[1]

A perusal of bonds, petitions, and other documents will show that many of the cruises of Massachusetts privateers were short, a few weeks only, and when they returned to port they were usually recommissioned. Some of them often changed owners and captains, perhaps particularly after unsuccessful cruises. It is noticeable that not only seafaring men but some merchants were rather apt to change their places of residence. While many of the vessels remained in home waters, others, a large number in the aggregate, were rovers in a real sense; they made long voyages and cruised in European or West Indian seas.

It has been possible to collect 1554 items, or separate commissions, for this work; a few of them, probably of doubtful authenticity. In addition to regularly bonded and commissioned privateers and letters of marque, it seems appropriate, in order to make a comprehensive list, to include certain classes of public vessels, state and national; and likewise the irregular private armed vessels, which sailed without commissions, in the few cases where their names are known. The public vessels included are: Washington's fleet of eight, manned by the army, which cruised in Massachusetts Bay in 1775 and 1776; the sixteen cruisers of the State Navy, many of which were bonded, and certain other vessels belonging to the State; a few vessels belonging to the United States, which also gave bonds.[2]

[1]. Mass. Archives, **169**, 231.
[2]. See above, pp. 43, 44.

Besides the main body of papers in the Massachusetts Archives, contained in 324 volumes, many other papers relating especially to the Revolution comprise a separate series, in 76 volumes, called the Revolutionary Rolls Collection. In referring to these papers in the present work, the numbers of the volumes in the main series are indicated by Arabic numerals in heavy type; the numbers of the volumes in the Revolutionary Rolls are indicated in Roman numerals; in both cases with the prefix M. A. (Massachusetts Archives). Most of the bonds are in volumes v, vi, and vii, a few in volume viii, and others in volume **139**. Reports of the trials of prizes, nearly all in 1777 and 1779, are in volume **159**. Most of the petitions will be found in volumes **164** to **172**; some in later volumes. Miscellaneous papers of interest relating to privateers are scattered through many other volumes. The manuscript records of the Council and of the General Court are important. To the State Archivist, Mr. John H. Edmonds, and his assistants, especially Miss Farnham, acknowledgments are due for valuable help and advice.

The privateer bonds among the Papers of the Continental Congress, in the Library of Congress and listed in *Naval Records of the American Revolution*, are designated by the letters C. C. in the present list. Inasmuch as this publication (*Naval Records*) is accessible in many libraries, the names on the bonds are here omitted, except those of the commanders. When necessary to indicate the home port, the owners also are given.

The "Maritime Court Records," "Early Court Files," and other papers in the Suffolk County Court House, give reports of a considerable number of prize cases, mostly for the later years of the war, and a few were found in a photostatic reproduction of the "Minutes of the Superior Court sitting as an Admiralty Court." Additional prize cases occur in "Notes of Evidence taken by Hon. Increase Sumner, Justice of the Supreme Court of Massachusetts, 1782–1797," in the manuscript collections of the Massachusetts Historical Society.

The Boston Marine Society was visited; also the Essex Institute and the Peabody Museum at Salem, and the manuscript collections of the Essex Institute were examined with some care. Mr. Benjamin J. Lindsey, of the Marblehead Historical Society, very kindly furnished a list of Marblehead vessels. The collections of the Massachusetts Historical Society have yielded data of great value. The compiler is greatly indebted to the custodians and other officials of all these societies and institutions; also to many other persons, especially Mr. O. L. Stone and Mr. H. C. Grafton.

Of printed material the most important is found in contemporary newspapers. The papers of Boston and Salem and the *London Chronicle* have furnished much information and have supplied many names of privateers not found elsewhere. The *Historical Collections of the Essex Institute* are very useful, especially the "Records of the Vice-Admiralty Court at Halifax," edited by Mr. George Francis Dow, and "Auction Sales in Salem, of Shipping and Merchandise," published respectively in the *Collections* for 1909 and for April, 1913. In some cases it has been difficult to decide to which state certain vessels should be credited and doubtless a few names have been admitted to this Massachusetts list which do not belong there; but it has seemed better to err on the safe side. In excluding such names great assistance has been given by Sheffield's *Rhode Island Privateers*, Middlebrook's *Maritime Connecticut during the American Revolution*, and the *Pennsylvania Archives*.

Banks' *History of Martha's Vineyard* and the *Collections of the Maine Historical Society* tell of some of the earliest warlike exploits of Massachusetts seamen during this war. Emmons' *Statistical History of the United States Navy* gives a list of privateers, "copied from official documents" for the most part, but with insufficient care and accuracy. Lists of Salem privateers will be found in Felt's *Annals of Salem*, Hunt's *Lives of American Merchants*, and Paine's *Ships and Sailors of Old Salem*. The authors doubtless had access to original documents, but they give no authorities, no dates, and in most cases extremely scanty data. More carefully prepared is a list of Beverly privateers compiled by Dr. O. T. Howe and published in Volume XXIV of the *Publications of the Colonial Society of Massachusetts*. There are other lists in town histories and elsewhere, including an unpublished one, compiled by William Leavitt, in the library of the *Essex Institute*. These various lists show evidence of having been more or less padded, are all open to suspicion, and should be used with caution.

A source of doubt which increases the difficulty of composing such a list is the confusion of different rigs by writers both contemporary and recent, and even occasionally in original documents. What is evidently the same vessel may be variously described as a ship or brig, schooner or sloop. Moreover, vessels were not infrequently converted from one rig to another.

MASSACHUSETTS PRIVATEERS OF THE REVOLUTION

1779 ABIGAIL, Sloop. *Guns*, 6; *Men*, 12.
Feb. 6   *Commander:* Daniel Smith.
    Bond: Continental, $5000; State, £4000.
    Bonders: Daniel Smith, mariner, principal; Henry Mitchell and Edmund Dunkin, of Boston, sureties.
    Bound to Hon. Henry Laurens, President, and other members of the Honorable Continental Congress; and to Henry Gardner, Esq., Treasurer of the State of Massachusetts Bay.
    Owners: Henry Mitchell and Edm[un]d Dunkin.
    Witnesses: Francis Johonnot, William Gould.
    M. A., v, 7, 10, **169**, 433; Andrews, *Guide to Public Record Office*, II, 334.

1776 ACTIVE, Schooner. *Guns*, 12; *Men*, 80.
Oct. 15   *Commander:* Andrew Gardner.
    Bond: Continental, $5000.
    Bonders: Andrew Gardner, principal; Joseph Pierce and Nehemiah Somes, all of Boston.
    Bound to John Hancock, President of Congress.
    Owners: Joseph Pierce, Nehemiah Somes, and others.
    Witnesses: Cha[rle]s Sigourney, Edmund Fowle.
    M. A., v, 19, XL, 129, XLIV, 438, **139**, 113, 127, **152**, 271, **165**, 358.

1777 ACTIVE, Brigantine. *Guns*, 12; *Men*, 70.
Oct. 13   *Commander:* John Foster Williams.
    Bond: Continental, $5000.
    Bonders: John Foster Williams, principal; Jacob Williams and Nehemiah Somes, of Boston.
    Owners: Nehemiah Somes, Jacob Williams, and others.
    Witnesses: W[illia]m Turner, Isaac Townsend.
    M. A., v, 6, **167**, 313.

1777 ACTIVE, Vessel of War.
Nov. 8   *Commander:* John Foster Williams.
  Bond: State, £2000.
  Bonders: Charles Sigourney, James Foster Condy, and John Foster Williams, of Boston.
  Bound to Henry Gardner.
  Owners: Charles Sigourney and James Foster Condy.
  Witnesses: John Furnass, John M. Furnass.
    M. A., **139**, 151 (Bond not to enlist "any Inhabitant of any of the New England States, other than the State of the Massachusetts Bay").

1779 ACTIVE, Brigantine. *Guns*, 18.
  Commander: John Allen Hallet.
  Massachusetts State Navy.

1780 ACTIVE, Brigantine. *Guns*, 10; *Men*, 24.
May 6   *Commander:* Benj[amin] Ellinwood.
  Bond: Continental, $10,000; State, £4000.
  Bonders: Benjamin Ellinwood, principal; Job Prince, jr., and William Creed, merchants, sureties—all of Boston.
  Owners: Job Prince and others.
  Witnesses: Samuel Holbrook, jr., John Avery, jr.
    M. A., v, 22, 24, VIII, 18, **171**, 148.

1780 ACTIVE, Brigantine. *Guns*, 12; *Men*, 60.
Dec. 13   *Commander:* Nathaniel Swasey, of Beverly.
  C. C. **196**, 1, 22; M. A., **171**, 314.

1781 ACTIVE, Brigantine. *Guns*, 14; *Men*, 60.
Apr. 9   *Commander:* John Pattin, of Beverly.
    C. C. **196**, 1, 20; M. A., **171**, 364; *Boston Gazette*, Dec. 8, 1783 (A prize of the *Active* to be tried Dec. 23, at the last session of the Maritime Court in Boston).

1782 ACTIVE, Brigantine. *Guns*, 11; *Men*, 50.
May 21   *Commander:* William Ross, of Salem.
  C. C. **196**, 1, 21.

1782 ACTIVE, Brigantine. *Guns*, 14; *Men*, 60.
  Commander: Johnson Briggs, of Salem.
  Salem Gazette, Dec. 5, 19, 1782; *Boston Gazette*, Dec. 16, 1782; Felt, II, 276.

Know all Men by these presents That We Nehemiah Somes Merchant and Andrew Gardner Mariner both of Boston in the County of Suffolk, are held and Stand firmly bound and Obliged unto Henry Gardner Esq. Treasurer of the State of Massachusetts Bay and his Successors in said Office in the full and just Sum of Six hundred pounds to be paid unto the said Henry Gardner Treasurer as aforesaid or his Successors in Said Office, to the which payment well and truly to be made we bind ourselves our heirs Executors and Administrators Jointly and Severally firmly by these presents Sealed with our Seals dated the Sixteenth day of April, In the Year of our Lord, One Thousand Seven hundred & Seventy Seven

The Condition of this present Obligation is Such That Whereas the Great & General Court of the State aforesaid on the Seventh of April Instant by their Resolve of that date did allow that the Inhabitants of any Town within said State who had raised their full proportion of the Continental Army to fit out private Vessels of War, but not to Ship or receive on board any Men that are the Inhabitants of any Town in said State that have not raised their proportion of said Army

If Therefore the said Nehemiah Somes & Andrew Gardner Shall not Ship or receive any Men on board the Schooner Active whereof the said Gardner is Commander that are the Inhabitants of any Town within the said State that have not raised their proportion of the Continental Army, then the above written Obligation to be void, but in default thereof to remain in full force & Virtue

Signed Sealed & Deld.
in the presence of

Jon.? Austin
Th. Furnass

Nehemiah Somes
And.w Gardner

Bond not to recruit in any Town which has not raised its Quota for the Continental Army

ACTIVE — ADVENTURE 67

1776 ADAM, Sloop.
July 15   *Commander:* George Creighton.
M. A., 165, 427: "The petition of John Winthrop and Stephen Bruce humbly sheweth that they are owners of the Sloop *Adam*, George Creighton Commander, now ready to sail for the Island of Hispanolia [*sic.*] and being desirous of procuring a quantity of Cannon and military Stores, they intend purchasing 'em at said Island, and for the better securing the same and defending the said Sloop, will have her well arm'd on her homeward passage and take on board an additional number of men with orders to proceed with all speed for some port on this Continent. Wherefore, as it's probable the said Vessel may meet with some belonging to our enemies and will be in a condition to make prizes of them, Your petitioners humbly pray that your Honors will commissionate the said Commander, to qualify him therefor and your petitioners as in duty bound shall ever pray. . . .

"In Council July 16, 1776. Read and committed to Moses Gill and Francis Dana, Esqrs. to report thereon. Jno. Avery, Dpty Sec'y." (No report of this committee has been preserved.)

1780 ADDITION, Brigantine (privateer).
June 17   *Commander:* Joseph Pratt, of Salem.
M. A., XL, 82.

1779 ADVENTURE, Brigantine. *Guns*, 6; *Men*, 15.
Jan. 5   *Commander:* John O'Brien.
Bond: Continental, $10,000; State, £4000.
Bonders: John Obrian, mariner, principal; Daniel Tappan and Enoch Moulton, of Cape Ann, sureties.
Owner: Caleb Tapping [Tappan?], of Newburyport.
Witnesses: John Toppan [Tappan?], Jo[seph?] Tappan.
Note. The commander signed his name Obrien.
M. A., V, 27, 28, **169**, 405.

1779 ADVENTURE, Brigantine. *Guns*, 8; *Men*, 30.
Jan. 15   *Commander:* Joseph Tripp.
Bond: Continental, $5000; State, £4000.
Bonders: Joseph Tripp, principal; Nathaniel Greene and Mungo Mackay, of Boston, sureties.

Owners: Nathaniel Greene and others.
Witnesses: T. Amory, jr., Mungo Mackay, jr.
M. A., v, 31, 32, **169**, 413½.

1779　ADVENTURE, Schooner. *Guns*, 6; *Men*, 35.
Sept. 8　　Commander: Robert Newman.
　　　　　Bond: Continental, $5000; State, £4000.
　　　　　Bonders: Robert Newman, mariner, principal; Larkin Thorndike and Sewall Tuck, of Beverly, sureties.
　　　　　Owners: Larkin Thorndike and others.
　　　　　Witnesses: Francis Rust [?], W. Harris.
　　　　　M. A., v, 29, 30, **159**, 317, **170**, 379.

1780　ADVENTURE, Schooner. *Guns*, 6; *Men*, 25.
May 11　　Commander: William James.
　　　　　Bond: Continental, $5000; State, £4000.
　　　　　Bonders: William James, mariner, of Beverly, principal; John Dyson and Benj[amin] Goldthwait, sureties.
　　　　　Owners: John Dyson and others, of Beverly.
　　　　　Witnesses: Jesse Goodnow, W[illia]m Goodnow.
　　　　　M. A., v, 5, 8, **171**, 159.

1780　ADVENTURE, Brigantine. *Guns*, 14; *Men*, 70.
Sept. 19　　Commander: James Morris, of Boston.
　　　　　C. C. **196**, 1, 37; M. A., **171**, 273.

1780　ADVENTURE, Ship. *Guns*, 6; *Men*, 45.
Nov. 22　　Commander: Hector McNeill.
　　　　　Owner: Hector McNeill, of Boston.
　　　　　C. C. **196**, 1, 36; M. A., **171**, 307.

1781　ADVENTURE, Ship. *Guns*, 8; *Men*, 20.
Nov. 30　　Commander: Edward Bacon, jr., of Barnstable.
　　　　　Owners: Stephen Higginson and others, of Boston.
　　　　　C. C. **196**, 1, 32; M. A., **172**, 75; *London Chronicle*, June 1, 1782.

[1781]　ADVENTURE, Brig. *Guns*, 4; *Men*, 10.
　　　　　Commander: J. Gardner, of Salem.
　　　　　Paine, 454.

1782　ADVENTURE, Brig. *Guns*, 4; *Men*, 10.
Aug. 20　　Commander: Jonathan Tucker, of Salem.
　　　　　C. C. **196**, 1, 41; *Salem Gazette*, Oct. 10, 1782: "Last Monday a Cartel with 62 prisoners belonging to this

ADVENTURE — ALEXANDER 69

place, Boston, and Gloucester, arrived here in fifteen days from Bermuda. Among the vessels lately captured by the enemy and carried to that island are the letter-of-marque ship *Thomas*, Capt. Palfray, the brig *Adventure*, Capt. Tucker, and the schooner *Chance*, Capt. Newell, from this port."

1782 ADVENTURE, Brig. *Guns*, 12; *Men*, 20.
Oct. 15   *Commander:* Joseph Chase, of Nantucket.
     Owners: Ebenezer Lane and others, of Boston.
     C. C. **196**, 1, 31; M. A., **172**, 205.

1782 ADVENTUROUS FISHERMAN, Schooner. *Guns*, 2; *Men*, 10.
Aug. 29   *Commander:* Nicholas Bartlett, of Marblehead.
     Owners: Fortesque Vernon and others, of Boston.
     C. C. **196**, 1, 30.

1780 ALEXANDER, Brigantine. *Guns*, 6, and 8 *swivels*; *Men*, 20.
Mar. 29   *Commander:* Alexander Coffin.
     Bond: Continental, $10,000; State, £4000.
     Bonders: Alex[ander] Coffin, mariner, principal; John Johnston and William Foster, of Boston, sureties.
     Owner: William Foster, merchant.
     Witnesses: James Yancey, Samuel Pitts.
     M. A., v, 42, 45, **171**, 107.

1781 ALEXANDER, Ship. *Guns*, 20; *Men*, 150.
Jan. 5   *Commander:* Thomas Simpson, of Portsmouth, N. H.
     Owners: Henry Mitchell and others, of Boston.
     C. C. **196**, 1, 46.

1781 ALEXANDER, Brigantine. *Guns*, 6; *Men*, 14.
Oct. 9   *Commander:* Gideon Crawford, jr., of Providence, R. I.
     Owners: William Foster and others, of Boston.
     C. C. **196**, 1, 45; M. A., **172**, $19\frac{1}{2}$.

1782 ALEXANDER, Ship. *Guns*, 14; *Men*, 60.
Jan. 5   *Commander:* Thomas Simpson.
     Owner: Henry Mitchell, of Boston.
     C. C. **196**, 1, 47.

1783 ALEXANDER, Ship. *Guns*, 17; *Men*, 50.
Jan. 4   *Commander:* John Foster Williams, of Boston.
     C. C. **196**, 1, 48; M. A., **172**, 275.

1780   AMAZON, Brigantine. *Guns*, 8; *Men*, 50.
Mar. 27   *Commander:* Noah Stoddard.
   Bond: Continental, $10,000; State, £4000.
   Bonders: Noah Stoddard, mariner of Boston, principal; Thomas Tillotson and Perez Morton, of Boston, sureties.
   Owners: Thomas Tillotson and Perez Morton.
   Witnesses: Dimond Morton, John Chaloner.
   M. A., v, 43, 363, **139**, 266, **171**, 106.

1776   AMERICA, Sloop. *Guns*, 10, and 12 *swivels*; *Men*, 70.
Sept. 6   *Commander:* Thomas Nicolson.
   Bond: Continental, $5000.
   Bonders: Thomas Nicolson and James Warren, of Plymouth; John Avery, jr., of Boston.
   Owners: Watson & Spooner, of Plymouth.
   Witnesses: Oakes Angier, Tho[ma]s Jones.
   M. A., v, 18, **165**, 211.

1776   AMERICA, Schooner. *Guns*, 10; *Men*, 80.
Sept. 13   *Commander:* Isaac Snow.
   Bond: Continental, $5000.
   Bonders: Isaac Snow, gentleman, of Harpswell, James Leach, shipwright, of Cape Elizabeth, and Ebenezer Prout, merchant, of Scarborough.
   Owners: Isaac Snow and others.
   Witnesses: Jona[than] Brown, Jeremiah Colburn.
   M. A., v, 21, **165**, 229.

1777   AMERICA, Schooner. *Guns*, 16; *Men*, 80.
Apr. 17   *Commander:* Daniel McNeill.
   Bond: Continental, $5000.
   Bonders: Daniel McNeill, principal; Thomas Harris and Samuel Thompson, sureties.
   Owners: Thomas Harris & Co., of Boston.
   Witnesses: Eben[eze]r Frothingham, John Wait.
   M. A., v, 41, **139**, 130, 154, **159**, 134, 137, **166**, 351, **181**, 217 (Petition of Thomas Harris, Sept. 9, 1776, for powder for the schooner *America*).

1777   AMERICA, Sloop. *Guns*, 12; *Men*, 67.
Sept. 20   *Commander:* William Coit.
   Bond: Continental, $5000; State, £500.
   Bonders: William Coit, of Connecticut, principal; Richard Gridley and Gabriel Johonnot, of Boston, sureties.

Owners: Eph[rai]m Spooner and W[illia]m Watson, of Plymouth.
Witness: Jno. Avery.
M. A., v, 9, 12, **167**, 242.

1777 **AMERICA**, Sloop. *Guns*, 8; *Men*, 35.
Dec. 4   *Commander:* Nathaniel Coit Webb.
Bond: Continental, $5000; State, £500.
Bonders: Nathaniel Coit Webb, of Salem, principal; Maj. James Swan and Capt. Silas Atkins, of Boston, sureties.
Owners: James Swan and others.
Witnesses: William Coleman, John Lowell.
M. A., v, 1, 2, **167**, 399.

1777 **AMERICA**, Brigantine. *Guns*, 16; *Men*, 80.
Dec. 24   *Commander:* John Allen Hallet.
Bond: Continental, $10,000; State, £500.
Bonders: John Allen Hallet, of Boston, principal; Thomas Harris and David Devens, of Boston, sureties.
Owners: Thomas Harris and David Devens.
Witness: W[illia]m Baker, jr.
M. A., v, 14, 15, **139**, 154, **168**, 113.

1778 **AMERICA**, Brigantine. *Tons*, 120; *Guns*, 16, and 14 *swivels;*
Aug. 28   *Men*, 80.
Commander: Nicholas Bartlett, jr.
Bond: Continental, $10,000; State, £4000.
Bonders: N[icholas] Bartlett, jr., mariner, principal; Thomas and Jona[than] Harris, sureties.
Owners: John Thomas, Jonathan Harris, David Devens, and others, of Boston.
Witnesses: Nicho[las] Lobdell, David Devens.
M. A., v, 16, 17, **139**, 209, **169**, 112.

1779 **AMERICA**, Brigantine. *Guns*, 6; *Men*, 18.
Apr. 22   *Commander:* Daniel McNeill.
Bond: Continental, $5,000; State, £4000.
Bonders: Daniel McNeill, mariner, principal; John Larkin and Tho[ma]s Harris, of Boston, sureties.
Owners: John Larkin and others.
Witnesses: Matt[he]w Clark, Isaac Townsend.
M. A., v, 20, 23, **170**, 62.

1779 AMERICA, Ship. *Guns,* 14; *Men,* 40.
Sept. 8   *Commander:* Anthony Shoemaker.
   Bond: Continental, $10,000; State, £4000.
   Bonders: Anthony Shoemaker, mariner, principal; Samuel Broome and Jos[eph] Head, of Boston, sureties.
   Owners: Samuel Broome and others.
   Witnesses: John Trumbull, John Frazier.
   M. A., v, 39, 40, **170**, 381.

1779 AMERICA, Brigantine. *Guns,* 8; *Men,* 25.
Nov. 2   *Commander:* Isaiah Simmons.
   Bond: Continental, $5000; State, £4000.
   Bonders: Isaiah Simmons, mariner, principal; Thomas Harris and Jonathan Harris, of Boston, sureties.
   Owners: Thomas Harris and others.
   Witnesses: Benj[amin] Goodwin, Isaac Townsend.
   M. A., v, 3, 4, **171**, 6.

1780 AMERICA, Ship.
June 9   *Commander:* John Somes.
   M. A., xl, 57; *Boston Gazette,* Sept. 4, 1780.

1780 AMERICA, Ship. *Guns,* 20; *Men,* 100.
Oct. 12   *Commander:* William Coffin, of Newburyport.
   Owners: John Coffin Jones and others, of Boston.
   C. C. **196**, 1, 52; M. A., xl, 58, **171**, 291.

1780 AMERICA, Schooner. *Guns,* 8; *Men,* 80.
   Commander: George Williams.
   Essex Institute, Miscellaneous Ship Papers.

1777 AMERICAN, Sloop. *Guns,* 10; *Men,* 55.
May 3   *Commander:* John Atwood.
   Bond: Continental, $5000.
   Bonders: John Atwood, mariner of Eastham, Stephen Sampson, of Plymouth, and Sam[ue]l A[llyne] Otis, of Boston.
   Owners: Stephen Sampson and others.
   Witnesses: Nath[anie]l Leonard, Seth Loring.
   M. A., v, 11, **166**, 380.

1778 AMERICAN, Sloop. *Guns,* 12; *Men,* 60.
May 26   *Commander:* Samuel Avery.
   Bond: Continental, $5000; State, £4000.
   Bonders: Samuel Avery, principal; Sam[ue]l Jackson and ——— ———, sureties.
   Owners: Samuel Jackson and others, of Boston.

Signers: Sam[ue]l Avery, Jonathan Waldron, Rob[er]t Williams.
Witnesses: William Baker (Continental), Sam[ue]l Dashwood (State), James Carter (both).
  Note. In the petition the name of the vessel is *America* and Jackson's residence is Plymouth.
M. A., v, 35, 36, **168**, 333.

1782   AMERICAN, Ship. *Guns,* 16; *Men,* 60.
July 9   *Commander:* Robert Caldwell, of Boston.
  Owners: John Donnaldson & Co., Philadelphia.
  C. C. **196**, 1, 51.

1782   AMERICAN HERO, Ship. *Guns,* 16; *Men,* 25.
Apr. 27   *Commander:* William Fairfield, of Salem.
    Note. This vessel was sometimes called *Hero.*
  C. C. **196**, 1, 54; M. A., 172, 142.

1779   AMERICAN REVENUE, Sloop. *Guns,* 12; *Men,* 60.
Sept. 13   *Commander:* William Jaggar.
  Bond: Continental, $5000; State, £4000.
  Bonders: William Jaggar, mariner, principal; Sam[ue]l Broome and Thomas Lamb, of Boston, sureties.
  Owner: Samuel Broome.
  Witnesses: John Frazier, Thomas Hunt.
  M. A., VII, 17, 18, **170**, 395.

1776   AMERICAN TARTAR, Ship. *Guns,* 24; *Men,* 150.
Nov. 29   *Commander:* John Grimes.
  Bond: Continental, $10,000.
  Bonders: John Grimes, principal; John Dean and Mungo Mackay, sureties — all of Boston.
  Owners: John Dean, Jos[eph] Barrell, and others.
  Witnesses: David Cobb, Joseph Barrell.
    M. A., VII, 49, **139**, 101, 131, **159**, 146, **166**, 67; Williams, *History of Liverpool Privateers,* 205 (quoting a Liverpool newspaper): The ship *Pole* of Liverpool, at sea on July 12, 1777, "fell in with the [*American*] *Tartar,* a rebel privateer. . . . She bore down on the *Pole* under English colours, enquired from whence she came and whether she was a King's ship. Being answered in the affirmative, the captain gave orders to hoist the Thirteen Stripes and fire away, on which the engagement began and continued from five until about twenty minutes past eight, when the privateer sheered off."

1780 AMERICAN TARTAR, Ship.
 Commander: David Porter, of Boston.
  Note. Doubtless the same as the *Tartar* (Oct. 18, 1779).
  M. A., **159**, 301 (The *American Tartar* captured the ship *Wallace* March 9, 1780, and brought her into Boston the next day. Mungo Mackay appeared in the Maritime Court March 14, in behalf of Captain Porter).

1782 AMIABLE EUNICE, Brigantine. *Guns*, 6; *Men*, 14.
Apr. 29 *Commander:* William Pearson, of Newburyport.
 Owners: Daniel Bell and others, of Boston.
 C. C. **196**, 1, 59; M. A., **172**, 143.

1779 AMSTERDAM, Brigantine. *Guns*, 10; *Men*, 30.
May 13 *Commander:* James Magee.
 Bond: Continental, $10,000; State, £4000.
 Bonders: James Magee, principal; Leonard Jarvis and Paschal N[elson] Smith, of Boston, sureties.
 Owners: Paschal N. Smith and Isaac Sears.
 Witnesses: Daniel Denison Rogers, James Thwing, jr.
 M. A., v, 33, 34, **170**, 93.

1780 AMSTERDAM, Brig.
Feb. 22 *Commander:* James Magee.
 Petitioners: Isaac Sears and Paschal N[elson] Smith.
 M. A., Council Records; *Boston Gazette*, Nov. 12, 1781: "Last week arrived a cartel schooner from Penobscot, in which came Capt. Magee, officers and crew of the *Amsterdam,* who inform they were captured the 19th ult. by the *Amphitrite* frigate, Capt. Biggs, and carried into Penobscot, where they received from Capt. Biggs and officers the greatest civility and generosity."

1778 ANGELICA, Ship. *Guns*, 16; *Men*, 98.
 Commander: —— ——.
 Gentleman's Magazine, XLVIII (1778), 330: "The *Andromeda,* in which ship General Howe came passenger [arriving at Portsmouth July 2, 1778], in her way home fell in with and took the *Angelica* privateer, from Boston, mounting sixteen guns, six pounders, and 98 men, and, after taking out the hands, set the ship on fire."

1778   ANGELICA, Private Vessel of War.
Aug. 23   *Commander:* William Dennis.
       Bond: State, £2000.
       Bonders: Adam Babcock and W[illiam] Dennis, of Boston.
       Owners: Adam Babcock and others.
       Witnesses: Jno. Furnass, J[ohn] M. Furnass.
           M. A., **139**, 181 (Bond not to enlist "any Inhabitant of any of the New England States, other than the State of the Massachusetts Bay").

1778   ANN, Brigantine.
May 20   *Commander:* James Magee.
       Bond: State, £2000.
       Bonders: Isaac Sears, merchant, "the major part of the owners," and John [signed James] Magee, both of Boston.
       Witnesses: W[illia]m Gardiner, Henry Alline, jr.
           M. A., **139**, 182 (Bond not to enlist any man in New England outside of Massachusetts).

1781   ANTELOPE, Brigantine. *Guns,* 10; *Men,* 18.
Oct. 29   *Commander:* Thomas Clouston, of Newburyport.
       C. C. **196**, 1, 67.

1782   ANTELOPE, Ship. *Guns,* 8; *Men,* 16.
Feb. 6   *Commander:* Edward Fettyplace, of Newburyport.
       C. C. **196**, 1, 68; M. A., **172**, 96.

1782   ANTI SMUGGLER, Galley. *Guns,* small arms; *Men,* 18.
Aug. 7   *Commander:* John Percival, of Barnstable.
       Owners: Nathaniel Freeman and others, of Sandwich.
       C. C. **196**, 1, 71; Maritime Court Records, 78; Sumner's Notes of Evidence (Mass. Hist. Soc. MS.), 1, 239.

1780   APOLLO, Ship. *Guns,* 10; *Men,* 20.
Oct. 2   *Commander:* Henry Skinner, of Boston.
       C. C. **196**, 1, 76; M. A., **171**, 286.

1782   APOLLO, Ship. *Guns,* 10; *Men,* 25.
Jan. 14   *Commander:* Bradbury Sanders, of Cape Ann.
       Owners: Thomas Dennie [Denney] and others, of Boston.
       C. C. **196**, 1, 75; M. A., **172**, 92.

1782   APOLLO, Ship. *Guns,* 6; *Men,* 25.
Dec. 13   *Commander:* Alexander Mackay, of Boston.
       C. C. **196**, 1, 74; M. A., **172**, 258.

1781 ARGO, Ship. *Guns*, 16; *Men*, 40.
Dec. 15   *Commander:* John Williamson, of Marblehead.
C. C. **196**, 1, 80.

1782 ARGO, Ship. *Guns*, 18; *Men*, not stated.
Commander: [Samuel?] Trevett.
Boston Gazette, Dec. 2, 1782 (Salem, Nov. 29): "On Thursday 21st instant, the letter of marque ship *Argo*, mounting 18 carriage guns and commanded by Capt. Trevett, was stranded near Old York Harbour."

1782 ASSURANCE, Sloop. *Guns*, 14; *Men*, 75.
Dec. 3   *Commander:* David Porter, of Boston.
C. C. **196**, 1, 83; M. A., **172**, 238.

1782 ASTREA, Ship. *Guns*, 20; *Men*, 50.
Dec. 19   *Commander:* John Derby, of Salem.
C. C. **196**, 1, 84; M. A., **172**, 260; *Salem Gazette*, Jan. 30, 1783: "The brigantine *Speedwell*, late commanded by Capt. John Ingersoll, of this place, arrived here on Sunday last. She was taken by the enemy on her homeward-bound passage from the West Indies and retaken off Halifax, by the letter of marque ship *Astrea*, Capt. John Derby, of this port."

1782 ATALANTA, Brig. *Guns*, 10; *Men*, 25.
Oct. 21   *Commander:* Cornelius Thompson, of Salem.
C. C. **196**, 1, 85; M. A., **172**, 210.

1778 AURORA, Schooner. *Guns*, 6, and 6 *swivels*; *Men*, 30.
Aug. 1   *Commander:* Redmond Hackett.
Bond: Continental, $5000; State, £4000.
Bonders: Redmond Hackett, mariner, principal; George Lynham and G[ené] Jolly, of Boston, sureties.
Owners: George Lynham and G[ené] Jolly.
Witnesses: William Baker, John Dall.
M. A., v, 37, 38, **169**, 56.

1780 AURORA, Ship.
Aug. 10   *Commander:* Thomas Collier.
M. A., **176**, 627 (Petition of Stephen Hooper and others, of Newburyport, that the ship may proceed on her cruise, embargo notwithstanding. Granted); *Boston Gazette*, June 26, 1780.

1780 AURORA, Ship. *Guns*, 10; *Men*, 20.
Oct. 2   *Commander:* David Porter, of Boston.
C. C. **196**, 1, 87; M. A., **171**, 285.

1781 AURORA, Ship of War.
June 16   *Commander:* David Porter.
Bond: £2000.
Bonders: John Cushing and Mungo Mackay, merchants of Boston, major part of owners, and David Porter, mariner.
Witnesses: George Burroughs, Charles Adams.
M. A., XL, 59, **139**, 279 (Bond not to enlist any man in New England outside of Massachusetts); *Boston Gazette*, Aug. 27, 1781: "The Privateers *Bellisarius*, Capt. James Munroe, and *Aurora*, Capt. David Porter, of this Port, are both captured by a 20-Gun Ship and two Brigs of 16 Guns each, and carried into New York."

1781 AURORA, Schooner. *Guns*, 6; *Men*, 20.
Nov. 2   *Commander:* René Chaloche, of Boston.
C. C. **196**, 1, 86; M. A., **172**, 58.

1781 AURORA, Brigantine. *Guns*, 6; *Men*, 12.
Dec. 27   *Commander:* George Williams, jr., of Salem.
C. C. **196**, 1, 88; M. A., **172**, 88.

1782 AURORA, Brig. *Guns*, 10; *Men*, 75.
Commander: [Robert?] Caldwell.
Essex Institute, Miscellaneous Ship Papers.

1782 BANTER, Sloop. *Guns*, 8; *Men*, 50.
May 25   *Commander:* Henry White, of Salem.
C. C. **196**, 1, 95; Sumner's Notes (Mass. Hist. Soc. MS.), 1, 52; M. A., **167**, 8; Andrews, *Guide to Public Record Office*, 11, 335 (Captured in Straits of Belle Isle, July, 1782).

1778 BATCHELOR, Schooner. *Guns*, 8, and 6 *swivels; Men*, 40.
Feb. 26   *Commander:* John Hays.
Bond: Continental, $5000; State, £500.
Bonders: John Hayes [signed Hays], principal; William Shattuck and [John Shattuck], sureties.
Owners: William Shattuck and others, of Boston.
Witnesses: William Dall, James Perkins.
Signatures: John Hays, William Shattuck, John Shattuck.
Note. The vessel's name is also spelled *Batchelder* and *Batcheldor*.
M. A., V, 81, 82, **139**, 157 (Bond not to enlist soldiers of the Continental Army), **168**, 192.

1779 BATCHELOR, Ship. *Guns*, 16; *Men*, 120.
Nov. 2   *Commander:* Alexander Holmes.
    Bond: Continental, $10,000; State, £4000.
    Bonders: Alexander Holmes, mariner, principal; William Erskine and Henry Mitchell, of Boston (on Continental bond), Martin Brimmer and Samuel Nicholson, of Boston (on State bond), sureties.
    Owners: William Erskine and others.
    Witnesses: Howard Barry [?] and Francis Sears [?] (on Continental bond), Henry Livingston and John Kean (on State bond).
    M. A., v, 61, 62, **139**, 261, **171**, 2.

1779 BEAVER, Schooner. *Tons*, 35; *Guns*, 2, and 8 *swivels*; *Men*, 30.
June 3   *Commander:* William Bootman.
    Petitioners: Joseph Lambert and Robert Stone, of Salem.
    M. A., **170**, 150.

1781 BEAVER, Ship. *Guns*, 6; *Men*, 20.
Jan. 31   *Commander:* William Russell, of Newburyport.
    C. C. **196**, 1, 99.

1781 BEAVER, Ship. *Tons*, 150; *Guns*, 6; *Men*, 20.
Feb. 5   *Commander:* William Russell.
    C. C. **196**, 1, 100; M. A., **171**, 339.

1779 BECCA, Brigantine. *Guns*, 8; *Men*, not stated.
Sept. 4, 18 *Commander:* John Willson.
    Bond: Continental, $5000; State, £4000.
    Bonders: John Willson, mariner, principal; William Shattuck and John Shattuck, of Boston.
    Owners: William and John Shattuck.
    Witnesses: James Perkins, Stephen H. Gray.
    Note. The State bond was signed two weeks later than the Continental bond.
    M. A., v, 96, 98, **170**, 404.

1778 BEHMUS, Ship. *Guns*, 4; *Men*, 13.
Dec. 28   *Commander:* Benjamin Hill.
    Bond: Continental, $10,000; State, £4000.
    Bonders: Benjamin Hill, mariner, principal; Samuel Bayley and Ralph Cross, jr., of Newburyport, sureties.
    Owners: Ralph Cross and others.
    Witnesses: Hannah Cross, John Herrick.
    M. A., v, 92, 95, **169**, 385.

1779 **BEHMUS**, Ship. *Guns*, 8; *Men*, 20.
Aug. 7   Commander: Samuel Bayley.
    Bond: Continental, ——; State, £4000.
    Bonders: Samuel Bailey [signed Bayley], principal; Moses Little and Joseph Moulton, jr., of Newburyport, sureties.
    Owners: Not stated.
    Witnesses: Jacob Boardman, Robert Stevenson.
    M. A., v, 63, 64, **170**, 308.

1781 **BELISARIUS**, Ship. *Tons*, 500; *Guns*, 20; *Men*, 200.
Apr. 14   Commander: James Munro, of Providence, R. I.
    Owners: William and John Shattuck, of Boston.
        Note. The vessel's name is often spelled *Bellisarius*.
    C. C. **196**, 1, 104; M. A., **171**, 370; *Boston Gazette*, Aug. 27, 1781 (See *Aurora*, Capt. Porter).

1777 **BELLONA**, Brigantine.
    Commander: Thomas Stevens.
    Boston Gazette, Sept. 22, 1777.

1778 **BELLONA**, Brigantine. *Guns*, 14; *Men*, 75.
Jan. 1   Commander: Nicholas Ogelbe.
    Bond: Continental, $5000; State, £500.
    Bonders: Nicholas Ogelbe, of Marblehead, principal; Maj. Sam[ue]l White, of Boston, and John Grush, of Marblehead, sureties.
    Owners: Samuel White and John Grush.
    Witnesses: Josh[ua] Bindon, W[illia]m McCarty.
    M. A., v, 67, 68, **168**, 218.

1779 **BENNINGTON**, Brigantine.
    Commander: William Tuck.
    Boston Gazette, Jan. 18, Feb. 15, 1779: "On Monday last [Jan. 11] arrived at Cape-Ann, the Privateer Brig *Bennington*, of Newbury; in her cruise she has taken a Ship from Jamaica laden with Rum and Sugar, also a Privateer Schooner of 12 guns, and several other vessels; the Ship arrived on Wednesday at Cape-Ann."

1779 **BENNINGTON**, Brigantine.
    Commander: John Hart.
        Note. This may have been a New Hampshire vessel.
    Boston Gazette, June 7, 1779.

1777 BETSEY, Sloop. *Guns, 4 swivels; Men,* 5.
June 21   *Commander:* John Palmer.
   Bond: Continental, $5000.
   Bonders: John Palmer, of New York, principal; Isaac Sears and Paschal N[elson] Smith, of Boston, sureties.
   Owner: Isaac Sears.
   Witnesses: Eliakim Raymond, Benjamin Jarvis.
   M. A., v, 56, **167**, 44.

1777 BETSEY, Sloop. *Guns,* 10; *Men,* 25.
Oct. 10   *Commander:* Enoch Coffin.
   Bond: Continental, $5000.
   Bonders: Tristram Dalton, of Newburyport, in behalf of Enoch Coffin; Samuel White and Job Prince, of Boston.
   Owner: Tristram Dalton.
   Witnesses: Tho[ma]s Prince, Jos[eph] Barrell.
   M. A., v, 87, **167**, 321.

1779 BETSEY, Brigantine. *Guns,* 6; *Men,* 20.
Jan. 1   *Commander:* Nathaniel Bently.
   Bond: Continental, $10,000; State, £4000.
   Bonders: Nathaniel Bently, mariner, principal; Joseph Laughton, of Boston, and John Tracy, of Newburyport, sureties.
   Owners: John Tracy and others.
   Witnesses: Isaiah Doane, Joseph Billings.
   M. A., v, 25, 26, **169**, 397.

1779 BETSEY, Sloop. *Guns,* 4; *Men,* 10.
Jan. 12   *Commander:* Elisha Smith.
   Bond: Continental, $5000; State, £4000.
   Bonders: Elisha Smith, principal; Philip Moore and Paschal N. Smith, of Boston, sureties.
   Owners: Isaac Sears and others, of Boston.
   Witnesses: Elia[ki]m Raymond, Joseph Skillin.
   M. A., v, 83, 84, **169**, 410.

1779 BETSEY, Schooner. *Guns,* 1 *swivel; Men,* 10.
June 10   *Commander:* René Chaloche.
   Bond: Continental, $5000; State, £4000.
   Bonders: René Chaloche, mariner, principal; John Larreguy and J. E. Dallet, merchants of Boston, sureties.
   Owners: John Larreguy and others.
   Witness: J[ohn] Dall.
   M. A., v, 75, 76, **170**, 165.

BETSEY

1780 BETSEY, Schooner.
May 16   *Commander:* George West, jr.
           M. A., XL, 95.

1780 BETSEY, Sloop. *Guns*, 6; *Men*, 7.
June 29 *Commander:* John Bishop.
           Bond: Continental, $5000; State, £4000.
           Bonders: John Bishop, mariner of Boston, principal;
             Elisha Doane and Stephen Bruce, of Boston, sureties.
           Owners: Stephen Bruce and others.
           Witnesses: James Lamb, jr., John M. Lovell.
           M. A., V, 77, 78.

1780 BETSEY, Brigantine. *Guns*, 6; *Men*, 20.
Sept. 26 *Commander:* Benjamin Willis, of Boston.
           C. C. **196**, II, 26.

1780 BETSEY, Brigantine. *Guns*, 4; *Men*, 9.
Nov. 29 *Commander:* Peter Wells, of Boston.
           C. C. **196**, II, 25; M. A., **171**, 311.

1781 BETSEY, Brigantine. *Guns*, 6; *Men*, 20.
Jan. 1   *Commander:* Barzillai Smith, of Cape Cod.
           Owners: Isaac Smith and others, of Boston.
           C. C. **196**, II, 24; M. A., **171**, 322.

1781 BETSEY, Sloop. *Guns*, 10; *Men*, 40.
Feb. 1   *Commander:* Benjamin Lurvy, of Amesbury.
           Owners: Tristram Dalton and others, of Newburyport.
           C. C. **196**, II, 18; M. A., **171**, 336.

1781 BETSEY, Ship. *Guns*, 20; *Men*, 130.
Feb. 2   *Commander:* Philemon Haskell, of Gloucester.
           C. C. **196**, II, 12; M. A., **171**, 338.

1781 BETSEY, Brig. *Guns*, 6; *Men*, 25.
June 16 *Commander:* Jesse Harding, of Boston.
           C. C. **196**, II, 13; M. A., **171**, 413; Andrews, *Guide to
             Public Record Office*, II, 334.

1783 BETSEY, Brig. *Guns*, 7; *Men*, 40.
Feb. 26 *Commander:* Patrick Maxfeld, of Boston.
           C. C. **196**, II, 19; M. A., **172**, 308.

           BETSEY, Ship. *Guns*, 8; *Men*, 40.
             Commander: Joseph Dennis.
             Essex Institute, Miscellaneous Ship Papers.

1776 BILBOA PACKET, Brigantine. *Guns,* 8; *Men,* 22.
Nov. 20   *Commander:* William Mein.
   Bond: Continental, $5000.
   Bonders: William Mein, mariner, Stephen Hooper and John Coffin Jones, merchants, all of Newburyport.
   Owners: Stephen Hooper and John Coffin Jones.
   Witnesses: Eben[eze]r Stocker, Will[ia]m Fisher.
      Note. Name spelled *Billboa* in the bond and *Bilboa* in the petition.
   M. A., v, 97, **166**, 60.

1777 BLACKBIRD, Schooner. *Guns,* 8; *Men,* 20.
Aug. 6   *Commander:* William Groves, of Salem.
   C. C. **196**, 11, 29; *Boston Gazette,* Oct. 6, 1777.

1777 BLACKBIRD, Schooner. *Guns,* 8 *swivels; Men,* 20.
Oct. 24   *Commander:* Joseph Pitman.
   Bond: Continental, $5000; State, £500.
   Bonders: Joseph Pitman, principal; Edw[ar]d Norice [signed Norris] and Daniel Hopkins, sureties.
   Owner: Edward Norris, of Salem.
   Witness: Joseph Batchelder, jr.
      Note. The name is written *Black Bird* on this bond and others in the State Archives.
   M. A., v, 86, 89, **167**, 376.

1778 BLACKBIRD, Schooner. *Guns,* 8 *swivels; Men,* 20.
Mar. 27   *Commander:* Nathaniel Reynolds.
   Bond: Continental, $5000; State, £500.
   Bonders: Nath[anie]l Reynolds, principal; Samuel Page and Walter Price Bartlett, of Salem, sureties.
   Owners: Samuel Page and Walter P. Bartlett.
   Witness: D[aniel] Hopkins.
   M. A., v, 69, 70, **168**, 233.

1778 BLACKBIRD, Armed Vessel.
   Commander: Nathaniel Harding.
   Boston Gazette, Nov. 30, 1778.

1779 BLACKBIRD, Schooner. *Guns,* 8 *swivels; Men,* 22.
Apr. 2   *Commander:* James Morton.
   Bond: Continental, $5000; State, £4000.
   Bonders: James Morton, mariner, principal; George I. [J.?] Yates [signed Yeates] and Simon Ellet [signed Eliot], "of Bristol in the County of Lincoln," sureties.

BILBOA PACKET — BLACK JOKE

Owners: "Belonging in the County of Lincoln."
Witnesses: Rich[ar]d Meagher, David Briant.
M. A., v, 73, 74, **170**, 50.

1777 BLACK EAGLE, Brig. *Guns,* 16.
Commander: John Brown.
London Chronicle, April 22, 1777 (Antigua, Feb. 22): "We have four privateers lying here now which have been taken within these three weeks; they are as follow: The brig *Black Eagle*, of 16 guns, John Brown, commander; *Royal African*, a snow of 14, Miles Baker; the *Neptune*, of 14, Charles Thompson; and the schooner *King Herod*, of 10, William Baker. They all had been out a long time and had taken several prizes, some of which they plundered and released, and others they sent for Boston."

1779 BLACKFISH, Sloop. *Guns,* 4; *Men,* 12.
Sept. 7 *Commander:* James Dilworth.
Bond: Continental, $5000; State, £4000.
Bonders: James Dilworth, principal; Enoch Ilsley and John Archer, of Falmouth, sureties.
Owner: Ebenezer Preble.
Witnesses: Eben[ezer] Preble, Tho[ma]s Saunders.
Note. Written *Black Fish* on the bond. Petition says Falmouth, Casco Bay.
M. A., VII, 258, 259, **170**, 378.

BLACKFORD, Schooner. *Guns,* 10.
Commander: —— ——.
Hunt, II, 48.

1779 BLACK JACK, Brigantine. *Guns,* 2; *Men,* 7.
Oct. 9 *Commander:* Stephen Sears.
Bond: Continental, $5000; State, £4000.
Bonders: Stephen Sears, mariner, principal; Edmund Howes and Amasa Davis, of Boston, sureties.
Owners: Thomas Denney and others.
Witnesses: David Bradlee, Joseph West.
M. A., v, 47, 48, **170**, 419.

1779 BLACK JOKE, Brigantine. *Guns,* 2; *Men,* 8.
May 14 *Commander:* Nathaniel Freeman.
Bond: Continental, $5000; State, £4000.
Bonders: Nathaniel Freeman, mariner, principal; Nathan Stone and W[illia]m Foster, of Boston, sureties.

Owners: William Foster and others.
Witnesses: William Payne, David Spear.
M. A., v, 54, 55, **170**, 105.

1778 BLACK PRINCE, Ship. *Tons*, 220; *Guns*, 18; *Men*, 130.
June 17 *Commander:* Elias Smith.
Bond: Continental, $10,000; State, £4000.
Bonders: Elias Smith, mariner, principal; William Pickman and William Orne, of Salem, sureties.
Owners: William Pickman, William Orne, Larkin Thorndike, and others.
Witness: Samuel Flagg.
M. A., v, 49, 51, **168**, 351.

1778 BLACK PRINCE, Brigantine. *Guns*, 14; *Men*, 70.
July 18 *Commander:* William Steward.
Bond: Continental, $10,000; State, £4000.
Bonders: William Steward, principal; Job Prince and Thomas Adams, of Boston, sureties.
Owners: Job Prince and others.
Witnesses: Tho[ma]s Prince, Benj[amin] Homer.
M. A., v, 65, 66, **139**, 201, **169**, 4.

1778 BLACK PRINCE, Ship. *Tons*, 220; *Guns*, 18; *Men*, 120.
Oct. 20 *Commander:* Nathaniel West.
Bond: Continental, $10,000; State, £4000.
Bonders: Nathaniel West, principal; Geo[rge] Williams and W[illia]m Pickman, of Salem, sureties.
Owners: George Williams and others.
Witnesses: Elias Smith, Joseph Moses.
  Note. On the Penobscot Expedition in 1779 and was destroyed to prevent capture.
M. A., v, 59, 60, XXXVII, 178, 280, **145**, 35, **169**, 236.

1782 BLACK PRINCE, Brigantine. *Guns*, 6; *Men*, 16.
Aug. 15 *Commander:* George Rendall, of York.
C. C. **196**, II, 32.

1777 BLACK SNAKE, Sloop. *Guns*, 12; *Men*, 60.
July 8 *Commander:* William Carlton, of Salem.
C. C. **196**, II, 39; *Boston Gazette*, Dec. 22, 1777; *Essex Inst. Hist. Coll.*, XXVII (1890), 127.

1777 BLACK SNAKE, Brig.
Commander: William Lecraw.
Marblehead Hist. Soc.

1778   BLACK SNAKE, Sloop. *Guns*, 12; *Men*, 60.
Jan. 21   *Commander:* Henry Phelps.
  Bond: Continental, $5000; State, £500.
  Bonders: Henry Phelps, principal; Simon Forrester [Samuel Forister on State bond] and Zachariah Burchmore, of Salem, sureties.
  Owners: Simon Forrester and Zachariah Burchmore.
  Witness: D[aniel] Hopkins.
  M. A., v, 71, 72, **168**, 155.

1782   BLACK SNAKE, Boat. *Guns*, "Swivels and musquets"; *Men*, 20.
Apr. 16   *Commander:* David Jenks, [of Kingston?].
  Owners: Peleg Wadsworth and others, of Boston and Kingston.
  C. C. **196**, II, 41; M. A., **172**, 137.

1783   BLACK SNAKE, Boat. *Guns*, 1; *Men*, 14.
Mar. 21   *Commander:* Barzillai Besse, of Plympton.
  Owners: David Rye and others, of Wareham.
  C. C. **196**, II, 38; M. A., **172**, 316.

1781   BLOODHOUND, Brig. *Guns*, 14; *Men*, 55.
  Commander: ———— ————.
  Essex Institute, Miscellaneous Ship Papers; Felt, II, 272; *Salem Gazette*, June 26, 1781 (Advertisement of the sale of "a prize taken by the Privateers *Bloodhound*, *Tyger*, *Captain*, and *Hero*").

1782   BLOOM, Schooner. *Guns*, 6; *Men*, 25.
Aug. 13   *Commander:* Silas Smith, of Salem.
  C. C. **196**, II, 43; M. A., **172**, 186.

1779   BODERVINE, Sloop. *Guns; swivels.*
  Commander: ———— ————.
  Essex Inst. Hist. Coll., XLIX, 118 (MS. Auctioneers' Sales Books in Essex Institute): "Nov. 2, 1779. Sold by order of H. Rust, agent for the privateer sloop *Bodervine*, viz.:— sloop *Bodervine*, £8100, to Nathan Nichols; cannon, swivel, 168 round shot," etc.

1782   BONTRAM, Sloop. *Guns*, 10.
  Commander: ———— White.
  London Chronicle, Sept. 7, 1782 (Stromness, Aug. 19): "The ship *Quebec* . . . arrived here this day and brought in with her a sloop privateer carrying 10 guns, called the *Bontram*, of Salem, commanded by Captain White."

1776 BOSTON, Schooner. *Guns*, 8, and 12 *swivels; Men*, 50.
Aug. 21 Commander: Silas Atkins, jr.
  Bond: Continental, $5000.
  Bonders: Silas Atkins, jr., Henry Bass, and John Bradford.
  Owners: Henry Bass & Co., of Boston.
  Witnesses: Jona[than] Foster, Jona[than] Brown.
  M. A., v, 94, **165**, 116.

1776 BOSTON, Ship. *Tons*, 400; *Guns*, 22; *Men*, 210.
Sept. 24 Commander: William Brown.
  Bond: Continental, $10,000.
  Bonders: William Brown, mariner, of Lincoln (Middlesex Co.); James Swan and Elias Parkman, merchants of Boston.
  Owners: Paul Dudley Sargent and others, of Boston.
  Witnesses: Elias Warner, Eben[ezer] Prout.
    M. A., v, 100, **159**, 60, 83, 95, 121, **165**, 271, **210**, 176; *Independent Chronicle*, Mar. 6, 1777: "Captain Brown, in the Privateer *Boston*, of this Port, has taken and sent into North Carolina a Ship and Schooner from Guinea with Negroes, bound to the West Indies; many of the poor Slaves perished soon after their arrival." *Boston Gazette*, Mar. 31, 1777: "Tuesday the privateer ship *Boston*, commanded by Capt. John Brown, returned into port; during her cruize she has taken six prizes, all of which are arrived in safe ports." [In the prize list published in the *Gazette* of Apr. 7, the captain's name is given as William Brown.]

1780 BOSTON. *Guns*, 18.
  Commander: Emanuel Smith.
    London Chronicle, Sept. 2, 1780: "An American privateer of 18 guns, six and nine pounders, called the *Boston* frigate and commanded by Emanuel Smith is taken on the Banks of Newfoundland, after half an hour's engagement, by the *Dolphin* privateer of Guernsey and carried into St. John's."

1781 BOSTON PACKET, Brigantine. *Guns*, 6; *Men*, 15.
July 6 Commander: William White, of Boston.
  C. C. **196**, 11, 46.

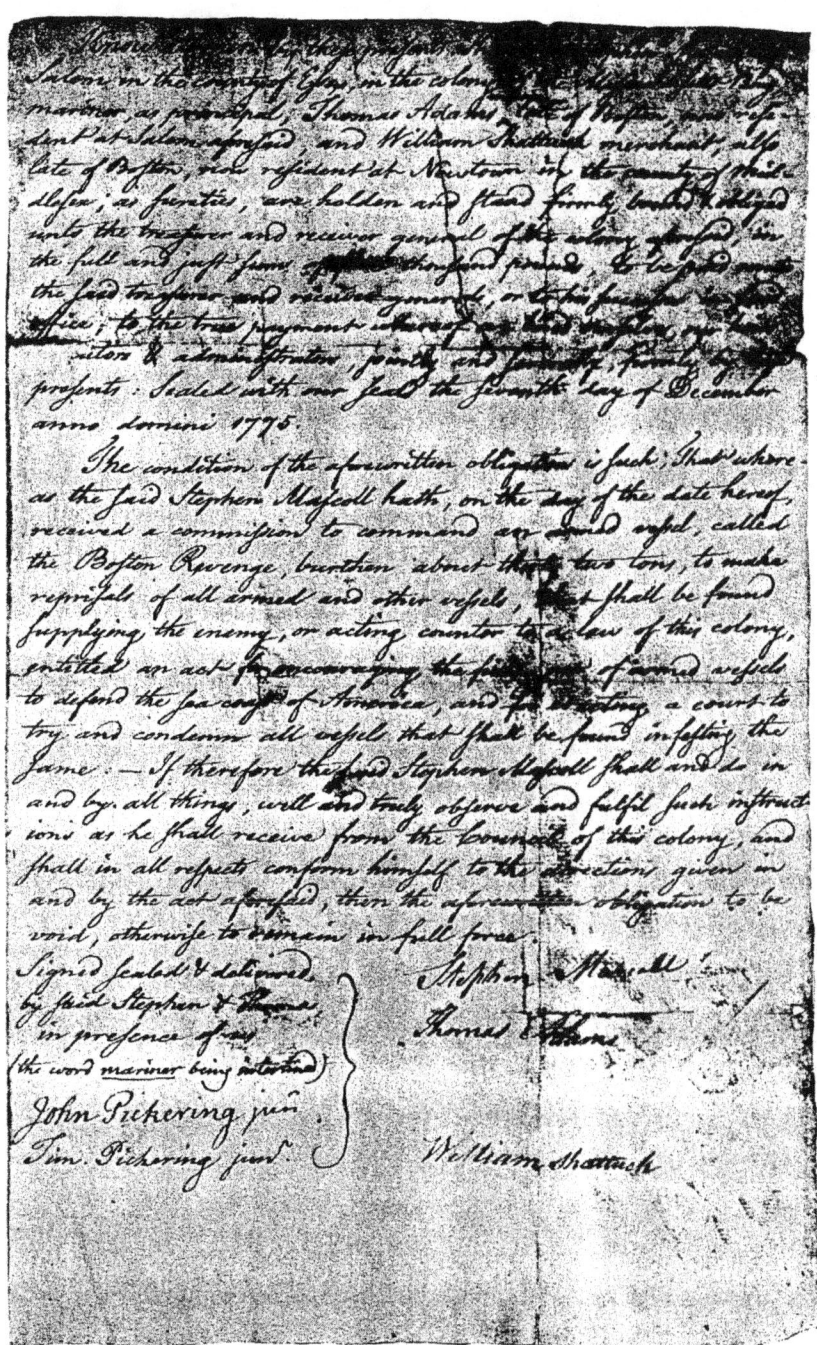

The First Massachusetts Privateer Bond in the Revolution

1781 BOSTON PACKET, Brig. *Tons*, 90; *Guns*, 6; *Men*, 15.
Aug. 3   *Commander:* John Young.
    Petitioners: Codman & Smith, of Boston.
    M. A., **171**, 440.

1775 BOSTON REVENGE, Armed Vessel (schooner). *Tons*, 32.
Dec. 7   *Commander:* Stephen Mascoll.
    Bond: £5000.
    Bonders: Stephen Mascoll, mariner of Salem, principal; Thomas Adams, mariner, late of Boston, now of Salem, and William Shattuck, merchant, late of Boston, now of Newtown, sureties.
    Bound to "the treasurer and receiver general of the colony aforesaid."
    Owners: Not stated.
    Witnesses: John Pickering, jr., Tim[othy] Pickering, jr.

> *Note.* This is believed to have been the first privateer bond issued in Massachusetts during the Revolution.

    M. A., VII, 48, **164**, 212, **209**, 53 (Apr. 22, 1776).

1778 BOWDOIN, Sloop. *Guns*, 8, and 9 *swivels; Men*, 45.
July 2   *Commander:* Thomas Stevens.
    Bond: Continental, $5000; State, £4000.
    Bonders: Thomas Stevens, principal; William West and Samuel Williams, of Salem, sureties.
    Owners: Samuel Williams and others.
    Witness: D[aniel] Hopkins.
    M. A., V, 79, 80, **168**, 399.

1782 BOWDOIN, Ship. *Guns*, 12; *Men*, 60.
    Commander: Peter Shorey.
    Essex Institute, Miscellaneous Ship Papers.

1783 BRANDYWINE, Brig. *Guns*, 6; *Men*, 30.
    Commander: —— ——.
    Essex Institute, Miscellaneous Ship Papers.

1778 BREDENOT. *Guns*, 16; *Men*, 140.
    Commander: John Stevens, of Salem.
    London Chronicle, June 16, 1778: "The *Bredenot* privateer, of Salem, mounting 16 guns and 140 men, John Stevens master, was taken off Bermudas by two armed transports, which two days after were at-

tacked by four American privateers of 14, 18, and two of 26 guns each, and which, after an engagement of six hours, took the two transports, with the *Bredenot*, and proceeded with them to America."

779 BRILLIANT, Brigantine. *Guns*, 10; *Men*, 30.
Sept. 4   *Commander:* Samuel Waters.
    Bond: Continental, $10,000; State, £4000.
    Bonders: Sam[ue]l Water [signed Waters], principal; Peter Aldoph and James Macduff, of Boston, sureties.
    Owner: James Macduff.
    Witness: J[ohn] Dall.
    M. A., v, 52, 53, **170**, 352.

781 BRUTUS, Ship. *Tons*, 206; *Guns*, 20; *Men*, 120.
July 10   *Commander:* William Cole [Coles?].
    Petitioners: George Williams and others, of Salem.
      Note. Called *Junius Brutus* in the endorsement and in the Council Records.
    M. A., **171**, 427; C. C. **196**, II, 49.

781 BUCCANEER, Ship. *Guns*, 18; *Men*, 150.
July 30   *Commander:* Hoysted Hacker, of Providence, R. I.
    Owners: John and Andrew Cabot, of Beverly.
    C. C. **196**, II, 51; M. A., **171**, 439.

782 BUCCANEER, Ship. *Guns*, 18; *Men*, 120.
Mar. 27   *Commander:* Jesse Fearson, of Boston.
    Owners: Andrew Cabot and others, of Beverly.
    C. C. **196**, II, 50; M. A., **172**, 126; *Boston Gazette*, Jan. 6, 1783: "The privateer ships *Buccanier*, *Revolution* [*Resolution*], and *Cicero*, belonging to Beverly and commanded by Captains Ferson, Webb, and Hill, have carried into France eight or nine sail of Jamaica ships."

777 BUCKRAM, Schooner. *Guns*, 8; *Men*, 45.
Apr. 25   *Commander:* William Morony.
    Bond: Continental, $5000.
    Bonders: William Marony [signed Morony], principal Thomas Adams, and Paul Dudley Sargent, all of Boston.
    Owners: Thomas Adams and others.
    Witness: Timothy Foster.
    M. A., v, 88, **139**, 109, **166**, 366.

1777 BUCKRAM, Schooner. *Guns*, 8; *Men*, 45.
June 4   *Commander:* Thomas Snoden.
   Bond: Continental, $5000.
   Bonders: Thomas Snoden, of Boston, principal; Daniel Martin and Thomas Adams, of Boston, sureties.
   Owners: Daniel Martin and Thomas Adams.
   Witnesses: Timothy Foster, William Lawrence.
   M. A., v, 85, **167**, 8.

1777 BUCKRAM, Schooner. *Guns*, 4; *Men*, 45.
Aug. 21   *Commander:* John Cross.
   Owners: John Blake and others, of Boston.
   C. C. **196**, II, 53; M. A., **139**, 142 (Bond, Sept. 9, 1777, not to enlist any man in New England outside of Massachusetts).

1781 BUCKRAM, Schooner. *Guns*, 5; *Men*, 20.
Sept. 19   *Commander:* John Obey, of Newburyport.
   Owners: William and James Bryant, of Boston.
   C. C. **196**, II, 54; M. A., **172**, 10.

1782 BUCKRAM, Schooner. *Guns*, 4; *Men*, 20.
Aug. 22   *Commander:* Samuel Trask [Trusk?], of Boston.
   C. C. **196**, II, 55.

1777 BUNKER HILL, Schooner. *Guns*, 6; *Men*, 35.
Aug. 12   *Commander:* Moses Lewis.
   Bond: Continental, $5000.
   Bonders: Moses Lewis, of Well Fleet, principal; Silas Atkins, jr., and Caleb Hopkins, of Boston, sureties.
   Owners: Silas Atkins and others.
   Witnesses: Benj[amin] Hammatt, jr., James Hughes.
   M. A., v, 91, **139**, 136, **167**, 155.

1778 BUNKER HILL, Schooner. *Guns*, 7; *Men*, 35.
May 4, 5   *Commander:* Isaac Cobb.
   Bond: Continental, $5000; State, £4000.
   Bonders: Isaac Cobb, principal; John Lowell and Silas Atkins, jr., sureties — all of Boston.
   Owners: John Lowell, Silas Atkins, Silas Atkins, jr., Ja[me]s Swan, and others.
   M. A., v, 90, 93, **139**, 170, **168**, 279.

1778 BUNKER HILL, Ship. *Guns*, 20.
      Commander: Edward Rolland.
      Boston Gazette, Sept. 14, 1778; Pickering Papers, XVII, 151 (William Pickman to Col. Pickering, May 27, 1778).

1778 BUNKER HILL, Ship. *Guns*, 18; *Men*, 100.
Oct. 27   *Commander:* Nicholas Ogelbe.
      Bond: Continental, $5000; State, £4000.
      Bonders: Nicholas Ogelby [signed Ogelbe], mariner of Marblehead, principle; Bartholomew Putnam and Jacob Ashton, of Salem, sureties.
      Owners: Bartholomew Putnam and Jacob Ashton.
      Witnesses: Stephen Higginson, James Jeffry.
      M. A., v, 57, 58, **169**, 292; Felt, II, 269 (Reported captured, Feb. 8, 1779).

1779 BUNKER HILL, Ship. *Guns*, 20; *Men*, 110.
      Commander: John Turner.
      Essex Institute, Miscellaneous Ship Papers.

1779 CADWALLADER, Ship. *Guns*, 14; *Men*, 60.
Mar. 23   *Commander:* Henry Johnson.
      Bond: Continental, $10,000; State, £4000.
      Bonders: Henry Johnson, mariner, principal; Francis Johonnot and George Stewart Johonnot, of Boston, sureties.
      Owners: Henry Mitchell and others.
      Witnesses: Mary Johonnot, Jona[than] Pollard.
      M. A., v, 148, 151, **170**, 28.

1781 CAESAR, Ship. *Tons*, 600; *Guns*, 26; *Men*, 70.
Dec. 26   *Commander:* Timothy Peirce.
      Petitioners: Jarvis & Russell, of Boston.
        Note. Name spelled *Caezar* in the petition.
        M. A., **172**, 86; *London Chronicle*, June 1, 1782: "The *Caesar*, of 26 guns, from Boston to the West Indies" captured and taken into New York.

1782 CAESAR, Boat. *Guns*, small arms; *Men*, 20.
Aug. 7   *Commander:* John Harvey, of Boston.
      C. C. **196**, II, 66; M. A., **172**, 184.

1782 CAESAR, Boat. *Guns*, small arms; *Men*, 20.
Aug. 29   *Commander:* Benjamin Slater, of Boston.
      C. C. **196**, II, 67.

1781 CAMBERWELL, Ship. *Guns*, 6; *Men*, 18.
Dec. 24   Commander: Silas Ewers, of Boston.
       C. C. **196**, II, 68; M. A., **172**, 85.

1781 CAPTAIN, Brigantine. *Guns*, 10; *Men*, 40.
Feb. 9   Commander: John Donaldson, of Salem.
       C. C. **196**, II, 72; M. A., **171**, 343; Mar. Court Rec., 74; *Salem Gazette*, Aug. 21, 1781: "Wednesday last returned into port the privateer brig *Captain*, John Dollanson, commander, after being out 24 hours, and brought in with him the famous Pomroy with his privateer, having 32 hands out from Penobscot." Felt, II, 271 (*Captain* captured in 1782).

1782 CATCHALL, Schooner. *Guns*, 6; *Men*, 15.
Nov. 10 Commander: Moses Chase.
       Owners: Miles Ward, jr., and others, of Salem.
       C. C. **196**, II, 78.

1779 CATO, Schooner. *Guns*, 2; *Men*, 20.
May 1   Commander: William Steward.
       Bond: Continental, $5000; State, £4000.
       Bonders: William Stewart [signed Steward], mariner, principal; James Swan, Silas Atkins, mariner, Andrew Oliver, hatter, and Jona[than] Nutting, painter — all of Boston, sureties.
       Owners: Jonathan Nutting and others.
       Witnesses: Robert Lash, Nath[anie]l Baker.
       M. A., v, 138, 141, **170**, 74.

1779 CATO, Schooner. *Guns*, 4, and 6 *swivels*; *Men*, 30.
Sept. 8 Commander: Samuel Trusk.
       Petitioners: Silas Atkins and others, of Boston.
       M. A., **159**, 236, 239, **170**, 380; *Boston Gazette*, Nov. 1, 1779.

1779 CATO, Snow. *Guns*, 10; *Men*, 30.
Sept. 18 Commander: Eleazer Giles.
       Petition signed by Job Prince in behalf of Andrew and John Cabot, of Beverly.
       M. A., **170**, 403.

1779 CATO, Schooner. *Guns*, 4; *Men*, 20.
Nov. 3   Commander: Noah Stoddard.
       Bond: Continental, $5000; State, £4000.
       Bonders: Noah Stoddard, mariner, principal; Thomas

Crafts and Dimond Morton, of Boston, sureties.
Owners: Thomas Crafts and others.
Witnesses: Rob[er]t Robins and Sam[uel] Paine.
M. A., v, 137, 139, **171**, 13.

1780 CATO, Schooner. *Guns*, 5; *Men*, 18.
Mar. 23   *Commander:* Timothy Weston.
Bond: Continental, $5000; State, £4000.
Bonders: Timothy Wheston [signed Weston], mariner, principal; Thomas Crafts and Dimond Morton, of Boston, sureties.
Owners: Dimond Morton and others.
Witnesses: Sarson Belcher, James Arnold.
M. A., v, 128, 131, **171**, 103.

1780 CATO, Schooner. *Guns*, 4; *Men*, 20.
Sept. 26   *Commander:* David Allen, of Boston.
C. C. **196**, II, 81; M. A., XL, 97, **171**, 282; Mar. Court Rec., 56.

1781 CATO, Ship. *Guns*, 10; *Men*, 40.
Feb. 5   *Commander:* Benjamin Lunt, of Newburyport.
C. C. **196**, II, 85; M. A., **171**, 339.

1781 CATO, Ship. *Guns*, 12; *Men*, 40.
Feb. 9   *Commander:* John Lee, of Newburyport.
C. C. **196**, II, 84.

1781 CATO, Brigantine. *Guns*, 16; *Men*, 60.
May 28   *Commander:* Jesse Fearson, of Salem.
C. C. **196**, II, 83; M. A., **171**, 400.

1781 CATO, Schooner.
Commander: William Morgan, of Boston.
Mar. Court Rec., 73 (The *Cato* captured the schooner *Sally* May 31, 1781, and brought her into Boston. The case was tried Aug. 27, 1781).

1781 CATO, Brigantine. *Guns*, 14; *Men*, 60.
Aug. 17   *Commander:* Johnson Briggs, of Salem.
C. C. **196**, II, 82; M. A., **171**, 463; *Boston Gazette*, Nov. 12, 1781: "A valuable Prize from Jamaica, loaded with Rum and Sugar, taken by Capt. Briggs in the *Cato* Privateer, was cast away, since our last, on Ipswich Bar; the Men were saved, but the Vessel and Cargo, excepting about thirty Hogsheads of Rum and a few

Hogsheads of Sugar, were lost." *Salem Gazette*, Nov. 22, 1781: "Last Monday arrived in a safe port the prize ship *St. Mary's Packet*, near 400 tons burthen, . . . bound from Jamaica to London, and was taken by the privateer brig *Cato*, Capt. Briggs, of this port." *Salem Gazette*, May 9, 1782: "The letter of marque brig *Cato*, Capt. Briggs, of this port, was taken on the 29th of March by a privateer brig of 16 guns and 75 men."

1781 CATO, Ship. *Guns*, 16; *Men*, 50.
Nov. 15   Commander: John Tittle, of Marblehead.
C. C. **196**, II, 88; M. A., **172**, 60; *Salem Gazette*, June 6, 1782 (New York, May 11): "Last Thursday arrived the ship *St. John*, Capt. Bowen. . . . This vessel struck without resistance to the *Fair American*, who the same day fought the ship *Cato*, Capt. Tittle. . . . It was a smart action lasting three glasses; the *Cato* was bravely defended against the united attacks of the *Fair American*, *Digby*, and *Prince William Henry*, cruisers. All the parties were greatly shattered and fortunately for Capt. Tittle, night and fog coming on enabled him to escape with flying colours. His antagonists give him the utmost credit for a very distinguished and truly gallant behaviour." *Ibid.*: "Among the many gallant actions which have distinguished the Commanders of American ships, during the present war, that lately fought by Captain Tittle, in the ship *Cato*, was one of the most brilliant. Notwithstanding what is said under the New York head, he had but 12 six-pounders and 35 men. With this small force he greatly damaged and finally beat off three privateers which to say the least were three times his strength. This brave officer (who belongs to Beverly) has, together with his officers and crew, the thanks of his owners and the applause of the public."

1782 CATO, Ship. *Guns*, 12; *Men*, 50.
May 6   Commander: Daniel Tappan, of Newburyport.
     Owners: Caleb and Joseph Tappan, of Newburyport.
        Note. A Massachusetts ship credited to Connecticut in *Naval Records of the Revolution*.
     C. C. **196**, II, 87.

1782 CATO, Schooner. *Guns*, 8; *Men*, 30.
July 30   *Commander:* James Pickman, of Salem.
   C. C. **196**, 11, 86.

1783 CATO, Schooner. *Tons*, 35; *Guns*, 6; *Men*, 25.
Jan. 1   *Commander:* Benjamin Green Mansfield.
   Petition signed by Miles Ward in behalf of Nathan Goodale and others, of Salem.
   M. A., **172**, 273.

1777 CENTIPEDE, Schooner. *Guns*, 2; *Men*, 40.
Dec. 5   *Commander:* William Langdell.
   Bond: Continental, $5000; State, £500.
   Bonders: William Langdon [signed Langdell], of Salem, principal; Elias Hasket Derby, Ichabod Nichols, and Joseph White, merchants of Salem, sureties.
   Owners: E. H. Derby and others.
   Witnesses: Robert Stone, Nehemiah Holt.
      Note. The vessel's name is spelled *Santapee*.
   M. A., VII, 137, 140, **168**, 105.

1778 CENTIPEDE, Schooner.
   Commander: [William?] Steward.
      Note. Name spelled *Cente-Pea*.
   Boston Gazette, May 11, 1778.

1778¾ CENTIPEDE, Schooner. *Guns*, 16 *swivels*; *Men*, 35.
May 21¾ *Commander:* Samuel Ingersoll.
   Bond: Continental, $5000; State, £4000.
   Bonders: Samuel Ingersoll, principal; Elias Hasket Derby, Joseph White, and others, of Salem, sureties.
   Owners: E. H. Derby, Joseph White, and others.
   Witnesses: Nath[anie]l Silsbee, Thomas Nichols.
      Note. Name spelled *Cente Pea*.
   M. A., V, 126, 129, **168**, 327.

1778 CENTIPEDE, SCHOONER. *Guns*, 16 *swivels*; *Men*, 35.
Sept. 29   *Commander:* Joseph Pratt.
   Bond: Continental, $5,000; State, £4000.
   Bonders: Joseph Pratt, principal; Miles Greenwood and Robert Stone, of Salem, sureties.
   Owners: Miles Greenwood and others.
   Witnesses: Joseph White and Sam[uel] Ward.
      Note. Name spelled *Cent a Pede*.
   M. A., V, 188, 189, **169**, 178.

1779 CENTIPEDE, Schooner. *Guns*, 4; *Men*, 50.
Aug. 3   *Commander:* Gideon Henfield.
   Bond: Continental, not stated; State, £4000.
   Bonders: Gideon Henfield, mariner, principal; Robert Stone and Simon Forrester, of Salem, sureties.
   Owner: Elias Hasket Derby.
   Witnesses: Jno. Fisk, Richard Manning.
       Note. Name spelled *Sentepe*.
   M. A., VII, 107, 108, **159**, 193, 274, **170**, 299; Mar. Court Rec., 28.

1780 CENTIPEDE, Schooner. *Guns*, 4; *Men*, 40.
Apr. 27   *Commander:* Joseph Pitman.
   Bond: Continental, £4000 (*sic*); State, £4000.
   Bonders: Joseph Pitman, of Salem, principal; Joseph White and Miles Greenwood, merchants of Salem, sureties.
   Owner: Joseph White.
   Witnesses: Eunice Goodwin, Eliza Elkins.
       Note. Name spelled *Cent a Pied*.
   M. A., V, 125, 127, **171**, 137.

1780 CENTIPEDE, Schooner.
   Commander: Samuel Croel.
       Note. Name spelled *Centipie*.
   Boston Gazette, June 26, 1780.

1780 CENTURION, Ship. *Guns*, 16; *Men*, 60.
Jan. 4   *Commander:* Gerald Forrester.
   Bond: Continental, $10,000; State, £4000.
   Bonders: Gerald Forrester, mariner, principal; Thomas Russell and Sam[ue]l Conant, jr., of Boston, sureties.
   Owner: Thomas Russell.
   Witnesses: Chambers Russell, Thomas Greene.
   M. A., V, 152, 155, **176**, 83.

   CERTIFICATE, Schooner. *Guns*, 6.
       Commander: —— ——.
   Hunt, II, 48.

1781 CHACE, Brigantine. *Guns*, 10; *Men*, 35.
Sept. 7   *Commander:* Cornelius Thompson, of Salem.
       C. C. **196**, II, 91; M. A., **172**, 3; Felt, II, 272: Captured May 29, 1782.

96 MASSACHUSETTS PRIVATEERS

1780 CHANCE, Sloop. *Tons,* 50; *Guns,* 6; *Men,* 12.
Apr. 10   *Commander:* William Almy.
    Petitioner: Samuel Dunn, jr. [of Boston].
    Owners: Samuel Dunn, jr., Mungo Mackay, and others.
    M. A., 171, 126.

1782 CHANCE, Schooner.
    Commander: —— Newell.
    Salem Gazette, Oct. 10, 1782 (See brig *Adventure,* Capt. Tucker).

1782 CHANCE, Brig (letter of marque).
    Commander: Zachariah Gage.
    Owners: Andrew and John Cabot, of Beverly.
    Note. Sold at Cape François in 1782.
    Publ. Colonial Society of Massachusetts, XXIV, 406.

1782 CHARLOTTE, Schooner.
    Commander: —— ——.
    Boston Gazette, Dec. 2, 1782: "In behalf of Henry Gallison and others, owners of the schooner *Charlotte,* alias *Nimble Shilling,* and all concerned therein" against the prize brigantine *Endeavor.*

1779 CHARMING NANCY, Brigantine. *Guns,* 8; *Men,* 20.
Nov. 23   *Commander:* William Faris.
    Bond: Continental, £4000 [*sic.*]; State, £4000.
    Bonders: Joseph Laughton and Tristram Barnard, of Boston, and William Faris, of Newburyport.
    Owner: John Tracy, of Newburyport.
    Witness: John Milliquet.
    M. A., V, 161, 162, 171, 29.

1776 CHARMING PEGGY, Brig. *Guns,* 12, and 12 *swivels; Men,* 25.
    Commander: J[oseph?] Jauncey.
    Note. Possibly a Connecticut vessel.
    Emmons, 131.

1779 CHARMING PEGGY, Brigantine. *Guns,* 10; *Men,* 40.
Oct. 26   *Commander:* John Phillips.
    Bond: Continental, $5000; State, £4000.
    Bonders: John Phillips, principal; John R. Livingston and Edm[un]d Dunkin, of Boston, sureties.
    Owner: John R. Livingston.
    Witnesses: Hector McNeill, Thomas Amory, jr.
    M. A., V, 163, 164, 139, 257.

1779 CHARMING POLLY, Schooner. *Guns,* 6; *Men,* 20.
June 26   *Commander:* John Palmer.
   Bond: Continental, $5000; State, £4000.
   Bonders: John Palmer, mariner, principal; Henry Livingston and William Erskine, of Boston, sureties.
   Owner: William Erskine.
   Witnesses: Sam[ue]l White, Edw[ar]d Davis.
      Note. On the Penobscot Expedition and destroyed to prevent capture.
   M. A., v, 201, 202, **145**, 1, **170**, 185.

1779 CHARMING POLLY, Sloop. *Guns,* 6; *Men,* 25.
Aug. 18   *Commander:* Phoenix Frazier.
   Bond: Continental, $5000; State, £4000.
   Bonders: Phoenix Frazier, mariner, principal; William Erskine and Joseph Russell, merchants of Boston, sureties.
   Owners: William Erskine and others.
   Witnesses: Samuel R[ussell] Gerry, W. Harris.
   M. A., v, 205, 206, **170**, 336.

1779 CHARMING POLLY, Brigantine. *Guns,* 6; *Men,* 20.
Dec. 24   *Commander:* George Shougherd.
   Bond: Continental, $10,000; State, £4000.
   Bonders: George Shougherd, mariner, principal; George Dodge, jr., and Eben[eze]r Parsons, of Boston and Salem, sureties.
   Owner: George Dodge, jr.
   Witnesses: And[rew] Henshaw, Oliver Peabody.
   M. A., v, 165, 166, **171**, 50.

1780 CHARMING POLLY, Brig (letter of marque).
   Commander: Daniel Bigelow.
   Felt, II, 271 (Captured September 19, 1780, and crew brought to Mill Prison).

1776 CHARMING SALLY, Sloop.
   Commander: Francis Brown.
   M. A., **159**, 66 (Captured the schooner *Betsey* December 6, 1776, and brought her into Beverly March 16, 1777. Jeremiah Platt and Paschal N. Smith, of Boston, appeared in the Maritime Court in behalf of Captain Brown); 92 (Captured the brigantine *Hannah* January 7, 1777, and brought her into Boston April 12, 1777. Abijah Dunham, of Tisbury, appeared in court for Captain Brown).

1777 CHARMING SALLY, Schooner. *Tons*, 70; *Guns*, 4, and 6
June 12   *swivels; Men*, 15.
    Commander: Joseph Tilden.
    Petitioner: William Shattuck, of Boston.
    M. A., **167**, 25.

1777 CHARMING SALLY, Schooner. *Guns*, 4, and 8 *swivels; Men*, 25.
Aug. 26   *Commander:* William Briggs.
    Bond: Continental, $5000.
    Bonders: William Briggs, mariner of Salem, Alex[ande]r Rose, of Charlestown, S. C., William Shattuck, of Boston, and Ab[raha]m Livingston, of New York.
    Owners: William Shattuck and others.
    Witnesses: John Parker, Mark Towell.
    M. A., v, 114, **139**, 140, **167**, 186.

1777 CHARMING SALLY, Brigantine. *Guns*, 4, and 2 *swivels; Men*, 10.
Dec. 31   *Commander:* Thomas Haws.
    Bond: Continental, $5000; State, £500.
    Bonders: Thomas Haws, principal; William Shattuck and William Dall, of Boston, sureties.
    Owners: William Shattuck and others.
    Witnesses: James Perkins, John Shattuck.
    M. A., v, 116, 119, **168**, 123.

1778 CHARMING SALLY, Sloop. *Guns*, 8; *Men*, 20.
Nov. 13   *Commander:* John Carey.
    Bond: Continental, $5000; *State*, £4000.
    Bonders: John Carey, mariner, principal, Shrimpton Hutchinson and W[illia]m Erskine, of Boston, sureties.
    Owners: William Erskine and others.
    Witness: Jno. Dall.
    M. A., v, 154, 156, **169**, 316.

1779 CHARMING SALLY, Ship. *Tons*, 300; *Guns*, 18; *Men*, 70.
Jan. 27   *Commander:* Alexander Holmes.
    Bond: Continental, $10,000; State, £4000.
    Bonders: Alexander Holmes, mariner, principal; W[illia]m Erskine and Edm[un]d Dunkin, of Boston, sureties.
    Owners: William Erskine and others.
    Witnesses: Daniel Smith, Francis Johonnot.
        Note. On the Penobscot Expedition and destroyed to prevent capture.
    M. A., v, 167, 168, xxxvii, 280, xlv, 190, **145**, 1, 40, **169**, 424.

1782 CHARMING SALLY, Ship. *Guns*, 10; *Men*, 30.
Dec. 21   *Commander:* Samuel Dunn, jr., of Boston.
C. C. 196, 11, 109; M. A., 172, 261.

1781 CICERO, Ship. *Tons*, 300; *Guns*, 16; *Men*, 60.
Jan. 15   *Commander:* Hugh Hill.
Petition signed by Job Prince, jr., in behalf of Andrew Cabot and others, of Beverly.
M. A., **171**, 332; *London Chronicle*, Aug. 23, 1781 (See brigantine *Rambler*, 1781); *Boston Gazette*, Dec. 31, 1781 (London, Aug. 24, 1781): "The passengers of both sexes, who were on board the *Mercury* packet, from Lisbon to Falmouth, prize to the *Cicero* privateer, of Salem in New England, Hugh Hill, commander, desire us to be the instruments of their gratitude, in publishing that as well from the captain and officers as the crew, they have received the most civil, humane, and even noble treatment." *Ibid.*, Jan. 28, 1782: "Capt. Hill, in the letter of marque ship *Cicero*, arrived at Beverly on Monday last, in six weeks from Bilboa. . . . In Captain Hill came Passengers, Col. John Trumbull, Son of his Excellency the Governor of Connecticut, and Master John [Quincy] Adams, Son of his Excellency John Adams, Esq., both of which Gentlemen arrived in this Town Yesterday." *Ibid.*, Jan. 6, 1783 (*See Buccaneer*, Jesse Fearson).

1782 CICERO, Ship. *Guns*, 18; *Men*, 120.
Commander: Anthony Diver.
Essex Institute, Miscellaneous Ship Papers.

1776 CIVIL USAGE, Brigantine. *Guns*, 12; *Men*, 80.
Sept. 18   *Commander:* Andrew Giddings.
Bond: Continental, $5000.
Bonders: Andrew Giddings [signed Giddinge], mariner, Jonathan Jackson, Nathaniel Tracy, John Tracy, Thomas Thomas, and John Coffin Jones, merchants, all of Newburyport.
Owners: Jonathan Jackson & Co.
Witness: Enoch Titcomb, 3rd.
M. A., v, 111, **165**, 244.

1778 CIVIL USAGE, Brigantine. *Guns*, 14, and 12 *swivels; Men*, 75.
Mar. 28   *Commander:* John Smith.
    Bond: Continental, $5000; State, £500.
    Bonders: John Smith, of Gloucester, principal; Joseph Barrell and Step[he]n Bruce, of Boston, sureties.
    Owners: Jackson Tracy and others, of Newburyport.
    Witnesses: Joseph Barrell, John Lowell, Thomas Russell, Jno. Winthrop, William Clough.
        M. A., v, 171, 173, **168**, 235.

1778 CIVIL USAGE, Schooner. *Guns*, 10 *swivels; Men*, 20.
Apr. 7   *Commander:* Anthony Diver.
    Bond: Continental, $5000; State, £500.
    Bonders: Anthony [signed Antoney] Diver, principal; Thomas Simmons and Robert Brookhouse, of Salem, sureties.
    Owners: Thomas Simmons and Robert Brookhouse.
    Witness: D[aniel] Hopkins.
        M. A., v, 169, 170, 184 (crew list), **168**, 247.

1781 CIVIL USAGE, Schooner. *Guns*, 6; *Men*, 25.
Apr. 23   *Commander:* Gregory Powers, of Salem.
        C. C. **196**, III, 6; M. A., **171**, 378.

1781 CIVIL USAGE, Schooner. *Guns*, 4; *Men*, 25.
July 26   *Commander:* Peter Martin, of Salem.
        C. C. **196**, III, 5; M. A., **171**, 435.

1777 CLEORA, Schooner. *Guns*, 4; *Men*, 14.
June 9   *Commander:* Richard Ellinwood.
    Bond: Continental, $5000.
    Bonders: Richard Ellinwood, of Boston, principal; Thomas Adams and W[illia]m Shattuck, sureties.
    Owner: Thomas Adams, of Boston.
    Witnesses: Eb[eneze]r Winship, Timothy Foster.
        M. A., v, 117, **167**, 17.

1779 CLINTON, Snow. *Guns*, 8; *Men*, 20.
Oct. 19   *Commander:* Edward Davis.
    Bond: Continental, $10,000; State, £4000.
    Bonders: Edward Davis, mariner, principal; Daniel Sargent and Step[he]n Higginson, of Boston, sureties.
    Owners: Daniel Sargent and others.
    Witnesses: Nathan Spink, jr., Jo[hn] Winthrop.
        M. A., v, 150, 153, **170**, 440.

To the Honorable the Council of the State of
Massachusetts Bay —

The Petition of Thomas Adams of Boston —
Humbly Sheweth —

That your Petitioner has fitted for Sea the Schooner called the Cleora Richard Ellenwood Master of the Burthen of about Sixty Tons, Armed with four Carriage & eight Swivel Guns Navigated by fourteen Men, Loaded with Articles and Lumber bound to the French West Indies. Your Petitioner prays your honor would grant a Commission for said Schooner as a Letter of Marque, as he intends said Schooner to be further Equipped in the West Indies to Cruze Against the Enemies of the United States of America, he giving Bond Agreeable to the Resolves of Congress — And as in Duty bound will ever pray —

Thomas Adams

In Council June 9th 1777
Read & Ordered that a Commission be Issued to the said Richd. Ellenwood as Commander of the Schooner Cleora, As a Letter of Marque he giving Bond Agreeable to the Resolves of Congress

Jno. Avery Dpy Secy

Petition for a Letter of Marque

CIVIL USAGE — COMMERCE 101

1780 COLUMBIA, Ship. *Guns*, 12; *Men*, 30.
Oct. 30   *Commander:* Jonathan Greely, of Boston.
   C. C. **196**, III, 9; M. A., **171**, 297.

1781 COLUMBIA, Ship.
   Commander: —— Newell.
      Note. It is not certain that this was a Massachusetts vessel.
      Boston Gazette, Feb. 19, 1781: "The ship *Columbia*, Capt. Newel, has taken a rich prize and both arrived at Guadaloup."

1781 COLUMBUS. *Guns*, 18; *Men*, 50.
   Commander: —— ——.
      London Chronicle, Aug. 28, 1781: "The *Monk*, Rogers, has taken the *Columbus*, of 18 guns and 50 men, with a valuable cargo, bound from Cadiz to Boston."

1781 COMET, Schooner. *Guns*, 9; *Men*, 29.
Mar. 31   *Commander:* Richard Elledge, of Salem.
   C. C. **196**, III, 15; M. A., **171**, 362.

1781 COMET, Brigantine. *Guns*, 6; *Men*, 15.
Nov. 23   *Commander:* Samuel Waters, of Salem.
   C. C. **196**, III, 22; M. A., **172**, 71.

1780 COMMERCE, Ship. *Guns*, 12; *Men*, 40.
July 6   *Commander:* Abraham Bartlett.
   Bond: Continental, $10,000; State, £4000.
   Bonders: Abraham Bartlett, mariner, of Boston, principal; Samuel Conant and John Codman, jr., sureties.
   Owners: Codman & Smith, merchants, of Boston.
   Witnesses: Jona[than] Webb, Sam[ue]l Henley.
      M. A., V, 130, 133, **171**, 192.

1780 COMMERCE, Sloop. *Tons*, 80; *Guns*, 6 (or 10); *Men*, 25.
Aug. 30   *Commander:* John Baptist Millet.
   Petitioners: Joshua Grafton and others, of Salem.
      M. A. **171**, 264; C. C. **196**, III, 27.

1780 COMMERCE, Ship. *Guns*, 12; *Men*, 40.
Oct. 31   *Commander:* Ignatius Webber, of Boston.
   C. C. **196**, III, 28; M. A., **171**, 306 (date of petition, Nov. 17).

1781 COMMERCE, Ship. *Tons*, 200; *Guns*, 14; *Men*, 50.
Jan. 15 *Commander:* Stephen Webb.
   Petition signed by Job Prince, jr., in behalf of Messrs. Cabot, of Beverly.
   M. A., **171**, 332.

1781 COMMERCE, Ship. *Guns*, 14; *Men*, 50.
Sept. 12 *Commander:* Abraham Bartlett, of Boston.
   C. C. **196**, III, 23; M. A., **172**, 8.

1782 COMMERCE, Ship. *Guns*, 14; *Men*, 40.
July 20 *Commander:* Ignatius Webber, of Boston.
   C. C. **196**, III, 29.

1782 COMMERCE, Brigantine. *Guns*, 6; *Men*, 12.
Aug. 30 *Commander:* Ephraim Emerton, of Salem.
   C. C **196**, III, 25.

1783 CONCLUSION, Schooner. *Guns*, 2; *Men*, 25.
Mar. 11 *Commander:* William Coles, of Beverly.
   C. C. **196**, III, 32.

1778 CONCORD, Privateer.
   Commander: Job Prince, jr.
   Calendar of Franklin Papers, I, 534, 539, III, 513, IV, 276; Smyth, *Writings of Franklin,* VII, 201, 202.

1782 CONCORD, Brig. *Guns*, 10; *Men*, 55.
   Commander: Ephraim Emerton.
   Essex Institute, Miscellaneous Ship Papers; Felt, II, 275 (Nov. 7, 1782).

1777 CONGRESS, Schooner. *Guns*, 6; *Men*, 30.
Oct. 24 *Commander:* John Martin.
   Bond: Continental, $5000; State, £500.
   Bonders: Not stated.
   Owners: John Farrey and Henry Newhall, of Boston.
   Signers: John Martin, John Farrey, Henry Newhall.
   Witness: Fitch Pool.
   M. A., V, 121, 122, **167**, 359.

1777 CONGRESS, Schooner. *Guns*, 4; *Men*, 20.
Dec. 19 *Commander:* Ephraim Emerton.
   Bond: Continental, $5000; State, £500.

COMMERCE — CONGRESS   103

 Bonders: Ephraim Emerton, of Salem, principal; Elias Hasket Derby, John Gardner, and Nathan Goodale, merchants of Salem, sureties.
 Owners: E. H. Derby and others.
 Witnesses: Bartho[lomew] Putnam, Jacob Ashton.
  M. A., v, 118, 120, **168**, 90.

1778   CONGRESS, Schooner. *Guns,* 8; *Men,* 40.
July 18   *Commander:* Samuel Hobbs.
 Bond: Continental, $5000; State, £4000.
 Bonders: Sam[ue]l Hobbs, mariner, Elias Hasket Derby, John Gardner, and Nathan Goodale, merchants — all of Salem.
 Owners: E. H. Derby, John Gardner, and Nathan Goodale.
 Witness: James Jeffry.
  M. A., v, 123, 124, **169**, 26.

1778   CONGRESS, Schooner. *Guns, swivels; Men,* 15.
July 18   *Commander:* Jabez West.
 Bond: Continental, $5000; State, £4000.
 Bonders: Jabez West, mariner, principal; Ebenezer Dorr and Henry Bass, of Boston, sureties.
 Owners: Ebenezer Dorr and Henry Bass.
 Witnesses: David Brewer, Stephen Hall.
  M. A., v, 132, 135, **169**, 5.

1778   CONGRESS, Schooner. *Guns,* 6, and 8 *swivels; Men,* 40.
July 30   *Commander:* John Guliker.
 Bond: Continental, $5000; State, £4000.
 Bonders: John Guliker, mariner, principal; William Mackay and John Mocketts [signed Jno. Mackett], of Boston, sureties.
 Owners: William Mackay and others.
 Witnesses: William Brown, Andrew Oliver.
  M. A., v, 146, 149, **139**, 197, **169**, 47.

1778   CONGRESS, Schooner. *Guns,* 4; *Men,* 12.
Nov. 3   *Commander:* Abraham Bartlett.
 Bond: Continental, $5000; State, £4000.
 Bonders: Abraham Bartlett, mariner, principal; John Hinckley [signed Hinkley] and Edward Procter, of Boston, sureties.
 Owners: John Hinkley and others.
 Witnesses: Solomon Lovell, Jonathan Metcalf.
  M. A., v, 186, 187, **139**, 227, **169**, 289.

1781 Congress, Ship. *Guns*, 20; *Men*, 130.
Mar. 14 Commander: David Ropes, of Salem.
C. C. **196**, III, 41; M. A., **171**, 350; *Boston Gazette*, Aug. 13, 1781: "We are sorry to inform our readers that the privateer Ship *Congress*, Capt. Ropes, belonging to Salem, is taken by the British Frigate *Bird*, and carried into St. John's."

1781 Congress, Brigantine. *Guns*, 6; *Men*, 14.
June 6 Commander: Seth Clark, of Salisbury.
C. C. **196**, III, 38; M. A., **171**, 406.

1782 Conquerant, Boat. *Guns, small arms*; *Men*, 20.
Aug. 7 Commander: Jeremiah Cushing, of Boston.
C. C. **196**, III, 42; M. A., **172**, 184.

1780 Constant, Ship. *Guns*, 10; *Men*, 30.
Commander: J. Grooves [Ichabod Groves?].
Emmons, 132.

1782 Constant, Brigantine. *Guns*, 4; *Men*, 12.
Apr. 16 Commander: Cornelius Fellows, of Boston.
C. C. **196**, III, 43; M. A., **172**, 135.

1778 Cornwall, Ship. *Guns*, 12; *Men*, 25.
Jan. 14 Commander: John Edmonds.
Bond: Continental, $10,000; State, £500.
Bonders: John Edmonds, mariner of Salem, principal; Mark Lafitte and Stephen Higginson, merchants of Salem, sureties.
Bound to Henry Gardner (both bonds).
Owner: Mark Lafitte.
Witnesses: Nath[anie]l Ropes, W. Prosser.
Note. The second part of the first bond is worded like a Continental bond and the amount is expressed in dollars; otherwise both documents resemble State bonds.
M. A., v, 140, 143, **168**, 146.

1777 Coulchester, Brig.
Commander: —— Coulchester.
Note. It is not certain that this was a Massachusetts vessel.
Boston Gazette, Oct. 6, 1777: "The Privateer Brig *Coulchester*, Capt. Coulchester, was spoke with in Latt. 39.50, Long. 55.30; all well and had taken three Prizes."

CONGRESS — COUNT D'ESTAING 105

1781 COUNT DE GRASSE, Ship. *Guns*, 14; *Men*, 40.
Dec. 24 *Commander:* Nicholas Johnson, of Newburyport.
C. C. **196**, III, 51.

1782 COUNT DE GRASSE, Sloop. *Guns*, 8; *Men*, 35.
May 4 *Commander:* Nathan Plimpton, of Boston.
C. C. **196**, III, 52.

1778 COUNT D'ESTAING, Brigantine. *Guns*, 16; *Men*, 100.
Dec. 16 *Commander:* John Kendrick.
Bond: Continental, $10,000; State, £4000.
Bonders: John Kendrick, principal; Isaac Sears and Paschal Nelson Smith, of Boston, sureties.
Owners: Isaac Sears and others.
Witnesses: W[illia]m Knox, Anthony Griffiths.
Note. The name is spelled *Count De Estaing.*
M. A., VIII, 10, 11, **139**, 237, **169**, 375.

1779 COUNT D'ESTAING, Schooner. *Guns*, 6; *Men*, 12.
Aug. 24 *Commander:* Oliver Davison.
Bond: Continental, $5000; State, £4000.
Bonders: Oliver Davison, mariner, principal; Shrimpton Hutchinson and Rich[ar]d Chilcott, of Boston, sureties (W[illia]m Hutchinson in place of Chilcott on State bond).
Owner: William Hutchinson, of Boston.
Witnesses: Nathaniel Brinley and Catherine Brinley (on Continental bond); Richard Chilcott and Nath[anie]l Brinley (on State bond).
M. A., VIII, 7, 12; **170**, 351.

1780 COUNT D'ESTAING, Brigantine. *Guns*, 6; *Men*, 10.
May 17 *Commander:* Matthew Wood.
Bond: Continental, $10,000; State, £4000.
Bonders: Matthew Wood, mariner of Barnstable, principal; James Swan and John Young, of Boston, sureties.
Owners: John Young and others.
Witnesses: Thornton Barrett, George Bunker.
Note. Name spelled *Count de Estaing.*
M. A., V, 172, 175, **171**, 162.

1780 COUNT D'ESTAING, Ship. *Guns*, 10; *Men*, 25.
Aug. 22 *Commander:* Elias Smith, of Beverly.
C. C. **196**, III, 53; M. A., **171**, 259.

1777 CREATURE, Brig. *Guns*, 14.
Commander: —— ——.
Boston Gazette, Sept. 8, 1777: "The *Creature*, a Privateer Brig of 14 6-pounders, owned at Salem and Beverly, has taken and carried in at a safe Port at the Eastward, a Ship of 600 Tons Burthen, laden with Sugar, etc. bound from Jamaica for London."

1777 CUMBERLAND, Ship. *Guns*, 20; *Men*, 180.
Sept. 12, 13 Commander: James Collins.
Bond: Continental, £10,000; State, £500.
Bonders: James Collins, Paul Dudley Sargent, and Nat[haniel] Crafts (Job Prince in place of Crafts on State bond).
Owners: Paul Dudley Sargent and others, of Boston.
Witnesses: Elisha Turner and Thomas Snowden (on Continental bond); Nat[haniel] Barber and Elisha Turner (on State bond).
Note. The captain is called Joseph Collins in *Boston Gazette*, Sept. 14, 1778. The pound sign on the Continental bond seems to be a clerical error.
M. A., v, 112, 115, **139**, 145, 187, **167**, 226.

1778 CUMBERLAND, Ship. *Tons*, 290; *Guns*, 20; *Men*, 150.
Dec. 14 Commander: John Manley.
Bond: Continental, $10,000; State, £4000.
Bonders: John Manley, principal; Edw[ar]d Carnes and Stephen Bruce, of Boston, sureties.
Owners: Edward Carnes and others.
Witnesses: Job Prince, R[ichar]d Salter.
M. A., v, 110, 113, **139**, 239, **169**, 367; *Independent Chronicle*, Mar. 4, 1779: "The private armed ship *Cumberland*, Capt. Manley, which sailed from this place about two months since, was taken soon after she left port by the *Juno*, an English frigate of 38 guns, and carried into Barbadoes." *Boston Gazette*, Mar. 8, 1779: "Capt. Manley, in the *Cumberland*, is taken [in January] by an English frigate which he fell in with in the night and engaged her before he found his mistake."

1777 CUTTER, Schooner. *Guns*, 8; *Men*, 20.
Aug. 6 Commander: Silas Smith, of Salem.
C. C. **196**, III, 57; *Boston Gazette*, Nov. 3, 1777.

1778 CUTTER, Schooner. *Guns*, 8 *swivels; Men*, 20.
Apr. 6   *Commander:* David Smith.
     Bond: Continental, $5000; State, £500.
     Bonders: David Smith, mariner, principal; Aaron Waitt [signed Wait] and Jeremiah Roals [signed Roale], of Salem, sureties.
     Owners: Aaron Waitt and others.
     Witness: Fitch Pool.
     M. A., v, 157, 158, **168**, 246.

1780 CUTTER, Schooner. *Guns*, 7; *Men*, 45.
Mar. 17   *Commander:* Samuel Croel.
     Bond: Continental, $5000; State, £4000.
     Bonders: Samuel Crowel [signed Croel], principal; John Page and Edward Norris, of Salem, sureties.
     Owners: John Page, Edward Norris, and others.
     Witnesses: Jona[than] Peele, jr., John Johnston.
     M. A., v, 134, 136, **171**, 100.

1780 CUTTER, Brigantine. *Guns*, 10; *Men*, 40.
July 25   *Commander:* Samuel Croel.
     Bond: Continental, $5000; State, £4000.
     Bonders: Samuel Crowell [signed Croel], mariner, principal; John Page and Sam[ue]l Ward, of Salem, sureties.
     Owners: Samuel Page and others.
     Witnesses: Eben Wales, Caleb Davis.
     M. A., v, 159, 160, **171**, 206.

1780 CUTTER, Brigantine. *Guns*, 10; *Men*, 45.
Nov. 3   *Commander:* George Ashby, jr., of Salem.
     C. C. **196**, III, 56; M. A., **171**, 299.

1782 CUTTER, Schooner. *Guns*, 6; *Men*, 30.
Sept. 27   *Commander:* Joseph Strout, of Salem.
     C. C. **196**, III, 58; M. A., **172**, 198.

1782 CYRUS, Ship. *Guns*, 12; *Men*, 45.
Mar. 19   *Commander:* John O'Brien, of Newburyport.
     C. C. **196**, III, 60.

1782 CYRUS, Ship. *Guns*, 10; *Men*, 20.
June 1   *Commander:* Jonathan Mason, jr., of Salem.
     C. C. **196**, III, 59; M. A., **172**, 170.

1776 DALTON, Brigantine. *Guns*, 18; *Men*, 120.
Oct. 7   Commander: Eleazar Johnson, jr.
   Bond: $10,000.
   Bonders: Eleazar Johnson, jr., mariner, Tristram Dalton and Stephen Hooper, merchants, all of Newburyport.
   Bound to Henry Gardner and payment, if made, to be "for the use of the United States."
   Owners: Tristram Dalton and Stephen Hooper.
   Witnesses: Joseph Cutler, Sam[ue]l Nowell.
      M. A., v, 191, **165**, 334; *N. E. Hist. and Gen. Reg.*, Apr., 1878; Livesey, *Prisoners of 1776* (The *Dalton* was captured and the crew sent to Mill Prison).

1779 DANIEL, Bark. *Guns*, 8; *Men*, 20.
Sept. 13 Commander: James Montaudevert.
   Bond: Continental, $10,000; State, £4000.
   Bonders: James Mountadere, mariner, principal; others not stated.
   Owners: Gustavus Fellows and others, of Boston.
   Witnesses: John Cathcart, Edward Tuckerman.
   Signers: J. Montaudevert, Daniel McNeill, Gustavus Fellows.
      M. A., v, 180, 183, **170**, 394.

1781 DART, Schooner. *Guns*, 2; *Men*, 25.
Aug. 28 Commander: Lemuel Perkins, of Salem.
   Owners: Nathaniel Brookhouse, of Marblehead, and others.
      C. C. **196**, III, 66.

1781 DART, Schooner. *Tons*, 25; *Guns*, 6; *Men*, 20.
Dec. 12 Commander: William Gray.
   Petition signed by Miles Ward in behalf of Nathan Goodale and others, of Salem.
      Note. Dated Dec. 24 in Council Records.
      M. A., **172**, 80.

1782 DART, Schooner. *Guns*, 10; *Men*, 25.
Mar. 5   Commander: Silas Smith, of Salem.
      C. C. **196**, III, 67; M. A., **172**, 113.

1782 DART, Schooner. *Guns*, 6; *Men*, 22.
July 10 Commander: Zenas Cook, of Salem.
      C. C. **196**, III, 63.

1782 DART, Schooner. *Guns*, 4; *Men*, 25.
Dec. 9   Commander: Thomas Dexter, of Salem.
C. C. **196**, III, 65; M. A., **172**, 255.

1779 DAUPHIN, Schooner. *Guns*, 6; *Men*, 12.
July 11   Commander: Thomas Powars.
Bond: Continental, $5000; State, £4000.
Bonders: Thomas Powars, mariner, principal; Dan[ie]l Den[niso]n Rogers and Benj[amin] Call, of Boston, sureties.
Owners: Benjamin Call and others.
Witnesses: John Browne Fitch, Samuel Call.
M. A., v, 196, 199, **170**, 216 (petition signed by Benjamin Call in behalf of John Rowe).

1782 DAUPHIN, Brig. *Guns*, 6; *Men*, 20.
Nov. 4   Commander: William Brown, of Boston.
C. C. **196**, III, 68; M. A., **172**, 218.

1780 DEANE, Ship. *Guns*, 30; *Men*, 210.
Dec. 9   Commander: Elisha Hinman.
Note. This vessel was owned in Connecticut, at least when she was bonded in that state, June 6, 1780 (C. C. **196**, III, 69).
M. A., XLIV, 392, 393: "Descriptive Roll of Men Belonging to the Privateer Ship *Deane*, Elisha Hinman, Commander. Boston, Novr. 1780," 392½: "Suffolk, Decr. 9th, 1780. then Elisha Hinman, Esqr. appeared and made oath that the foregoing is a Just and true discriptive list of the officers, marines, and mariners belonging to the Ship *Deane*, commanded by himself. Before me, Joseph Greenleaf, Justice peace."

1780 DECOY, Schooner. *Guns*, 7; *Men*, 25.
May 11   Commander: Silas Howell.
Bond: Continental, $5000; State, £4000.
Bonders: Silas Howell, of Manchester, principal; Nathan Nichols and Jerathmeel Pierce [signed Peirce], of Salem, sureties.
Owners: Nathan Nichols and Jerathmeel Peirce.
Witness: Dan[iel] Hopkins.
M. A., v, 194, 197, **171**, 156.

1779 DEEPFALL.
  Commander: —— ——.
  London Chronicle, Aug. 28, 1779: "The *Deepfall* privateer, of Salem, is taken by the *Nancy* letter of marque, after an engagement of two hours, and carried into New York."

1779 DEFENCE, Boat. *Tons*, 8; *Guns*, 6 *swivels; Men*, 15.
May 13 Commander: Silas Hatch, jr.
  Bond: Continental, $5000; State, £4000.
  Bonders: Silas Hatch, jr., principal; Nathaniel Freeman and Joseph Dimick [signed Dimuck], of Falmouth.
  Owners: Joseph Dimuck and others.
  Witnesses: N. Bodfish, E[benezer?] Nye.
    M. A., v, 174, 177, 170, 95 (Intention of petitioner to cruise on Vineyard Sound).

1779 DEFENCE, Brigantine. *Tons*, 170; *Guns*, 16; *Men*, 100.
July 6 Commander: John Edmonds.
  Bond: Continental, $5000; State, £4000.
  Bonders: John Edmonds, principal; Andrew Cabot and Moses Brown, merchants of Beverly, sureties.
  Owner: Andrew Cabot.
  Witness: Job Prince, jr.
    Note. On the Penobscot Expedition and destroyed to prevent capture.
    M. A., v, 144, 147, xxxvii, 178, 280, 170, 209.

1780 DEFENCE, Brigantine. *Guns*, 14; *Men*, 50.
Mar. 24 Commander: John Edmonds.
  Bond: Continental, $10,000; State, £4000.
  Bonders: John Edmonds, mariner, principal; Andrew Cabot and Job Prince, jr., of Beverly and Boston, sureties.
  Owner: Andrew Cabot.
  Witness: Samuel Colesworthy, jr.
    M. A., v, 142, 145, 171, 104.

1781 DEFENCE, Ship. *Guns*, 16; *Men*, 50.
  Commander: John Edmonds.
    Salem Gazette, Jan. 16, 1781: For Bilboa. "The Ship *Rambler*, Benjamin Lovet, Commander, carries 16 six Pounders and 50 Men. The Ship *Defence*, John Edmonds, Master, carries 16 four Pounders and 50 Men

Will sail by the first of February. . . . For Particulars apply to Capt. Job Prince, at Boston, or the Commanders on board, or John and Andrew Cabot. Beverly, Jan. 1, 1781." (Advertisement.)

1781 DEFENCE, Sloop.
Commander: James Nivens.
Massachusetts State Navy.

1781 DEFENCE, Brigantine. *Guns*, 10; *Men*, 16.
Nov. 18   Commander: Robert Rentoul, of Salem.
Note. The captain's name is also spelled Rantoul and Rentall.
C. C. **196**, III, 74; M. A., **172**, 63.

1782 DEFENCE, Brigantine. *Guns*, 10; *Men*, 16.
Oct. 26   Commander: John Barr, of Salem.
C. C. **196**, III, 71.

1779 DEFIANCE, Brigantine. *Guns*, 6; *Men*, 15.
Jan. 4   Commander: Jonathan Parsons.
Bond: Continental, $10,000; State, £4000.
Bonders: Jonathan Parsons, mariner, principal; Nathaniel Tracy, of Newburyport, surety.

Owner: Nathaniel Tracy.
Witnesses: Joseph Chapman, jr., William Payne.
Note. Bond signed also by William Foster.
M. A., V, 104, 105, **169**, 400.

1779 DEFIANCE. *Guns*, 12.
Commander: —— ——.
London Chronicle, June 24, 1779: "The *Defiance*, an American privateer of 12 guns, belonging to Salem, is taken by a letter of marque after an engagement of two hours and carried into New York."

1782 DEFIANCE, Boat. *Guns, small arms; Men*, 9.
Oct. 12   Commander: William Read, of Freetown.
C. C. **196**, III, 78; M. A., **172**, 204.

1780 DELIGHT, Schooner. *Tons*, 60; *Guns*, 10; *Men*, 50.
Aug. 28   Commander: Seth Story.
Petitioners: Nath[anie]l Silsbee and others, of Salem.
M. A., **171**, 263.

1781 DELIGHT, Brigantine. *Guns,* 8; *Men,* 15.
Jan. 6   *Commander:* Moses Hale, of Gloucester.
   Owners: Eben[ezer] Parsons and others, of Boston.
   C. C. **196**, III, 85; M. A., **171**, 325.

1781 DELIGHT, Brigantine. *Guns,* 8; *Men,* 20.
Aug. 16   *Commander:* Nathaniel Sargent, of Cape Ann.
   Owners: William Parsons and others, of Boston.
   C. C. **196**, III, 90; M. A., **171**, 459.

1781 DELIGHT, Schooner. *Guns,* 4; *Men,* 10.
Dec. 18   *Commander:* Ebenezer Lakeman, of Ipswich.
      Note. In the petition the captain's name is Lateman.
   C. C. **196**, III, 87; M. A., **178**, 218.

1782 DELIGHT, Brig. *Guns,* 6; *Men,* 20.
Aug. 29   *Commander:* Nathaniel Goodwin, of Boston.
   C. C. **196**, III, 84.

1781 DIAMOND, Ship. *Guns,* 16; *Men,* 45.
Dec. 29   *Commander:* Zebulon Babson, of Newburyport.
   C. C. **196**, III, 108; M. A., **172**, 89.

1779 DIANA, Brigantine. *Guns,* 4; *Men,* 12.
May 22   *Commander:* William Haydon.
   Bond: Continental, $10,000; State, £4000.
   Bonders: William Hayden [signed Haydon], mariner, principal; Joseph Russell and Leonard Jarvis, of Boston, sureties.
   Owners: Leonard Jarvis and others.
   Witnesses: John Peck Rathburne [signed Rathbun], B[enjami]n Jarvis.
   M. A., v, 182, 185, **170**, 132.

1779 DIANA, Brigantine. *Guns,* 10; *Men,* 25.
June 16   *Commander:* Andrew Giddings.
   Bond: Continental, $5000; State, £4000.
   Bonders: And[re]w Giddings [signed Gidding], mariner, principal; Ebenezer Parsons and Daniel Sargent, of Newburyport, sureties.
   Owner: William Foster.
   Witnesses: Eben[eze]r Lane, John Babson.
   M. A., v, 99, 101, **170**, 169.

1780 DIANA, Brigantine. *Guns*, 4; *Men*, 12.
Mar. 6   *Commander:* Richard Chilcott.
    Bond: Continental, $10,000; State, £4000.
    Bonders: Richard Chilcot [signed Chilcott], mariner, principal; Leonard Jarvis and Joseph Russell, of Boston, sureties.
    Owners: Leonard Jarvis and Joseph Russell.
    Witnesses: Philip Jarvis, William Seymour.
    M. A., v, 176, 179, **171**, 93.

1780 DIANA, Snow. *Guns*, 8; *Men*, 23.
Sept. 19   *Commander:* William Herrick, of Salem.
    Owner: John Loviet, of Beverly.
    C. C. **196**, III, 103; M. A., XL, 75, **171**, 275.

1781 DIANA, Brig. *Guns*, 6; *Men*, 15.
Jan. 17   *Commander:* William Knapp, of Newburyport.
    C. C. **196**, III, 104.

1781 DIANA, Schooner. *Guns*, 4; *Men*, 20.
Aug. 20   *Commander:* Richard Lakeman, of Ipswich.
    Owners: Joseph Swazey and others, of Beverly.
    C. C. **196**, III, 105; M. A., **171**, 464.

1781 DIANA, Brigantine. *Guns*, 6; *Men*, 16.
Dec. 12   *Commander:* Robert Barker, of Salem.
    C. C. **196**, III, 94; M. A., **172**, 80.

1782 DIANA, Brig. *Guns*, 8; *Men*, 25.
Apr. 20   *Commander:* Robert Cushing, of Boston.
    C. C. **196**, III, 99; M. A., **172**, 140.

1782 DIANA, Brig. *Guns*, 8; *Men*, 18.
Aug.   *Commander:* Thorndike Deland, of Salem.
    C. C. **196**, III, 100; *Salem Gazette*, Sept. 26, 1782 (See ship *General Greene*, Capt. Aaron Croel).

1783 DIANA, Ship. *Guns*, 10; *Men*, 30.
Jan. 20   *Commander:* Richard Chilcott, of Boston.
    C. C. **196**, III, 97; M. A., **172**, 278 (Jan. 7).

1775 DILIGENT, Schooner. *Men*, 30.
Aug. 21   *Commander:* Jeremiah O'Brien.
        Note. A British prize taken in July, 1775, at Machias. The *Diligent* and *Machias Liberty*, as provided in the legislation quoted below, formed the beginning of the Massachusetts State Navy.

M. A., Rec. Gen. Court. (On petition of Benjamin Foster and Jeremiah O'Brien.) "In the House of Representatives Aug. 21, 1775. Whereas the Inhabitants of Machias have been at considerable expense in fixing two Armed Vessels for the Defense of the Sea coasts. . . . Therefore Resolved that proper Officers be commissioned to take Command of said Vessels . . . and that Said Officers and Seamen shall be under such Pay of this Colony as shall hereafter be allowed . . . [Aug. 23] Resolved that there be Paid out of the Public Treasury of this Colony to Capt. Jeremiah Obrian, appointed Commander of the armed Schooner *Diligent* and of the Sloop *Machias Liberty*, now lying in the Harbour of Machias, . . . the Sum of One Hundred and Sixty Pounds . . . for supplying the Men with Provisions." *Amer. Archives*, 4th Ser., III, 346, 354; *Mass. Spy*, Aug. 16, 1775.

1776 DILIGENT, Schooner. *Guns*, 5, and 20 *swivels; Men*, 50.
Commander: John Lambert.
Note. The same vessel as the above.
M. A., **138**, 298 (Feb. 24, 1776), 302 (Mar. 18, 1776), **158**, 12 (Mar. 22, 1776), **165**, 448 (July 13, 1776), **181**, 235 (Sept. 11, 1776), **208**, 166 (Feb. 7, 1776), 168 (Feb. 2, 1776), **210**, 322, 323 (Oct. 10, 11, 1776).

1781 DISCOVERY, Ship. *Guns*, 20; *Men*, 80.
Mar. 2   Commander: Francis Brown, of New Haven, Conn.
Owners: James Jarvis & Co., of Boston.
C. C. **196**, III, 109.

1781 DISDAIN, Ship. *Guns*, 20; *Men*, 100.
June 13 Commander: William Patterson, of Salem.
C. C. **196**, III, 111; M. A., **171**, 411; *Salem Gazette*, Aug. 7, 1781: "The privateer ship *Disdain*, Capt. Patterson, of this port, has taken a schooner." *Boston Gazette*, Sept. 10, 1781: "Thursday last arrived at a safe Port a Brig from Fayal, laden with Wine, taken by the *Disdain* belonging to Salem." Felt, II, 272 (The *Disdain* captured by the enemy).

1781 DISDAIN, Schooner. *Guns*, 4; *Men*, 15.
July 7   Commander: Stephen Hall, of Boston.
C. C. **196**, III, 110; M. A., **171**, 426.

1776 DISPATCH, Ship (letter of marque). *Tons*, 250.
    Commander: Stephen Cleveland.
    Agent: William Bartlett.
       Note. The name is spelled *Despatch*.
       Publ. Colonial Society of Mass., XXIV, 331 (Letter of Gen. Artemas Ward. The *Dispatch* was a prize called the *Hannah*).

1778 DISPATCH, Brigantine. *Guns*, 4, and 6 *swivels;* *Men*, 11.
Apr. 2   *Commander:* John Browne.
    Bond: Continental, $10,000; State, £500.
    Bonders: John Brown [signed Browne], principal; Jo[hn] Bradford [Continental Agent], and Thomas Jackson, of Boston, sureties.
    Owner: The United States of America.
    Witnesses: David Dickson, William Bradford.
       Note. The name is spelled *Despatch*.
    M. A., V, 203, 204, **168**, 234.

1779 DISPATCH, Sloop. *Guns*, 2; *Men*, 12.
Aug. 20   *Commander:* Silvanus Coleman.
    Bond: Continental, $5000; State, £4000.
    Bonders: Silvanus Coleman, mariner, principal; Benj[amin] Blyth and John Coles, of Salem, sureties.
    Owner: Benjamin Blyth.
    Witnesses: Daniel Malloon, Eben[eze]r Peirce.
       Note. The name is spelled *Despatch*.
    M. A., V, 198, 200, **170**, 345.

1780 DISPATCH, Brigantine. *Guns*, 14; *Men*, 30.
July 26   *Commander:* James Thompson.
    Bond: Continental, $10,000; State, £4000.
    Bonders: James Thompson, mariner, Thomas Adams and James Swan, merchants, all of Boston.
    Owners: James Swan and others.
    Witnesses: Edw[ar]d Sands, Thomas Adams, John Keyes.
       Note. The name is spelled *Despatch*.
    M. A., V, 106, 107, **171**, 208.

1780 DISPATCH, Brigantine. *Guns*, 8; *Men*, 12.
Sept. 22   *Commander:* Daniel Jacobs, of Boston.
    C. C. **196**, IV, 5; M. A., XL, 83, **171**, 278.

1781 Dispatch, Schooner. *Tons*, 30; *Guns*, 8; *Men*, 25.
Nov. 28   Commander: Silas Smith.
       Petitioner: Nath[anie]l Coit Webb, of Salem.
       M. A., **172**, 69.

1782 Dispatch, Ship. *Guns*, 10; *Men*, 60.
Apr. 9   Commander: John Felt, of Salem.
       C. C. **196**, iv, 2; Felt, ii, 273.

1782 Dispatch, Sloop. *Guns*, 4; *Men*, 14.
Nov. 27   Commander: John Burke, of Boston.
       C. C. **196**, iv, 1; M. A., **172**, 235.

1782 Dolly, Brigantine. *Guns*, 6; *Men*, 10.
July 10   Commander: Edward Davis, of Boston.
       C. C. **196**, iv, 9.

1775 Dolphin, Schooner. *Tons*, 17; *Guns* and *Men*, not stated.
Dec. 15   Commander: Richard Masury.
       Bond: State, £5000.
       Bonders: Richard Masury, principal; Bartholomew Putnam, Joseph Sprague, Joshua Ward, jr., merchants, sureties — all of Salem. (Petition signed by Henry Rust in addition to the above.)
       Bound to "the Treasurer and Receiver General of the Colony of Massachusetts Bay."
       Owners: Not stated, but doubtless the petitioners.
       Witnesses: Jona[than] Webb, Jer[emia]h Shepard.
          Note. The petition, dated Dec. 1, 1775, was probably the first privateer petition presented in Massachusetts. On Dec. 8 this petition and that for the *Boston Revenge* (dated Dec. 7) were granted by the Council.
       M. A., v, 108, **164**, 211.

1776 Dolphin, Schooner. *Guns*, 8 *swivels*; *Men*, 25.
Aug. 13   Commander: Samuel Waters.
       Bond: Continental, $2000.
       Bonders: Samuel Waters, mariner, Joseph Sprague, and Samuel Ward, all of Salem.
       Owners: Joseph Sprague and Samuel Ward.
       Witnesses: Josh[ua] Dodge, Peter Lander.
       M. A., viii, 17, **165**, 46, **181**, 223.

1776 Dolphin, Schooner. *Guns*, 8 *swivels*; *Men*, 25.
Sept. 30   Commander: John Leach.
       Bond: Continental, $5000.

DISPATCH — DOLPHIN 117

Bonders: John Leach, principal, Samuel Ward, and Joseph Sprague, all of Salem.
Owners: Samuel Ward and Joseph Sprague.
Witnesses: Benj[amin] Ward, jr., William Marston.
M. A., v, 109, **159**, 168, 180, **165**, 299.

1777 DOLPHIN, Schooner. *Guns*, 10; *Men*, 60.
May 26 *Commander:* Edward Fettyplace, jr.
Bond: Continental, $5000.
Bonders: Edward Fettyplace, jr., principal; William Williams and Samuel Russell Gerry, sureties — all of Marblehead.
Owners: Samuel R. Gerry and others.
Witnesses: Joshua Woodbridge, Timothy Foster.
M. A., v, 190, **152**, 362, **166**, 421.

1778 DOLPHIN, Schooner. *Guns*, 2, and 10 *swivels; Men*, 30.
Aug. 28 *Commander:* John Carrick.
Bond: Continental, $5000; State, £4000.
Bonders: John Carwick [signed Carrick], principal; Henry Rust and Joseph Sprague, of Salem, sureties.
Owners: Henry Rust and Joseph Sprague.
Witness: D[aniel] Hopkins.
M. A., v, 102, 103, **169**, 107.

1779 DOLPHIN, Schooner. *Guns*, 8; *Men*, 20.
Apr. 30 *Commander:* Nathaniel Harding.
Bond: Continental, $5000.
Bonders: Nathaniel Harding, principal; Samuel Pitts and James Swan, of Boston, sureties.
Owners: Not stated.
Witnesses: Eleazer Homer, Thornton Barrett.
M. A., v, 195, **170**, 73.

1780 DOLPHIN, Schooner. *Guns*, 6; *Men*, 30.
Mar. 13 *Commander:* Benjamin Hammond.
Bond: Continental, $5000; State, £4000.
Bonders: Benjamin Hammond, mariner, principal; William West, jr., and David Felt, of Salem, sureties.
Owner: Joseph Grafton, of Salem.
Witnesses: Joseph Grafton, Nath[anie]l Perry.
M. A., vi, 66, 68, **171**, 94.

1780 DOLPHIN, Brigantine. *Tons*, 100; *Guns*, 6; *Men*, 20.
May 19 *Commander:* David Ingersoll.
Petitioners: Nathaniel Silsbee and others, of Salem.
M. A., XL, 41, **171**, 163.

1780 DOLPHIN, Brigantine. *Tons*, 90; *Guns*, 8; *Men*, 20.
Aug. 28   *Commander:* Abner Parret.
             Petitioners: Nathaniel Silsbee and others, of Salem.
             M. A., **171**, 263; *Boston Gazette*, Nov. 13, 1780.

1780 DOLPHIN, Schooner. *Guns*, 8; *Men*, 20.
Sept. 9   *Commander:* David Ropes, of Salem.
             C. C. **196**, IV, 30; M. A., **171**, 271.

1780 DOLPHIN, Sloop. *Guns*, 9; *Men*, 40.
Nov. 29   *Commander:* John G. Scranton, of Boston.
             C. C. **196**, IV, 31; M. A., **172**, 236.

1781 DOLPHIN, Schooner. *Guns*, 6; *Men*, 35.
July 14   *Commander:* Joseph Knowlton, of Beverly.
             C. C. **196**, IV, 24; M. A., **171**, 430.

1781 DOLPHIN, Schooner. *Guns*, 6; *Men*, 20.
Dec. 12   *Commander:* William Gray, of Salem.
             C. C. **196**, IV, 22; *Boston Gazette*, Mar. 18, 1782: "Capt. Gray, in a privateer schooner of Salem, arrived there from a cruise on Tuesday last. On the 19th ult. he carried a prize sloop into one of the harbours of New Jersey and the next day sent a boat with seven men in pursuit of a brig, which lay near the bar; but the boat was lost and all the men were unfortunately drowned."

1782 DOLPHIN, Brigantine. *Guns*, 6; *Men*, 12.
Mar. 15   *Commander:* David Felt, jr., of Salem.
             C. C. **196**, IV, 19; M. A., **172**, 119.

1782 DOLPHIN, Brigantine. *Guns*, 8; *Men*, 25.
Apr. 4   *Commander:* Samuel Babson, of Cape Ann.
             C. C. **196**, IV, 11.

1782 DOLPHIN, Schooner. *Guns*, 8; *Men*, 30.
Apr. 16   *Commander:* Gregory Powers, of Salem.
             C. C. **196**, IV, 28; M. A., **172**, 134; *Boston Gazette*, Aug. 5, 1782: "Lately arrived in a safe port a prize ship, of about 250 tons, from Quebec bound to New York. The gallantry exhibited in the capture of this ship deserves to be particularly noticed. She mounted 10 four-pounders and 4 sixes and had on board 24 men. She was attacked by Capt. Gregory Powars in a privateer belonging to this place [Salem] called the

Dolphin, a schooner of 30 tons, mounting 6 small carriage guns and carrying 25 men and boys. After an engagement of three glasses the ship struck. Capt. Gordon, who commanded her, received a wound in his hand but lost none of his men in the action. Capt. Powars had three men killed and one badly wounded. The cargo of the ship consists principally of lumber. The *Dolphin* in returning from her cruise was lost on Cape Sables, but the men were all saved and arrived here yesterday."

1782 DOLPHIN, Boat. *Guns*, not stated; *Men*, 10.
May 8   *Commander:* Jabez Meigs, of Plymouth.
     C. C. **196**, IV, 26; M. A., **172**, 150.

1782 DOLPHIN, Schooner. *Guns*, 8; *Men*, 18.
May 25 *Commander:* William Chaple, of Salem.
     C. C. **196**, IV, 16; M. A., **172**, 162.

1782 DOLPHIN, Schooner. *Guns*, 8; *Men*, 18.
Aug. 13 *Commander:* Francis Benson, of Salem.
     C. C. **196**, IV, 13; M. A., **172**, 185.

1782 DOLPHIN, Brigantine. *Guns*, 4; *Men*, 16.
Sept. 10 *Commander:* Benjamin Baker, of Boston.
     C. C. **196**, IV, 12.

1782 DOLPHIN, Sloop. *Tons*, 35; *Guns*, 9; *Men*, 40.
Nov. 27 *Commander:* John [G.] Scranton.
     Petitioner: William de Luce, of Boston.
     M. A., **172**, 236.

1782 DON GALVEZ, Brig. *Guns*, 6; *Men*, 16.
Feb. 28 *Commander:* Silas Jones, of Nantucket.
     Owners: N[athan] Goodale and others, of Salem.
     C. C. **196**, IV, 37; M. A., **172**, 104.

1776 DOVE, Schooner.
     Commander: Hugh Hill.
     M. A., **292**, 12 (Maritime Court, Salem, May 16, 1776; prize of the *Dove* libelled by Jonathan Glover).

1776 DOVE.
     Commander: Robert Haskell.
     Note. Called a privateer on endorsement of orders.
     M. A., **195**, 110 (July 15, 1776, orders to cruise off Nova Scotia, to gain intelligence).

1782 DRAGON, Brig. *Guns*, 6; *Men*, 20.
Oct. 3   *Commander:* John Adams, of Boston.
C. C. **196**, IV, 44.

1780 DRAKE, Brigantine. *Guns*, 6; *Men*, 14.
Nov. 7   *Commander:* Nathaniel Newman, of Newburyport.
C. C. **196**, IV, 48.

1782 DREADNOUGHT, Lugger. *Guns*, 2; *Men*, 35.
May 11   *Commander:* Amos Potter, of Boston.
C. C. **196**, IV, 51; M. A., **172**, 155; Sumner's Notes (Mass. Hist. Soc. MS.), III, 10.

1779 DRIVER, Sloop. *Guns*, 8; *Men*, 20.
Sept. 1   *Commander:* Daniel Adams.
Bond: Continental, $5000; State, £4000.
Bonders: Daniel Adams, principal; Josiah Batchelder, jr., and Livermore Whittridge, of Beverly, sureties.
Owner: Josiah Batchelder.
Witnesses: William Ellinwood, Joanna Batchelder.
M. A., V, 192, 193, **170**, 368.

1782 DUKE OF LEINSTER, Ship. *Guns*, 14; *Men*, 25.
Aug. 30   *Commander:* Robert Caldwell, of Boston.
C. C. **196**, IV, 52; M. A., **171**, 479.

1776 EAGLE, Schooner. *Tons*, 60; *Guns*, 8; *Men*, 60.
Oct. 16   *Commander:* Barzillai Smith.
Petitioner: Elijah Freeman Payne, of Boston.
M. A., **159**, 32, 37, **165**, 360; Min. Sup. Court, 40.

1777 EAGLE, Schooner. *Guns*, 8; *Men*, 50.
May 10   *Commander:* Samuel Avery.
Bond: Continental, $5000.
Bonders: Samuel Avery, principal; Paul Dudley Sargent and John Winthrop, of Boston, sureties.
Owners: P. D. Sargent and John Winthrop.
Witnesses: Leo[nard] Jarvis, Martin Brimmer.
M. A., V, 220, **166**, 400.

1778 EAGLE, Brigantine. *Guns*, 8, and 6 *swivels*; *Men*, 45.
Mar. 10, 11 *Commander:* Elijah Luce.
Bond: Continental, $5000; State, £500.
Bonders: Elijah Luce, principal; John Hinckley [signed Hinkley] and Dimond Morton, of Boston, sureties.
Owners: John Hinkley, Dimond Morton, and others.
Witnesses: R[obert?] Robins, John Channing.
M. A., V, 219, 222, **139**, 159, **168**, 204.

1780   EAGLE, Ship. *Guns*, 10; *Men*, 40.
June 2   *Commander:* Daniel McNeill.
            Bond: Continental, $10,000; State, £4000.
            Bonders: Daniel McNeill, mariner of Boston, principal; Ebenezer Parsons and Stephen Higginson, merchants of Boston, sureties.
            Owners: Stephen Higginson and others.
            Witnesses: Moses Pike, Daniel Sargent, jr.
            M. A., v, 211, 212, **171**, 168.

1780   EAGLE, Ship.
June 17   *Commander:* William Groves, of Beverly.
            M. A., XL, 84; *Pub. Colonial Society of Mass.*, XXIV, 408.

1780   EAGLE, Brig. *Guns*, 14.
            Commander: Ambrose James.
            Independent Chronicle, Sept. 14, 1780: "The ship *Harlequin* of 18 guns, ship *Jack* of 14, and the brig *Eagle* of 14, all belonging to Salem, are taken by the enemy in the river St. Lawrence and carried to Quebec." Essex Institute Miscellaneous Ship Papers (schooner *Eagle*, probably the same vessel).

1780   EAGLE, Ship. *Guns*, 10; *Men*, 40.
Nov. 8   *Commander:* Nathaniel Sargent.
            Owner: Stephen Higginson, of Boston.
            C. C. **196**, IV, 61; M. A., **171**, 301.

1782   EAGLE, Brig. *Guns*, 20; *Men*, 110.
            Commander: John Leach.
            Paine, 455; Marblehead Hist. Soc. (1782).

1780   EDWARD, Brigantine. *Guns*, 3; *Men*, 12.
Nov. 5   *Commander:* Alexander Wilson, of Boston.
            C. C. **196**, IV, 64; M. A., **171**, 301.

1778   EFFINGHAM, Ship. *Tons*, 350; *Guns*, 8; *Men*, 24.
Sept. 17   *Commander:* Joseph Costin.
            Bond: Continental, $10,000; State, £4000.
            Bonders: Joseph Costin, mariner, principal; James Swan and John Codman, of Boston, sureties.
            Owners: James Swan and others.
            Witness: Benj[amin] Greene.
            M. A., v, 213, 214, **169**, 163.

1779 Elizabeth, Brigantine. *Guns*, 6; *Men*, 15.
Dec. 16   *Commander:* Simon Mansis.
   Bond: Continental, $10,000; State, £4000.
   Bonders: Simon Mansis, mariner, principal; Thomas Russell and Sam[ue]l Conant, jr., of Boston, sureties.
   Owners: Thomas Russell & Co.
   Witnesses: Chambers Russell, Thomas Greene.
   M. A., v, 207, 208, **171**, 44.

1780 Elizabeth, Brigantine. *Guns*, 8; *Men*, 20.
Aug. 15   *Commander:* Michael Hopkins.
   Petitioner: Thomas Russell, of Boston.
   M. A., **171**, 246; C. C. **196**, iv, 72.

1781 Elizabeth, Schooner. *Guns*, 4; *Men*, 10.
Nov. 1   *Commander:* Samuel West, of Salem.
   C. C. **196**, iv, 74; M. A., **172**, 55.

1781 Elizabeth, Ship. *Guns*, 8; *Men*, 25.
Dec. 1   *Commander:* Nathaniel Cutting, of Newburyport.
   C. C. **196**, iv, 71.

1781 Elizabeth, Schooner. *Guns*, 4; *Men*, 10.
Dec. 20   *Commander:* Clifford Byrne, of Salem.
   C. C. **196**, iv, 68.

1782 Elizabeth, Brig. *Guns*, 6; *Men*, 15.
July 31   *Commander:* Ichabod Clarke.
   Owners: Job Prince, jr., and others, of Boston.
   C. C. **196**, iv, 69; M. A., **172**, 182.

1779 Endeavour, Brigantine. *Guns*, 8; *Men*, 30.
Aug. 10   *Commander:* George May.
   Bond: Continental, $5000; State, £4000.
   Bonders: George May, mariner, principal; William Erskine and Henry Mitchell, of Boston, sureties.
   Owners: William Erskine and others.
   Witnesses: Samuel Breck, W[illia]m Bright.
   M. A., v, 221, 224, **170**, 317.

1778 Enterprize, Schooner. *Guns*, 4, and 10 *swivels; Men*, 30.
Sept. 2   *Commander:* Joseph Leach.
   Bond: Continental, $5000; State, £4000.
   Bonders: Joseph Leach, mariner, principal; Benj[amin] Blyth and John Cole [signed Coles], of Salem, sureties.

ELIZABETH — EXCHANGE 123

Owners: Benj. Blyth, John Coles, and others.
Witness: D[aniel] Hopkins.
M. A., v, 215, 216, **169**, 130.

1782 ENTERPRIZE, Brigantine. *Guns*, 14; *Men*, 14.
Mar. 9 *Commander:* Ebenezer Nickerson, of Boston.
C. C. **196**, IV, 85; M. A., **172**, 115.

1780 ESSEX, Ship. *Guns*, 20; *Men*, 140.
May 6 *Commander:* John Cathcart.
Bond: Continental, $10,000; State, £4000.
Bonders: John Cathcart, principal; William Creed and Job Prince, jr., of Boston, sureties.
Owners: Job Prince and others.
Witness: Eben[eze]r I. Thayer.
M. A., v, 217, 218, **171**, 148; *Salem Gazette and General Advertiser*, Jan. 2, 1781: "Last Friday se'nnight arrived here from a cruise the privateer ship *Essex*, Capt. Cathcart, having captured three valuable prizes, all homeward bound, which are daily expected. The above vessels were captured on the coast of Ireland."

1781 ESSEX, Ship. *Guns*, 20; *Men*, 150.
Apr. 14 *Commander:* John Cathcart, of Salem.
Owners: Jonathan Jackson, Joseph Lee, and others, of Newburyport.
C. C. **196**, IV, 86; M. A., **171**, 369.

1781 EXCHANGE, Ship. *Guns*, 20; *Men*, 60.
Mar. 6 *Commander:* John Collins, of Salem.
C. C. **196**, IV, 88; M. A., **171**, 348; Mar. Court Rec., 53.

1781 EXCHANGE, Schooner. *Guns*, 2; *Men*, 15.
Oct. 12 *Commander:* Henry Tibbets, of Damariscotta.
Owners: William Long and others, of Salem.
C. C. **196**, IV, 90; M. A., **172**, 25.

1782 EXCHANGE, Ship. *Guns*, 20; *Men*, 40.
Feb. 12 *Commander:* Simon Forrester, of Salem.
C. C. **196**, IV, 89; M. A., **172**, 99; *Salem Gazette*, Apr. 4, 1782: "The ship *Exchange*, Capt. Forrester, and the brig *Revolt*, Capt. Phelps, both belonging to this port, are taken and carried into New York."

1780 EXPEDITION, Brigantine. *Guns,* 10; *Men,* 20.
Dec. 23   *Commander:* Henry Atkins, of Boston.
C. C. **196**, IV, 102; M. A., **171**, 319.

1781 EXPEDITION, Brig. *Guns,* 10; *Men,* 25.
June 16   *Commander:* Ephraim Lombard, of Truro.
Owners: Isaac Smith and Codman & Smith, of Boston.
C. C. **196**, IV, 91; M. A., **171**, 413.

1779 EXPERIMENT, Brigantine. *Guns,* 6; *Men,* 25.
Mar. 30   *Commander:* John Porter.
Bond: Continental, $10,000; State, £4000.
Bonders: John Porter, mariner, principal; Stephen Higginson and Job Prince, jr., of Boston, sureties.
Owners: George Cabot and others [of Beverly].
Witnesses: Thomas Prince, Mungo Mackay, jr.
M. A., V, 209, 210, **170**, 42.

1781 EXPERIMENT, Brigantine. *Guns,* 10; *Men,* 20.
Apr. 16   *Commander:* Samuel Ingersoll, of Salem.
C. C. **196**, IV, 94; M. A., **171**, 373.

1782 EXPERIMENT, Brigantine. *Guns,* 6; *Men,* 14.
Apr. 6   *Commander:* Samuel Ingersoll, of Salem.
C. C. **196**, IV, 95; Mar. Court Rec., 95.

1782 EXPERIMENT, Brigantine. *Guns,* 6; *Men,* 14.
July 13   *Commander:* Phineas Parker, of Salem.
C. C. **196**, IV, 97.

1782 EXPERIMENT, Ship. *Guns,* 4; *Men,* 14.
July 16   *Commander:* William Noyes, of Newburyport.
C. C. **196**, IV, 96.

1782 EXPERIMENT, Brig. *Guns,* 6; *Men,* 12.
Dec. 7   *Commander:* George Williams, jr., of Salem.
C. C. **196**, IV, 100; M. A., **172**, 252.

1779 FAIRFIELD, Brigantine.
Commander: Joseph Tripp.
Boston Gazette, Apr. 19, 1779.

1776 FAIR LADY, Schooner. *Guns,* 1, and 4 *swivels; Men,* 20.
Aug. 23   *Commander:* Jacob Martin.
Bond: Continental, $5000.
Bonders: Jacob Martin, principal; Michael Farley and Asa Lawrence, gentlemen, sureties.

Owners: Capt. Daniel Goodhue and others, of Ipswich.
Witnesses: B. Chadbourn, Jno. Molineux.
M. A., v, 284, **165**, 144, 148.

1776 FAIR LADY, Schooner. *Guns*, 2, and 4 *swivels; Men*, 20.
Oct. 10   *Commander:* Joseph Dennis.
Bond: Continental, $5000.
Bonders: Joseph Dennis, principal; Michael Farley, of Ipswich, and Eleazer Johnson, of Newburyport, sureties.
Owners: Nath[anie]l Farley, Jacob Treadwell, and others, of Ipswich.
Witnesses: Seth Loring, Joseph Rowe.
M. A., v, 286, **165**, 333.

1777 FAIR PLAY, Brigantine. *Guns*, 12; *Men*, 60.
July 17   *Commander:* Isaac Somes, of Gloucester.
Owner: Tristram Dalton, of Newburyport.
Note. In *Boston Gazette*, Oct. 6, 1777, the captain's name appears as Isaac Sobries.
C. C. **196**, IV, 113; Court Files, 102633.

1778 FAIR PLAY, Brigantine. *Guns*, 12; *Men*, 70.
Oct. 19   *Commander:* Andrew Giddings.
Bond: Continental, $5000; State, £4000.
Bonders: Andrew Giddings [signed Giddinge], mariner, principal; Eben[ezer] Parsons and Joseph Marquand, sureties.
Owners: Dan[ie]l Sargent and others, of Cape Ann.
Witnesses: W[illia]m Coombs, Eben[ezer] Lane.
M. A., v, 235, 238, **169**, 238.

1780 FAIR PLAY, Brigantine. *Guns*, 6; *Men*, 8.
July 24   *Commander:* Elias Davis.
Bond: Continental, $5000; State, £4000.
Bonders: Elias Davis, mariner of Cape Ann, principal; John Coffin Jones and Ebenezer Parsons, merchants of Boston, sureties.
Owners: Daniel Sargent and others, merchants of Boston.
Witnesses: Stephen Higginson, Daniel Sargent.
M. A., v, 229, 232, **171**, 205.

1782 FAIR TRADER, Schooner. *Guns*, 4; *Men*, 14.
July 5   *Commander:* Peter Geyer, of Boston.
C. C. **196**, v, 1; M. A., **172**, 179.

1782 FALMOUTH, Boat. *Guns*, 7; *Men*, 30.
May 8   *Commander:* Barakiah Bassett, of Plymouth.
   Owners: Joseph Demick [Dimuck] and others, of Falmouth.
   C. C. **196**, v, 2; M. A., **172**, 150.

1779 FAME, Brigantine. *Guns*, 16; *Men*, 100.
Apr. 15   *Commander:* Samuel Hobbs.
   Bond: Continental, $10,000; State, £4000.
   Bonders: Samuel Hobbs, mariner, principal; Elias Hasket Derby and Nath[anie]l Silsbee, of Salem, sureties.
   Owners: E. H. Derby and others.
   Witnesses: Bartho[lomew] Putnam, Stephen Webb.
   M. A., v, 294, 295, **159**, 225, 346, **170**, 59.

1779 FAME, Brigantine. *Guns*, 10; *Men*, 30.
Oct. 19   *Commander:* Abraham Bartlett.
   Bond: Continental, $10,000; State, £4000.
   Bonders: Abraham Bartlett, mariner, principal; John Codman and William Smith, of Boston, sureties.
   Owners: John Codman and others.
   Witnesses: Martin Bicker, John Hutchinson, jr.
   M. A., v, 298, 299, **170**, 436.

1780 FAME, Brig. *Guns*, 18; *Men*, 30.
Apr. 18   *Commander:* Nicholas Lamprell.
   Bond: Continental, $10,000; State, £4000.
   Bonders: Nicholas Lamprell, mariner, principal; Elias Hasket Derby and Nath[anie]l Silsbee, sureties.
   Owner: E. H. Derby, of Salem.
   Witness: Nath[aniel] Coit Webb.
   M. A., v, 290, 291, **171**, 130.

1780 FAME, Brigantine. *Guns*, 12; *Men*, 30.
Apr. 22   *Commander:* Joseph Costin.
   Bond: Continental, $10,000; State, £4000.
   Bonders: Joseph Costin, mariner, principal; Codman & Smith, and Thomas Russell, of Boston, sureties.
   Owners: Codman & Smith, of Boston.
   Witnesses: Chambers Russell, Samuel Conant, jr.
   M. A., v, 227, 230, **171**, 133; Mar. Court Rec., 32.

1777 FANCY, Brigantine. *Guns*, 12; *Men*, 75.
May 20   *Commander:* John Lee.
   Bond: Continental, $10,000.

State of Massachusetts Bay } To the Hon'ble the Council of said State.

The Petition of Daniel McNeill Commander of the Armed Brigantine Hancock Burthen One Hundred and Forty Tons — Mounting Twelve Carriage Guns & Eighteen Swivels, In behalf of himself and Owners of the said Brig.— Humbly Shews that the said Brigantine was fitted at a very Great Expence Victualed Mand & fitt for Sea before the said Brig.— left the Port of Newberry except Wood, which was on Board and had Actually sailed before any embargo took place, with proper Papers below all the Forts in this Harbour, and was entirely ready to proceed to Sea ———

That in complyance with a Requisition of the Hon'ble Council of this State & that alone said Brig. Return'd to the Harbour of Boston & is there now lying at a very Great Expence entirely fit for the Sea, and that many Valuable Articles of Provision are now Perishing on Board her ——— Your Petitioner therefore Humbly prays that your Honours would take the Premises into your Wise Consideration & Grant him Liberty to proceed on his intended Cruise and your Petitioners as in duty bound shall ever Pray ———

Dan'l McNeill for Self Mess.rs Mercer Moor & Co.

Petition for Liberty to sail notwithstanding Embargo

FALMOUTH — FANNY

Bonders: John Lee, of Newburyport, principal; John Tracy and William Titcomb, sureties.
Owners: Jona[than] Jackson, John Tracy, and others, of Newburyport.
Witnesses: Sam[ue]l White, Tim[othy] Foster.
   Note. The vessel's name is spelled *Fancey*.
M. A., v, 280, 159, 182, 166, 417.

1777 FANCY, Schooner. *Guns*, 6; *Men*, 30.
May 26   *Commander:* John Farrey.
Bond: Continental, $5000.
Bonders: John Farrey, principal; Henry Newhall and William Shattuck, of Boston, sureties.
Owners: John Farrey and Henry Newhall.
Witnesses: Timothy Foster, Edward Bassett.
   Note. The *Boston Gazette*, Sept. 22, 1777, mentions the *Fanny*, Capt. Ferry, probably the same vessel.
M. A., v, 283, 159, 159, 162, 166, 422.

1779 FANCY, Ship. *Guns*, 10; *Men*, 24.
Aug. 7   *Commander:* Jonathan Jewett.
Bond: Continental, $10,000; State, £4000.
Bonders: Jonathan Jewett, mariner, principal; Moses Little and Robert Stevenson, of Newburyport, sureties.
Owners: Moses Little and others.
Witnesses: Jacob Boardman, Joseph Moulton, jr.
   Note. The ship is called the *Fanny* in Council Records.
M. A., v, 251, 254, 170, 308.

1780 FANCY, Ship. *Guns*, 10; *Men*, 25.
Dec. 28   *Commander:* Samuel Coffin, of Newburyport.
Owners: Jonathan Hamilton, of Berwick, and Robert Stevenson, of Kittery.
C. C. 196, v, 13.

1781 FANCY, Ship. *Guns*, 8; *Men*, 25.
Aug. 13   *Commander:* Samuel Rice, of Kittery.
C. C. 196, v, 12.

1777 FANNY, Brigantine. *Guns*, 18; *Men*, 100.
May 26   *Commander:* John Kendrick.
Bond: Continental, $10,000.
Bonders: John Kendrick, of Wareham, principal; Adam Babcock and Archibald Blair, of Dartmouth, sureties.
Owners: Adam Babcock and Archibald Blair.

Witnesses: Jno. Avery, jr., W[illia]m Baker, Jere[mia]h Mayhew, John Pease, 3rd.

M. A., v, 270, **166**, 123, 420, **167**, 45 (Petition of Adam Babcock, June 23, 1777, that the *Fanny*, now lying at Dartmouth, be permitted to go to sea and to Martha's Vineyard and Nantucket. Granted), **169**, 231 (The *Fanny* was called the *Boston* while in France); Stevens's *Facsimiles*, 1661, 1664, 1801; Wharton, *Dipl. Corres. Rev.*, II, 381, 496. See above, Introduction, 59.

1778 FANNY, Snow. *Guns*, 6; *Men*, 12.
Jan. 14   *Commander:* Richard Ober.
    Bond: Continental, $10,000; State, £500.
    Bonders: Rich[ar]d Obear [signed Ober], mariner, principal; Mark Lafitte and Step[hen] Higginson, of Salem, sureties.
    Bound to Henry Gardner (both bonds).
    Owner: Mark Lafitte.
    Witnesses: Nath[anie]l Ropes, W. Prosser.
    M. A., v, 282, 285, **168**, 145.

1780 FANNY, Brigantine. *Guns*, 6; *Men*, 15.
Aug. 19   *Commander:* Herbert Woodberry, of Beverly.
    C. C. **196**, v, 17; M. A., XL, 85.

1781 FANNY, Brigantine. *Guns*, 4; *Men*, 12.
May 16   *Commander:* Samuel Tucker, of Salem.
    C. C. **196**, v, 16; M. A., **171**, 394.

1778 FAVOURITE, Vessel of War (brigantine).
May 27   *Commander:* John Lamb.
    Bond: State, £2000.
    Bonders: William Shattuck, merchant of Boston, John Lamb, mariner of Norwich, Conn., and Patrick Moore, of Martinique, W. I.
    Witnesses: Jno. Furnass, Jno. M. Furnass, Tho[ma]s Appleton.
    M. A., **139**, 172, 221 (Bond not to enlist any man in New England outside of Massachusetts); *Boston Gazette*, Aug. 17, 1778.

1778 FAVORITE, Schooner. *Guns*, 8; *Men*, 16.
Oct. 14   *Commander:* John Guliker.
    Bond: Continental, $5000; State, £4000.

Bonders: John Guliker, mariner, principal; Thomas Adams and Daniel Clark, of Boston, sureties.
Owners: Thomas Adams and others.
Witnesses: Both bonds unwitnessed.
M. A., v, 237, 240, **169**, 225.

1779 FAVORITE, Schooner. *Guns,* 8; *Men,* 15.
Sept. 21   *Commander:* David McLeod.
Bond: Continental, $5000; State, £4000.
Bonders: David McCleod, mariner, principal; Daniel Clark, of Boston, and Hon. Abraham Fuller, of Newton, sureties.
Owner: Daniel Clark.
Witnesses: Jonathan Metcalf, Jo[hn] Dall.
M. A., v, 223, 226, **170**, 409.

1779 FAVOURITE, Brig. *Tons,* 100; *Guns,* 8; *Men,* 20.
Dec. 14   *Commander:* Isaac Somes.
Petitioners: Daniel Sargent and others, of Boston.
M. A., **176**, 53; *Boston Gazette,* July 30, 1781.

1780 FAVORITE, Ship. *Guns,* 10; *Men,* 30.
Mar. 22, 23   *Commander:* Jonathan Oakes.
Bond: Continental, $10,000; State, £4000.
Bonders: Jonathan Oakes, principal; William Shattuck and David Tilden, of Boston, sureties.
Owner: William Shattuck, of Boston.
Witnesses: John Shattuck, James Perkins.
M. A., v, 239, 242, **171**, 102.

1781 FAVOURITE, Brig. *Guns,* 10; *Men,* 20.
Dec. 6   *Commander:* Elias Davis, of Boston.
C. C. **196**, v, 20; M. A., **172**, 79.

1782 FAVOURITE, Brigantine. *Guns,* 11; *Men,* 50.
May 21   *Commander:* William Patterson, of Salem.
C. C. **196**, v, 22; M. A., **172**, 161.

1782 FAVOURITE, Ship. *Guns,* 6; *Men,* 20.
Nov. 21   *Commander:* Nathaniel Sargent, of Gloucester.
Owners: Daniel Sargent and others, of Boston.
C. C. **196**, v, 23; M. A., **172**, 234.

1782 FELICITY, Brig. *Guns,* 8; *Men,* 40.
Commander: —— ——.
Essex Institute, Miscellaneous Ship Papers.

1782 FIREBRAND, Brigantine. *Guns,* 10; *Men,* 35.
Oct. 6   *Commander:* Phoenix Frazier, of Boston.
C. C. **196**, v, 32; M. A., **172**, 211 (Petition dated Oct. 25); *Boston Gazette,* Apr. 14, 1783: "Wednesday last arrived here the Brig *Firebrand,* Capt. Frazier, in 35 Days from Amsterdam, but last from Dover in 29 Days."

1779 FISH HAWK, Sloop. *Guns,* 8; *Men,* 40.
Sept. 8   *Commander:* William Groves.
Bond: Continental, $5000; State, £4000.
Bonders: William Groves, mariner, principal; Nathan Leech and Livermore Whittridge, mariners of Beverly, sureties.
Owners: Josiah Batchelder and others, of Beverly.
Witnesses: Benj[amin] Herkimer [?], Joseph Wyer.
M. A., v, 265, 266, **159**, 198, **170**, 368.

1779 FISH HAWK, Sloop. *Guns,* 8; *Men,* 16.
Dec. 1   *Commander:* Samuel Foster.
Bond: Continental, $5000; State, £4000.
Bonders: Samuel Foster, principal; Nathan Leach [signed Leech] and Livermore Whittredge, of Beverly, sureties.
Owners: Josiah Batchelder, jr., and others, of Beverly.
Witnesses: Tho[ma]s Stephens, William Leach.
M. A., v, 267, 268, **171**, 35.

1780 FISH HAWK, Sloop. *Guns,* 8; *Men,* 16.
Sept. 1   *Commander:* Israel Ober, of Beverly.
C. C. **196**, v, 36; M. A., **177**, 45.

1781 FISH HAWK, Sloop. *Guns,* 6; *Men,* 40.
May 2   *Commander:* Samuel Foster, of Beverly.
C. C. **196**, v, 35; M. A., **171**, 381.

1779 FLORA, Schooner. *Guns,* 4; *Men,* 12.
July 28   *Commander:* Eleazar Ingals.
Bond: Continental, $5000; State, £4000.
Bonders: Ellis [signed Eleazar] Ingals, mariner, principal; Peter Joseph Lion and John Larreguy, of Boston, sureties.
Owner: Peter Joseph Lion, of the Island of Guadeloupe.
Witness: J[ohn] Dall.
M. A., v, 273, 276, **170**, 278.

1781   FLORA, Brigantine. *Guns,* 14; *Men,* 25.
Feb. 14   *Commander:* Elisha Turner, of Boston.
   C. C. 196, v, 42; M. A., **171**, 344.

1781   FLORA, Brigantine. *Guns,* 10; *Men,* 30.
Oct. 10   *Commander:* Jacob Dunnell, of Boston.
   C. C. 196, v, 40; M. A., **172**, 21.

1782   FLORA. *Guns,* 26.
   Commander: —— ——.
   London Chronicle, Aug. 31, 1782: "The *Industry* . . . was taken the 28th of June by the *Flora,* American frigate of 26 twelve pounders . . . and sent for Boston."

1778   FLY, Sloop. *Guns,* 4, and 8 *swivels; Men,* 50.
Aug. 28, 29   *Commander:* John Marsh.
   Bond: Continental, $5000; State, £4000.
   Bonders: John Marsh, mariner, principal; Benj[amin] Lovett and Mansel Alecock [signed Alcock], of Beverly and Salem, sureties.
   Owners: Benjamin Lovett, and others, of Beverly.
   Witnesses: D[aniel] Hopkins, James Bott.
   M. A., v, 256, 259, **169**, 117.

1779   FLY, Schooner. *Guns,* 8; *Men,* 25.
Mar. 23   *Commander:* Joshua Burges.
   Bond: Continental, $5000; State, £4000.
   Bonders: Joshua Burgis [signed Burges], mariner, principal; Henry Mitchell and Francis Johonnot, of Boston, sureties.
   Owners: Henry Mitchell and others.
   Witnesses: Henry Johnson, W[illia]m Miller.
   M. A., v, 269, 272, **139**, 243, **170**, 28.

1779   FLY, Schooner. *Guns,* 2; *Men,* 25.
July 6   *Commander:* Nathaniel Bently.
   Bond: Continental, $5000; State, £4000.
   Bonders: Nathaniel Bentley [signed Bently], mariner, principal; Joseph Head and Henry Swan, of Boston, sureties.
   Owner: Sam[ue]l Batchelder, of Newburyport.
   Witnesses: W[illia]m Knapp, Peter Roberts.
   M. A., v, 278, 279, **170**, 208.

1780 FLY, Schooner. *Guns,* 10; *Men,* 25.
Sept. 22   *Commander:* Silas Smith, of Salem.
C. C. **196**, v, 56; M. A., XLIV, 450, **171**, 277.

1781 FLY, Boat. *Guns, Small arms; Men,* 9.
Aug. 22   *Commander:* John Perry, of St. Georges.
C. C. **196**, v, 52; M. A., **171**, 465.

1782 FLY, Schooner. *Guns,* 6; *Men,* 25.
Feb. 12   *Commander:* Christopher Babbidge, of Salem.
C. C. **196**, v, 43.

1782 FLY, Schooner. *Guns,* 4; *Men,* 30.
June 4   *Commander:* William Molloy, of Salem.
C. C. **196**, v, 50; M. A., **172**, 172.

1782 FLY, Boat. *Guns,* 1; *Men,* 14.
June 29   *Commander:* John Perry, of St. Georges.
Owners: Israel Mead and others, of Boston.
C. C. **196**, v, 53; M. A., **178**, 438; *Boston Gazette,* June 10, 1782.

1781 FLYING FISH, Brigantine. *Guns,* 6; *Men,* 15.
Feb. 1   *Commander:* Anthony Divers, of Salem.
C. C. **196**, v, 60; M. A., **171**, 337.

1781 FLYING FISH, Brigantine. *Tons,* 80; *Guns,* 12; *Men,* 50.
May 28   *Commander:* John Gavett.
Owners: John Moriarty and others, of Salem.
C. C. **196**, v, 61; M. A., **171**, 397; *Boston Gazette,* July 16, 1781 (Halifax, June 26). "Last Saturday was sent in here by the *Charlestown* Frigate the Rebel Privateer Brig *Flying Fish,* mounting 10 Guns, lately built at Salem."

1777 FORTUNE, Ship. *Guns,* 22.
Commander: —— Simpkins.
Almon's *Remembrancer,* v, 174 (Nantucket, May 15, 1777): "The 11th inst. Capt. Simpkins, commander of the *Fortune,* Provincial ship of war of 22 guns, 4 cohorns and 18 swivels, fell in with the English brig *Boscawen,* of 18 six-pounders, near this port, and after an engagement of upwards of an hour the latter was taken and carried for Boston. We saw the action, which was continued a considerable time very resolute by both parties and seemed to us rather doubtful. The Captain of the brig was wounded and the officer that was second in command was killed."

1779 FORTUNE, Brigantine. *Guns*, 8; *Men*, 18.
June 28   *Commander:* Francis Boardman.
   Bond: Continental, not stated; State, £4000.
   Bonders: Francis Bowman [signed Boardman], mariner of Salem, principal; Miles Greenwood, of Salem, and John Dyson, of Beverly, merchants, sureties.
   Owners: Miles Greenwood and John Dyson.
   Witnesses: Betsy Elkins, Sarah Batchelder.
   M. A., v, 296, 297, **170**, 190.

1780 FORTUNE, Ship. *Guns*, 8; *Men*, 20.
Feb. 26   *Commander:* Edward Jarvis.
   Bond: Continental, $10,000; State, £4000.
   Bonders: Edward Jarvis, mariner, principal; John Welch, jr., [signed Welsh] and Joseph Whiting, of Boston, sureties.
   Owners: John Welsh and others.
   Witnesses: John Larkin, John Boies.
   M. A., v, 243, 246, **171**, 91.

1780 FORTUNE, Brigantine. *Guns*, 8; *Men*, 30.
Apr. 24   *Commander:* Jesse Fearson.
   Bond: Continental, £4000 (*sic.*); State, £4000.
   Bonders: Jesse Fearson, mariner, principal; Miles Greenwood and John Brooks, merchants, sureties — all of Salem.
   Owners: Francis Boardman, John Brooks, and others.
   Witnesses: Joseph White, Eliza Elkins.
   M. A., v, 258, 260, **171**, 136.

1780 FORTUNE, Brig. *Guns*, 14; *Men*, 70.
   Commander: John Cathcart.
   Essex Institute, Miscellaneous Ship Papers.

1781 FORTUNE, Schooner. *Guns*, 8; *Men*, 30.
Mar. 19   *Commander:* Joshua Burges, of Newburyport.
   C. C. **196**, v, 65; M. A., **171**, 352.

1781 FORTUNE, Brig. *Guns*, 14; *Men*, 60.
July 3   *Commander:* Benjamin Ives, of Salem.
   C. C. **196**, v, 66; M. A., **171**, 421; Felt, II, 271.

1781 FORTUNE, Sloop. *Guns*, 3; *Men*, 12.
Aug. 10   *Commander:* James Brown, of Boston.
   C. C. **196**, v, 64; M. A., **171**, 452.

1781 FORTUNE, Brigantine. *Guns*, 7; *Men*, 15.
Nov. 7   Commander: Richard Ober, of Beverly.
   C. C. **196**, v, 67.

1782 FORTY-FIVE, Ship. *Guns*, 14; *Men*, 70.
Nov. 11   Commander: John Beach, of Gloucester.
   C. C. **196**, v, 69.

1778 Fox, Sloop. *Guns*, 1; *Men*, 20.
Feb. 19   Commander: Jonathan Tuksbery.
   Bond: Continental, $5000; State, £4000.
   Bonders: Jonat[han] Tukesbery [signed Tuksbery], principal; Sam[ue]l Page and John Page [of Salem], sureties.
   Owners: Samuel and John Page.
   Witness: D[aniel] Hopkins.
   M. A., v, 257, 364, **168**, 183.

1780 Fox, Brigantine. *Guns*, 8; *Men*, 15.
July 14   Commander: Israel Johnson, of Salem.
   Bond: Continental, $10,000; State, £4000.
   Bonders: Israel Johnson, principal; Benj[amin] Lovett, jr., of Salem, and Stephen Higginson, of Boston, sureties.
   Owners: Stephen Higginson and others.
   Witnesses: Dan[ie]l McNeill, Geo[rge] Burroughs.
   M. A., v, 225, 228, **171**, 196.

1780 Fox, Sloop. *Guns*, 8; *Men*, 40.
Nov. 15   Commander: Levi Doane, of Boston.
   C. C. **196**, v, 77; M. A., XL, 104.

1781 Fox, Ship. *Guns*, 8; *Men*, 20.
Jan. 15   Commander: Joshua Stone, of Falmouth, Cumberland County.
   C. C. **196**, v, 92; M. A., **171**, 334.

1781 Fox, Schooner. *Guns*, 2; *Men*, 20.
Aug. 24   Commander: Daniel Howland, of Newburyport.
   C. C., **196**, v, 81.

1781 Fox, Schooner. *Guns*, 6; *Men*, 75.
Aug. 25   Commander: Jeremiah Lousvay, of Salem.
   Note. Jeremiah Lousvay and Germain Langevain were probably the same person. See *Surprize,* Mar. 15, 1782.
   C. C. **196**, v, 83; M. A., **171**, 473.

1781　　Fox, Brigantine. *Guns*, 10; *Men*, 50.
Aug. 29　　*Commander:* Jonathan Neall, of Salem.
　　　　C. C. **196**, v, 86; M. A., **171**, 480; *Boston Gazette*, Jan. 7, 1782: "Last Monday a large Prize Ship, lately taken by Capt. Niel in the *Fox* Privateer, of Salem, arrived from an Eastern Port, where she had been waiting for a Wind. Her Cargo consists of about 300 Hogsheads of Rum and Sugar, with a considerable Quantity of Cotton and Coffee." *Ibid.*, June 10, 1782: "Since our last, arrived in a safe port a prize sloop . . . captured by Capt. Neill, in the privateer brig *Fox*, of Salem."

1781　　Fox, Sloop. *Guns*, 4; *Men*, 35.
Sept. 7　　*Commander:* David Allen, of Boston.
　　　　C. C. **196**, v, 72; M. A., **172**, 4.

1782　　Fox, Brigantine. *Guns*, 12; *Men*, 60.
Apr. 12　　*Commander:* John Donaldson [Dollenson?], of Salem.
　　　　C. C. **196**, v, 78; M. A., **172**, 128.

1782　　Fox, Ship. *Guns*, 8; *Men*, 20.
May 8　　*Commander:* Israel Johnson, of Portsmouth, N. H.
　　　　Owners: Benjamin Lovett and others, of Beverly.
　　　　C. C. **196**, v, 82; M. A., **172**, 152.

1782　　Fox, Schooner. *Guns*, 8; *Men*, 30.
June 18　　*Commander:* James Sellars, of Newburyport.
　　　　C. C. **196**, v, 89.

1782　　Fox, Ship. *Guns*, 12; *Men*, 30.
July 22　　*Commander:* Greenfield Pote, of Falmouth, Cumberland County.
　　　　C. C. **196**, v, 88.

1782　　Fox, Schooner. *Guns*, 6; *Men*, 20.
Nov. 16　　*Commander:* John Porter, of Boston.
　　　　C. C. **196**, v, 87; M. A., **172**, 226.

1782　　Fox, Brigantine. *Guns*, 8; *Men*, 30.
Nov. 20　　*Commander:* Willliam Gray, of Salem.
　　　　C. C. **196**, v, 80.

1775　　FRANKLIN, Schooner.
Oct. 16　　*Commander:* John Selman.
　　　　Note. Afterwards commanded successively by Samuel Tucker, James Mugford, and John Skimmer. Washington's Fleet.

1778 FRANKLIN, Brigantine. *Tons*, 200; *Guns*, 18; *Men*, 100.
Apr. 20 Commander: Thomas Connoly.
  Bond: Continental, $10,000; State, £4000.
  Bonders: Thomas Connoly, principal; Francis Cabot and Tho[ma]s Prince, sureties.
  Owners: Francis Cabot and others.
  Witness: John Leach.
  M. A., v, 233, 236, **168**, 264.

1778 FRANKLIN, Brigantine. *Tons*, 200; *Guns*, 18; *Men*, 120.
Oct. 14 Commander: John Leach, jr.
  Bond: Continental, $10,000; State, £4000.
  Bonders: John Leach, jr., mariner, Elias Hasket Derby, Bartho[lomew] Putnam, and Jacob Ashton, merchants, all of Salem.
  Owners: E. H. Derby and others.
  Witnesses: James Jeffry, N[athan] Goodale.
  M. A., v, 263, 264, **169**, 229; *Ind. Chronicle*, Feb. 4, 1779: "On the 4th of November the Privateer brig *Franklin*, Capt. John Leach, sailed from Salem on a cruize and on the 17th he took a snow with 300 quintals of fish; the 22d he took a brig from England for Antigua, mounting 16 guns, laden with dry goods — she gave the *Franklin* a broadside which was quickly returned, which killed several of her hands and she immediately struck; and on the 25th he took a brig with eighty tons of butter, which last is safe arrived at Salem. The *Franklin* was left cruizing off Cape-Finisterre, all well on board, not having lost a man since she left port."

1779 FRANKLIN, Brigantine. *Guns*, 18; *Men*, 100.
Mar. 30 Commander: Joseph Robinson.
  Bond: Continental, $10,000; State, £4000.
  Bonders: Joseph Robinson, mariner, principal; Elias Hasket Derby and Bartho[lomew] Putnam, of Salem, sureties.
  Owners: E. H. Derby and others.
  Witnesses: Jno. Fisk, N[athan] Goodale (Continental bond); Benj[amin] Moses, Tho[ma]s Palfray (State bond).
  M. A., v, 231, 234, **170**, 43.

1779 FRANKLIN, Ship. *Guns*, 18; *Men*, 120.
Sept. 10   *Commander:* Joseph Robinson.
   Bond: Continental, $10,000; State, £4000.
   Bonders: Joseph Robinson, mariner, principal; Stephen Cleveland and Stephen Higginson, of Boston, sureties.
   Owners: Nathan Goodale, of Salem, and others.
   Witnesses: John F[oster] Williams, John Tucker.
      M. A., v, 249, 252, **159**, 343, **170**, 391.

1779 FRANKLIN, Brigantine. *Guns*, 4; *Men*, 15.
Sept. 23   *Commander:* Robert Birrell.
   Bond: Continental, $10,000; State, £4000.
   Bonders: Robert Birrell, mariner, principal; Samuel Clarke and [Antoine Tatagay], of Boston, sureties.
   Owner: Samuel Clarke.
   Witnesses: Stephen Hills, Henry Newman.
      Note. Tatagay's name is omitted from the list of bonders, but he signed the bond.
      M. A., v, 288, 289, **170**, 398.

1780 FRANKLIN, Ship. *Guns*, 18; *Men*, 100.
Mar. 23   *Commander:* John Turner, jr.
   Bond: Continental, $10,000; State, £4000.
   Bonders: John Turner, jr., mariner, principal; Daniel Sargent and Isaac Somes, sureties.
   Owner: Nathan Goodale, merchant of Salem.
   Witness: Jo[hn] Winthrop.
      M. A., v, 241, 244, **171**, 105; *Boston Gazette*, May 28, 1781: "Last Sunday arrived at Salem, the privateer ship *Franklin*, Capt. Turner, of that port, having had the misfortune to have her mainmast disabled in an engagement of 40 minutes with a large ship from Liverpool bound to N. York, which proved a valuable prize but is not yet arrived. The *Franklin* had one man killed and one wounded; on board the prize was two killed and eight wounded."

1781 FRANKLIN, Ship. *Guns*, 18; *Men*, 100.
June 22   *Commander:* John Allen Hallet, of Boston.
   Owners: George and Andrew Cabot and Bartholomew Putnam, of Salem.
      C. C. **196**, v, 98; M. A., XL, 15, **171**, 415; *Boston Gazette*, Oct. 22, 1781: "We hear Capt. Hallet, in the

Franklin Privateer, is safe arrived at an Eastern Port from a Cruize, during which he has taken four Prizes."

1781 FRANKLIN, Ship. *Guns*, 18; *Men*, 25.
Dec. 14   *Commander:* Silas Devol.
   Owners: Bartholomew Putnam and others, of Salem.
   C. C. **196**, v, 97; M. A., **172**, 81.

1777 FREE AMERICAN, Schooner. *Tons*, 90; *Guns*, 10; *Men*, 70.
Apr. 29   *Commander:* John Buffinton.
   Petition signed by George Dodge, jr., of Salem, in behalf of Andrew Cabot & Co.
   Note. This vessel is sometimes called *True American*.
   M. A., **166**, 372 (In the petition the word *True* is crossed out and *Free* substituted).

1776 FREEDOM, Sloop.
Sept. 4   *Commander:* John Clouston.
   Bond: State, £2000.
   Bonders: John Clouston, mariner of Dighton, Jerathmeel Bowers, of Swansea, and George Codding, of Dighton.
   Owners: "Belonging to the said State."
   Witnesses: Cha[rle]s Cushing, Joseph Hosmer.
      Note. One of the first vessels built for the State Navy. She was soon converted into a brigantine.
   M. A., **139**, 125, **159**, 114, 118, 171, 185.

1777 FREEDOM, Schooner. *Guns*, 10; *Men*, 70.
May 5   *Commander:* James Colven.
   Bond: Continental, $5000.
   Bonders: James Colven, principal; Philip Moore and Archibald Blair, of Boston, sureties.
   Owners: Philip Moore and Archibald Blair.
   Witnesses: Job Prince, Benj[amin] Hammatt, jr.
   M. A., v, 281, **166**, 387.

1780 FREEDOM, Brigantine. *Guns*, 7; *Men*, 15.
Sept. 7   *Commander:* Benjamin Ober, of Salem.
   C. C. **196**, v, 101; M. A., **171**, 268.

1778 FREE MASON, Brigantine. *Tons*, 100; *Guns*, 14; *Men*, 80.
July 27   *Commander:* John Conway.
   Bond: Continental, $10,000; State, £4000.

Bonders: John Conway, mariner, principal; Edmund Lewis and David Devens, of Marblehead and Boston, sureties.
Owners: Edmund Lewis and others.
Witness: J[ohn] Dall.
M. A., v, 261, 262, **169**, 42.

1778 FREE MASON, Brigantine. *Guns,* 14; *Men,* 70.
Oct. 6 *Commander:* William Dennis.
Bond: Continental, $5000; State, £4000.
Bonders: William Dennis, mariner, principal; Will[iam] R. Lee and Samuel Trevett, of Marblehead, sureties.
Owners: W[illia]m R. Lee and others.
Witnesses: Edm[un]d Lewis, Benj[amin] I. Reed.
M. A., v, 253, 255, **169**, 201; *Independent Chronicle,* Nov. 27, 1778: "The Privateer brig *Free Mason* of 16 guns, which sailed from Marblehead the 5th instant and was taken by the *Savage* frigate about 20 hours after she sailed, was retaken by the *Speedwell* privateer of this port."

1779 FREE MASON, Brigantine. *Tons,* 120; *Guns,* 14; *Men,* 65.
Feb. 10 *Commander:* William Dennis.
Bond: Continental, $10,000; State, £4000.
Bonders: W[illia]m Dennis, mariner, principal; Sam[ue]l R. Trevett and Edw[ar]d Fettyplace, jr., of Marblehead, sureties.
Owners: Samuel R. Trevett and others.
Witnesses: John Dixey, Edm[un]d Lewis.
M. A., v, 292, 293, **169**, 437; Roads, *History and Traditions of Marblehead,* 391.

1779 FREE MASON, Snow. *Guns,* 6; *Men,* 12.
Oct. 20 *Commander:* Benjamin Boden.
Bond: Continental, $5000; State, £4000.
Bonders: Benjamin Boden, mariner, principal; Joseph Lee and Richard Hinckley, of Marblehead, sureties.
Owner: Richard Hinckley.
Witnesses: David Ross, Tho[ma]s Butman, jr.
M. A., v, 247, 250, **170**, 441; Roads, *History and Traditions of Marblehead,* 185.

1781 FREE MASON, Schooner. *Guns,* 4; *Men,* 20.
July 26 *Commander:* Noah Stoddard, of Boston.
C. C. **196**, v, 103; M. A., **171**, 434.

140   MASSACHUSETTS PRIVATEERS

1782 FREE MASON, Schooner. *Guns*, 6; *Men*, 25.
Apr. 18   *Commander:* Ebenezer Coombes, of Boston.
C. C. **196**, v, 102; M. A., **172**, 138.

1777 FRIEND, Schooner. *Guns*, 10 *swivels; Men*, 30.
Sept. 11   *Commander:* William Lawrence.
Bond: Continental, $5000; State, £500.
Bonders: Will[ia]m Lawrence, of Boston, principal; Henry Newell [signed Newhall] and Jona[than] Nutting, of Boston, sureties.
Owners: Henry Newhall and Jonathan Nutting.
Witnesses: Samuel Hastings, W[illia]m Gowen.
M. A., v, 275, 277, **167**, 225.

1780 FRIENDS ADVENTURE, Brigantine. *Tons*, 200; *Guns*, 10;
Dec. 13   *Men*, 25.
Commander: Thomas Fossey.
Petitioners: Joseph Barrell and others, of Boston.
M. A., **177**, 285.

1779 FRIENDSHIP, Schooner. *Guns*, 6; *Men*, 12.
June 3   *Commander:* Edward Wigglesworth.
Bond: Continental, $5000; State, £4000.
Bonders: Edward Wigglesworth, mariner, of Newburyport, principal; John Coffin Jones, of Newburyport, and Joseph Laughton, of Boston, merchants, sureties.
Owner: Nath[anie]l Tracy, of Newburyport.
Witnesses: Step[he]n Bruce, Nat[haniel] Peirce.
M. A., v, 271, 274, **170**, 151.

1779 FRIENDSHIP, Ship. *Guns*, 6; *Men*, 60.
Dec. 16   *Commander:* Isaac Smith.
Bond: Continental, $10,000; State, £4000.
Bonders: Isaac Smith, mariner, principal; Thomas Russell and Samuel Conant, jr., of Boston, sureties.
Owners: Thomas Russell & Co., of Boston.
Witnesses: Chambers Russell, Thomas Greene.
M. A., v, 245, 248, **171**, 44.

1780 FRIENDSHIP, Ship. *Tons*, 300; *Guns*, 18; *Men*, 60.
Aug. 15   *Commander:* Simon Mansis, of Boston.
Note. The captain's name is Mansir on the bond, Mansis on the petition.
C. C. **196**, v, 115; M. A., **171**, 246.

1781 FRIENDSHIP, Ship. *Guns,* 16; *Men,* 70.
Jan. 30   *Commander:* Daniel Waters, of Boston.
C. C. **196**, v, 118; M. A., **171**, 335.

1781 FRIENDSHIP, Ship.
Commander: Thomas Tracy.
Boston Gazette, May 7, 1781.

1781 FRIENDSHIP, Brigantine. *Guns,* 8; *Men,* 20.
Oct. 3   *Commander:* Isaac Elwell, of Cape Ann.
C. C. **196**, v, 111; M. A., **172**, 16.

1782 FRIENDSHIP, Ship. *Guns,* 6; *Men,* 20.
Nov. 16   *Commander:* Gideon Henfield, of Salem.
C. C. **196**, v, 113.

FRIENDSHIP, Ship. *Guns,* 12; *Men,* 75.
Commander: Thomas Simmons.
Essex Institute, Miscellaneous Ship Papers.

1775 GAMECOCK, Armed Vessel. *Tons,* 20.
Dec. 11   *Commander:* Peter Roberts.
Bond: State, £5000.
Bonders: Peter Roberts, mariner, and Abner **Greenleaf**, merchant, both of Newburyport.
Owners: Not stated.
Witnesses: William Cooper, Perez Morton.
M. A. **139**, 117.

1781 GAMECOCK, Schooner. *Tons,* 30; *Guns,* 8; *Men,* 30.
Aug. 27   *Commander:* Richard Smith, of Salem.
C. C. **196**, VI, 3; M. A., **171**, 472.

1783 GAMECOCK, Schooner. *Tons,* 20; *Guns,* 4; *Men,* 15.
Jan. 1   *Commander:* Thomas Coburn.
Petitioners: Miles Ward and others, of Salem.
M. A., **172**, 274.

1778 GATES, Sloop. *Guns,* 10, and 10 *swivels; Men,* 30.
June 23   *Commander:* Thomas Smith.
Bond: Continental, $5000; State, £4000.
Bonders: Thomas Smith, mariner, principal; Henry Rust and Sam[ue]l Ward, of Salem, sureties.
Owners: Henry Rust, and others.
Witness: D[aniel] Hopkins.
M. A., v, 355, 356, **168**, 382.

1779 GATES, Brigantine. *Guns*, 12; *Men*, 25.
Jan. 21, 25   *Commander:* Philip Marett.
   Bond: Continental, $10,000; State, £4000.
   Bonders: Philip Marett, mariner of Boston, principal; Stephen Hooper and Thomas Gates, of Newburyport, sureties.
   Owners: Stephen Hooper and Thomas Gates.
   Witnesses: Joseph Cutler, William Fisher.
   M. A., v, 341, 343, **169**, 427.

1779 GATES, Sloop.
   Commander: [William?] Jaggar.
   Boston Gazette, Aug. 9, 1779.

1780 GATES, Brigantine.
   Commander: Joseph Newman.
   Petitioners: Joseph Cutler, merchant, and others of Newburyport.
   M. A., **176**, 628 (Petition, dated Aug. 10, 1780, that the *Gates* be permitted to sail on a cruise, embargo notwithstanding. Granted); *Boston Gazette,* Nov. 13, 1780.

1777 GENERAL ARNOLD, Schooner. *Guns*, 4, and 4 *swivels; Men*, 25.
Dec. 20   *Commander:* John Willson.
   Bond: Continental, $5000; State, £500.
   Bonders: John Wilson [signed Willson], principal; William Shattuck and Alex[ander] Rose, of Boston, sureties.
   Owners: William Shattuck and Alexander Rose.
   Witnesses: W[illia]m Dall, James Perkins.
   M. A., v, 321, 324, **168**, 96.

1778 GENERAL ARNOLD, Ship. *Guns*, 22; *Men*, 120.
Apr. 16   *Commander:* Moses Brown.
   Bond: Continental, $10,000; State, £4000.
   Bonders: Moses Brown, principal; Sam[ue]l Newhall and Stephen Cross, of Newburyport, sureties.
   Owners: Samuel Newhall, Nathaniel Tracy, and others.
   Witnesses: Moses Little, Thomas Brooks.
   M. A., v, 315, 316, **168**, 263.

1778 GENERAL ARNOLD, Brigantine. *Guns*, 20; *Men*, 120.
May 11   *Commander:* James Magee, of Boston.
   C. C. **196**, VI, 8; M. A., **139**, 235; *Boston Gazette,* Oct. 26, 1778; *Ind. Chronicle,* Jan. 7, 1779: "On Friday the 25th ult. at 6 A.M., the wind to the Westward,

sailed from this port [Boston] the brig *General Arnold*, James Magee commander; and about meridian the wind chop'd round to N. E. and looking likely for a gale, they thought best to put into Plymouth and came to anchor in a place called the Cow-Yard. On Saturday, the gale encreasing, she started from her anchor and stuck on the White Flatt. They then cut both cables and masts away in hopes to drive over, but she immediately bilged; it being low water left her quarter deck dry, where all hands got for relief. A schooner lying within hail heard their cries, but could not assist them. On Sunday the inhabitants were cutting ice most of the day before they got on board, when they saw 75 of the men had perished and 34 very much froze, which they got on shore; and on Monday they got on shore and buried the dead. Great part of their stores, etc., will be saved. Some evil minded persons report that she was plundered by the inhabitants, which is entirely false, as they behaved with the greatest humanity."

1778 GENERAL ARNOLD, Schooner. *Guns*, 4, and 8 *swivels; Men*, 25.
June 8   Commander: Isaac Dunton.
    Bond: Continental, $5000; State, £4000.
    Bonders: Isaac Dunton, mariner, principal; William Shattuck and John Shattuck, of Boston, sureties.
    Owners: William Shattuck and others.
    Witnesses: James Perkins, William Dall.
    M. A., v, 317, 318, **139**, 189, **168**, 354.

1779 GENERAL ARNOLD. *Guns*, 18.
    Commander: —— Roach [Francis Roch?].
    London Chronicle, July 6, 1779: "The *General Arnold* American privateer, Capt. Roach, of 18 Guns, belonging to Salem, is taken by a letter of marque and carried into St. Augustine."

1778 GENERAL GADSDEN, Brigantine. *Tons*, 150; *Guns*, 16; *Men*,
Aug. 19   70.
    Commander: John Horn.
    Bond: Continental, $10,000; State, £4000.
    Bonders: John Horn, mariner, principal; William Erskine and Jno. Donaldson, of Boston, sureties.
    Owners: John Horn and others, of Providence, R. I.

Witnesses: Nath[anie]l Cudworth, J[ohn] Dall.
Note. The vessel's name is spelled *Gasden* in the bond.
M. A., v, 303, 304, **139**, 208, **169**, 85.

1782 GENERAL GALVEZ, Ship. *Guns,* 18; *Men,* 40.
Nov. 20   *Commander:* Thomas Smith, of Salem.
C. C. **196**, VI, 10; M. A., **172**, 233; *Boston Gazette,* May 5, 1783 (Salem, May 1): "Last Monday the ship *General Galvez,* Capt. Smith, arrived here in 36 days from Bourdeaux."

1776 GENERAL GATES, Schooner. *Guns,* 8; *Men,* 40.
Aug. 8   *Commander:* William Carlton.
Bond: Continental, $2000.
Bonders: William Carlton, principal, John Gardner, jr., and Benjamin Goodhue, sureties, all of Salem.
Owners: John Gardner, jr., and partners.
Witnesses: Andrew Cabot, Michael Hearn.
M. A., v, 322, **165**, 40, **181**, 170.

1778 GENERAL GATES, Brigantine. *Guns,* 4; *Men,* 15.
Feb. 9   *Commander:* Joseph Tilden.
Bond: Continental, $5000; State, £500.
Bonders: Joseph Tilden, principal; William Shattuck and Winthrop Sargent, of Boston, sureties.
Owners: William Shattuck and Winthrop Sargent.
Witness: John Shattuck.
M. A., v, 300, 301, **168**, 174.

1778 GENERAL GATES, Brig. *Guns,* 10; *Men,* 55.
Commander: —— Skinner.
Note. Possibly the sloop of war (ship) *General Gates* of the Continental Navy, commanded in 1778 by Captain John Skimmer and in 1779 by Captain Daniel Waters. She is called a privateer in the *Independent Chronicle,* Feb. 25, 1779.
Essex Institute, Miscellaneous Ship Papers.

1781 GENERAL GATES, Ship.
Commander: —— ——.
London Chronicle, Dec. 27, 1781: "The *General Gates,* an American armed ship, laden with flour and wheat, bound to the Havannah from Boston, is taken by Admiral Hood's cruisers and sent into Barbadoes."

1779 GENERAL GLOVER. Brigantine, *Guns,* 14; *Men,* 80.
Mar. 2   *Commander:* Samuel Horton.
   Bond: Continental, $10,000; State, £4000.
   Bonders: Sam[ue]l Horton, mariner, principal; John Lewis and John Waite, of Marblehead, sureties.
   Owners: John Waite [signed Waitt] and others.
   Witnseses: Nath[anie]l Shiverick, Eph[rai]m Starkweather.
   M. A., v, 346, 365, **170**, 1; *Boston Gazette,* Aug. 9, 1779.

1779 GENERAL GLOVER, Brigantine. *Guns,* 14; *Men,* 50.
Aug. 26   *Commander:* Nicholas Bartlett.
   Bond: Continental, $10,000; State, £4000.
   Bonders: Nicholas Bartlett, mariner, principal; John Grush and John Lewis, of Marblehead, sureties.
   Owner: John Grush.
   Witnesses: John Selman, Burrill Devereux.
   M. A., v, 335, 338, **170**, 272.

1781 GENERAL GREEN, Sloop. *Guns,* 8; *Men,* 25.
Oct. 11   *Commander:* Isaiah Simmons, of Boston.
   C. C. **196**, vi, 24; M. A., **172**, 22.

1782 GENERAL GREENE, Ship. *Guns,* 16; *Men,* 80.
May 15   *Commander:* Samuel Croel, of Salem.
   C. C. **196**, vi, 20; M. A., **172**, 159; Felt, ii, 274; *Boston Gazette,* July 1, 1782 (Salem, June 27): "Yesterday arrived in a safe port the prize brig *Olive Branch* . . . captured on her passage from New York to Quebec by the privateer ship *General Greene,* Capt. Crow, of this port."

1782 GENERAL GREENE, Ship. *Guns,* 16; *Men,* 90.
Aug. 9   *Commander:* Aaron Croel, of Salem.
   Note. Listed as a brig by Felt and Hunt.
   C. C. **196**, vi, 19; *Salem Gazette,* Sept. 26, 1782: "The privateer ship *General Greene,* commanded by Capt. Crowell, and the brig *Diana,* commanded by Capt. Deland, both belonging to this port and captured by the British frigate *Perseverance,* were carried into New York on the 3d instant."

1782 GENERAL GREEN, Schooner. *Guns,* 6; *Men,* 8.
Nov. 16   *Commander:* Daniel Adams, of Boston.
   C. C. **196**, vi, 16; M. A., **172**, 230.

1778 GENERAL HANCOCK, Ship. *Tons*, 200; *Guns*, 18, and 6 *swi-*
June 23   *vels; Men*, 130.
    Commander: Ishmael Hardy.
    Bond: Continental, $10,000; State, £4000.
    Bonders: Ishmael Hardy, mariner, principal; John Cushing and Joseph Barrell, of Boston, sureties.
    Owners: John Cushing and others.
    Witness: J[ohn] Dall.
        M. A., VI, 7, 10, **168**, 378; Almon's *Remembrancer*, VII, 168; *Independent Chronicle*, Sept. 3, 1778; *Continental Journal*, Sept. 24, 1778: "Monday last the privateer ship *Hancock*, of 20 guns, returned into port from a cruize in which she fell in with and fought the *Levant*, a letter of marque ship from Jamaica bound to Bristol, of 24 guns and 97 men; and after a smart conflict which was maintained for some time with equal bravery on both sides, the *Levant* blew up and every soul perished, except 18 which the *Hancock* took up. Capt. Hardy of the *Hancock* and four of his men were killed in the engagement."

1778 GENERAL HEATH, Schooner. *Guns*, 2, and 6 *swivels; Men*, 25.
June 25   *Commander:* Isaiah Simmons.
    Bond: Continental, $5000; State, £4000.
    Bonders: Isaiah Simmons, principal; William Shattuck and [John Foster Williams], sureties.
    Owners: William Shattuck and others, of Boston.
    Witness: J[ohn] Dall.
        M. A., V, 319, 320, **139**, 191, **168**, 390.

1778 GENERAL HEATH, Schooner. *Guns*, 2; *Men*, 25.
Sept. 29   *Commander:* John Willson.
    Bond: Continental, $5000; State, £4000.
    Bonders: John Wilson [signed Willson], principal; William Shattuck and John Shattuck of Boston, sureties.
    Owners: William Shattuck and others.
    Witnesses: W[illia]m Dall, James Perkins.
        M. A., V, 327, 328, **139**, 216, **169**, 179.

1779 GENERAL HEATH, Schooner. *Guns*, 2; *Men*, 8.
Mar. 18   *Commander:* John Prout Sloan.
    Bond: Continental, $5000; State, £4000.
    Bonders: John Prout Sloan, mariner, principal; William Shattuck and John Shattuck, of Boston, sureties.

Owners: William and John Shattuck.
Witnesses: James Perkins, Stephen H. Gray.
M. A., v, 336, VIII, 9, 170, 19.

1777 GENERAL LINCOLN, Ship.
Commander: Jacob Cole.
M. A., 270, 30 (Mar. 8, 1777), 292, 109.

1777 GENERAL LINCOLN, Schooner. Guns, 10; Men, 50.
Dec. 22   Commander: John Margeson.
Bond: Continental, $5000; State, £500.
Bonders: John Margeson, principal; Philip Moore and Samuel White, of Boston, sureties.
Owner: Philip Moore.
Witnesses: Ezek[ie]l Price, Nalbro Frazier.
M. A., v, 323, 326, 139, 153, 168, 97.

1778   GENERAL LINCOLN, Schooner. Guns, 10; Men, 50.
July 31   Commander: Joseph Griffin.
Bond: Continental, $5000; State, £4000.
Bonders: Joseph Griffin, mariner, principal; Job Prince and Thomas Prince, of Boston, sureties.
Owners: Job Prince and others.
Witnesses: H. Welch, Benj[amin] Homer.
M. A., v, 307, 308, 139, 205, 169, 53.

1778   GENERAL LINCOLN, Schooner. Guns, 10, and 2 *swivels;*
Aug. 31   Men, 45.
Commander: William Meserve.
Bond: Continental, $5000; State, £4000.
Bonders: W[illia]m Meserve, mariner, principal; Job Prince and [Job Prince, jr.], of Boston, sureties.
Owners: Job Prince and others.
Witnesses: Tho[ma]s Prince, Benjamin Homer.
M. A., v, 331, 332, 139, 210, 169, 122.

1778 GENERAL LINCOLN, Schooner.
Commander: John Blackler.
Marbehead Hist. Soc.

1779   GENERAL LINCOLN, Brigantine. Guns, 14; Men, 75.
Aug. 31   Commander: John Carnes.
Bond: Continental, $10,000; State, £4000.
Bonders: John Carnes, mariner, principal; John Fisk and John Norris, of Salem, sureties.

Owner: John Norris.
Witnesses: John Gardner, 3rd, Samuel Waters.
M. A., v, 337, 340, **159**, 320, **170**, 367.

1777 GENERAL MERCER, Brig. Guns, 16; Men, 100.
Apr. 30   Commander: James Babson.
Bond: Continental, $10,000.
Bonders: James Babson, principal; Winthrop Sargent, of Gloucester, and John Winthrop, of Boston, sureties.
Owners: Winthrop Sargent and John Winthrop.
Witness: Timothy Foster.
M. A., v, 325, **166**, 375, **169**, 231 (The *General Mercer* was called the *Hancock* while in France); Stevens's *Facsimiles*, 1661, 1664, 1801; Wharton, *Dipl. Corres. Rev.*, II, 381, 496. See above, Introduction, 59.

1780 GENERAL MERCER, Brig. Guns, 10; Men, 25.
Oct. 11   Commander: Joseph Foster, of Cape Ann.
C. C. **196**, VI, 30; M. A., **177**, 181.

1776 GENERAL MIFFLIN, Ship. Tons, 350; Guns, 26; Men, 120.
Oct. 28   Commander: William Day.
Bond: Continental, $10,000.
Bonders: W[illia]m Day, principal; Philip Moore and Archibald Mercer, of Boston, sureties.
Owners: Philip Moore and Archibald Mercer.
Witnesses: Jacobus Van Landt, Nath[anie]l Hazard.
M. A., v, 333, **159**, 153, **166**, 6.

1778 GENERAL MIFFLIN, Ship. Guns, 20; Men, 150.
Mar. 18   Commander: Daniel McNeill.
Bond: Continental, $10,000; State, £500.
Bonders: Daniel McNeill, principal; Philip Moore and [James Craig], of Boston, sureties.
Owners: Philip Moore and others.
Witnesses: John R. Livingston, Ezek[ie]l Price.
Note. At Brest, in July, 1777, the *General Mifflin* gave to the French admiral a salute, which was returned. This has generally been credited to Capt. McNeill, but the dates of the bonds would indicate that Capt. Day was in command at the time. An additional bond may be missing.
M. A., v, 329, 330, **139**, 160, **168**, 217; Stevens's *Facsimiles*, 1599; Wharton, *Dipl. Corres. Rev.*, II, 381; Almon's *Remembrancer*, v, 203; Williams, *Liverpool*

Privateers, 210; *Independent Chronicle*, Nov. 27, 1778 (by a vessel which sailed from Nantes Sept. 28): "The Privateer *Mifflin* from this port, Captain McNeil has taken 13 prizes in her way to Europe." *Boston Post*, Feb. 20, 1779: "The armed Snow, of 16 Carriage Guns, lately captured by Capt. McNeal, in the *Mifflin* Privateer, is safe arrived at an Eastern Port."

1780 GENERAL MIFFLIN, Ship.
Aug. 7
  Commander: George Waith Babcock.
  Bond: State, £2000.
  Bonders: Mungo Mackay and Samuel Dunn, jr., merchants of Boston and major part of the owners, and George Wait [Waith] Babcock, mariner of Boston.
  Witnesses: James Boyd, Tho[ma]s Porter.
  M. A., XL, 17, 139, 275 (Bond not to enlist any man in New England outside of Massachusetts), 177, 76 (Sept. 11, 1780. Petition of Mungo Mackay for pass to proceed to sea): "Ordered that the Naval Officer of the Port of Boston be and hereby is directed to clear out the Ship *Mifflin*, George W. Babcock, Commander, for her intended Cruise against the enemies of these States, any Embargo to the contrary notwithstanding." *Boston Gazette*, Oct. 25, 1779: "Saturday last arrived here the Privateer Ship *General Mifflin*, Capt. Babcock in 10 Weeks from France. On his Passage hither he took two Prizes and retook another. On the 7th ult. the *Mifflin* engaged a Sloop of War three Glasses, had three Men killed and seven wounded; and being much disabled in her Masts and Rigging, was obliged to bear away." *Salem Gazette*, Jan. 16, 1781 (New York, Dec. 18): "The ship *General Mifflin*, of 20 guns and 150 men, is taken off Charlestown by his Majesty's ship *Raleigh*, as also two prizes she had in her possession that belonged to the Cork fleet."

1778 GENERAL MONTGOMERY, Sloop. *Guns*, 6; *Men*, 30.
Feb. 3
  Commander: William Steward.
  Bond: Continental, $5000; State, £500.
  Bonders: William Steward, principal; Thomas Adams and [Michael Pruddock], sureties.
  Owners: Thomas Adams and others, of Boston.
  Witnesses: Both bonds unwitnessed.
  M. A., V, 309, 310, 168, 168.

1781 GENERAL MONTGOMERY, Brigantine. *Guns*, 14; *Men*, 60.
June 4   *Commander:* Samuel Hobbs, of Salem.
C. C. **196**, VI, 33; M. A., **171**, 402; *Salem Gazette*, Aug. 7, 1781: "Last Thursday returned here from a cruise the privateer *Montgomery*, Capt. Hobbs, of this port."

1778 GENERAL PICKERING, Brig.
Sept. 30   *Commander:* Jonathan Haraden.
Petitioner: George Williams.
M. A., Council Records.

1779 GENERAL PICKERING, Ship. *Guns*, 16; *Men*, 100.
Apr. 24   *Commander:* Jonathan Haraden.
Bond: Continental, $10,000; State, £4000.
Bonders: Jonathan Haraden, mariner, principal; George Williams and John Fisk, of Salem, sureties.
Owners: George Williams and others.
Witnesses: Jona[than] Mason, J. Grafton.
M. A., VI, 258, 261, **159**, 195, 331, 335, 338, 342, **169**, 183; Hunt, II, 34–42; Pickering MSS., XXXIX, 179 (Letter from Capt. Haraden, Cape Henlopen, Oct. 1, 1779): "I left the Capes at Sundown on Tuesday last and at Sunrising on Wednesday Morning I discovered two sail to the windward. The Winds being light I hove out two Draggs to keep my Ship from going ahead and made all the Sail I could, as though I was running from them. They both gave Chace and at 5 P.M. they got nigh enough to discover that I was a cruising Vessel. They both hove about and haul'd their Wind, I immediately hove about after them, they crowded all the Sail they could and rowed at the same time. At sundown the Wind breezed up a little and as Night came on, I kept Sight of them with my Night Glass; at 8 P.M. they parted, one stood to the Northward and the other to the Southward. I kept in chace of the largest and at 9 P.M. She Hove about, being to the Windward; as she past me I hail'd her, but had no answer. Then I gave her a Broadside, but without any effect that I could perceive; then I Tackt Ship and gave her another Broadside and hail'd her. She answered from N. York. I order'd her to haul down the Colours, which they obey'd instantly; very peaceable people, . . .

though they had 14 6 and 4 pounders and 38 Men. She proves to be the *Royal George* Cutter, a Letter of Marque out of New York last Tuesday Morning bound to the West Indies and was in Company with a Sloop of 8 Carriage Guns from the same place, she being clean and a fast Sailor got off clear." *Boston Gazette*, Dec. 20, 1779; *Ind. Chronicle*, Aug. 17, 1780: "By letters just received from Spain, we are informed that Capt. Jonathan Harriden in the ship *Pickering*, of sixteen 6-pounders and 48 men and boys, on his passage from Salem to Bilboa fell in with a British cruiser mounting twenty long 9-pounders, and after engaging her for five glasses obliged her to sheer off. In this engagement the *Pickering* suffered great damages. In a few days after this he met with and after a warm engagement captured a privateer from England, of fourteen 9 and six 4-pounders and 60 men and put 10 of his men on board her. With this prize Capt. Harriden was making the best of his way to Bilboa, when he was pursued by a very large Lugger [the *Achilles*]; but supposing himself by no means a match for such a vessel as this appear'd to be, he endeavour'd to keep clear of her and gave a signal to his prize to do the same; but she came up and took her and soon after came up with him also. A most violent contest ensued and continued for two hours and a half, during which time the Captain, officers and crew of the *Pickering* managed their ship with such address and fought with such unexampled bravery and heroism that the Lugger, large and stout as she was, was glad to leave them. They then pursued their prize and took her again, in sight of their vanquish'd enemy. By the people on board they were informed that the vessel they had engaged was the largest of the kind that had ever been fitted out from Great Britain, that she mounted, upon two decks, twenty-one long 9-pounders, six 18-pounders, fourteen brass 4-pounders, and two brass 2-pounders, having in all 43 guns and 130 men."

1776 GENERAL PUTNAM, Schooner. *Guns*, 8; *Men*, 60.
Aug. 28   *Commander:* Stephen Mascoll.
   Bond: Continental, $5000.

Bonders: Stephen Mascoll, mariner of Salem, principal; Joseph Lambert, mariner, and William Becket, shipwright, both of Salem, sureties.
Bound to "the President of the Honourable Congress of the United States of America."
Owners: William Becket, Joseph Lambert, Samuel Webb, Henry Williams, Ebenezer Peirce, Stephen Mascoll, John Gardner, jr., Ebenezer Beckford, Josiah Orne, Samuel Ward, James Diman, jr., George Williams, jr., and John McMillan [spelled MacMillion], all of Salem.
Witnesses: George Williams, jr., Samuel Webb.
M. A., v, 302, **165**, 170.

1779 GENERAL PUTNAM, Ship. *Tons,* 350; *Guns,* 20; *Men,* 60.
July 9 *Commander:* Daniel Waters.
Owner: Nathaniel Shaw.
Note. On the Penobscot Expedition and destroyed to prevent capture.
M. A., xxxvii, 242, 280, **145**, 8, 33, 43; Council Records, July 2, 9, 10, 11, 1779.

1777 GENERAL STARK, Brigantine.
Commander: John Allen Hallet.
Bond: State, £2000.
Bonders: John Allen Hallet, mariner, David Devens and Jonathan Harris, merchants, of Boston.
Witnesses: Samuel Adams, Richard Call, John Furnass, Henry Alline, jr.
Note. The name is commonly spelled *Starks,* sometimes *Starke.*
M. A., **139**, 144 (Bond, dated Sept. 29, 1777, not to enlist any man in New England outside of Massachusetts).

1778 GENERAL STARK, Brig. *Guns,* 10, and 8 *swivels; Men,* 50.
June 15 *Commander:* John Willson.
Bond: Continental, $5000; State, £4000.
Bonders: John Wilson [signed Willson], mariner, principal; Thomas Harris and John Harris, jr., of Boston, sureties.
Owners: Thomas and John Harris and others.
Witnesses: And[re]w Newell, David Townsend.
M. A., v, 311, 312, **139**, 195, **168**, 370; Mar. Court Rec., 16.

State of Massachusetts Bay

Council Chamber Boston July 2d 1779

Whereas it appears to this Board that it is absolutely necessary to compleat a sufficient Naval Force for the Penobscot Expedition, That the Ship General Putnam now in this Harbour should be taken into that Service immediately & the Owners thereof being at a Distance therefrom

Ordered That the Sheriff of the County of Suffolk be & he hereby is impowered & directed to impress the Ship General Putnam with her Tackle & Apparel & Appurtenances and deliver her — — to this Board of War to fit her immediately for a two Months Cruize, to Sail on an Expedition to Penobscot, to dispossess the Enemy of the United States there & This shall be your sufficient Warrant hereof fail not & make due Return of this Warrant with your doings therein forthwith —

In the Name & behalf of the Council

John Avery D. Secy   Jer. Powell Presid.

Suffolk ss July 3d 1779 Agreeable to the above Warrant I have Impressed the Ship General Putnam with her Tackle & appurtenances & delivered the same to the Board of War

Wm Greenleaf Sheriff

Warrant for Impressment of a Vessel for the Penobscot Expedition

1778 GENERAL STARK, Ship. *Tons,* 220; *Guns,* 18; *Men,* 150.
Aug. 14   *Commander:* William Coas.
   Bond: Continental, $10,000; State, £4000.
   Bonders: William Coas, mariner, principal; Winthrop Sargent and David Parse [signed Pearce], of Gloucester, sureties.
   Owners: Winthrop Sargent and others, of Cape Ann.
   Witnesses: Winthrop Allen, FitzWilliam Sargent.
   M. A., v, 313, 314, **169**, 76; Babson, *History of Gloucester,* 418–422.

1778 GENERAL STARK, Sloop.
Dec. 3   *Commander:* Benjamin Pierce, of Taunton.
   Bond: State, £2000.
   Bonders: Nathan Miller, of Warren, R. I., merchant, major part of the owners, and Benjamin Pierce, mariner.
   Witnesses: W[illia]m Tyley, Henry Alline, jr.
   M. A., **139**, 230 (Bond not to enlist any man in New England outside of Massachusetts); Mar. Court Rec., 16; *Independent Chronicle,* Jan. 7, 1779: "In the storm which we had last Saturday se'ennight, the private armed sloop called the *General Starks* and which sailed from hence some time since, was cast ashore at Nantucket and about 20 hands perished."

1779 GENERAL STARK, Brigantine. *Guns,* 2; *Men,* 8.
Sept. 22   *Commander:* Matthias Rich.
   Bond: Continental, $10,000; State, £4000.
   Bonders: Matthias Rich, mariner, principal; David Devens and Tho[ma]s Harris, of Boston, sureties.
   Owners: Thomas Harris and others.
   Witnesses: Matth[e]w Clark, And[re]w Newell.
   M. A., v, 339, 342, **170**, 408.

1779 GENERAL STARK, Ship. *Guns,* 20; *Men,* 120.
Oct. 27   *Commander:* James Pearson.
   Bond: Continental, $10,000; State, £4000.
   Bonders: James Pearson, mariner, principal; David Parse [signed Pearce] and Winthrop Sargent, of Gloucester, sureties.
   Owner: Winthrop Sargent, of Cape Ann.
   Witnesses: Jona[than] Elwell, John Chapman.
   M. A., v, 305, 306, **170**, 446.

1781 GENERAL STARK, Ship. *Guns*, 22; *Men*, 100.
July 3   *Commander:* William Coas, of Gloucester.
           C. C. **196**, VI, 42; M. A., **171**, 423; *Essex Inst. Hist. Coll.*, XLV, 175 (Captured Oct. 8, 1781, in Boston Bay, by H. M. S. *Chatham*).

1781 GENERAL TITCOMB, Ship. *Guns*, 18; *Men*, 50.
Feb. 27 *Commander:* Jeremiah Pearson, jr., of Newburyport.
           C. C. **196**, VI, 44.

1780 GENERAL WADSWORTH, Schooner.
           Commander: Timothy Weston.
           Boston Gazette, Oct. 23, 1780.

1781 GENERAL WADSWORTH, Sloop. *Tons*, 110; *Guns*, 12; *Men*, 80.
Feb. 5   *Commander:* Paul Reed, jr., of Boothbay.
           Owners: Moses and Ebenezer Little, of Newburyport.
           C. C. **196**, VI, 45; M. A., **171**, 339.

1775 GENERAL WARD, Armed Vessel. *Tons*, 20.
Dec. 19 *Commander:* Mathew Kelly.
           Bond: State, £5000.
           Bonders: Eben[ezer] Parsons and Joseph Foster, merchants of Gloucester, and Timothy Jackman, of Rowley, gentleman.
           Bound to "the Treasurer and Receiver General" of the Colony.
           Witnesses: Jacob Boardman, Levi Rounsevell.
           M. A., V, 334, **164**, 218.

1777 GENERAL WASHINGTON, Brigantine. *Guns*, 18; *Men*, 130.
July 25, *Commander:* William Rogers, of Boston, Mass., and
Nov. 10   Wilton, Conn.
           Bond: Continental (July 25), $10,000; State (Nov. 10), £2000.
           Bonders (Nov. 10): William Rogers; Isaac Sears and Paschal N. Smith, of Boston, and Samuel Broome, of Wethersfield, Conn., merchants.
           Owners (July 25): Isaac Sears and others.
           Witnesses (Nov. 10): Tim[othy] Austin; Jno. Furnass.
           C. C. **196**, VI, 47 (July 25. Called a Connecticut vessel). M. A., **139**, 150 (Nov. 10. A Massachusetts bond, not to enlist any man in New England outside of Massachusetts); *Boston Gazette*, Apr. 20, 1778.

1779 GENERAL WASHINGTON, Brigantine. *Guns*, 10; *Men*, 30.
Oct. 18   *Commander:* Robert Caldwell.
       Bond: Continental, $10,000; State, £4000.
       Bonders: Robert Caldwell, mariner, principal; Samuel Dunn, jr., and Mungo Mackay, of Boston, sureties.
       Owner: Mungo Mackay.
       Witnesses: Thomas Porter, Mungo Mackay, jr.
       M. A., VII, 307, 308, **170**, 435.

1780 GENERAL WASHINGTON, Ship. *Guns*, 20; *Men*, 75.
Apr. 24   *Commander:* Richard Whellen.
       Bond: Continental, $10,000; State, £4000.
       Bonders: Richard Whellen, mariner, principal; Samuel Broome and John Walker, jr., of Boston, sureties.
       Owner: John Walker, jr.
       Witnesses: Samuel Barrett, Nathaniel Barrett.
       M. A., VII, 303, 304, **171**, 134.

1782 GENERAL WASHINGTON, Brig. *Guns*, 6; *Men*, 16.
Aug. 22   *Commander:* Thomas Powars, of Boston.
       C. C. **196**, VI, 46.

1780 GENERAL WAYNE, Brigantine. *Guns*, 8; *Men*, 25.
Feb. 3   *Commander:* Richard Quatermass.
       Bond: Continental, $5000; State, £4000.
       Bonders: Richard Quartermass [signed Quatermass], principal; Samuel Page and Daniel Parker, of Salem, sureties.
       Owners: Samuel Page and others.
       Witness: William Davis.
       M. A., VII, 337, 340, **171**, 78.

1780 GENERAL WAYNE, Brig (letter of marque).
June 17   *Commander:* John Leech.
       M. A., XL, 88; *Boston Gazette*, Sept. 4, 1780.

1776 GEORGE, Ship.
       Commander: Caleb Hopkins.
       Boston Gazette, Aug. 5, 1776; Min. Sup. Court, 121 (The *George* captured the ship *Queen of England*).

1777 GEORGE, Schooner. *Guns*, 8; *Men*, 40.
Dec. 22   *Commander:* John Moulton.
       Bond: Continental, $5000; State, £500.
       Bonders: John Moulton, principal; Philip Moore and Sam[ue]l White, of Boston, sureties.

Owner: Philip Moore.
Witnesses: Ezek[ie]l Price, Nalbro Frazier.
M. A., v, 359, 360, **168**, 98.

1779 GEORGE, Brigantine. *Guns,* 8; *Men,* 20.
Sept. 7   *Commander:* Alexander Mackay.
Bond: Continental, $5000; State, £4000.
Bonders: Alexander Mackay, mariner, principal; Mungo Mackay and Sam[ue]l Dunn, jr., of Boston, sureties.
Owners: Mungo Mackay and others.
Witnesses: Thomas Amory, jr., Luther Turner.
M. A., VI, 3, 6, **170**, 371.

1779 GEORGE, Ship. *Guns,* 16; *Men,* 60.
Dec. 16   *Commander:* William Hayman.
Bond: Continental, $10,000; State, £4000.
Bonders: William Hayman, principal; Thomas Russell and Samuel Conant, jr., of Boston, sureties.
Owners: George Meade & Co., of Philadelphia.
Witnesses: Chambers Russell, Thomas Greene.
M. A., V, 347, 348, **171**, 44.

1781 GEORGE AND FANNY, Brigantine. *Guns,* 6; *Men,* 16.
Feb. 6   *Commander:* John Adams, of Boston.
C. C. **196**, VI, 60; M. A., **171**, 340; *Salem Gazette,* Dec. 6, 1781 (See brig *Phoenix,* Capt. Clay).

1782 GEORGE AND FANNY, Brigantine. *Guns,* 6; *Men,* 20.
Jan. 21   *Commander:* Moses Hale, of Gloucester.
Owners: Stephen Higginson and others, of Boston.
C. C. **196**, VI, 61; M. A., **172**, 94.

1779 GERARD, Brigantine. *Guns,* 12; *Men,* 50.
Mar. 23   *Commander:* William Williams.
Bond: Continental, $10,000; State, £4000.
Bonders: William Williams, mariner, principal; Thomas Barclay and Henry Mitchell, of Boston, sureties.
Owners: Henry Mitchell and others.
Witnesses: Francis Johonnot, Joshua Blanchard, jr.
   Note. The vessel's name is spelled *Gerrard*.
M. A., VI, 5, 8, **170**, 28.

1777 GLORIOSA, Schooner. *Guns,* 10; *Men,* 50.
July 22   *Commander:* John Babson, of Amesbury.
Owners: Jackson, Tracy & Tracy, of Newburyport.
C. C. **196**, VI, 65.

1777 GLORIOSA, Schooner. *Guns*, 8; *Men*, 45.
Sept. 17   *Commander:* Daniel Parsons.
  Bond: Continental, $5000; State, £500.
  Bonders: Daniel Parsons, principal; Joseph Lawton [signed Laughton], of Boston, and John Tracy, of Newburyport, merchants, sureties.
  Owners: Joseph Laughton and John Tracy.
  Witnesses: Jno. Avery, jr., W[illia]m Baker, jr.
  M. A., v, 357, 358, **167**, 236.

1777 GLOUCESTER, Brigantine. *Guns*, 18; *Men*, 130.
June 28   *Commander:* John Coulston.
  Bond: Continental, $10,000.
  Bonders: John Coulston, principal; David Pearce and Daniel Warner, of Gloucester, sureties.

  Owners: David Pearce and others.
  Witnesses: Thomas Sparling, Barnett Haskin.
    Note. The vessel's name is spelled *Glocester*.
  M. A., v, 362, **152**, 362.

1777 GLOUCESTER, Brigantine. *Guns*, 18; *Men*, 130.
July 17   *Commander:* John Coulston, of Gloucester.
    Note. The vessel's name is spelled *Glouster*.
  C. C. **196**, vi, 68.

1780 GLOUCESTER PACKET, Ship. *Guns*, 16; *Men*, 45.
Dec. 28   *Commander:* John Beach, of Gloucester.
  C. C. **196**, vi, 66; M. A., **171**, 320.

1782 GLOUCESTER PACKET, Ship. *Guns*, 16; *Men*, 40.
Jan. 11   *Commander:* John Osborne Sargent, of Gloucester.
  C. C. **196**, vi, 67; M. A., **172**, 91.

1780 GOOD INTENT, Boat.
  Commander: Cornelius Thompson.
  Boston Gazette, July 3, 1780.

1782 GOOD LUCK, Ship. *Guns*, 8; *Men*, 20.
Sept. 23   *Commander:* Jonathan Neall, of Salem.
  C. C. **196**, vi, 72.

1778 GRAMPUS, Sloop. *Guns*, 8, and 8 *swivels*; *Men*, 25.
Jan. 14   *Commander:* Ishmael Hardy.
  Bond: Continental, $5000; State, £500.

Bonders: Ishmael Hardy, principal; Isaac White and Daniel Hopkins, of Salem, sureties.
Owners: Isaac White and others.
Witness: John Dall.
   M. A., V, 349, 350, **168**, 143.

1780 GRAMPUS, Schooner.
May 27 *Commander:* Thomas Holmes.
   M. A., XL, 100; *London Chronicle*, Sept. 7, 1782: "... Two American privateers, one called the *Shark* and the other the *Grampus*, are both taken by his Majesty's cruisers and are carried into St. John's. They had taken within a fortnight four vessels just off the Banks and sent them for Salem."

1780 GRAND MONARCH, Ship. *Guns*, 16; *Men*, 45.
Dec. 12 *Commander:* David Coats, of Newburyport.
   Note. Name spelled *Monarque*.
   C. C. 196, VI, 81.

1781 GRAND MONARCH, Ship. *Guns*, 18; *Men*, 120.
July 27 *Commander:* John Lee, of Newburyport.
   C. C. 196, VI, 80; M. A., **171**, 436.

1781 GRAND TURK, Ship. *Guns*, 28; *Men*, 140.
June 13 *Commander:* Thomas Simmons, of Salem.
   C. C. 196, VI, 84; M. A., **171**, 410.

1781 GRAND TURK, Ship. *Guns*, 24; *Men*, 100.
Sept. 27 *Commander:* Joseph Pratt, of Salem.
   C. C. 196, VI, 82; M. A., **172**, 13, 216 (Nov. 2, 1782. Petition of Edward Bacon and others, American prisoners who have come from Halifax on parole. If not exchanged they must return, and there are not enough British prisoners for exchange. Certain British prisoners have entered on board the *Grand Turk*. The petitioners beg that these may be used for exchange); *Boston Gazette*, Oct. 22, 1781: "The Copper bottomed private armed Ship *Grand Turk*, Capt. Pratt, belonging to Salem, which sailed from thence on Wednesday last, returned the next Day, having in that Time captured the Privateer Brig *Providence* . . . mounting fourteen four-pound cannon and navigated by 65 Men." *Ibid.*, May 6, 1782, May 5, 1783; *Salem Gazette*, Apr. 3, 1783: "A prize

ship, which arrived here on Tuesday last, sailed from England about the 11th of February and was captured in the West Indies on the 12th ult. by the privateer ship *Grand Turk*, Capt. Joseph Pratt of this port. This prize . . . is near 400 tons burthen and though when taken she mounted 22 nine-pounders and carried 70 men, she struck without firing a gun." See above, Introduction, 57.

1778 GREYHOUND, Schooner. *Guns*, 2, and 12 *swivels; Men*, 30.
Apr. 21   *Commander:* Benjamin Hammond, jr.
  Bond: Continental, $5000; State, £4000.
  Bonders: Benjamin Hammond, jr., principal; Aaron Wait and John Dutch, sureties.
  Owners: Aaron Wait and others. Place not stated.
  Witness: Jno Dall.
    Note. The name is usually written *Grey Hound.*
  M. A., v, 353, 354, **168**, 265.

1778 GREYHOUND, Schooner. *Guns*, 2, and 12 *swivels; Men*, 30.
Oct. 6   *Commander:* John Pearce.
  Bond: Continental, $10,000; State, £4000.
  Bonders: John Pearce, principal; Aaron Wait and Jerathmeel Peirce, of Salem, sureties.
  Owners: Aaron Wait and Jerathmeel Peirce.
  Witness: D[aniel] Hopkins.
  M. A., v, 361, vi, 2, **169**, 199.

1779 GREYHOUND, Schooner. *Guns*, 10; *Men*, 30.
Mar. 17   *Commander:* Benjamin Hammond.
  Bond: Continental, $5000; State, £4000.
  Bonders: Benjamin Hammond, mariner, principal; Nathan Pierce [signed Peirce] and John Wait, of Boston and Salem, sureties.

  Owners: Nathan Peirce and others, of Salem.
  Witnesses: David Townsend, Isaac Townsend.
  M. A., vi, 1, 4, **159**, 351, **170**, 18.

1779 GREYHOUND, Schooner. *Guns*, 6; *Men*, 11.
Oct. 13   *Commander:* Samuel Croel.
  Bond: Continental, $5000; State, £4000.
  Bonders: Samuel Croel, principal; Aaron Wait and Jerathmeel Peirce, of Salem, sureties.
  Owners: Aaron Wait and Jerathmeel Peirce.

MASSACHUSETTS PRIVATEERS

Witness: Dan[ie]l Hopkins.
Note. The name is spelled *Greyhown*.
M. A., v, 351, 352, **170**, 424; *Essex Inst. Hist. Coll.*, xxi (1884), 127 (Capt. Croel's commission).

1781 GREYHOUND, Schooner. *Guns*, 8; *Men*, 35.
May 7   *Commander:* Jacob Wilds, of Salem.
C. C. **196**, vi, 91; M. A., **171**, 384.

1782 GREYHOUND, Schooner. *Guns*, 8; *Men*, 35.
May 25   *Commander:* Jacob Wilds, of Salem.
C. C. **196**, vi, 92; M. A., **172**, 164.

1782 GREYHOUND, Schooner. *Guns*, 8; *Men*, 35.
Sept. 9   *Commander:* John Cooke, of Salem.
C. C. **196**, vi, 86; Felt, ii, 270.

1783 GREYHOUND, Schooner. *Guns*, 6; *Men*, 25.
Feb. 13   *Commander:* Levi Doane, of Boston.
C. C. **196**, vi, 87; M. A., **172**, 294.

1780 GRIFFIN, Brigantine. *Guns*, 14; *Men*, 65.
May 16   *Commander:* Gideon Henfield.
Bond: Continental, $5000; State, £4000.
Bonders: Gideon Henfield, Josiah Orne, and Peter Lander, all of Salem.
Owners: Josiah Orne and Peter Lander.
Witnesses: Samuel Flagg, Will[ia]m Northey.
M. A., v, 344, 345, **171**, 161.

1782 GUSTAVUS, Ship. *Guns*, 16; *Men*, 70.
Dec. 3   *Commander:* James Magee, of Boston.
C. C. **196**, vi, 95; M. A., **172**, 238.

1777 HAMMOND, Schooner. *Guns*, 2, and 12 *swivels; Men*, 25.
Dec. 10   *Commander:* Jacob Oliver.
Bond: Continental, $5000; State, £500.
Bonders: Jacob Oliver, principal; Robert Shillaber and D[aniel] Hopkins, sureties.
Owner: Robert Shillaber, of Danvers.
Witnesses: Josiah Austin, Samuel Whittemore.
M. A., vi, 109, viii, 4, **168**, 75.

1777 HAMMOND, Schooner. *Guns*, 2; *Men*, 25.
Dec. 24   *Commander:* Jonathan Woodman.
Bond: Continental, $5000; State, £500.

Bonders: Jonathan Woodman, principal; Daniel Hopkins and Robert Foster, sureties.
Owners: Robert Shillaber and others, of Danvers.
Witness: John Dall.
M. A., VI, 108, VIII, 16, **168**, 112.

HAMMOND, Brig. *Guns*, 14.
   Commander: —— ——.
Hunt, II, 48.

1777   HAMPDEN, Brigantine. *Guns*, 14; *Men*, 100.
July 7   *Commander:* Benjamin Warren.
   Bond: Continental, $10,000.
   Bonders: Benjamin Warren, of Salem, George Cabot and Francis Cabot, of Beverly.
   Owners: George and Francis Cabot and others.
   Witness: John Doul.
   M. A., VI, 110, **152**, 362, **167**, 67.

1777   HAMPDEN, Schooner. *Guns*, 8 *swivels; Men*, 20.
Oct. 23   *Commander:* John Lander.
   Bond: Continental, $5000; State, £500.
   Bonders: John Lander, principal; Aaron Waitt [signed Wait] and Daniel Hopkins, sureties — all of Salem.
   Owners: Aaron Wait and Daniel Hopkins.
   Witness: Fitch Pool.
      Note. The vessel's name is spelled *Hamden.*
   M. A., VI, 96, 97, **167**, 356.

1777   HAMPDEN, Brigantine. *Guns*, 14; *Men*, 60.
Nov. 29   *Commander:* John Bartlett.
   Bond: Continental, $10,000; State, £500.
   Bonders: John Bartlett, of Marblehead, principal; George Cabot, of Beverly, and Jonathan Ingersoll, of Salem, sureties.
   Owners: Jonathan Ingersoll and others.
   Witnesses: William Lander, jr., Daniel Hathorne.
   M. A., VI, 100, 103, **168**, 54.

1778   HAMPDEN, Schooner. *Guns*, 6; *Men*, 40.
July 16   *Commander:* John Ashton.
   Bond: Continental, $10,000; State, £4000.
   Bonders: John Ashton, mariner, principal; George Dodge, jr., and Joshua Dodge, of Salem, sureties.

Owners: Joshua Dodge and others.
Witnesses: Stephen Floyd, Reuben Alley (State bond); Daniel Bancroft, Jonathan Symonds (Continental bond).
M. A., VI, 48, 49, **168**, 446.

1776 HANCOCK, Schooner.
Jan. 1   *Commander:* John Manley.
Note. Afterwards commanded by Samuel Tucker. Washington's Fleet.

1776 HANCOCK, Brigantine.
Commander: Wingate Newman.
Boston Gazette, Sept. 2, 1776.

1776 HANCOCK, Brig. *Guns*, 12; *Men*, 60.
Nov. 29   *Commander:* Daniel McNeill.
Bond: Continental, $5000.
Bonders: Daniel McNeill, principal; Arch[ibal]d Mercer and Philip Moore. Place not stated.
Owners: Archibald Mercer and Philip Moore.
Witnesses: Jona[than] Hastings, jr., Mary Cotton.
M. A., VI, 78, **166**, 69; Council Records, Dec. 17, 1776 (The *Hancock* had sailed and returned to port; and was held in port by an embargo. A petition that she be allowed to proceed on her cruise was not granted).

1777 HANCOCK, Sloop. *Guns*, 8; *Men*, 50.
June 11   *Commander:* James Sellers.
Bond: Continental, $5000.
Bonders: James Sellers, of Dartmouth, principal; Israel Ferring [signed Fearing], and Ebenezer White, sureties.
Owners: Israel Fearing and others, of Wareham.
Witnesses: Oliver Prescott, John Tyler.
M. A., VI, 57, **167**, 19.

1777 HANCOCK, Sloop. *Guns*, 8; *Men*, 45.
Sept. 11   *Commander:* John Sellers.
Bond: Continental, $5000; State, £500.
Bonders: John Sellers, of Wareham, principal; John Gibbs and David Nye, sureties.
Owners: John Gibbs and David Nye, of Wareham.
Witness: Eben[eze]r Davis.
M. A., VI, 56, VIII, 13, **167**, 227.

1778 HANCOCK, Ship of War.
Apr. 3   *Commander:* Thomas Snoden.
   Bond: State, £2000.
   Bonders: Mungo Mackay and Samuel White, merchants, major part of the owners, and Thomas Snoden, mariner — all of Boston.
   Witnesses: Edw[ar]d Holyoke, Tho[ma]s Oliver.
   M. A., **139**, 161 (Bond not to enlist any man in New England outside of Massachusetts).

[1783] HANCOCK, Sloop. *Guns,* 10.
   Commander: James Southard.
      Note. Probably the same vessel as those of 1777 above.
      Rochester's Official Bi-Centennial Record. 1879 (Address of N. W. Everett), 42: "Also a ten-gun sloop, named the *Hancock,* owned by John Carver, Nathan Bassett, and others was fitted out from this place [Wareham] as a privateer, commanded by James Southard."

1775 HANNAH, Schooner.
Sept. 2   *Commander:* Nicholson Broughton.
   Washington's Fleet.

1779 HANNAH, Schooner. *Guns,* 6.
   Commander: —— ——.
      Note. On the Penobscot Expedition and destroyed to prevent capture. Seems to have been an armed transport.
      M. A., **145**, 42a, 199, 201; Weymouth Hist. Soc. (No. 1: 1881), 57.

1780 HANNAH, Brigantine. *Guns,* 8; *Men,* 20.
Feb. 26   *Commander:* William Haydon.
   Bond: Continental, $10,000; State, £4000.
   Bonders: William Hayden [signed Haydon], mariner, principal; Leonard Jarvis and Joseph Russell, of Boston, sureties.
   Owners: Jarvis & Russell, merchants.
   Witnesses: W[illia]m Seymour, B[enjami]n Jarvis.
   M. A., VI, 91, 94, **171**, 90.

1780 HANNAH, Brigantine. *Guns,* 8; *Men,* 18.
Dec. 28   *Commander:* Samuel Gill, of Connecticut.
   Owners: Leonard Jarvis and others, of Boston.
   C. C. **196**, VI, 107; M. A., **171**, 321.

1776 HANNAH AND MOLLY, Schooner. *Tons*, 25; *Guns*, 8 swi-
July 31   vels; *Men*, 13.
    Commander: Agreen Crabtree.
    Bond: State, £2000.
    Bonders: Agreen Crabtree, mariner of Frenchman's Bay, Lincoln Co., Timothy McDaniell, merchant of Scarborough, Cumberland Co., and Francis Shaw, jr., of Gouldsborough, Lincoln Co.
    Owner: Agreen Crabtree.
    Witnesses: John Taylor, Nicholas Dike.
    M. A., **139**, 124 (July 31, 1776), 141 (Aug. 29, 1777. Bond not to enlist any man in New England outside of Massachusetts), **165**, 477 (July 30, 1776. Petition); Min. Sup. Court, 7, 16.

1780 HANNIBAL, Ship. Guns, 24; *Men*, 130.
Sept. 8   *Commander:* Jeremiah O'Brien, of Newburyport.
    C. C. **196**, VII, 2; M. A., **171**, 269.

1779 HAPPY RETURN, Snow. *Guns*, 4; *Men*, 20.
Nov. 24   *Commander:* Samuel Davis.
    Bond: Continental, $10,000; State, £4000.
    Bonders: Samuel Davis, mariner, principal; Justus Bellamy and Lavis Sisson, of Boston, sureties.
    Owners: Davis & Benson, of Boston.
    Witnesses: Lavis Sisson, Simon Davis.
    M. A., VI, 44, 45, **171**, 31.

1780 HAPPY RETURN, Sloop. *Tons*, 75; *Guns*, 6; *Men*, 12.
Apr. 17   *Commander:* Ichabod Halloway.
    Petitioner: Peter Guyer [signed Geyer], of Boston.
    M. A., **171**, 128.

1776 HARLEQUIN, Schooner. *Guns*, 8; *Men*, 60.
Aug. 8   *Commander:* John Tucker.
    Bond: Continental, $2000.
    Bonders: John Tucker, principal; John Gardner, jr., and Benjamin Goodhue, sureties — all of Salem.
    Owners: John Gardner, jr., and partners.
    Witnesses: Andrew Cabot, Michael Hearn.
    M. A., VI, 118, **159**, 1, 7, **165**, 37.

1777 HARLEQUIN, Schooner. *Guns*, 10; *Men*, 60.
June 3   *Commander:* James Dennis.
    Bond: Continental, $5000.

Know all Men by these presents That I Agreen Crabtree of a place called Frenchmans Bay in the County of Lincoln and State of the Massachusetts Bay Mariner, Sole Owner of the Privateer Schooner called Hannah and Molley and also Commander of said Privateer am held and stand firmly bound and Obliged unto Henry Gardoner of Boston in the County of Suffolk, and State aforesaid Esq.r Treasurer and Receiver General of the said State, in the full and Just Sum of Two Thousand pounds to be paid unto the said Henry Gardoner, or his Successors in said Office to and for the use of the said State, to the which payment well and truly to be made I bind myself my heirs Executors & Administrators firmly by these presents, Sealed with my Seal dated the Twenty ninth day of August, In the year of our Lord One Thousand, Seven hundred and Seventy Seven.

The Condition of this present Obligation is Such That Whereas the Great and General Court of the State aforesaid on the Nineteenth day of April last; in and by a Certain Resolve allowing private persons to fit out Vessels of War did among other things restrict them from Shipping on board said Privateers any Inhabitant of any of the New England States other than the State of Massachusetts Bay. If Therefore the above bounden Agreen Crabtree Owner and Commander of the said Privateer Hannah & Molley shall not inlist or take on board said Privateer any Inhabitant of any of the New England States, other than the State of the Massachusetts Bay, then this Obligation to be null & void, otherwise to remain in full force & Virtue.

Signed Sealed & Deliv.d
in the presence of
  Uriah Oakes
  Henry Alline jun.r

Agreen Crabtree

Bonders: James Dennis, principal; Richard Derby, jr., and Jerathmeel Peirce, sureties — all of Salem.
Owner: Jerathmeel Peirce.
Witnesses: John Adams, Will[iam] Harris.
M. A., vi, 112, **167**, 3.

1777 HARLEQUIN, Schooner. *Guns*, 10, and 16 *swivels; Men*, 55.
Aug. 22   *Commander:* Agreen Crabtree.
Bond: Continental, $5000.
Bonders: Agreen Crabtree, mariner, of Frenchman's Bay, Lincoln Co., Benjamin Hichborn, of Boston, and Daniel Ilsley, of Falmouth, Cumberland Co.
Owners: Agreen Crabtree and others.
Witnesses: John [?] Austin, James Hughes.
M. A., vi, 9, **167**, 171.

1777 HARLEQUIN, Schooner. *Guns*, 10; *Men*, 60.
Nov. 12   *Commander:* Francis Bowden Dennis.
Bond: Continental, $5000; State, £500.
Bonders: Francis Bowden Dennis, principal; Jerathmeel Peirce and John Leach. Place not stated.
Owners: Jerathmeel Peirce and John Leach.
Witness: Fitch Pool.
M. A., vi, 93, 95, **168**, 7.

1778 HARLEQUIN, Schooner. *Guns*, 9, and 8 *swivels; Men*, 40.
Aug. 4   *Commander:* Charles Hamilton.
Bond: Continental, $5000; State, £4000.
Bonders: Charles Hamilton, mariner, principal; William Shillaber, and Eben[eze]r Beckford, sureties — all of Salem.
Owners: William Shillaber and others.
Witness: D[aniel] Hopkins.
M. A., vi, 52, 53, **169**, 59.

1779 HARLEQUIN, Sloop. *Guns*, 4; *Men*, 10.
Mar. 16   *Commander:* Caleb Hopkins.
Bond: Continental, $5000; State, £4000.
Bonders: Caleb Hopkins, mariner, principal; Mungo Mackay and James Billings, of Boston, sureties.
Owners: Mungo Mackay and others.
Witnesses: Laz[aru]s Goodwin, Josh[ua] Billings, jr.
M. A., vi, 117, 120, **170**, 16.

1779 HARLEQUIN, Ship. *Guns,* 18; *Men,* 90.
Apr. 9   *Commander:* Francis Bowden Dennis.
   Bond: Continental, $10,000; State, £4000.
   Bonders: Francis Bowden Dennis, principal; Aaron Wait [signed Waitt] and John Tucker, of Salem, sureties.
   Owners: John Tucker, Aaron Wait and others.
   Witness: D[aniel] Hopkins.
      M. A., VI, 38, 39, **170**, 57; Mar. Court Rec., 22.

1779 HARLEQUIN, Ship. *Guns,* 20; *Men,* 100.
Aug. 4   *Commander:* Putnam Cleaves.
   Bond: Continental, $5000; State, £4000.
   Bonders: Putnam Cleves [signed Cleaves], mariner, principal; Caleb Low and Samuel Tucker, of Danvers and Salem, sureties.
   Owners: Caleb Low and others.
   Witness: J[ohn] Dall.
      M. A., VI, 40, 41, **159**, 215, 219, 222, **170**, 300; *Independent Chronicle,* Sept. 14, 1780 (See brig *Eagle*).

1780 HARLEQUIN, Ship. *Guns,* 18; *Men,* 60.
Dec. 19   *Commander:* Daniel Needham, of Salem.
      C. C. **196**, VII, 13; M. A., **171**, 315; *Salem Gazette,* Aug. 7, 1781: "The privateer ship *Harlequin,* Capt. Needham, who lately sailed from hence, has captured three prizes, all of which are safe arrived." *Ibid.,* Jan. 3, 1782 (See ship *Thorn,* Captain Tucker).

1782 HARPEY, Galley. *Guns,* 2; *Men,* 18.
May 16   *Commander:* Phineas Smith, of Salem.
      C. C. **196**, VII, 112; M. A., **172**, 158.

HARRIET, Schooner. *Guns,* 14.
   Commander: —— ——.
   Hunt, II, 48.

1782 HARRIOT, Ship. *Guns,* 16; *Men,* 20.
Jan. 21   *Commander:* John Beach, of Gloucester.
      C. C. **196**, VII, 16; M. A., **172**, 93.

1775 HARRISON, Schooner.
Oct. 29   *Commander:* William Coit.
      Note. Afterwards commanded by Charles Dyar. Washington's Fleet.

1780 HARRISON, Ship.
  Commander: James Johnson [Johnston?].
  Note. This may have been a New Hampshire vessel
  Boston Gazette, June 26, 1780.

1779 HARRY, Brigantine. *Guns,* 4; *Men,* 20.
Oct. 12 *Commander:* John Baptist Millet.
  Bond: Continental, $10,000; State, £4000.
  Bonders: John Baptist Millet, mariner, principal; Henry Williams and Pasturin & Terundet, of Salem and Boston, sureties.
  Owner: John Baptist Millet.
  Witness: Jno. Dall.
  M. A., VI, 87, 90, **170**, 422.

1780 HARRY, Schooner. *Guns,* 4; *Men,* 12.
Feb. 29 *Commander:* William Cowell.
  Bond: Continental, $5000; State, £4000.
  Bonders: William Cowell, mariner, principal; Daniel Hubbard and Adam Babcock, of Boston, sureties.
  Owner: Adam Babcock.
  Witnesses: Thomas G. Hubbard, Gabriel Helme.
  M. A., VI, 63, 65, **171**, 92.

1780 HASKET AND JOHN, Brigantine. *Guns,* 18; *Men,* 24.
Mar. 22 *Commander:* John Collins.
  Bond: Continental, $10,000; State, £4000.
  Bonders: John Collen [signed Jno. Collins], mariner, principal; Elias Hasket Derby and Nehemiah Felt, sureties.
  Owner: Elias Hasket Derby, of Salem.
  Witness: Joseph Chandler.
  M. A., VI, 71, 74, **171**, 101.

1780 HASKET AND JOHN, Brigantine. *Tons,* 150; *Guns,* 10; *Men,* 35.
Aug. 7 *Commander:* Benjamin Crowninshield.
  Bond: Continental, $10,000; State, £4000.
  Bonders: Benjamin Crowninshield, mariner, principal; Elias Hasket Derby and John Collins, sureties.
  Owners: Elias Hasket Derby and others, of Salem.
  Witness: Joseph Chandler.
  M. A., VI, 24, 25, **171**, 226.

1781 HASKET AND JOHN. Brigantine.
  Commander: Adam Wellman.
  Boston Gazette, July 16, 1781; Felt, II, 271.

1776 HAWKE, Schooner. *Guns*, 6; *Men*, 30.
Aug. 10   *Commander:* John Lee.
  Bond: Continental, $5000.
  Bonders: John Lee, mariner, Jona[than] Jackson, Nathaniel Tracy, and John Tracy, merchants, all of Newburyport.
  Owners: Jackson, Tracy & Tracy (first bond), Martha Lee, Joseph Lee, and Jackson, Tracy & Tracy (second bond).
  Witnesses: John Mulliken, Enoch Titcomb, 3rd (first bond), Enoch Titcomb, 3rd, Stephen Holland (second bond).
    Note. Two Continental bonds of same date and identical except names of owners and witnesses.
    M. A., VI, 77, 80, **159**, 45, 52, **165**, 45; *Annual Register*, XIX (1776), 261; Wharton, *Dipl. Corres. of Rev.*, II, 175, 195, 208, 379; Stevens's *Facsimiles*, 587, 589, 590.

1776 HAWKE, Brigantine. *Guns*, 10; *Men*, 80.
Nov. 3   *Commander:* Jonathan Oakes.
  Bond: Continental, $5000.
  Bonders: Jonathan Oakes, principal; Daniel Parker and Ezra Sargent [signed Sargeant], sureties.
  Owners: Uriah Oakes and William Shattuck, of Boston.
  Witnesses: Jos[eph] Cushing, Cha[rle]s Stockbridge.
    M. A., VI, 20, **139**, 128, **159**, 150, **166**, 11, **182**, 341; *Independent Chronicle*, July 10, 1777: "Last Tuesday arrived at a safe Port a Prize Brig laden with Rum. She was from Jamaica, bound to Liverpool, and was captured by Capt. Oaks in the private armed Brig *Hawk*."

1777 HAWKE, Schooner. *Guns*, 10, and 8 *swivels; Men*, 60.
June 18   *Commander:* Jeremiah Hibbert.
  Bond: Continental, $5000.
  Bonders: Jeremiah Hibbert, of Marblehead, principal; William Lee, of Marblehead, and Martin Brimmer, of Boston, sureties.
  Owners: Nathaniel Tracy and others, of Newburyport.
  Witnesses: Timothy Foster, Stephen Parker.
    M. A., VI, 111, **167**, 37.

1777 HAWK, Brigantine. *Guns*, 12; *Men*, 80.
Sept. 25, 27   *Commander:* Thomas Parker.
    Bond: Continental, $5000; State, £500.
    Bonders: Thomas Parker, principal; William Shattuck and Daniel Parker, sureties.
    Owners: William Shattuck and others, of Boston.
    Witnesses: Moses Hall (State bond), Joseph Tilden (Continental bond).
    M. A., VI, 98, 101, **139**, 143, **167**, 269.

1777 HAWK, Sloop. *Guns*, 10 *swivels; Men*, 25.
Dec. 10   *Commander:* Samuel Waters.
    Bond: Continental, $5000; State, £500.
    Bonders: Samuel Waters, principal; John Fisk and Henry Williams, of Salem, sureties.
    Owners: John Fisk and Henry Williams.
    Witnesses: William Gray, jr., William Shirley.
    M. A., VI, 119, 122, **168**, 69.

1778 HAWK, Brigantine. *Guns*, 12, and 8 *swivels; Men*, 80.
Apr. 4   *Commander:* Jonathan Oakes.
    Bond: Continental, $10,000; State, £500.
    Bonders: Jonathan Oakes, mariner, principal; William Shattuck and Uriah Oakes, of Boston, sureties.
    Owners: William Shattuck, Uriah Oakes, and others.
    Witnesses: William Dall, James Perkins.
    M. A., VI, 113, 114, **139**, 175, **168**, 243.

1778 HAWKE, Schooner. *Guns*, 10; *Men*, 60.
July 21   *Commander:* John Vallison.
    Bond: Continental, $5000; State, £4000.
    Bonders: John Vallison [signed Vilson], mariner, principal; Joseph Laughton, of Boston, and Joseph Choate, of Newburyport, sureties.
    Owners: Joseph Laughton and others.
    Witnesses: John Avery, jr., Jno. Dall.
    M. A., VI, 11, 13, **169**, 28.

1778 HAWK, Schooner. *Guns*, 6, and 6 *swivels; Men*, 40.
Aug. 4   *Commander:* Coas Gardner.
    Bond: Continental, $5000; State, £4000.
    Bonders: Coas Gardner, mariner, principal; Eben[eze]r Parsons and John Low, jr., of Cape Ann, sureties.
    Owners: Winthrop Sargent and others, of Cape Ann.
    Witnesses: Step[he]n Bruce, William Clough.
    M. A., VI, 50, 51, **169**, 58.

1778 HAWKE, Brigantine. *Guns*, 12; *Men*, 70.
Sept. 28 Commander: Thomas Hawes.
   Bond: Continental, $5000; *State*, £4000.
   Bonders: Thomas Hawes [signed Hawse], principal; William Shattuck and [John Shattuck] of Boston.
   Owners: William Shattuck and others.
   Witnesses: William Dall, Joseph Tilden.
      M. A., VI, 28, 29, **139**, 214, **169**, 169.

1778 HAWK, Schooner. *Guns*, 10; *Men*, 35.
Nov. 17 Commander: John Calef.
   Bond: Continental, $5000; State, £4000.
   Bonders: John Calef, mariner, principal; Samuel Tucker and John Head, of Newburyport and Boston, sureties.
   Owners (*Petitioners*): Jona[than] Jackson, Nath[anie]l Tracy, and John Tracy, of Newburyport.
   Witnesses: Abraham Whipple, Nathaniel Pearce.
      M. A., VI, 32, 33, **169**, 315.

1779 HAWK, Brigantine. *Guns*, 10; *Men*, 40.
Mar. 23 Commander: William Taylor.
   Bond: Continental, $10,000; State, £4000.
   Bonders: William Taylor, mariner, principal; Thomas Barclay and Henry Mitchell, of Boston, sureties.
   Owners: Henry Mitchell and others.
   Witnesses: Francis Johonnot, Nathaniel Thwing.
      M. A., VI, 85, 88, **170**, 28.

1779 HAWKE, Schooner. *Guns*, 4; *Men*, 12.
Aug. 25 Commander: Enoch Howes.
   Bond: Continental, $5000; State, £4000.
   Bonders: Enoch Howes, mariner, principal; William Shattuck and John Shattuck, of Boston, sureties.
   Owner: William Shattuck.
   Witnesses: Silas C. Brenton, James Perkins.
      M. A., VI, 69, 72, **170**, 354.

1779 HAWK, Schooner. *Guns*, 6; *Men*, 15.
Nov. 1 Commander: William Holland.
   Bond: Continental, $5000; State, £4000.
   Bonders: William Holland, mariner, principal; Isaiah Doane and William Baker, jr., of Boston, sureties.
   Owners: Thomas Davis and others, of Plymouth.
   Witnesses: Jona[than] Webb, Jno. Dall.
      M. A., VI, 59, 62, **171**, 1.

1780   HAWK, Schooner. *Guns*, 4; *Men*, 25.
July 22   *Commander:* Cornelius Thompson.
         Bond: Continental, $5000; State, £4000.
         Bonders: Cornelius Thompson, of Salem, principal; William Shattuck and John Shattuck, merchants of Boston, sureties.
         Owners: William Creed and others, of Salem.
         Witnesses: William Crafts, jr., Thomas Perkins.
         M. A., VI, 115, 116, **171**, 203.

1782   HAWK, Schooner. *Guns*, 6; *Men*, 15.
May 2   *Commander:* John Barbaroux, of Salem.
         C. C. **196**, VII, 21; M. A., **172**, 146.

1782   HAWK, Boat. *Guns*, 4; *Men*, 13.
Aug. 24   *Commander:* Zebulon Roe, of Essex County.
         C. C. **196**, VII, 24.

1782   HAWKE, Schooner. *Guns*, 4; *Men*, 30.
Nov. 20   *Commander:* Jacob Wilds, of Salem.
         C. C. **196**, VII, 28; M. A., **172**, 232.

1782   HAWK, Schooner. *Guns*, 4; *Men*, 20.
Dec. 3   *Commander:* Elijah Ayer, of Machias.
         C. C. **196**, VII, 20; M. A., **172**, 237.

1777   HAZARD, Brig. *Guns*, 14.
         Commander: Simeon Samson.
         Massachusetts State Navy.

1779   HAZARD, Schooner. *Guns*, 6; *Men*, 30.
May 14   *Commander:* Joshua Pilsbury.
         Bond: Continental, $5000; State, £4000.
         Bonders: Joshua Pilsbury [signed Pilsberry], mariner, principal; Shrimpton Hutchinson and Nathaniel Greenough, of Boston, sureties.
         Owners: William and Godfrey Hutchinson, merchants.
         Witnesses: Isaac Davis, John Call.
         M. A., VI, 99, VIII, 6, **170**, 102.

1779   HAZARD, Brigantine. *Guns*, 18; *Men*, 100.
Sept. 7   *Commander:* Joseph Olney.
         Bond: Continental, $5000; State, £4000.
         Bonders: Joseph Olney, mariner, principal; Mungo Mackay and Samuel Dunn, jr., of Boston, sureties.
         Owners: Mungo Mackay and others.
         Witnesses: Thomas Amory, jr., Luther Turner.
         M. A., VI, 83, 86, **170**, 371.

1779 HAZARD, Schooner. *Guns*, 6; *Men*, 30.
Oct. 20   *Commander:* Samuel Johnson.
    Bond: Continental, not stated; State, £4000.
    Bonders: Samuel Johnson, mariner, principal; Joseph Head and George S[tewart] Johonnot, of Boston, sureties.
    Owners: George S. Johonnot and others.
    Witnesses: John Frazier, Thomas Hunt.
    M. A., VI, 79, 82, **170**, 437.

1781 HAZARD, Brigantine. *Guns*, 6; *Men*, 14.
Feb. 5   *Commander:* Enoch Coffin, of Newburyport.
    C. C. **196**, VII, 31; M. A., **171**, 339.

1781 HAZARD, Brigantine. *Guns*, 6; *Men*, 12.
May 30   *Commander:* Samuel Coffin, of Newburyport.
    C. C. **196**, VII, 32.

1781 HAZARD, Sloop. *Guns*, 4; *Men*, 25.
July 10   *Commander:* Nathaniel Coit Webb, of Salem.
    C. C. **196**, VII, 37; M. A., **171**, 427; Court Files, 104074.

1781 HAZARD, Sloop. *Tons*, 35; *Guns*, 6; *Men*, 25.
Aug. 24   *Commander:* James Cheever.
    Petitioners: George Williams and others, of Boston.
    M. A., **171**, 470.

1781 HAZARD, Schooner. *Guns*, 8; *Men*, 25.
Nov. 17   *Commander:* Benjamin Knight, of Salem.
    C. C. **196**, VII, 35; M. A., **172**, 62.

1782 HAZARD, Sloop. *Guns*, 4; *Men*, 25.
Mar. 5   *Commander:* Edward Smith, jr., of Salem.
    C. C. **196**, VII, 38; M. A., **172**, 113; *Salem Gazette*, May 16, 1782: "Last Sunday the privateer *Hazard*, Capt. Smith, of this port, arrived from a cruise, having taken 4 prizes consisting of schooners and sloops."

1782 HAZARD, Schooner. *Guns*, 4; *Men*, 25.
June 21   *Commander:* John Harmon, of York.
    Owners: Benjamin Harrod and others, of Newburyport.
    C. C. **196**, VII, 33.

1782 HAZARD, Sloop. *Guns*, 6; *Men*, 25.
Aug. 22   *Commander:* Hugh Helme, of Salem.
    C. C. **196**, VII, 34.

1783 HAZARD, Schooner. *Guns*, 4; *Men*, 14.
Feb. 10   *Commander:* Samuel Barnes, of Salem.
   Owners: Mungo Mackay and others, of Boston.
   C. C. **196**, VII, 30; M. A., **172**, 293.

1777 HECTOR, Brig. *Guns*, 8; *Men*, 12.
Mar. 27   *Commander:* Zachariah Burchmore.
   Bond: Continental, $10,000.
   Bonders: Zachariah Burchmore, of Salem, principal; George Cabot and William Bartlet, merchants of Beverly, sureties.
   Owners: George Cabot and William Bartlet.
   Witnesses: Joshua Cleaves, D[aniel] Hopkins.
   M. A., VI, 106, **166**, 333.

1779 HECTOR, Ship. *Tons*, 220; *Guns*, 20; *Men*, 120.
June 22   *Commander:* John Carnes.
   Bond: Continental, $10,000; State, £4000.
   Bonders: John Carnes, mariner, principal; Thomas Mason and Jona[than] Peele, jr., of Salem, sureties.
   Owners: George Williams and others, of Salem.
   Witnesses: Jere[mia]h Shepard, Tho[ma]s Palfray.
      Note. On the Penobscot Expedition and destroyed to prevent capture.
   M. A., VI, 42, 43, XXXVII, 178, 280, **145**, 35, **170**, 180.

1782 HECTOR, Schooner. *Guns*, 6; *Men*, 15.
Nov. 5   *Commander:* John Cartwright, of Salem.
   C. C. **196**, VII, 40; M. A., **172**, 220.

1781 HENDRICK, Ship. *Tons*, 200; *Guns*, 18; *Men*, 90.
Aug. 16,   *Commander:* Thomas Benson.
   20   Petition signed by Henry Rust in behalf of John Fisk and others, of Salem.
      Note. The vessel is called *Kendrick* in *Naval Records of the Revolution*. Listed as a schooner by Hunt. Called *Hendrick Hudson* in Essex Institute, Miscellaneous Ship Papers.
   M. A., **171**, 461; C. C. **196**, IX, 13; Mar. Court Rec., 82; *Salem Gazette*, Feb. 28, 1782: "It is said that the privateer ship *Hendrick* . . . has made several prizes in the West Indies." *Ibid.*, Mar. 7: "Last Monday the privateer ship *Hendrick*, Capt. Benson, of this port, arrived from a cruise. She sailed from Martinico on the 3d ult." *Ibid.*, Oct. 24, 1782: "The

privateer ship *Mohawk*, Captain Carnes, from Beverly, and the privateer ship *Hendrick*, Captain Benson, from this place, are captured by the enemy and carried into New York."

1779 HENRY, Ship. *Guns*, 12; *Men*, 60.
Nov. 2   *Commander:* William Burke.
Bond: Continental, $10,000; State, £4000.
Bonders: William Burke, mariner, principal; Henry Mitchell and William Erskine, of Boston (Continental bond), Martin Brimmer and Samuel Nicholson, of Boston (State bond), sureties.
Owners: William Erskine and others.
Witnesses: Nathaniel Thwing, William Williams (Continental bond); Henry Livingston, John Kean (State bond).
M. A., VI, 36, 37, **171**, 2.

1780 HENRY, Schooner. *Guns*, 4; *Men*, 10.
Commander: John Baptist Millet.
Felt, II, 271; Paine, 456.

1781 HERCULES, Ship. *Guns*, 20; *Men*, 120.
July 31   *Commander:* Thomas Dissmore, of Newburyport.
Owners: John Coffin Jones and others, of Boston.
C. C. **196**, VII, 46; M. A., **171**, 438.

1781 HERMIONE, Sloop. *Guns*, 6; *Men*, 12.
Aug. 20   *Commander:* Silas Rand, of Nantucket.
Owners: Isaac Sears and others, of Boston.
C. C. **196**, VII, 49; M. A., **171**, 462.

1781 HERMIONE, Sloop. *Tons*, 60; *Guns*, 6; *Men*, 15.
Dec. 30   *Commander:* James Magee.
Petitioners: Isaac Sears and others (Sears & Smith), of Boston.
M. A., **172**, 90.

1777 HERO, Ship. *Guns*, 28; *Men*, 200.
July 16   *Commander:* James Tracy, of Newburyport.
C. C. **196**, VII, 62; M. A., **167**, 176 (Boston, Aug. 21, 1777. Petition of Robert Tracy, in behalf of Capt. James Tracy, "that he is now in this Harbour ready for Sea, but the naval Officer refuses to give him a Pass without a Certificate from the Treasurer, which

must be founded on Bonds given by the major Part of his Owners, who are not here. Your Petitioner conceives that since the Repeal of the Embargo Bill, no such Bonds are necessary. . . . He prays your Honours would be pleased to direct the naval Officer to give him such a Pass as will enable him forthwith to proceed to Sea." Petition granted).

1779 HERO, Schooner. *Tons*, 50; *Guns*, 4, and 10 *swivels; Men*, 40.
May 21   *Commander:* Nicholas Bartlett, jr.
   Bond: State, £4000.
   Bonders: Nicholas Bartlett, jr., mariner, principal; John Waitt and James Dennis, of Marblehead, sureties.
   Owners: John Waitt and James Dennis.
   Witness: Jno. Dall.
   M. A., VIII, 8, **170**, 129.

1781 HERO, Brigantine. *Guns*, 12; *Men*, 50.
May 5   *Commander:* Silas Smith, of Salem.
   C. C. **196**, VII, 60; M. A., **171**, 383; *Essex Inst. Hist. Coll.*, XLV, 180 (Captured July 4, 1781, by H. M. S. *Charlestown*, in Gut of Canso).

1781 HERO, Schooner. *Guns*, 2; *Men*, 20.
Aug. 24   *Commander:* Silas Smith, of Salem.
   C. C. **196**, VII, 61; M. A., **171**, 469.

1781 HERO, Schooner. *Guns*, 4; *Men*, 40.
Sept. 10   *Commander:* John G. Scranton, of Boston.
   C. C. **196**, VII, 58; M. A., **172**, 5.

1781 HERO, Schooner. *Guns*, 4; *Men*, 15.
Oct. 24   *Commander:* Nathan Plimpton, of Boston.
   C. C. **196**, VII, 55; M. A., **172**, 42.

1782 HERO, Schooner. *Guns*, 9; *Men*, 25.
May 28   *Commander:* G[eorge] W[aith] Babcock, of Boston [?].
   C. C. **196**, VII, 50; M. A., **172**, 165; Mar. Court Rec., 87; Court Files, 103255; *Boston Gazette*, July 15, 1782: "Captains Babcock of the *Hero*, Stoddard of the *Scammel*, Woodbury [Woodberry] of the *Hope*, and Tibbets of the *Swallow*, [a New Hampshire vessel], having determined to surprize and possess themselves of Lunenburgh, an elegantly situated Town, ten Leagues West of Halifax, landed Ninety Men two Miles below it, under the Command of Lieut. Barte-

man, on Monday the first Day of July Instant at half after Seven o'Clock A.M. This gallant Corps with amazing Rapidity reached the Town and, amidst many heavy Discharges of Musquetry from the Enemy, burnt the Commanding Officer's House, a Blockhouse in the North West Part of the Town, spik'd up two 24 pounders, and forc'd the Enemy into the South Blockhouse, from whence they kept up a brisk and animating Fire and declared their Intention to hold out to the last Extremity. But their Animation subsided upon the Receipt of a few 4-pound Shot from the *Hero* and they reluctantly surrendered themselves Prisoners of War. The victorious Party with a natural and pleasing Vivacity fell to plundering, and quickly emptied the Stores of a Variety and considerable Quantity of Dry Goods, twenty Puncheons of good West-India Rum, and the King's Beef, Pork and Flour. Upon the near Approach of the Combined Fleet, two 18 pounders were spiked up and dismounted and the Royal Magazine was safely deposited in the Hold of the *Scammel*. The strictest Decorum was observed towards the Inhabitants and their Wearing Apparel and Household Furniture inviolably preserv'd for their Use. The Town was ransomed for a Thousand Pounds Sterling and Colonel Creighton with some of the principal Inhabitants were shipped on board the *Scammel*. On the Side of the brave Sons of Liberty, three were wounded slightly, one dangerously; on the Part of the Abettors of Oppression and Despotism, the Number of slain and wounded unknown, only one of their slain being found."

1782   HERO, Ship. *Guns*, 4; *Men*, 20.
July 11   *Commander:* Alexander Coffin, of Nantucket.
   Owner: William Foster, of Boston.
   C. C. **196**, VII, 52.

1782   HERO, Boat. *Guns*, small arms; *Men*, 20.
Aug. 7   *Commander:* John G. Scranton, of Boston.
   C. C. **196**, VII, 59; M. A., **172**, 184.

1782   HERO, Schooner. *Guns*, 9; *Men*, 25.
Aug. 9   *Commander:* Oliver Reed, of Boston.
   C. C. **196**, VII, 56.

1782 HERSEY, Ship. *Guns*, 14; *Men*, 75.
 Commander:
 Essex Institute, Miscellaneous Ship Papers.

1777 HIBERNIA, Brig.
 Commander: Moses Foster.
 Almon's *Remembrancer*, v, 142 (Boston, N. E., April 24, 1777): "This morning the Provincial brig of War *Hibernia*, Moses Foster, commander, arrived from Curaçoa, with a cargo of muskets, pistols, cannon-balls, powder, etc."

1779 HIBERNIA, Schooner. *Guns*, 10; *Men*, 50.
May 17 *Commander:* John O'Brien.
 Bond: Continental, $5000; State, £4000.
 Bonders: John Obrian [signed Obrien], mariner, principal; Benja[min] Jepson and John Nutting, of Boston, sureties.
 Owners: Benjamin Jepson and others.
 Witnesses: John Avery, jr., W[illiam] Baker, jr.
  Note. The *Hibernia* was a prize captured from the British.
  M. A., VI, 102, 105, **139**, 249, **159**, 266, **170**, 115; Mar. Court Rec., 26, 28, 59; *Boston Post*, May 22, July 31, 1779.

1780 HIBERNIA, Brigantine.
 Commander: William O'Brien.
 Boston Gazette, July 10, 1780.

1780 HIBERNIA, Brigantine.
 Commander: Enoch Titcomb, jr.
  M. A., **176**, 600 (Aug. 7, 1780. Petition of Enoch Titcomb, jr., of Newburyport, in behalf of the owners, that the vessel may proceed on her cruise, the embargo notwithstanding. Granted).

1781 HIBERNIA, Brigantine. *Guns*, 10; *Men*, 60.
May 28 *Commander:* Jeremiah O'Brien, of Newburyport.
 C. C. **196**, VII, 79.

1782 HIBERNIA, Brigantine. *Guns*, 4; *Men*, 15.
July 16 *Commander:* Joseph Atkins, of Newburyport.
 C. C. **196**, VII, 73.

1782 HIBERNIA, Schooner. *Guns*, 6; *Men*, 20.
Aug. 7 *Commander:* George Smith, of Boston.
 C. C. **196**, VII, 81.

1782 HIBERNIA, Schooner. *Guns*, 6; *Men*, 20.
Oct. 2   *Commander:* Joseph Darbey, of Boston.
C. C. **196**, VII, 78.

1781 HIND, Brig.
Commander: [Gamaliel?] Hodges.
Salem Gazette, Aug. 7, 1781: "Since our last arrived in this harbour the Letter of Marque brig *Hyne*, Capt. Hodges, in 17 days from Port-au-Prince."

1782 HIND, Brigantine.
Commander: Joseph Leach.
Boston Gazette, Apr. 29, May 20, 1782 (Salem, Apr. 26): "Yesterday arrived in a safe port the prize brig *Peggy* taken by Capt. Leach in the letter-of-marque brig *Hind*, belonging to this port." *Salem Gazette*, May 2, 1782.

1782 HIND, Brigantine. *Guns*, 8; *Men*, 16.
July 3   *Commander:* Benjamin Dunham, of Salem.
C. C. **196**, VII, 53; M. A., **172**, 178.

1782 HIND, Brigantine. *Guns*, 8; *Men*, 16.
Nov. 19   *Commander:* Francis Boardman, of Salem.
Note. The vessel's name is spelled *Hynde*.
C. C. **196**, VIII, 31; M. A., **172**, 229.

1779 HIRAM, Schooner. *Guns*, 6; *Men*, 16.
May 5   *Commander:* Samuel Butler.
Bond: Continental, $5000; State, £4000.
Bonders: Samuel Butler, mariner, principal; Philip Marett and John Codman, of Boston, sureties.
Owners: Samuel Butler and others.
Witnesses: Silas Burbank, Stephen Fowler (Continental bond); Stephen Fowler, W. Baker (State bond).
M. A., VI, 58, 60, **170**, 80.

1779 HODSHON, Schooner. *Guns*, 6; *Men*, 12.
Dec. 11   *Commander:* Robert Stonehouse.
Bond: Continental, $5000; State, £4000.
Bonders: Robert Stonehouse, mariner, principal; James Bowdoin, jr., and Andre Carente, of Boston, sureties.
Owner: James Bowdoin, jr.
Witnesses: John Read, John Read, jr.
M. A., VI, 61, 64, **171**, 43.

1776 HOPE, Schooner. *Guns*, 5; *Men*, 45.
Sept. 26   *Commander:* Walter Hatch.
   Bond: Continental, $5000.
   Bonders: Walter Hatch, principal, Simeon Sampson (signed Samson) and Samuel Nutting, all of Plymouth.
   Owners: Watson & Spooner, Jackson & Gray, and others, of Plymouth.
   No witnesses.
   M. A., VI, 75, **165**, 286.

1778 HOPE, Brigantine. *Tons*, 110; *Guns*, 12; *Men*, 40.
Sept. 16   *Commander:* William Friend.
   Bond: Continental, $10,000; State, £4000.
   Bonders: William Friend, mariner, principal; Joseph Laughton and Joseph Choate, of Newburyport, sureties.
   Owners: John Tracy and others, of Newburyport.
   Witness: Jonath[an] Greenleaf.
   M. A., VI, 30, 31, **169**, 162.

1778 HOPE, Schooner. *Guns*, 4; *Men*, 20.
Oct. 14   *Commander:* William Woodberry.
   Bond: Continental, $5000; State, £4000.
   Bonders: William Woodberry, principal; Joshua Dodge, of Salem, and Thomas Knox, of Boston, sureties.
   Owners: Joshua Dodge and others, of Salem.
   Witness: D[aniel] Hopkins.
   M. A., VI, 46, 47, **169**, 223.

1779 HOPE, Schooner. *Guns*, 6; *Men*, 18.
Apr. 6   *Commander:* John Carey.
   Bond: Continental, $5000; State, £4000.
   Bonders: John Carey, mariner, principal; Samuel Greenough and Joshua Winslow, of Boston, sureties.
   Owners: William and Godfrey Hutchinson.
   Witnesses: Nathaniel Greenough, Nalbro Frazier.
   M. A., VI, 104, 107, **170**, 53.

1780 HOPE, Brig. *Guns*, 4; *Men*, 11.
Feb. 9   *Commander:* Thomas Palfrey.
   Bond: Continental, $5000; State, £4000.
   Bonders: Thomas Palfrey [signed Palfray], John Fisk, and John Norris, all of Salem.
   Owners: John Fisk and John Norris.
   Witness: Bartho[lemew] Putnam.
   M. A., VI, 22, 23, **171**, 79.

1780 HOPE, Brigantine. *Guns*, 6; *Men*, 20.
Aug. 31 *Commander:* Robert Wormsted, of Marblehead.
C. C. **196**, VII, 110; M. A., **171**, 265.

1780 HOPE, Brigantine. *Guns*, 4; *Men*, 10.
Oct. 2 *Commander:* Ezekiel Burroughs, of Boston.
C. C. **196**, VII, 89; M. A., **171**, 285.

1780 HOPE, Schooner. *Guns*, 10; *Men*, 20.
Nov. 29 *Commander:* Nathaniel Goodwin, of Boston.
C. C. **196**, VII, 98; M. A., **171**, 309.

1781 HOPE, Schooner. *Guns*, 8; *Men*, 30.
Feb. 20 *Commander:* Samuel Trask [Trusk], of Boston.
C. C. **196**, VII, 107; M. A., **171**, 346.

1781 HOPE, Brigantine. *Guns*, 8; *Men*, 30.
May 17 *Commander:* Phoenix Frazier, of Philadelphia.
Note. Owned in Philadelphia, but two Boston men signed the bond and she is called a Massachusetts vessel in *Naval Records of the Revolution*.
C. C. **196**, VII, 94; M. A., **171**, 389.

1781 HOPE, Schooner. *Guns*, 6; *Men*, 25.
May 18 *Commander:* Nathan Plimpton, of Boston.
C. C. **196**, VII, 106.

1781 HOPE, Schooner. *Guns*, 8; *Men*, 25.
Sept. 10 *Commander:* Robert Wormsted, of Salem.
C. C. **196**, VII, 111; M. A., **172**, 6.

1781 HOPE, Brigantine. *Guns*, 8; *Men*, 15.
Sept. 22 *Commander:* Anthony Furnes, of Marblehead.
C. C. **196**, VII, 95; M. A., **172**, 11.

1781 HOPE, Brig. *Guns*, 8; *Men*, 15.
Sept. 24 *Commander:* Joseph Hinckley, of Marblehead.
C. C. **196**, VII, 102.

1782 HOPE, Brigantine. *Guns*, 6; *Men*, 35.
May 28 *Commander:* Herbert Woodberry, of Beverly.
C. C. **196**, VII, 109; M. A., **172**, 167; *Boston Gazette*, July 15, 1782 (At Lunenburgh, see *Hero*, Capt. Babcock); *Ibid.*, Sept. 30, 1782: "Wednesday arrived at Beverly a Brig of 16 Guns, late in the Service of his Britannic Majesty. The Crew of the *Hope* (a small Privateer lately captured by her) being Prisoners on

Know all Men by these presents That We Nathaniel Bently of Taunton in the County of Bristol and State of the Massachusetts Bay Mariner and Commander of the Private Schooner of War called Hornet and Samuel Batchelder of Newbury Port in the County of Essex and State aforesaid Merchant the Major part of the Owners of said Private Vessel of War are held and Stand firmly bound and Obliged unto Henry Gardner of Boston in the County of Suffolk Esq. Treasurer and Receiver General of the State aforesaid in the full & just sum of Two Thousand pounds Lawful money to be paid unto the said Henry Gardner or his Successors in said Office, to and for the use of the said State, to the which payment well and truly to be made we bind ourselves our heirs Executors & Administrators Joyntly and Severally firmly by these presents Sealed with our Seals dated the Sixth day of March, In the year of our Lord One Thousand Seven hundred and Seventy Eight. —

The Condition of this present Obligation is Such That if the above bounden Nathaniel Bently Commander and Samuel Batchelder the Major part of the Owners of said Private Schooner of War shall not Inlist or take on board said Privateer any Soldier or Soldiers belonging to the Continental Army of the United States of America than this Obligation to be null & void, otherwise to remain in full force and Virtue.

Signed Sealed & Deliv'd
in the presence of

Samuel Brownell
Henry Alline jun'r

Nath'l Bently
Sam'l Batchelder

Bond not to enlist Continental Soldiers

See page 42

board her, to the number of 21, rose upon the Brig's People, in number 62, while laying in a small Harbour on the Labrador Shore, which they had the good Fortune to arrive safe in Port with."

1782 HOPE, Schooner. *Guns*, 6; *Men*, 10.
Sept. 20   *Commander:* John Palmer, of Salem.
       C. C. **196**, VII, 105.

1782 HOPEWELL, Schooner. *Guns*, 2; *Men*, 18.
July 26   *Commander:* Cornelius Dunham, of Beverly.
       C. C. **196**, VIII, 3.

1782 HOPEWELL, Schooner. *Guns*, 10; *Men*, 20.
Oct. 21   *Commander:* Martin Brewster, of Beverly.
       C. C. **196**, VIII, 1; M. A., **172**, 209.

1779 HORATIO, Sloop. *Guns*, 8; *Men*, 20.
Oct. 22   *Commander:* Thomas Eskridge.
       Bond: Continental, $5000; State, £4000.
       Bonders: Thomas Eskridge, mariner, principal; William Shattuck and Joseph Head, of Boston, sureties.
       Owner: Samuel Broome, of Boston.
       Witnesses: Oliver Greenleaf, Thomas Munro.
       M. A., VI, 121, 124, **170**, 443.

1778 HORNETT, Schooner. *Guns*, 10, and 8 *swivels; Men*, 50.
Jan. 22   *Commander:* Nathaniel Bently.
       Bond: Continental, $5000; State, £500.
       Bonders: Nathaniel Bentley [signed Bently], principal, John Tracy, of Newburyport, and Sam[ue]l White, of Boston, sureties.
       Owners: John Tracy and Samuel White.
       Witnesses: John Marston, Tho[ma]s Dennie.
       M. A., VI, 54, 55, **139**, 158, **168**, 156.

1778 HORNET, Brig. *Guns*, 8, and 8 *swivels; Men*, 45.
June 5   *Commander:* John Sellers.
       Bond: Continental, $5000; State, £4000.
       Bonders: John Sellers, principal; Henry Williams and Samuel Ward, of Salem, sureties.
       Owners: Henry Williams and Samuel Ward.
       Witness: D[aniel] Hopkins.
       M. A., VI, 16, 19, **168**, 353.

1778 HORNET, Schooner. *Guns*, 2, and 16 *swivels; Men*, 60.
June 10   *Commander:* Nathaniel Reynolds.
   Bond: Continental, $5000; State, £4000.
   Bonders: Nath[anie]l Reynolds, principal; John Norris and Nath[anie]l Peirce, of Salem, sureties.
   Owners: John Norris and others.
   Witness: D[aniel] Hopkins.
   M. A., VI, 18, 21, **168**, 361.

1778 HORNET, Schooner. *Guns*, 2, and 16 *swivels; Men*, 45.
Aug. 28   *Commander:* Nehemiah Buffinton.
   Bond: Continental, $5000; State, £4000.
   Bonders: Nehemiah Buffington [signed Buffinton], principal; John Norris and Jno. Dutch, of Salem, sureties.
   Owners: John Norris and John Dutch.
   Witness: D[aniel] Hopkins.
   M. A., VI, 73, 76, **169**, 113.

1778 HORNET, Schooner. *Guns*, 8; *Men*, 30.
Sept. 15   *Commander:* William Springer.
   Bond: Continental, $5000; State, £4000.
   Bonders: William Springer, mariner, principal; Joseph Laughton, of Boston, and Joseph Choate, of Newburyport, sureties.
   Owner: John Tracy, of Newburyport.
   Witness: W. Baker, jr.
   M. A., VI, 12, 15, **169**, 161.

1778 HORNET, Schooner. *Guns*, 2, and 6 *swivels; Men*, 10.
Dec. 29   *Commander:* George Osborn.
   Bond: Continental, $5000; State, £4000.
   Bonders: George Orsborn [signed Osborn], principal; Isaac Needham and John Dutch, of Salem, sureties.
   Owners: Isaac Needham and John Dutch.
   Witness: D[aniel] Hopkins.
   M. A., VI, 14, 17, **169**, 394.

1779 HORNET, Schooner. *Guns*, 4; *Men*, 13.
June 15   *Commander:* Robert Brookhouse.
   Bond: Continental, $5000; State, £4000.
   Bonders: Rob[er]t Brookhouse, mariner, principal; John Norris and Bartholomew Putnam, of Salem, sureties.
   Owner: Bartholomew Putnam.
   Witnesses: Nathan Peirce, Joseph Grafton.
   M. A., VI, 67, 70, **159**, 259, **170**, 168.

1779 HOUND, Brigantine.
Oct. 11   *Commander:* William Bunker.
           Bond: State, £2000.
           Bonders: Thomas Russell, of Boston, merchant and major part of the owners, and William Bunker, mariner of Nantucket.
           Witnesses: Peter Collas, Henry Alline, jr.
           M. A., **139**, 255 (Bond not to enlist any man in New England outside of Massachusetts).

1781 HOUND, Brigantine. *Guns,* 6; *Men,* 20.
Apr. 14   *Commander:* Nathaniel Hathaway, of Dartmouth.
           Owners: Samuel Emery and others, of Boston.
           C. C. **196**, VIII, 11; M. A., **171**, 365.

1781 HOUND, Brigantine. *Guns,* 14; *Men,* 50.
Apr. 16   *Commander:* John Adkison, of Salem.
           Note. In the petition the captain's name is spelled Adkinson.
           C. C. **196**, VIII, 9; M. A., **171**, 375.

1781 HOUND, Brigantine. *Guns,* 14; *Men,* 20.
Oct. 8   *Commander:* Ephraim Emerton, of Salem.
           C. C. **196**, VIII, 10; M. A., **172**, 19.

           How, Brig. *Guns,* 8; *Men,* 40.
           Commander: —— ——.
           Hunt, II, 48.

1780 HUMBIRD, Brigantine. *Guns,* 8; *Men,* 20.
Aug. 7   *Commander:* Samuel Ingersoll.
           Bond: Continental, $5000; State, £4000.
           Bonders: Samuel Ingersoll, of Salem, principal; Nath[anie]l Silsbee and John Collins, sureties.
           Owners: Nathaniel Silsbee and others, of Salem.
           Witness: Benj[amin] Cook.
           M. A., VI, 89, 92, **171**, 227.

1779 HUNTER, Ship. *Tons,* 160; *Guns,* 18; *Men,* 110.
Apr. 15   *Commander:* Nathan Brown.
           Bond: Continental, $10,000; State, £4000.
           Bonders: Nathan Brown, mariner, principal; Elias Hasket Derby and Bartho[lomew] Putnam, of Salem, sureties.
           Owners: Elias Hasket Derby and others.

Witnesses: Stephen Webb, John Battan.
  Note. On the Penobscot Expedition and captured by the British.
  M. A., VI, 81, 84, XXXVII, 178, 280, **145**, 35, **170**, 59.

1779 HUNTER, Sloop. *Guns*, 8; *Men*, 40.
July 23   *Commander:* Alexander Thomson Ogilvie.
  Bond: Continental, $5000; State, £4000.
  Bonders: Alex[ander] Thompson [signed Thomson] Ogilvie, mariner, principal; Thomas Parker and Elisha Sigourney, merchants of Boston, sureties.
  Owners: Thomas Parker and others.
  Witnesses: W. Harris, Jno. Dall.
  M. A., VI, 123, 126, **170**, 266, 267.

1781 HUNTER, Brigantine. *Guns*, 6; *Men*, 15.
Oct. 18   *Commander:* David Lawrence, of Boston.
  C. C. **196**, VIII, 18; M. A., **172**, 35.

1779 HUNTINGTON, Brigantine. *Guns*, 6; *Men*, 16.
Dec. 7   *Commander:* John Adams.
  Bond: Continental, $5000; State, £4000.
  Bonders: John Adams, mariner, principal; John Wait and Jonathan Ingersoll, sureties.
  Owners: John Wait and others, of Boston.
  Witnesses: Hugh McClallen, Jos[eph] Williams.
  M. A., VI, 164, 165, **171**, 42.

1780 HUNTINGTON, Brigantine. *Guns*, 4; *Men*, 15.
May 20   *Commander:* Cornelius Fellows.
  Bond: Continental, $5000; State, £4000.
  Bonders: Cornelius Fellows [signed Fellowes], mariner, principal; Samuel Perkins and John Wait, of Boston, sureties.
  Owners: Samuel Perkins and John Wait, merchants.
  Witnesses: Edward Rumney, Thomas Ridgway.
  M. A., VI, 26, 27, **176**, 367.

1780 HUNTINGTON, Brigantine. *Guns*, 6; *Men*, 15.
Sept. 21   *Commander:* Samuel Skinner, of Boston.
  Note. In the petition the captain's name is spelled Skimmer.
  C. C. **196**, VIII, 26; M. A., **171**, 276.

1782   HYDER ALLY, Galley. *Guns*, 2; *Men*, 40.
May 4   *Commander:* Benjamin Conner, of Newburyport.
    Owners: John Cushing and others, of Boston.
        Note. The vessel's name is spelled *Heyder Ally.*
    C. C. 196, VII, 71; M. A., **172**, 148.

1782   HYDER ALLY, Schooner. *Guns*, 12; *Men*, 40.
May 30   *Commander:* William Baldwin, of Salem.
        Note. Spelled *Heyder Ally.*
    C. C. 196, VII, 70; M. A., **172**, 168; *Salem Gazette*, Nov. 29, 1782: "Capt. Baldwin, in the *Hyder Ali* privateer" has "been lately taken and carried into Halifax." *Essex Inst.* XLV, 182 (Captured Oct. 31, 1782, on Georges Bank by H. M. S. *Chatham*).

1776   INDEPENDENCE, Brigantine.
July 26   *Commander:* Simeon Samson.
    Bond: State, £2000.
    Bonders: Simeon Sampson [signed Samson], mariner, and James Warren, merchant, both of Plymouth, and Richard Derby, jr., merchant of Salem.
    Owners: "Belonging to the said State of the Massachusetts Bay."
    Witnesses: Jno. F. Williams, John Clouston, William Cooper, John Browne.
        Note. One of the first vessels built for the Massachusetts State Navy.
    M. A., **139**, 122.

1776   INDEPENDENCE, Schooner. *Guns*, 4; *Men*, 35.
Aug. 8   *Commander:* John Gill.
    Bond: Continental, $5000.
    Bonders: John Gill, of Salem, mariner, Thomas Adams and Paul Dudley Sargent, of Boston, merchants.
    Owners: Thomas Adams, Paul Dudley Sargent, and William Shattuck.
    Witnesses: Gustavus Fellows, John Marston.
    M. A., VI, 128, **165**, 34.

1776   INDEPENDENCE, Schooner. *Guns*, 6; *Men*, 25.
Sept. 23   *Commander:* William Nichols.
    Bond: Continental, $5000.
    Bonders: William Nichols, mariner, Stephen Hooper and Samuel Batchelder, merchants, all of Newburyport.

>
> *Owners:* Stephen Hooper, Samuel Batchelder, and William Nichols.
> *Witnesses:* Joseph Cutler, Thomas Roberts.
> M. A., VI, 127, **165**, 275.

1777 INDEPENDENCE, Sloop.
> *Commander:* James Magee.
> *Boston Gazette,* Jan. 13, 1777.

1777 INDEPENDENCE, Brigantine. *Guns,* 6; *Men,* 18.
Nov. 25
> *Commander:* Nicholas Johnson.
> *Bond:* Continental, $5000; State, £500.
> *Bonders:* Nicholas Johnson, principal; Tristram Dalton and Thomas Thomas, of Newburyport, sureties.
> *Owner:* Tristram Dalton.
> *Witnesses:* Eben[ezer] Parsons, Joseph Marquand.
>> *Note.* The captain's name, Nicholas, is written over the name William, which is partially erased, on both bonds. In the petition the name is William Johnson.
>
> M. A., VI, 152, 153, **168**, 42.

1777 INDEPENDENCE, Sloop. *Guns,* 10; *Men,* 55.
Dec. 31
> *Commander:* Peter Pollard.
> *Bond:* Continental, $5000; State, £500.
> *Bonders:* Peter Pollard, principal; Isaac Sears and Paschal N[elson] Smith, of Boston, sureties.
> *Owners:* Isaac Sears and Paschal N. Smith.
> *Witnesses:* A[nthony?] Griffiths, Elia[ki]m Raymond, Joseph Skillin.
> M. A., VI, 131, 134, **139**, 265, **168**, 124; *Independent Chronicle,* Apr. 2, 1778: "Last Thursday arrived safe in Port a Prize Ship of 10 Guns and 20 Men. She was bound from New York for the West Indies for a Cargo of Rum for Howe's Troops at New York, but taken by the Privateer Sloop *Independence,* of this Port, Capt. Peter Pollard, after an obstinate Engagement of five Glasses. The Captain of the Ship is badly wounded in two Places and the brave Captain Pollard had Five of his Hands wounded though not dangerous."

1778 INDEPENDENCE, Brigantine. *Guns,* 6; *Men,* 13.
Nov. 7
> *Commander:* Paul Newman.
> *Bond:* Continental, $5000; State, £4000.
> *Bonders:* Paul Newman, principal; Ralph Cross, jr., and Benjamin Loring, of Newbury, sureties.

Owners: Samuel Batchelder and William Nichols, of Newbury.
Witness: Jno. Dall.
M. A., VI, 129, 130, **169**, 302.

1779 INDEPENDENCE, Sloop. *Guns*, 4; *Men*, 10.
Jan. 12
Commander: Francis Brown.
Bond: Continental, $5000; State, £4000.
Bonders: Francis Brown, mariner, principal; Samuel Broome and Paschal N[elson] Smith, of Boston, sureties.
Owners: Isaac Sears and others, of Boston.
Witnesses: E[liaki]m Raymond, Joseph Skillin.
M. A., VI, 125, 132, **169**, 410.

1778 INDUSTRY, Sloop.
Commander: Henry Coffin.
M. A., **168**, 153 (Petition of Nathaniel Barber, jr.): "that Henry Coffin late Master of the Sloop *Industry*, was taken by the Enemy five months ago and is now a prisoner in Newport. Capt. Coffin's Wife and Children are in such circumstances as to want him at home. Your petitioner begs your Honours will allow Captn Cockran to go to Providence and be exchanged for him." 154: "In Council, Jany 24, 1778. Read and Ordered that the Commissary of Prisoners be and hereby is directed to permit Capt. Cockran to proceed to Providence, . . . to go in a Flagg from thence to Newport, . . . provided the Honble Major Genl Spencer indulges him with a Flagg for that Purpose, he giving his Parole that upon his Arrival at Newport to procure the Liberation of Henry Coffin, late master of the Sloop *Industry*, detained as a Prisoner in New Port, or in case said Coffin should have been released, then to return a Person of Equal Rank or return Personally in the Term of one Month from the Date hereof."

1779 INDUSTRY, Brigantine. *Tons*, 75; *Guns*, 4, and 4 *swivels;*
Oct. 19
Men, 18.
Commander: Samuel Smith.
Petitioners: Samuel Bartlett, of Plymouth, and Isaiah Doane, of Boston.
M. A., **170**, 439.

1781 INDUSTRY, Schooner. *Tons*, 70; *Guns*, 12; *Men*, 15.
Aug. 9   *Commander:* Duncan Piper.
   Petition signed by William Wier in behalf of Capt. James Pearson & Co., of Cape Ann.
   Note. In *Naval Records of the Revolution* the captain's name is spelled Doneen Pyper.
   M. A., **171**, 448; C. C. **196**, VIII, 48.

1782 INDUSTRY, Schooner. *Guns*, 4; *Men*, 12.
May 25   *Commander:* Charles Cole, of Boston.
   C. C. **196**, VIII, 42; M. A., **172**, 160.

1779 INTREPID.
   Commander: —— ——.
   London Chronicle, May 15, 1779: "The *Intrepid* privateer, of Boston, has taken the *Nancy*, Woolman, from Jamaica to Georgia, and sent her into Salem."

1781 INTREPID. Brigantine, *Guns*, 4; *Men*, 12.
Sept. 14   *Commander:* Obadiah Rich, of Wellfleet.
   Owners: John Pringle and others, of Philadelphia.
   C. C. **196**, VIII, 54; M. A., **172**, 9.

1782 INTREPID, Ship. *Guns*, 20; *Men*, 160.
Apr. 8   *Commander:* Moses Brown of Newburyport.
   C. C. **196**, VIII, 52.

1782 IRIS, Ship. *Guns*, 8; *Men*, 20.
June 28   *Commander:* Stephen Clay, of Boston.
   C. C. **196**, VIII, 55.

1782 IRIS, Brigantine. *Guns*, 8; *Men*, 30.
July 4   *Commander:* Alexander Smiley, of Philadelphia.
   Owner: James Jarvis, of Boston.
   C. C. **196**, VIII, 56; M. A., **172**, 180; *Salem Gazette*, Apr. 17, 1783 (Richmond, Va., Mar. 15): "The brig *Iris*, a letter of marque of 8 six pounders and 42 men, commanded by Captain Smiley, which sailed from the Havana the 23d of January bound into this river, was chased on Cape Charles by the *Amphion* frigate and privateer *Admiral Digby* in the evening of the 7th ult. The *Iris* unexpectedly struck upon a small spit of sand, in coming round the Cape, and the *Digby*, being very near, grounded also within pistol shot; a few minutes previous to which an engagement began, which continued as they lay parallel to each other, about two hours and a half, when the

Digby, having been often hulled by the more fortunate shot of the *Iris*, had seven feet water in her hold and surrendered. She was commanded by Captain Laughton from New York, armed with fourteen double fortified four pounders, four short nine pounders and had 54 men on board, 4 of which were killed and 12 wounded in the action. Captain Wing and upwards of twenty American prisoners were on this occasion happily released. The *Iris* had her spars, rigging and sails much damaged and but four people wounded, who will probably recover. Exertions were made with great appearance of success the next day to heave off the *Iris*, but the wind and surf rising in the evening destroyed both vessels and exceedingly endangered the lives of about fifty people, who however were happily saved."

1782 IRIS, Ship. *Guns*, 9; *Men*, 18.
Dec. 23   *Commander:* Robert Rentoul, of Salem.
C. C. **196**, xv, 39; M. A., **172**, 263.

1782 ISABELLA, Brig. *Guns*, 2; *Men*, 10.
Sept. 19   *Commander:* Joseph Cunningham, of Boston.
C. C. **196**, viii, 58; M. A., **172**, 197.

1779 JACK, Ship. *Guns*, 14; *Men*, 75.
Sept. 14   *Commander:* Nathan Brown.
Bond: Continental, $10,000; State, £4000.
Bonders: Nathan Brown, mariner, principal; John Norris and Jon[a]th[an] Mason, of Salem, sureties.
Owners: John Norris and others.
Witnesses: John Leach, jr., Nat[haniel] West.
M. A., vi, 143, 146, **159**, 270, 327, **170**, 396; *Independent Chronicle*, Sept. 14, 1780 (Captured. See brig *Eagle*).

1781 JACK, Boat. *Guns*, 1; *Men*, 10.
Aug. 14   *Commander:* Nathaniel Arnold, of Salisbury.
Owners: Luke Webster and others, of Newburyport.
C. C. **196**, viii, 61.

1781 JACK, Ship. *Guns*, 14; *Men*, 60.
Sept. 6   *Commander:* David Ropes, of Salem.
Note. The 14-gun sloop in Felt's list was probably the same vessel.
C. C. **196**, viii, 62; M. A., **172**, 2; *Essex Inst. Hist. Coll.*, xlv, 182; *Salem Gazette*, July 11, 1782 (Narrative of

William Gray, first lieutenant of the *Jack*, of an engagement with the British brigantine *Observer*, 12 guns and 173 men): "It was our misfortune to have our worthy commander, Capt. Ropes, mortally wounded by the first broadside. I was slightly wounded at the same time. . . . The action was maintained on both sides, close, severe and without intermission, for upwards of two hours, in which time we had seven killed, several wounded, and many abandoned their quarters. Our rigging was so destroyed that not having command of our yards, the *Jack* fell with her larboard bow foul of the brig's starboard quarter, when the enemy made an attempt to board us, but they were repulsed by a very small number compared with them. We were engaged in this position about a quarter of an hour, in which time I received a wound by a bayonet fixed on a musket and which was hove with such force as, entering the fore part of my right thigh and passing through close to the bone, entered the carriage of a bow gun, where I was fastened, and it was out of my power to get clear till assisted by one of the prize masters. We then fell round and came with our broadsides to each other, when we renewed the action with powder and balls, but our match rope . . . being all expended, . . . we bore away, making a running fight. The brig being far superior in her number of men, was able to get soon repaired and completely ready to renew the action, indeed had constantly kept up a chasing fire, for we had not been out of reach of her musketry. She was now close alongside of us again with 50 men picked out for boarding. I therefore called Mr. Glover and the rest together and found we had but ten upon deck and two of them besides myself wounded. I had been repeatedly desired to strike, but I mentioned the sufferings of a prison ship and made use of every other argument in my power for continuing the engagement. All the foreigners however deserted their quarters every opportunity. At 2 o'clock P.M. on the 29th I had the inexpressible mortification to deliver up the vessel." See *The Connoisseur*, February, 1925, for a picture of this battle.

1782   JACKALL, Schooner. *Guns*, 8; *Men*, 35.
May 31   *Commander:* Adam Wellman, of Salem.
            C. C. **196**, VIII, 68; M. A., **172**, 169; Mar. Court Rec., 71.

1782   JACKALL, Schooner. *Guns*, 8; *Men*, 45.
Oct. 22   *Commander:* Thomas Holmes, of Salem.
            C. C. **196**, VIII, 66.

1780   JACK AND HARRY, Ship. *Guns*, 10; *Men*, 25.
Dec. 12   *Commander:* Nathaniel Nowell, of Newburyport.
            C. C. **196**, VIII, 63.

1782   JACK O'LANTHORN, Boat. *Tons*, 10; *Guns*, small arms;
Sept. 14   *Men*, 10.
            Commander: Edward Smith, jr.
            Petitioners: Edward Smith and others, of Salem.
            M. A., **172**, 194.

1779   JAMES, Ship. *Guns*, 6; *Men*, 25.
Jan. 12   *Commander:* Samuel Gill.
            Bond: Continental, $10,000; State, £4000.
            Bonders: Samuel Gill, mariner, principal; Isaac Sears
              and Paschal N[elson] Smith, of Boston, sureties.
            Owners: Isaac Sears and others.
            Witnesses: Elia[ki]m Raymond, Joseph Skillin.
            M. A., VI, 145, 148, **169**, 410.

1783   JAMES, Brigantine. *Guns*, 8; *Men*, 25.
Jan. 15   *Commander:* Ebenezer Atwood, of Cape Cod.
            Owner: Henry Mitchell, of Boston.
            C. C. **196**, VIII, 70; M. A., **172**, 280.

1781   JANUS, Ship. *Tons*, 150; *Guns*, 11; *Men*, 25.
May 14   *Commander:* John Clark.
            Petition signed by Nathaniel West in behalf of George
              and Joshua Dodge, of Salem.
                Note. In the *Naval Records of the Revolution* this vessel
                  is listed as the *James*, Capt. John Clarke. The ship
                  James on Felt's list was very likely the same vessel.
            M. A., **171**, 388; C. C. **196**, VIII, 71.

1779   JASON, Ship. *Guns*, 18; *Men*, 120.
June 2   *Commander:* John Manley.
            Bond: Continental, $10,000; State, £4000.
            Bonders: John Manley, mariner, principal; Mungo
              Mackay and Herman Brimmer, of Boston, sureties.
            Owners: Mungo Mackay and others.

Witnesses: Ivory Hovey, Samuel Avery.

M. A., VI, 149, 151, **139**, 251, **159**, 229, **170**, 148; *Boston Post,* July 31, 1779; *Boston Gazette,* Nov. 29, 1779; *Narrative of Joshua Davis* (Boston, 1811), 4–12: The *Jason,* recently captured from the British, sailed June 19 and soon encountered a thunder squall. "When the squall struck us it hove us all aback, when we clued down. In ten seconds the wind shifted on our starboard beam and shivered our sails. In a few seconds more the wind shifted on the starboard quarter and struck us with such force that hove us on our beam ends and carried away our three masts and bowsprit. She immediately righted and the squall went over." The ship was re-rigged at sea, continued her cruise, and fell in with two British privateer brigs of sixteen and eighteen guns. "The enemy hove upon the wind with his larboard tacks on board, run up his courses, hoisted his colours and gave us a broadside. Our Captain ordered the sailing master to get the best bower anchor out, so that the bill of it should take into the fore shrouds of the enemy. It was quickly done. The Captain ordered the helm hard a-port, which brought us alongside. The anchor caught their fore rigging. Our Captain then said: 'fire away, my boys.' We then gave them a broadside which tore her off side very much and killed and wounded some of them. The rest all ran below, except their captain, who stood on the deck like one amazed." The brig was then boarded and captured. "When we got disentangled we bore away for the other privateer, that began to run from us. We gave her a few shot from our bow chasers and she hove too," and surrendered. Some months later the *Jason* was chased by a British frigate of 28 guns and 230 men. "Our captain would not let us fire until they got abreast of us. They gave us another broadside, which cut away some of our running rigging and drove some of our men from the tops. We gave them a broadside which silenced two of her bow guns. The next we gave her cut away her maintopsail and drove her maintop-men out of it. Both sides continued the fire until one o'clock [A.M.]. Our studding sails and booms, our sails, rigging, yards, etc. were so cut away that they were useless. Lanterns were hung at the ship's side, between the guns, on nails, but they soon fell on deck at the shaking of the guns; which made it so dark that the men could not see to load the guns. They broke the fore hatches open and ran below. Our captain sent the sailing master forward to see why the bow guns did not keep the fire up, but he never returned. The captain then sent the master's mate on the same errand and he never returned. It was therefore thought needless to stand it any longer and the captain took the trumpet and called out for quarters." *Salem Gazette,* Nov. 29, 1781, Jan. 3, 1782. See ship *Thorn,* Captain Tucker.

1780 JASON, Ship. *Guns,* 10; *Men,* 25.
June 8   *Commander:* Simon Forrester.
    Bond: Continental, $10,000; State, £4000.
    Bonders: Simon Forrester, mariner of Salem, principal; Bartholomew Putnam and Jacob Ashton, merchants, sureties.
    Owners: Bartholomew Putnam and others, of Salem.
    Witnesses: N[athan] Goodale, W[illia]m Cleveland.
    M. A., VI, 147, 150, **171**, 173.

1780 JASON, Ship. *Guns,* 10; *Men,* 25.
Oct. 20   *Commander:* Thomas Dissmore, of Boston.
    C. C. **196**, VIII, 79; M. A., **171**, 294.

1781 JASON, Ship. *Guns,* 16; *Men,* 70.
Mar. 30   *Commander:* Charles Hamilton, of Salem.
    Note. In the petition the captain's name is spelled Hambleton.
    C. C. **196**, VIII, 80; M. A., **171**, 361; Felt, II, 273.

1779 JOHN, Brigantine. *Guns,* 4; *Men,* 12.
Dec. 7   *Commander:* Jonathan Ingersoll.
    Bond: Continental, $10,000; State, £4000.
    Bonders: Jonathan Ingersoll, mariner, principal; John Wait and John Adams, of Boston, sureties.
    Owners: John Heard and others, of Ipswich.
    Witnesses: Hugh McClallen, Jos[eph] Williams.
    M. A., VI, 135, 138, **171**, 40.

1782 JOHN, Ship. *Guns,* 16; *Men,* 90.
    Commander: Jonathan Ingersoll.
    Essex Institute. Miscellaneous Ship Papers.

1779 JOHN AND SALLY, Schooner. *Guns*, 6; *Men*, 18.
Aug. 14   Commander: Benjamin Humphreys.
    Bond: Continental, $5000; State, £4000.
    Bonders: Benjamin Humphreys, principal; John Wait [signed Waitt] and Thomas Bootman, jr. [signed Buttman], sureties.
    Owner: John Waitt, of Marblehead.
    Witnesses: Sam[ue]l Swett, jr., Jno. Dall.
        M. A., VI, 154, 155, 170, 327.

1780 JOHN AND SALLY, Brigantine. *Tons*, 80; *Guns*, 6; *Men*, 14.
May 6   Commander: Benjamin Humphreys.
    Bond: Continental, $5000; State, £4000.
    Bonders: Benjamin Humphries [signed Humphreys], principal; John Wait [signed Waitt], of Marblehead, and John Wait of Boston, sureties.
    Owners: John Waitt and Samuel Wait [Waitt?], of Marblehead.
    Witness: John Avery, jr.
        M. A., VI, 156, 157, 171, 151.

1779 JOHNSON SMITH, Brigantine.
Jan. 6   Commander: Andrew Paton.
    Bond: State, £2000.
    Bonders: John Bradford, of Boston, "the major part of the owners," and Andrew Patten [signed Paton], mariner.
    Witnesses: George Lobb, David Dickson.
        M. A., 139, 241 (Bond not to enlist any man in New England outside of Massachusetts).

1780 JONATHAN, Sloop.
Oct.   Commander: Christopher Babbidge, of Salem.
        M. A., XL, 106.

1777 JOSEPH, Sloop.
    Commander: Thomas West.
    Boston Gazette, Jan. 13, 1777.

1777 JOSEPH, Brigantine. *Guns*, 8; *Men*, 25.
July 23   Commander: Christopher Babbidge, of Salem.
        C. C. 196, VIII, 105; *Boston Gazette*, June 15, 1778.

1781 JOSEPH, Brigantine. *Guns*, 6; *Men*, 20.
Sept. 12   Commander: Peter Wells, of Boston.
        C. C. 196, VIII, 107; M. A., 172, 7.

1782 JOSEPH, Brigantine. *Guns*, 8; *Men*, 15.
July 19   *Commander:* Henry Higginson, of Salem.
   Owners: Ebenezer Parsons and others, of Boston.
   C. C. **196**, VIII, 106.

1780 JUDITH, Sloop. *Guns*, 8; *Men*, 20.
June 9   *Commander:* George Southward.
   Bond: Continental, $10,000; State, £4000.
   Bonders: George Southward, mariner, principal; Will[ia]m Creed, of Salem, and John Shattuck, of Boston, merchants, sureties.
   Owner: William Creed.
   Witnesses: Tho[ma]s Lee, Stephen H. Gray.
   M. A., VI, 158, 159, **171**, 174.

1781 JULIET, Brigantine. *Guns*, 6; *Men*, 15.
July 24   *Commander:* Samuel Smith, of Boston.
   C. C. **196**, VIII, 108; M. A., **171**, 441.

1780 JULIUS CAESAR, Brig. *Guns*, 10; *Men*, 50.
May 11   *Commander:* Nathaniel Bently.
   Bond: Continental, $5000; State, £4000.
   Bonders: Nath[anie]l Bentley [signed Bently], mariner, principal; John Fletcher and Robert Stevenson, sureties.
   Owners: Wingate Newman and others, merchants of Newburyport.
   Witnesses: Jo[seph] Swasey, John Rand.
   M. A., VI, 139, 142, **171**, 158.

1781 JULIUS CAESAR, Ship. *Guns*, 14; *Men*, 25.
Jan. 17   *Commander:* Anthony Knap, of Newburyport.
   C. C. **196**, VIII, 111.

1782 JULIUS CAESAR, Ship. *Guns*, 14; *Men*, 40.
Apr. 11   *Commander:* Jonathan Haraden, of Salem.
   C. C. **196**, VIII, 110; M. A., **172**, 145; Felt, II, 274, 275.

1783 JULIUS CAESAR, Ship. *Guns*, 14; *Men*, 100.
Mar. 4   *Commander:* Thomas Benson, of Salem.
   C. C. **196**, VIII, 109; M. A., **172**, 309.

1781 JUNIUS, Ship. *Guns*, 10; *Men*, 25.
Aug. 13   *Commander:* Nathaniel West, of Salem.
   C. C. **196**, VIII, 112.

1780 JUNIUS BRUTUS, Ship. *Guns*, 20; *Men*, 120.
May 23   *Commander:* John Leach.
  Bond: Continental, $10,000; State, £4000.
  Bonders: John Leach, mariner of Salem, principal; Andrew Cabot, of Beverly, and Henry Rust, of Salem, merchants, sureties.
  Owners: Joshua Ward, Henry Rust, and others, of Salem.
  Witness: Thomas Prince.
  M. A., VI, 141, 144, **171**, 166; Felt, II, 270.

1780 JUNIUS BRUTUS, Ship. *Guns*, 20; *Men*, 120.
Aug. 23   *Commander:* John Brooks, of Salem.
  C. C. **196**, IX, 2, 3; M. A., **171**, 260; *Essex Inst. Hist. Coll.*, I (1859), 111 (list of crew); *Salem Gazette*, June 26, 1781: "Yesterday arrived in this harbour the privateer ship *Junius Brutus*, Capt. John Brooks, from a successful cruise, having captured 5 prizes."

1781 JUNIUS BRUTUS, Ship.
  Commander: Robert Leach [Leech].
  Boston Gazette, Apr. 30, 1781.

1781 JUNIUS BRUTUS, Ship. *Guns*, 20; *Men*, 120.
Oct. 25   *Commander:* Nathaniel Brookhouse, of Salem.
  C. C. **196**, IX, 1; M. A., **172**, 44; *Salem Gazette*, Feb. 21, 1782: "Last Tuesday arrived at a safe port the prize ship *Experiment*, Daniel Sinclair late master, captured on the 23d ult. on her passage from England to Jamaica by the privateer ship *Junius Brutus*, Capt. Brookhouse, of this port."

1782 JUNIUS BRUTUS, Ship. *Guns*, 18; *Men*, 100.
June 15   *Commander:* John Brooks, of Salem.
  C. C. **196**, IX, 4; M. A., **172**, 175; Felt, II, 272, 273; *Salem Gazette*, Oct. 10, 1782: "By several men who escaped from Newfoundland and arrived here since our last, we have advice that the privateer ship *Junius Brutus*, Capt. John Brooks, the *Raven*, Capt. Needham, and another privateer, all belonging to this port, have been lately captured by the enemy and carried to that island." *Boston Gazette*, Oct. 21, 1782: "Last Wednesday evening arrived at Salem a Cartel, in 12 days from Newfoundland, and bro't in 292 American prisoners, among whom are the crews of the *Junius Brutus* and other privateers from that port, lately captured by the enemy."

1779   JUNO, Ship. *Guns*, 12; *Men*, 30.
Oct. 6   *Commander:* Samuel Gill.
         Bond: Continental, ——; State, £4000.
         Bonders: Samuel Gill, mariner, principal. [Sureties omitted; bonds signed by Joseph Russell and Paschal N. Smith.]
         Owner: Leonard Jarvis, of Boston.
         Witnesses: Elia[ki]m Raymond, Ben[jamin] Jarvis.
             M. A., VI, 133, 136, **170**, 405.

1780   JUNO, Ship. *Guns*, 12; *Men*, 25.
Oct. 20   *Commander:* William Haydon, of Boston.
             C. C. **196**, IX, 9; M. A., **171**, 295.

1781   JUNO, Brigantine. *Guns*, 6; *Men*, 17.
Sept. 11   *Commander:* Philip Aubin, of Newburyport.
             C. C. **196**, IX, 5.

1782   JUNO, Brig. *Guns*, 12; *Men*, 16.
Aug. 20   *Commander:* John Felt, of Salem.
             C. C. **196**, IX, 8.

1779   JUPITER, Brigantine. *Guns*, 6; *Men*, 12.
Nov. 20   *Commander:* Peter Roberts.
         Bond: Continental, $10,000; State, £4000.
         Bonders: Peter Roberts, mariner, principal; Jonathan Titcomb and Stephen Cross, of Salem and Newbury, sureties.
         Owners: Jonathan Titcomb and others, of Newburyport.
         Witnesses: Christopher Bassett, Benaiah Titcomb.
             M. A., VI, 137, 140, **171**, 27.

1782   JUPITER, Ship. *Guns*, 14; *Men*, 40.
Apr. 27   *Commander:* William Orne, of Salem.
             C. C. **196**, IX, 12; M. A., **172**, 144.

1781   KENSINGTON, Brigantine. *Guns*, 14; *Men*, 60.
May 7   *Commander:* Samuel Smith.
         Owners: John Pringle & Co., of Philadelphia.
             C. C. **196**, IX, 16; M. A., **171**, 385 (May 7, 1781. Petition of Thomas Russell, of Boston, for commission for Samuel Smith).

1781   KENSINGTON, Brigantine. *Tons*, 150; *Guns*, 14; *Men*, 25.
Oct. 23   *Commander:* James Degge.
         Petitioner: Thomas Russell, of Boston.
         Owners: John Pringle & Co., of Philadelphia.

Note. In *Naval Records of the Revolution* the first *Kensington* is listed as a Massachusetts vessel, the second as a Pennsylvania vessel. They are evidently the same.
M. A., **172**, 41 (Boston, Oct. 23, 1781. Petition to the Governor and Council of Massachusetts for a commission for James Degge); C. C. **196**, IX, 14 (Oct. 24, 1781).

1780 KING HENDRICK, Schooner. *Guns*, 6; *Men*, 25.
June 12   *Commander:* Shubael Gorham.
Bond: Continental, $5000; State, £4000.
Bonders: Shubael Gorham, mariner, principal; Stephen Higginson and Ebenezer Parsons, merchants of Boston, sureties.
Owners: Stephen Higginson and Ebenezer Parsons.
Witnesses: George Burroughs, David Spear, jr.
M. A., VI, 160, 161, **171**, 175.

1777 KING HEROD, Schooner. *Guns*, 10.
Commander: William Baker.
London Chronicle, Apr. 22, 1777. See *Black Eagle*.

1782 LADY GREENE, Brig.
Commander: —— ——.
Salem Gazette, Jan. 17, 1782: "A prize brig of four carriage guns is arrived at a safe port, captured by the privateer brig *Lady Greene*."

1778 LADY'S FAVORITE, Schooner.
Oct. 28   *Commander:* John Guliker.
Bond: State, £2000.
Bonders: Thomas Adams, merchant of Boston, David Clark, of Newton, and John Guliker, mariner.
Owners: Thomas Adams and David Clark.
Witnesses: Ph[ilip?] Ryley, jr., Henry Alline.
M. A., **139**, 223 (Bond not to enlist any man in New England outside of Massachusetts).

1776 LADY WASHINGTON, Schooner. *Guns*, 4, and 12 *swivels;*
May 7   *Men*, 20.
Commander: Joseph Cunningham.
Bond: Continental, $5000.
Bonders: Joseph Cunningham, Ebenezer Dorr, and Joseph Gardner, all of Boston.

Owner: John G. Frazier, of the Parish of St. Johns, County of King William, Virginia.
Witnesses: Daniel Malcom, Henry Prentiss.

M. A., VII, 291, 164, 325 (Apr. 22, 1776. In the petition the owner's name is spelled Frazer. He apparently intended at first to command the vessel himself); *Boston Gazette,* May 27, 1776: Captain James Mugford, commanding the schooner *Franklin,* of Washington's Fleet in Boston harbor, on May 19 "in company with capt. Cunningham in the *Lady Washington,* a small privateer armed with swivels, blunderbusses and muskets, fell down in order to go out in the bay. The enemy observed their sailing and fitted out a fleet of boats for the purpose of surprizing and taking them in the night; and the *Franklin's* running aground in the Gut gave them a good opportunity for executing their plan. The *Lady Washington* came to anchor near capt. Mugford and between 9 and 10 o'clock he discovered a number of boats which he hailed and received for answer that they were from Boston. . . . Capt. Mugford instantly fired and was followed by all his men, and cutting his cable bro't his broadside to bear, when he discharged his cannon loaded with musket ball directly in upon them. Before the cannon could be charged a second time, 2 or 3 boats were alongside, each of them supposed to have as many men on board as the *Franklin,* which were only 21, including officers. By the best accounts there were not less than 13 boats in all, many of them armed with swivels and having on board, at the lowest computation, 200 men. Capt. Mugford and his men plied those alongside with fire arms and spears and with such intrepidity, activity and success, that two boats were soon sunk and all the men either killed or drowned. But while the heroic Mugford, with outstretched arms, was righteously dealing death and destruction to our base and unnatural enemies, he received a fatal ball in his body, which in a few minutes put a period to a life from which, had it been spared, his oppressed country would undoubtedly have reaped very eminent advantages. . . . The number of boats which attacked the *Franklin* was about 8 or 9. The remainder, to the number of 4 or 5, at the same time attacked Capt. Cunningham in the *Lady Washington*, who then had on board only 6 men besides himself. This brave little company gave the boats such a warm reception that the enemy were soon glad to give over the contest. . . ." See *Mass. Hist. Soc. Collections*, LXXV, 270.

1777 LADY WASHINGTON, Sloop.
  Commander: Ishmael Hardy.
  M. A., **159**, 89 (The *Lady Washington* captured the ship *Weathrill*, Jan. 24, 1777, and brought her into Boston Mar. 5, 1777. Francis Dana, of Cambridge, appeared in Court Mar. 21, in behalf of Captain Hardy); *Boston Gazette*, Apr. 7, 1777.

1777 LADY WASHINGTON, Sloop. *Guns*, 12; *Men*, 40.
Aug. 12 *Commander:* Richard Weeden.
  Bond: Continental, $5000.
  Bonders: Richard Weeden, principal; Samuel Brown and Samuel Vernon, sureties — all of Providence, R. I.
  Owners: Samuel Brown and Samuel Vernon.
  Witnesses: Thomas Russell, Elisha Ballard.
  M. A., VII, 296, **139**, 139 (Aug. 23, 1777. Bond to enlist no inhabitant of New England outside of Massachusetts. Weeden and Brown "both residing in Boston"), **167**, 156 (Aug. 12, 1777. Petition of Brown and Vernon, of Providence, to Massachusetts Council for commission).

1778 LADY WASHINGTON, Sloop. *Guns*, 6; *Men*, 20.
Sept. 23 *Commander:* Benjamin Dunn.
  Bond: Continental, $5000; State, £4000.
  Bonders: Benjamin Dunn, mariner, principal; Henry Mitchell and Edmund Dunkin, of Boston, sureties.
  Owners: Henry Mitchell and others.
  Witnesses: Nat[haniel] Barber, Jno. Dall.
  M. A., VII, 293, 294, **169**, 165.

1782 LADY WASHINGTON, Brigantine. *Guns*, 6; *Men*, 15.
July 20 *Commander:* William White, of Boston.
  C. C. **196**, IX, 30.

1783 LADY WASHINGTON, Brigantine. *Guns*, 6; *Men*, 15.
Jan. 16 *Commander:* Naler Hatch, of Boston.
  C. C. **196**, IX, 29; M. A., **172**, 281.

1780 LA MANETTE, Schooner.
    Commander: Jean Baptiste [John Baptist] Millet.
    Note. This vessel seems also to have been called *Manete.*
    Boston Gazette, Sept. 4, 1780.

1776 LANGDON, Schooner. *Guns*, 6, and 10 *swivels; Men*, 50.
Aug. 28   *Commander:* Jacob Allen.
    Bond: Continental, $5000.
    Bonders: Jacob Allen, principal; John Codman and David Peirce [signed Pearce], sureties.
    Owners: John Codman, of Boston, and others belonging to Cape Ann.
    Witnesses: John Smith, Joseph Allen.
    M. A., VI, 208, **165**, 152, **181**, 213.

1776 LANGDON, Schooner. *Guns*, 6; *Men*, 50.
Oct. 22   *Commander:* Samuel Robinson.
    Bond: Continental, $5000.
    Bonders: Samuel Robinson, principal; David Pearce and John Smith, sureties — all of Cape Ann.
    Owners: David Pearce, John Smith, and others.
    Witnesses: Samuel Whittemore, Joseph Allen.
    M. A., VI, 215, **165**, 368.

1781 LANGUEDOCK, Schooner. *Tons*, 40; *Guns*, 4, and 8 *swivels;*
Mar. 16   *Men*, 25.
    Commander: Jeremiah Hegerty.
    Owners: John Moriarty and others, of Salem.
    Note. The captain's name is variously spelled Haggerty, Heggerty, Higgerty.
    C. C. **196**, IX, 33; M. A., **171**, 351.

1781 LANGUEDOC, Schooner. *Guns*, 4; *Men*, 25.
July 3   *Commander:* John Augusta Dunn, of Salem.
    C. C. **196**, IX, 32; M. A., **171**, 420.

1781 LANGUEDOC, Schooner. *Guns*, 8; *Men*, 25.
Nov. 2   *Commander:* Reuben Yearman, of Salem.
    Note. In *Naval Records of the Revolution* the captain's name is spelled Yeomans.
    C. C. **196**, IX, 34; M. A., **172**, 57; Felt, II, 272.

1781 LANGUEDOC. *Guns*, 6; *Men*, 25.
    Commander: Benjamin Hammond.
    Salem Gazette, Jan. 3, 1782: "Last Friday the *Languedoc* privateer, Capt. Hammond, arrived here from a cruise." Essex Institute, Miscellaneous Ship Papers.

1782 LANGUEDOC.
    Commander: Zenas Cook.
    Boston Gazette, June 3, 1782; *Salem Gazette*, May 23, 1783: "Last week was sent into port by the *Languedoc*, Capt. Cook, of this port, a re-captured sloop."

1778 LARK, Schooner. *Guns*, 12 *swivels; Men*, 30.
Mar. 18   *Commander:* William Munday.
    Bond: Continental, $5000; State, £500.
    Bonders: William Munday, principal; John Dutch and Jerathmeel Peirce, of Salem, sureties.
    Owners: Jerathmeel Peirce and John Dutch.
    Witness: D[aniel] Hopkins.
    M. A., VI, 194, 196, **168**, 223.

1781 LARK, Brigantine. *Guns*, 4; *Men*, 13.
June 28   *Commander:* Robert Stonehouse, of Boston.
    C. C. **196**, IX, 39; M. A., **171**, 418.

1781 LARK, Brigantine. *Guns*, 4; *Men*, 12.
Oct. 1   *Commander:* Joseph Tilden, of Boston.
    C. C. **196**, IX, 40; M. A., **172**, 15.

1782 LARK, Brigantine. *Guns*, 4; *Men*, 15.
May 11   *Commander:* Offin Boardman, jr., of Newburyport.
    C. C. **196**, IX, 35.

1782 LARK, Sloop. *Guns*, 10; *Men*, 15.
June 13   *Commander:* Thomas Newson, of Wethersfield, Conn.
    Note. Owned in Connecticut, but called a Massachusetts vessel in *Naval Records of the Revolution*.
    C. C. **196**, IX, 38.

1782 LARK, Schooner. *Guns*, 12 *swivels*.
    Commander: N. Tilden.
    Essex Institute, Miscellaneous Ship Papers.

1775 LEE, Schooner.
Oct. 29   *Commander:* John Manley.
    Note. Afterwards commanded by Daniel Waters. Washington's Fleet.

1776 LEE, Schooner. *Guns*, 8; *Men*, 45.
Nov. 27   *Commander:* Nathaniel Odiorne.
    Bond: Continental, $5000.
    Bonders: Nathaniel Odiorne, of Portsmouth, N. H., principal; Jonathan Jackson, of Newburyport, and John Adams, of Boston, sureties.

LANGUEDOC — LEE   203

  Owners: John Coffin Jones, Jonas Marquand, and others, of Newburyport.
  Witnesses: Alex[ander] Gray, Seth Loring.
  M. A., VI, 213, **166**, 66.

1777   LEE, Schooner. *Guns,* 10; *Men,* 54.
Mar. 12   *Commander:* John Skimmer.
  Bond: Continental, not stated.
  Bonders: John Skimmer, Tho[ma]s Jackson and John Bradford.
  Owner: "The United States of America."
  Witnesses: John F. Osgood, W[illia]m Addiscott.
   Note. Formerly of Washington's Fleet — see above (Oct. 29, 1775).
   M. A., VI, 216, **159**, 104, 108, **166**, 327 (Petition of John Bradford, Continental Agent, that Capt. Skimmer be commissioned as successor to Capt. Waters).

1778   LEE, Schooner. *Guns,* 10; *Men,* 50.
May 4   *Commander:* John Hyer.
  Bond: Continental, $5000; State, £4000.
  Bonders: John Hyer, principal; Dan[ie]l Martin and Paul D[udley] Sergeant [signed Sargent], of Boston, sureties.
  Owners: Paul Dudley Sargent, Joseph Barrell, Tho[ma]s Adams, and Daniel Martin, of Boston.
  Witness: William Baker, jr.
   M. A., VI, 174, 175, **139**, 169, **168**, 238; *Independent Chronicle*, Sept. 3, 1778: "Saturday last returned into Port from a Cruise the Privateer Schooner *Lee,* commanded by Capt. Hyer, during which she has taken six prizes."

1778   LEE, Schooner. *Guns,* 10; *Men,* 50.
Nov. 4   *Commander:* William Steward.
  Bond: Continental, $5000; State, £4000.
  Bonders: William Steward, principal; Job Prince and Thomas Adams, of Boston, sureties.
  Owners: Job Prince and Thomas Adams.
  Witness: Jno. Dall.
   M. A., VI, 206, 209, **139**, 229, **169**, 290.

1779   LEE, Schooner. *Guns,* 6, and 4 *swivels; Men,* 23.
June 3   *Commander:* James Thompson.
  Bond: Continental, $5000; State, £4000.

Bonders: James Thompson, of Boston, mariner, principal; Thomas Adams and Daniel Martin, of Boston, sureties.
Owners: Daniel Martin and others.
Witnesses: Fran[cis] Archbald, Joseph Wheaton.
M. A., VI, 187, 211, **170**, 152.

1780 LEE, Schooner. *Guns,* 10; *Men,* 14.
May 25   *Commander:* James Hopkins, of Connecticut.
Owners: Adams & Dexter, of Boston.
Note. Called a Connecticut vessel in *Naval Records of the Revolution.*
C. C. **196**, IX, 45.

1782 LEE, Schooner. *Guns,* 6; *Men,* 25.
Mar. 25   *Commander:* John Conway, of Marblehead.
C. C. **196**, IX, 44; M. A., **172**, 121.

1782 LEE, Schooner. *Guns,* 6; *Men,* 30.
July 12   *Commander:* William James, of Marblehead.
C. C. **196**, IX, 46.

1778 LEXINGTON, Schooner. *Guns,* 16 swivels; *Men,* 25.
Apr. 10   *Commander:* Joseph Cook.
Bond: Continental, $5000; State, £4000.
Bonders: Joseph Cooke [signed Cook], principal; Elias Hasket Derby [and Ichabod Nichols], of Salem, sureties.
Owners: Elias Hasket Derby and others.
Witnesses: Nathaniel Silsbee, Nehemiah Holt.
M. A., VI, 172, 173, **168**, 253.

1778 LEXINGTON, Schooner.
May 8   *Commander:* David Masury.
Petitioner: Marshal Mansfield.
M. A., Council Records.

1778 LEXINGTON, Schooner.
Commander: Benjamin Cook.
Boston Gazette, Nov. 2, 1778.

1779 LEXINGTON, Schooner. *Guns,* 4; *Men,* 12.
Apr. 27   *Commander:* Nicholas Lamprel.
Bond: Continental, $5000; State, £4000.
Bonders: Nicholas Lamprel, of Salem, principal; Jonathan Ingersoll and Job Prince, jr., of Salem and Boston, sureties.
Owners: Jonathan Ingersoll and others.
Witnesses: Timothy Penny, Ladurantie.
M. A., VI, 162, 163, **170**, 70.

1780 LEXINGTON, Brig. *Guns*, 6; *Men*, 15.
Apr. 18   *Commander:* David Smith, jr.
    Bond: Continental, $5000; State, £4000.
    Bonders: David Smith, jr., mariner, principal; Elias Hasket Derby and Nathaniel Silsbee, sureties.
    Owner: Elias Hasket Derby, merchant of Salem.
    Witness: Nehemiah Holt.
        M. A., VI, 218, 219, **171**, 130.

1781 LEXINGTON, Brig. *Guns*, 10; *Men*, 20.
Nov. 26   *Commander:* David Smith, jr., of Salem.
        C. C. **196**, IX, 51; M. A., **172**, 84.

1782 LEXINGTON, Brigantine. *Guns*, 14; *Men*, 50.
May 9   *Commander:* Benjamin Crowninshield, of Salem.
        C. C. **196**, IX, 50; M. A., **172**, 154.

1779 L'HEUREUSE RENCONTRE, Schooner. *Guns*, 6 *swivels; Men,*
Sept. 30   20.
    Commander: Jean Dàguin.
    Bond: Continental, $5000; State, £4000.
    Bonders: John Daggin [signed Jean Dàguin], mariner, principal; Peter Durbergier [signed P^{ere} Dubergier] and Dansel [signed D'Ansel], of Boston, sureties.
    Owner: Pierre Dubergier.
    Witnesses: Dombléder, B^t Merlino Desaint Pry.
        M. A., VI, 178, 179, **170**, 412.

1776 LIBERTY, Sloop. *Guns*, not stated; *Men*, 37.
Mar. 7   *Commander:* Benjamin Smith.
        Note. This vessel, "a small sloop called the *Liberty*," was hastily manned at Edgartown for the capture of a British transport, which was successfully accomplished.
        M. A., **181**, 78, **194**, 275, 281; Banks, *History of Martha's Vineyard*, 405, 406.

1776 LIBERTY, Schooner. *Guns*, 6; *Men*, 25.
Sept. 24   *Commander:* Ebenezer Peirce.
    Bond: Continental, $5000.
    Bonders: Ebenezer Peirce and Samuel Webb, mariners, and Samuel Flagg, merchant, all of Salem.
    Owners: Samuel Webb, Samuel Flagg, and others.
    Witnesses: Joseph Lambert, Daniel Hopkins.
        M. A., VI, 210, **165**, 262.

1778   LIBERTY, Brigantine.
       Commander: Thomas Herbert.
       Boston Gazette, Feb. 23, 1778.

1781   LIBERTY, Schooner. *Guns,* 4; *Men,* 25.
Mar. 17   *Commander:* William Preston, of Newburyport.
       C. C. **196**, IX, 57.

1781   LIBERTY, Ship. *Guns,* 4; *Men,* 12.
Dec. 22   *Commander:* William Russell, of Newburyport.
       C. C. **196**, IX, 58.

1782   LIBERTY, Ship. *Guns,* 6; *Men,* 20.
May 23   *Commander:* William Russell, of Newburyport.
       C. C. **196**, IX, 59.

1780   LIGHTFOOT, Brigantine. *Tons,* 60; *Guns,* 4; *Men,* 10.
Feb. 22   *Commander:* Bradbury Saunders.
       Petitioner: Daniel Sargent, of Boston.
       M. A., **171**, 182.

1779   LINCOLN, Galley. *Guns,* 4 *swivels.*
       Commander: Joseph Ingraham.
       Massachusetts State Navy.
       M. A., **271**, 187.

1777   LION, Brigantine. *Guns,* 18; *Men,* 130.
Aug. 19   *Commander:* Ishmael Hardy.
       Bond: Continental, $5000.
       Bonders: Ishmael Hardy, mariner of Salem, principal; Tho[mas] Gardner, jr., and Jona[than] Peale, jr. [signed Peele], merchants of Salem, sureties.
       Owner: Jonathan Peele, jr.
       Witnesses: Miles Greenwood, William Young.
       Note. The vessel's name is spelled *Lyon.*
       M. A., VI, 191, **167**, 168.

1777   LION, Brigantine. *Guns,* 16; *Men,* 100.
Nov. 28   *Commander:* Benjamin Warren.
       Bond: Continental, $10,000; State, £500.
       Bonders: Benjamin Warren, principal; Jonathan Peele, jr., and John Fisk, of Salem, sureties.
       Owners: Jonathan Peele, jr., John Fisk and others.
       Witnesses: Samuel Buffum, Nathaniel Cheever.
       Note. The name is spelled *Lyon.*
       M. A., VI, 197, 198, **168**, 49.

1778 LION, Brig. *Guns*, 16; *Men*, 100.
June 9 *Commander:* John Carnes.
  Bond: Continental, $10,000; State, £4000.
  Bonders: John Carnes, mariner, principal; Jonathan Peele, jr., and Thomas Mason, of Salem, sureties.
  Owners: Jonathan Peele and others.
  Witnesses: George Williams, Samuel Very.
    Note. The name is spelled *Lyon.*
  M. A., VI, 184, 185, **168**, 360.

1781 LION, Brig. *Guns*, 10; *Men*, 45.
July 3 *Commander:* Jonathan Mason, of Salem.
  C. C. **196**, IX, 65; M. A., **171**, 422.

1781 LION, Ship. *Guns*, 22; *Men*, 120.
July 14 *Commander:* Wingate Newman, of Newburyport.
    Note. The name is spelled *Lyon.*
  C. C. **196**, IX, 104; M. A., XL, 62, **171**, 431.

1782 LION, Ship. *Tons*, 400; *Guns*, 26; *Men*, 90.
Mar. 14 *Commander:* William Tuck, of Salem.
    Note. The name is spelled *Lyon.* Petition dated Feb. 14; granted Mar. 6.
  C. C. **196**, IX, 106; M. A., **172**, 114.

1782 LITTLE BACHELOR, Sloop. *Guns*, 4; *Men*, 20.
Dec. 6 *Commander:* Miller Johnston, of Boston.
  Owner: John Lawhorn, of North Carolina.
  C. C. **196**, IX, 67; M. A., **172**, 249.

1778 LITTLE BETSEY, Brigantine. *Tons*, 150; *Guns*, 14; *Men*, 70.
Feb. 24 *Commander:* Jean Baptiste Hugounene.
  Petitioner: Jean Baptiste Hugounene, of Martinique.
  Bonders (proposed): James Price and William McCarty, merchants.
  M. A., **168**, 328, 329.

1781 LITTLE DAN, Schooner. *Guns*, 4; *Men*, 25.
Aug. 9 *Commander:* Daniel Young, of Cape Ann.
  C. C. **196**, IX, 69; M. A., **171**, 450.

1779 LITTLE JOHN, Sloop. *Tons*, 40; *Guns*, 6, and 8 *swivels;*
Aug. 23 *Men*, 30.
  Commander: Charles Anderson.
  Petitioners: John Wait and others, of Boston.
  M. A., **170**, 350.

1781 LITTLE PORGA, Brigantine. *Guns,* 10; *Men,* 60.
Apr. 30   *Commander:* William Armstrong, of Newburyport.
   C. C. **196**, IX, 74; M. A., **171**, 380.

1781 LITTLE VINCENT, Sloop. *Guns,* 4; *Men,* 6.
Apr. 27   *Commander:* René Chaloche, of Boston.
   C. C. **196**, IX, 76; M. A., **171**, 379.

1781 LITTLE VINCENT, Sloop. *Guns,* 10; *Men,* 16.
Dec. 4   *Commander:* Israel F. Ober, of Beverly.
   Owners: E[tienne] Dombléder and others, of Boston.
   C. C. **196**, IX, 77; M. A., **172**, 78.

1781 LITTLE VINCENT, Brig. *Guns,* 8; *Men,* 25.
   Commander: N[athan?] Poor.
   Emmons, 150.

1778 LITTLE WEASEL, Schooner. *Guns,* 4, and 10 *swivels; Men,* 20.
Aug. 7   *Commander:* Abel Gore.
   Bond: Continental, $5000; State, £4000.
   Bonders: Abel Gore, mariner, principal; Mungo Mackay and [William Shattuck], of Boston, sureties.
   Owners: Mungo Mackay and William Shattuck.
   Witnesses: William Baker, Jno. Dall.
   Note. Name spelled *Weesel* and *Wheesel.*
   M. A., VI, 202, 205, **169**, 68.

1777 LIVELY, Schooner. *Guns,* 6; *Men,* 25.
July 4   *Commander:* Michael Dupuy, of Marblehead.
   Owner: Nathaniel Tracy, of Newburyport.
   C. C. **196**, IX, 85.

1777 LIVELY, Schooner. *Guns,* 2; *Men,* 40.
Oct. 7   *Commander:* Thomas Benson.
   Bond: Continental, $5000; State, £500.
   Bonders: Thomas Benson, of Salem, principal; Samuel Page and Edward Norris, sureties.
   Owners: Samuel Page and Walter P[rice] Bartlett, of Salem.
   Witnesses: Nathaniel Cudworth, Edward Baker.
   M. A., VI, 189, 192, **167**, 317.

1777 LIVELY, Schooner. *Guns,* 2, and 14 *swivels; Men,* 30.
Dec. 22   *Commander:* Thomas Simmons.
   Bond: Continental, $5000; State, £500.
   Bonders: Thomas Simmons, principal, Samuel Page and Walter [Price] Bartlett, of Salem, sureties.

LITTLE PORGA — LIVELY

    Owners: Samuel Page and Walter P. Bartlett.
    Witnesses: Joshua Grafton, D[aniel] Hopkins.
    M. A., VI, 193, 195, **168**, 107.

1778   LIVELY, Schooner. *Guns*, 2, and 14 *swivels; Men*, 14.
Apr. 14   *Commander:* Robert Brookhouse.
    Bond: Continental, $5000; State, £4000.
    Bonders: Robert Brookhouse, principal; Samuel Page and Josiah Orne, sureties — all of Salem.
    Owners: Samuel Page and Josiah Orne.
    Witness: D[aniel] Hopkins.
    M. A., VI, 186, 188, **168**, 258.

1778   LIVELY, Schooner. *Guns*, 14 *swivels; Men*, 40.
Aug. 14   *Commander:* David Ropes.
    Bond: Continental, $5000; State, £4000.
    Bonders: David Ropes, principal; Peter Lander and John Dutch, sureties — all of Salem.
    Owners: Peter Lander and John Dutch.
    Witnesses: Richard Ward, T. White.
        M. A., VI, 180, 181, **169**, 74; *Essex Inst. Hist. Coll.*, XLV, 225 (Captured Nov. 10, 1778, off Jeddore, N. S., by the armed sloop *Howe*).

1779   LIVELY, Brigantine. *Guns*, 6; *Men*, 16.
May 13   *Commander:* John Adams.
    Bond: Continental, $5000; State, £4000.
    Bonders: John Adams, mariner, principal; Samuel Page and Jonathan Watson, of Salem and Boston, sureties.
    Owner: Samuel Page.
    Witness: William Baker, jr.
    M. A., VI, 170, 171, **159**, 309, **170**, 100.

1779   LIVELY, Brigantine. *Guns*, 6; *Men*, 26.
Dec. 20   *Commander:* John Leach.
    Bond: Continental, $5000; State, £4000.
    Bonders: John Leach, mariner, principal; Stephen Bruce and Samuel Page, of Boston and Salem, sureties.
    Owner: Samuel Page.
    Witness: William Baker, jr.
    M. A., VI, 166, 167, **171**, 48.

1780   LIVELY, Brigantine. *Guns*, 6; *Men*, 16.
Aug. 7   *Commander:* Benjamin Dunham.
    Bond: Continental, $5000; State, £4000.

Bonders: Benjamin Dunham, mariner, of Salem, principal; William Tuck and Francis Clarke, sureties.
Owners: Samuel Page and others, of Salem.
Witnesses: C. Rea, Jos[eph] Henfield.
M. A., VI, 168, 169, **171**, 228.

1781 LIVELY, Schooner. *Guns,* 8; *Men,* 35.
May 21   *Commander:* George Ashby, of Salem.
C. C. **196**, IX, 79; M. A., **171**, 392.

1781 LIVELY, Ship. *Guns,* 14; *Men,* 30.
July 5   *Commander:* Nathaniel Goodwin, of Boston.
C. C. **196**, IX, 86; M. A., **171**, 424.

1781 LIVELY, Sloop. *Guns,* 6; *Men,* 30.
Oct. 26   *Commander:* John Augusta Dunn, of Salem.
C. C. **196**, IX, 79; M. A., **172**, 43; *Essex Inst. Hist. Coll.,* XLV, 225 (Captured May 8, 1782, in Annapolis Basin by the armed schooner *Buckram*).

1782 LIVELY, Sloop. *Guns,* 10; *Men,* 35.
Apr. 20   *Commander:* Daniel Adams, of Boston.
C. C. **196**, IX, 78; M. A., **172**, 141; Mar. Court Rec., 66; Sumner's Notes (Mass. Hist. Soc. MSS.), III, 10.

1783 LIVELY, Brig. *Guns,* 10; *Men,* 50.
Mar. 8   *Commander:* Nathaniel Brookhouse, of Salem.
C. C. **196**, IX, 83; M. A., **172**, 310; *Salem Gazette,* Apr. 3, 1783: "Yesterday returned into port the privateer brig *Lively,* Capt. Brookhouse, who sailed on the 25th ult. He . . . captured two small privateers," which "being taken after the day on which hostilities were to cease, must be returned to the original owners."

1782 LIVE OAK, Sloop. *Guns,* 6; *Men,* 20.
Nov. 8   *Commander:* Samuel Tucker, of Salem.
C. C. **196**, IX, 89.

1780 LIVERPOOL, Sloop.
May 17   *Commander:* Nehemiah Story, of Manchester.
M. A., XL, 107.

1776 LIZARD, Armed Vessel (Sloop). *Tons,* 32.
Feb. 8   *Commander:* Benjamin Gorham.
Bond: State, £1000.

Bonders: Benj[ami]n Gaham [signed Gorham], mariner, Isaiah Doane, merchant, Michael [signed Micah] Nichols, cooper, of Cohasset, Sturgis Gaham [signed Gorham], of Barnstable, merchant.
Bound to "the Treasurer and Receiver General of the Colony of the Massachusetts Bay."
Owners: Not stated.
Witnesses: Isaac Bartlett, Lusitanus Stephenson.
Note. The vessel's name is spelled *Lyzard*.
M. A., VI, 212, **164**, 239 (Jan. 12, 1776).

1777 LIZARD, Schooner. *Guns,* 4; *Men,* 30.
Sept. 23   *Commander:* William Steward.
Bond: Continental; amount not stated.
Bonders: William Steward, principal; Mungo Mackay and Thomas Adams, sureties.
Owners: Mungo Mackay and Thomas Adams, of Boston.
Witnesses: Unsigned.
M. A., VI, 190, **167**, 243.

1778 LIZARD, Schooner. *Guns,* 6, and 8 *swivels; Men,* 25.
Mar. 27   *Commander:* John Blackler.
Bond: Continental, $5000; State, £500.
Bonders: John Blacker [signed Blackler], principal; Thomas Adams and Mungo Mackay, of Boston, sureties.
Owners: Thomas Adams and others.
Witnesses: James Ingels, John Cloon.
Note. Name spelled *Lizzard*. Bond signed by John Brown, in behalf of Mungo Mackay.
M. A., VI, 176, 177, **168**, 231.

1778 LIZARD, Schooner. *Guns,* 4, and 10 *swivels; Men,* 30.
July 31   *Commander:* John Barnard.
Bond: Continental, $5000; State, £4000.
Bonders: John Barnard, mariner, principal; Mungo Mackay and William Shattuck, of Boston, sureties.
Owners: Mungo Mackay and William Shattuck.
Witnesses: Jona[than] Webb, Fitch Pool.
M. A., VI, 182, 183, **139**, 203, **169**, 51.

1782 LORD STIRLING, Schooner. *Guns,* 4; *Men,* 30.
Feb. 16   *Commander:* Wingate Newman, of Newburyport.
C. C. **196**, IX, 93.

MASSACHUSETTS PRIVATEERS

1782 LORD STIRLING, Schooner. *Guns*, 6; *Men*, 35.
June 5   *Commander:* Paul Stevens, of Newburyport.
            C. C. 196, IX, 94.

1782 LOUIS LE GRAND, Ship. *Guns*, 18; *Men*, 100.
            Commander: —— ——.
            Essex Institute, Miscellaneous Ship Papers.

1778 LOYAL AMERICAN, Sloop. *Guns*, 10; *Men*, 45.
Feb. 4   *Commander:* William Grinnell.
            Bond: Continental, $5000; State, £500.
            Bonders: William Grinnell, of Boston, principal; Philip Moore and Briggs Hallowell, sureties.
            Owner: Philip Moore, merchant of Boston.
            Witnesses: Samuel Pitts, Job Prince, jr.
            M. A., VI, 204, 207, **139**, 156, **168**, 171.

1779 LOYALTY.
            Commander: —— ——.
            London Chronicle, Aug. 28, 1779: "The *Sally*, Capt. Lucas, from Newfoundland to Oporto, is taken by the *Loyalty*, American privateer, and sent for Boston."

1780 LUCY, Brigantine. *Guns*, 12; *Men*, 25.
Nov. 8   *Commander:* Stephen Clay, of Boston.
            Owners: Benjamin West and others, of Salem.
            C. C. 196, IX, 96; M. A., **171**, 303.

1777 LYDIA, Brigantine. *Guns*, 4; *Men*, 20.
Dec. 22   *Commander:* Joshua Grafton.
            Bond: Continental, $5000; State, £500.
            Bonders: Joshua Grafton, principal; Samuel Page and Walter P[rice] Bartlett, of Salem, sureties.
            Owners: Samuel Page and Walter P. Bartlett.
            Witnesses: Thomas Simmons, D[aniel] Hopkins.
            M. A., VI, 200, 203, **168**, 106.

1778 LYDIA, Schooner.
            Commander: Thomas Simmons.
            Boston Gazette, Apr. 20, 1778.

1775 LYNCH, Schooner.
Oct. 16   *Commander:* Nicholson Broughton.
            Note. Afterwards commanded by John Ayres.
            Washington's Fleet.

Know all Men by these presents That
I Stephen Mascoll of Salem in the County
of Essex Mariner am held & stand firmly bound
& Obliged unto Henry Gardner Esq'r Treasurer of the
Colony of Massachusetts Bay in New England
in the full and just Sum of One hundred pounds
to be paid to the said Henry Gardner Esq'r or his
Successor in said Office for the use of the Colony.
To the which payment well & truly to be made
I bind my self Heirs Executors & Administrators
firmly by these presents Sealed with my Seal dated
at Boston this twenty second day of April Anno Domini
One thousand seven hundred & seventy 5 —

The Condition of the above Obligation is such
that Whereas I the said Stephen Mascoll Master
of the Schooner Boston Revenge now bound from
said Boston to Salem have this day received a
permit (from Nath'l D——— Esq'r regularly appointed for that purpose) to take onboard said
Schooner now in the harbour of said Boston the
following Articles viz — Two hundred Canvas Sheets
two hundred weight musket ball Six Bolts Oznabrigs
one hundred & seventy bush Beans one Box Tea one
empty Case one Small Box eight hundred Bread
to be landed at said Salem Now if the said Stephen
shall truly & faithfully carry from hence & deliver
said Goods at the port of Salem aforesaid (Dangers of
Seas & British Pirates excepted) without fraud Cover
or further delay then the above written Obligation
to be void & of none effect otherwise to abide &
remain in full force & virtue —

Signed Sealed & Delivered
in presence of
Eunice Marston
Martha Ethend

Steph'n Mascoll

Bond for a Voyage to Salem with Military Stores

1779 MACARONI, Brigantine. *Guns*, 14; *Men*, 70.
June 15 *Commander:* William Patterson.
    Bond: Continental, $10,000; State, £4000.
    Bonders: William Patterson, mariner, principal; Bartho[lomew] Putnam and Jona[than] Lambert, of Salem, sureties.
    Owners: Bartholomew Putnam and Jonathan Lambert.
    Witness: Joshua Phippen.
    Note. The vessel's name is spelled *Mackaroni*.
    M. A., VI, 282, 283, **170**, 168; Felt, II, 270.

1775 MACHIAS LIBERTY, Sloop.
Aug. 21 *Commander:* Jeremiah O'Brien.
    Note. Formerly the sloop *Unity*, which on June 12, 1775, captured the British schooner *Margaretta*, off Machias.
    M. A., Rec. Gen. Court (Aug. 21, 1775). See *Diligent*.

1776 MACHIAS LIBERTY, Sloop.
July 25 *Commander:* Jeremiah O'Brien.
    Bond: State, £2000.
    Bonders: Jeremiah O'Brien [signed Obrien], mariner of Machias, Benjamin Balch, of Danvers, and Francis Shaw, of Goldboro' [Gouldsborough?], Lincoln County.
    Owners: "In the Colony Service of the Massachusetts Bay and fitted out by order of the Great and General Court."
    Witnesses: Caleb Wilder, John Furnass, Joseph Noyes.
    M. A., **139**, 121. See references under *Diligent*, Captain Lambert.

1780 MANETE, Schooner. *Guns*, 6; *Men*, 16.
Aug. 30 *Commander:* John Daccaretta, of Salem.
    C. C. **196**, IX, 114; M. A., **171**, 264.

1778 MARIA, Ship. *Tons*, 240; *Guns*, 8; *Men*, 20.
Nov. 24 *Commander:* Timothy Peirce.
    Bond: Continental, $10,000; State, £4000.
    Bonders: Timothy Peirce, mariner, principal; Leonard Jarvis and Joseph Russell, of Boston, sureties.
    Owners: Leonard Jarvis and others.
    Witnesses: Joseph Urann, Samuel Drinkwalter.
    M. A., VI, 331, 332, **169**, 329.

1779 MARIA, Sloop. *Tons*, 50; *Guns*, 8; *Men*, 17.
Nov. 29   *Commander:* Joseph Dodge.
        Petitioner: Joseph Head, in behalf of Samuel Broome, [of Boston].
        M. A., **171**, 34.

1781 MARIA, Brigantine. *Guns*, 7; *Men*, 20.
Jan. 12   *Commander:* Patrick Maxfield, of Dartmouth.
        Owners: Leonard Jarvis and others, of Boston.
        C. C. **196**, x, 4; M. A., **171**, 331.

1781 MARIA, Ship. *Guns*, 12; *Men*, 35.
Nov. 26   *Commander:* Stephen Hills, of Boston.
        C. C. **196**, x, 2; M. A., **172**, 73.

1780 MARIANNE, Brigantine. *Guns*, 16; *Men*, 65.
Dec. 16   *Commander:* John Kendrick, of Wareham, Mass.
        Owner: John Williams, of Worcester, Mass.
        Note. Called a Rhode Island vessel in *Naval Records of the Revolution.*
        C. C. **196**, x, 7.

1777 MARISHEETE, Schooner. *Tons*, 30; *Guns*, 4, and 8 *swivels;*
Apr. 7   *Men*, 12.
        Commander: Joshua Wing.
        Bond: Continental, $5000.
        Bonders: Joshua Wing, mariner, John Allan, late of Cumberland, N. S., Continental Agent for the Eastern Indians, and Elijah Ayer, farmer of Cumberland, N. S.
        Owner: The United States of America.
        Witnesses: Nathaniel Reynolds, Robert Foster.
        Note. For the use of John Allan in the Indian service.
        M. A., VI, 335, **159**, 141, **166**, 291, $291\frac{1}{2}$.

1778 MARISHEET, Schooner. *Guns*, 6; *Men*, 15.
Nov. 23   *Commander:* William Ray.
        Bond: Continental, $5000; State, £4000.
        Bonders: William Ray, mariner, principal; Francis Shaw and John Preble, of Boston and Machias, sureties.
        Owner: Not stated; still in the service of the United States.
        Witnesses: John Fulton, James Archibald, Jonathan Metcalf.
        M. A., VI, 276, 277; **169**, 327, 328 (Petition of John Preble in behalf of Col. John Allan).

1779 MARKINDER. *Guns*, 12, and 16 *swivels; Men*, 120.
  Commander: ———— ————.
  London Chronicle, June 12, 1779: "The *Markinder* privateer of Salem, mounting 12 six and nine pounders and 16 swivels besides a number of cohorns, and 120 men on board, on the 24th of March last fell in with a ship bound to Gambia from the West Indies, where she had been to sell her slaves, boarded her and sent her to Salem."

1778 MARLBOROUGH, Ship of War.
Sept. 8 *Commander:* George Waith Babcock.
  Bond: State, £2000.
  Bonders: James Godfrey, mariner of Taunton, James Swan, merchant of Boston, the major part of the owners, and George Waith Babcock, mariner of Exeter, R. I.
  Witnesses: John Furnass, Nathaniel Furnass.
    M. A., **139**, 212 (Bond not to enlist any man in New England outside of Massachusetts); *Providence Gazette*, June 13, 1778: "Since our last the Privateer Ship *Marlborough*, Capt. Babcock, of this place, arrived in Port from a successful Cruize, having taken 28 Prizes. Six of the most valuable were manned and three of them have arrived; the others were sunk or destroyed. She brought in with her a Ship laden with dry Goods, Wine, Porter, etc. and a Brig with Provisions; a large Guineaman, having on board 300 Slaves, was ordered to South-Carolina." *Independent Chronicle*, Dec. 24, 1778: "Last Sunday returned from a cruise the private armed ship *Marlborough*, having taken three prizes."

1779 MARLBOROUGH, Ship. *Guns*, 14; *Men*, 40.
May 28 *Commander:* William Chace.
  Bond: Continental, $10,000; State, £4000.
  Bonders: William Chace, mariner, principal; James Bowdoin, jr., and James Price, of Boston, sureties.
  Owner: James Bowdoin, jr.
  Witnesses: John Rogers, Christopher Rophey.
    M. A., VI, 327, 328, **170**, 136.

1780 MARQUIS, Ship. *Guns*, 10; *Men*, 20.
Sept. 19 *Commander:* Nathaniel West, of Salem.
    C. C. **196**, x, 10; M. A., **171**, 274.

1781 MARQUIS, Ship. *Guns*, 16; *Men*, 80.
Apr. 16   *Commander:* Richard Cowell, of Salem.
    C. C. **196**, x, 9; M. A., **171**, 375.

1779 MARQUIS DE LA FAYETTE, Schooner. *Guns*, 6; *Men*, 12.
Jan. 21   *Commander:* Seth Thomas.
    Bond: Continental, $5000; State, £4000.
    Bonders: Seth Thomas, mariner, principal; Thomas Thomas and Stephen Hooper, merchants of Newburyport, sureties.
    Owners: Thomas Thomas and Stephen Hooper.
    Witnesses: Eben[eze]r Stocker, W[illia]m Titcomb.
    M. A., vi, 199, 201, **169**, 417.

1779 MARQUIS DE LA FAYETTE, Ship. *Guns*, 10; *Men*, 30.
Nov. 23   *Commander:* John Tittle.
    Bond: Continental, $10,000; State, £4000.
    Bonders: John Tittle, mariner, principal; Samuel Flagg and John Buffinton, sureties — all of Salem.
    Owners: Samuel Flagg and others.
    Witnesses: Josiah Orne, W. Prosser.
    M. A., vi, 214, 217, **171**, 30.

1781 MARQUIS DE LA FAYETTE, Brigantine. *Guns*, 6; *Men*, 15.
Jan. 11   *Commander:* Seth Thomas, of Newburyport.
    C. C. **196**, x, 17; M. A., **171**, 329.

1781 MARQUIS DE LA FAYETTE, Ship. *Guns*, 16; *Men*, 100.
Aug. 13   *Commander:* Ebenezer Reed, of Salem.
    C. C. **196**, x, 15; M. A., **171**, 455; Felt, ii, 272: "Reported as having attacked a brig of 32 guns upwards of two glasses, but drew off much damaged with 8 killed, 14 wounded, and the enemy with 17 killed besides others wounded."

1781 MARQUIS DE LA FAYETTE, Brigantine. *Guns*, 6; *Men*, 15.
Sept. 1   *Commander:* Joseph Wells, of Newburyport.
    C. C. **196**, x, 19.

1782 MARQUIS DE LA FAYETTE, Ship. *Guns*, 16; *Men*, 100.
Mar. 15   *Commander:* John Buffinton, of Salem.
    C. C. **196**, x, 11; M. A., **172**, 120; *Boston Gazette*, Aug. 26, 1782: "Friday last arrived at Salem the Ship *Mars* [called *Le Marquis de la Fayette* in the prize list in the same paper], Capt. John Buffinton, and carried in with him a Prize Brig."

1783 MARQUIS DE LA FAYETTE, Brigantine. *Guns*, 6; *Men*, 15.
Jan. 3   *Commander:* Arnold Comerais, of Boston.
C. C. **196**, x, 12; M. A., **172**, 276.

1777 MARS, Ship. *Tons*, 280; *Guns*, 22; *Men*, 150.
May 24   *Commander:* Thomas Truxtun.
Bond: Continental, $15,000.
Bonders: Thomas Truxton [signed Truxtun], of New York, principal; Col. Isaac Sears and Paschal N[elson] Smith, merchants of Boston, sureties.
Owners: Isaac Sears and Paschal N. Smith.
Witnesses: Adam Babcock, Elia[ki]m Raymond.
M. A., VI, 311, **166**, 419.

1777 MARS, Sloop. *Guns*, 8; *Men*, 40.
July 7   *Commander:* Frederick Shannon.
Bond: Continental, $5000.
Bonders: Frederick Shannon, William Corlis, and James Swan.
Owners: Samuel Dunn and James Swan, of Boston.
Witnesses: Josiah Bacon, Spencer Walker.
M. A., VI, 293, **167**, 65.

1778 MARS, Ship of War. *Guns*, 22; *Men*, 130.
May 23   *Commander:* Gilbert Ash.
Bond: State, £2000.
Bonders: Isaac Sears, merchant, the major part of the owners, and Gilbert Ash, mariner, both of Boston.
Owners: Isaac Sears, of Boston, and others.
Witnesses: John Furnass, Thomas Appleton.
M. A., **139**, 184, 233 (Bonds not to enlist any man in New England outside of Massachusetts); C. C. **196**, x, 20 (May 11, 1778. Called a Connecticut vessel in *Naval Records of the Revolution*).

1779 MARS, Brigantine (Letter of marque).
Aug. 9   *Commander:* Joshua Ellingwood.
Owner: Mark Lafitte, of Salem.
M. A., **170**, 313, 314 (Petition to be allowed to sail notwithstanding embargo. Granted).

1781 MARS, Ship. *Guns*, 20; *Men*, 150.
Apr. 23   *Commander:* James Nivens.
Bond: State, Twenty Thousand Spanish Milled Dollars.

> *Bonders:* James Nivens, mariner of Boston, principal; Isaac Phillips, of Boston, and Nathaniel Gorham, of Charlestown.
> *Owners:* Commonwealth of Massachusetts.
> *Witnesses:* Nathaniel Foster, Onesiphorus Tileston.
> > *Note.* This vessel was purchased in 1780 for the Massachusetts State Navy.
>
> M. A., **139**, 278.

1781   MARS, Ship. *Guns,* 6; *Men,* 20.
Nov. 8   *Commander:* Samuel Daggett, of Martha's Vineyard.
> *Owners:* Gower [Gawen?] Brown & Co., of Boston.
> C. C. **196**, x, 22; M. A., **178**, 169.

1781   MARS, Ship. *Guns,* 14; *Men,* 45.
Dec. 18   *Commander:* Ignatius Webber, of Gloucester.
> *Owners:* Codman & Smith, of Boston.
> C. C. **196**, x, 30.

> MARS, Ship. *Guns,* 16; *Men,* 75.
> > *Commander:* William Woodberry.
> > Paine, 457; *Publ. Colonial Society of Mass.,* XXIV, 435.

1777   MARY, Brigantine. *Guns,* 6; *Men,* 20.
Dec. 22   *Commander:* William Gray.
> *Bond:* Continental, $5000; State, £500.
> *Bonders:* William Gray, principal; George Crowninshield and Henry Williams, of Salem, sureties.
> *Owners:* George Crowninshield and Henry Williams.
> *Witnesses:* Nathaniel Gould, Joshua Grafton.
> M. A., VI, 290, 291, **168**, 114.

1779   MARY, Ship. *Guns,* 10; *Men,* 25.
Aug. 16   *Commander:* Robert Stonehouse.
> *Bond:* Continental, $10,000; State, £4000.
> *Bonders:* Robert Stonehouse, mariner, principal; William Greenleaf and Daniel Bell, sureties — all of Boston.
> *Owner:* William Greenleaf.
> *Witnesses:* D. Jeffries, James Foster.
> M. A., VI, 274, 275, **170**, 328.

1776   MASSACHUSETTS, Brigantine.
> *Commander:* Daniel Souther.
> Massachusetts State Navy.

MARS — MERCURY 219

1780 MASSACHUSETTS, Brigantine. *Guns*, 16; *Men*, 30.
Nov. 23   *Commander:* John Calef, of Boston.
           Owners: Nathaniel and John Tracy, of Newburyport.
           C. C. **196**, x, 39; M. A., **171**, 310.

1781 MEDIUM, Schooner. *Guns*, 4; *Men*, 25.
Mar. 21 *Commander:* Benjamin Withem, of Cape Ann.
           Note. In the petition the captain's name is spelled Witham.
           C. C. **196**, x, 44; M. A., **171**, 359.

1783 MENTOR, Brig. *Guns*, 10; *Men*, 15.
Jan. 6   *Commander:* Samuel Smith, of Barnstable.
           Owners: Isaiah Doane and others, of Boston.
           C. C. **196**, x, 46; M. A., **172**, 277.

1777 MERCURY. *Guns*, 22.
           Commander: [Gamaliel?] Hodges.
           London Chronicle, June 5, 1777: "A letter received from Salem says an American privateer called the *Mercury*, of 22 guns, —— Hodges Commander, has taken an armed tender commanded by a Lieutenant of the navy which belonged to Lord Howe's squadron . . . and carried her into the above port."

1779 MERCURY, Brigantine. *Guns*, 8; *Men*, 20.
May 17   *Commander:* William Brown.
           Bond: Continental, $10,000; State, £4000.
           Bonders: William Brown, mariner, principal; John Merchant and Samuel Clarke, of Boston, sureties.
           Owners: Samuel Clarke and others.
           Witnesses: John Fenno, John Brown.
           M. A., VI, 288, 289, **170**, 114.

1780 MERCURY, Ship (letter of marque).
           Commander: Nicholas Johnston.
           Note. The captain's name was probably Johnson.
           Boston Gazette, Sept. 4, 1780.

1781 MERCURY, Brig. *Guns*, 6; *Men*, 15.
June 1   *Commander:* William Faris, of Newburyport.
           Note. In the petition the captain's name is spelled Parris and in *Naval Records of the Revolution*, Farris.
           C. C. **196**, x, 48; M. A., **171**, 417 (June 25, 1781).

1781 MERCURY, Ship. *Guns*, 12; *Men*, 25.
Sept. 1   *Commander:* Seth Thomas, of Newburyport.
          C. C. **196**, x, 55.

1782 MERCY, Schooner. *Guns*, 4; *Men*, 10.
Dec. 16   *Commander:* Jacob Adams, of Boston.
          C. C. **196**, x, 56; M. A., **172**, 259.

1777 MERMAID, Brigantine.
          Commander: David Bray.
          Owner: Arnold Welles.
             Note. It is not certain that the *Mermaid* was an armed vessel.
             M. A., **167**, 114 (Petition of Arnold Welles in behalf of Capt. David Bray, July 21, 1777).

1782 MERMAID, Brig. *Guns*, 14; *Men*, 11.
Nov. 15   *Commander:* Jonathan Tucker, of Salem.
          C. C. **196**, x, 58.

1781 MEY, Brigantine. *Guns*, 4; *Men*, 12.
July 26   *Commander:* Abraham Edwards, of Newburyport.
          C. C. **196**, x, 59.

1779 MIFFLIN, Ship. *Guns*, 20; *Men*, 130.
Mar. 31   *Commander:* George W[aith] Babcock.
          Bond: Continental, $10,000; State, £4000.
          Bonders: George W. Babcock, mariner, principal; Mungo Mackay and Philip Moore, of Boston, sureties.
          Owners: Mungo Mackay and others.
          Witnesses: Thomas Amory, jr., James Eldred.
             Note. The name is spelled *Miflin;* she was doubtless the same vessel as the *General Mifflin.*
             M. A., vi, 286, 287, **139**, 244, **159**, 233, **170**, 47; *Independent Chronicle*, Aug. 5, 1779: "Saturday last arrived here the Prize Ship *Tartar*, mounting 26 Carriage Guns besides Cohorns and Swivels and had 130 Hands; taken by the *Mifflin* of 20 Guns, Capt. Babcock, of this Port, and only 100 Hands. She was fitted out of Ireland for the Purpose of taking an American Frigate and she happened to catch a Tartar. The *Tartar* had her Captain and 22 Hands killed besides some wounded. The *Mifflin* had two Men killed. The *Mifflin* had also taken four other Prizes."

1778 MINERVA, Ship of War. *Guns*, 20 (9-pounders).
Apr. 3   *Commander:* John Grimes.
   Bond: State, £2000.
   Bonders: John Cushing and Samuel White, merchants, major part of the owners, and John Grimes, mariner, all of Boston.
   Witnesses: Edward Holyoke, Thomas Oliver.
      M. A., **139**, 162 (Bond not to enlist any soldier of the Continental Army); Mar. Court Rec., 1, 3, 5, 7; British Admiralty Records, Admirals' Despatches, **488**, 57 (April 23, 1778. Description of the *Minerva* and other vessels).

1779 MINERVA, Brigantine. *Tons*, 120; *Guns*, 14; *Men*, 80.
Sept. 14   *Commander:* Stephen Hills.
   Bond: Continental, $10,000; State, £4000.
   Bonders: Stephen Hills, mariner, principal; Samuel Clarke and John Merchant, of Boston, sureties.
   Owner: Samuel Clarke.
   Witnesses: Jos[eph] Gardner, Nath[anie]l By[fiel]d Lyde.
      M. A., VI, 284, 285, **159**, 263 (On Oct. 20, 1779, the *Minerva*, called in the Court Records the *Mercury*, captured the sloop *Mary and Fanny* and brought her into Boston; Nov. 3, 1779, Samuel Clarke and John Merchant, merchants of Boston, appeared in Court in behalf of Capt. Stephen Hills). **170**, 398 (Petition of Samuel Clarke and Thomas Cushing, jr.; in this petition the vessel is called both *Minerva* and *Mercury*.)

1780 MINERVA, Brigantine. *Guns*, 8; *Men*, 24.
Feb. 11   *Commander:* Samuel McCobb.
   Bond: Continental, $10,000; State, £4000.
   Bonders: Samuel McCobb, mariner, principal; Simeon Mayo and Elias Parkman, of Boston, sureties.
   Owners: Samuel Mayo and others.
   Witnesses: Jno. Clarke, A[llen?] Hallet.
      M. A., VI, 272, 273, **171**, 80.

1780 MINERVA, Brigantine. *Guns*, 8; *Men*, 20.
June 8   *Commander:* Henry Johnson.
   Bond: Continental, $10,000; State, £4000.
   Bonders: Henry Johnson, mariner, principal; Simeon Mayo and Gawen Brown, jr., merchants, sureties — all of Boston.

Owners: Samuel Mayo and others.
Witnesses: Stephen Bruce, Elisha Turner.
M. A., VI, 325, 326, **176**, 428.

1781 MINERVA, Ship. *Guns*, 16; *Men*, 60.
Feb. 24 *Commander:* Moses Brown, of Newburyport.
C. C. **196**, X, 64.

1781 MINERVA, Ship. *Guns*, 16; *Men*, 40.
Dec. 15 *Commander:* George Rapall, of Newburyport.
Note. The ship is called *Minerve* in *Naval Records of the Revolution*.
C. C. **196**, X, 74.

1781 MINERVA, Ship. *Guns*, 16; *Men*, 50.
Dec. 22 *Commander:* John Lee, of Newburyport.
C. C. **196**, X, 72.

1782 MINERVA, Brigantine. *Guns*, 16; *Men*, 35.
Feb. 28 *Commander:* [John] Allen Hallet, of Boston.
C. C. **196**, X, 70; M. A., **172**, 102.

1782 MINERVA, Sloop. *Guns*, 6; *Men*, 10.
Aug. 3 *Commander:* Nehemiah Buffington, of Salem.
Note. On other bonds the captain signed his name Buffinton.
C. C. **196**, X, 65.

1783 MINERVA, Ship. *Tons*, 180; *Guns*, 10; *Men*, 25.
Jan. 20 *Commander:* Jacob Cole.
Petitioner: William Smith, of Boston.
M. A., **172**, 282.

MINERVA, Schooner. *Guns*, 12; *Men*, 60.
Commander: Hugh Helme.
Essex Insitute, Miscellaneous Ship Papers.

1779 MODERN PILGRIM.
Commander: —— ——.
London Chronicle, May 18, 1779: "The *Modern Pilgrim* privateer, of Salem, has taken the *William*."

1779 MODESTY, Schooner. *Tons*, 90; *Guns*, 10, and 4 *swivels;*
Aug. 6 *Men*, 45.
Commander: William Carlton.
Bond: Continental, $5000; State, £4000.
Bonders: William Carlton, mariner, principal; John Marston and Samuel White, of Boston, sureties.

MINERVA — MONMOUTH 223

Owners: Benjamin Warren and others [of Salem].
Witnesses: Charles Jarvis, Joseph Robinson.
M. A., VI, 323, 324, **170**, 287 (Petition dated Salem, July 30, 1779, and signed by Benjamin Warren and William Carlton).

1782 MODESTY, Brig. *Guns*, 8.
Commander: —— ——.
Essex Institute, Miscellaneous Ship Papers.

1781 MOHAWK, Ship. *Tons*, 250; *Guns*, 20; *Men*, 130.
Nov. 8 *Commander:* Elias Smith, of Beverly.
C. C. **196**, x, 76; M.A., **172**, 59; *Salem Gazette*, Apr. 18, 1782: "On Tuesday last also arrived at Beverly in 23 days from Martinico, the ship *Daniel*, Capt. [Benjamin] Bickford. This ship was formerly called the *Salem Packet* and belonged to this port, but was captured in her homeward-bound passage from Bilboa. She is now prize to the *Mohawk*, being one of the vessels lately taken by her in the West Indies." *Boston Gazette*, Apr. 22, 1782: "Saturday se'nnight the privateer ship *Mohawk*, Capt. Smith, arrived at Beverly from a cruize in the West Indies. By the arrival of this vessel we are advised that the privateer ship *Rhodes*, belonging to Salem and commanded by Capt. Nehemiah Buffington, was some time since taken and carried into Barbadoes. The privateer ship *Scourge*, Capt. Parker, belonging to Beverly, has been also captured and carried into the same island."

1782 MOHAWK, Ship. *Guns*, 20; *Men*, 80.
Sept. 6 *Commander:* John Carnes, of Beverly.
C. C. **196**, x, 75; *Salem Gazette*, Oct. 24, 1782 (See *Hendrick*).

1778 MONMOUTH, Brig. *Guns*, 10; *Men*, 60.
Oct. 13 *Commander:* Samuel Ingersoll.
Bond: Continental, $10,000; State, £4000.
Bonders: Samuel Ingersoll, mariner, principal; Elias Hasket Derby and Ichabod Nichols, of Salem, sureties.
Owners: Elias Hasket Derby and others.
Witnesses: Jona[than] Ingersoll, Daniel Hathorne.
M. A., VI, 278, 279, **169**, 214.

1778 MONMOUTH, Ship. *Guns*, 20; *Men*, 120.
Nov. 1   *Commander:* William Nichols.
    Bond: Continental, $10,000; State, £4000.
    Bonders: William Nichols, mariner, principal; John Coffin Jones, Joseph Marquand, and Samuel Batchelder, of Newburyport, sureties.
    Owners: Not stated.
    Witnesses: James Coffin, William Springer.
    M. A., VI, 309, 312, **169**, 298.

1779 MONMOUTH, Ship. *Guns*, 20; *Men*, 120.
Feb. 9   *Commander:* Thomas Collyer.
    Bond: Continental, $5000; State, £4000.
    Bonders: Thomas Collyer, mariner, of Newburyport, principal; Stephen Bruce and Joseph Marquand, of Newburyport and Boston, sureties.
    Owners: Samuel Batchelder, Lee & Jones, and Joseph Marquand.
    Witnesses: William Clough, N. Fosdick.
    M. A., VI, 280, 281, **169**, 434.

1779 MONMOUTH, Ship. *Tons*, 250; *Guns*, 20; *Men*, 120.
June 28   *Commander:* Alexander Ross.
    Petitioners: John Coffin Jones and others, of Newburyport.
        Note. On the Penobscot Expedition and destroyed to prevent capture.
    M. A., **170**, 189.

1779 MONMOUTH, Brigantine. *Guns*, 12; *Men*, 65.
Sept. 4   *Commander:* John Revell.
    Bond: Continental, $5000; State, £4000.
    Bonders: John Revell, mariner, principal; Peter Lander and William Pickman, of Salem, sureties.
    Owner: Job Prince, jr.
    Witnesses: Joseph Grafton, Richard Ward.
    M. A., VI, 333, 334, **159**, 324, **170**, 372; Felt, II, 270.

1781 MONMOUTH, Ship. *Guns*, 8; *Men*, 30.
Apr. 14   *Commander:* Paul Newman, of Newburyport.
    C. C. **196**, X, 85.

1782 MONMOUTH, Brigantine. *Guns*, 6; *Men*, 20.
Nov. 7   *Commander:* David Ingersoll, of Salem.
    C. C. **196**, X, 84.

1778 MONTGOMERY, Brigantine. *Guns*, 16, and 6 *swivels; Men*,
Feb. 5   100.
   Commander: Nathan Brown.
   Bond: Continental, $10,000; State, £500.
   Bonders: Nathan Brown, principal; George Williams and Joshua Ward, jr., of Salem, sureties.
   Owners: George Williams and Joshua Ward, jr.
   Witness: D[aniel] Hopkins.
     M. A., VI, 292, 295, **168**, 172.

1778 MONTGOMERY, Brigantine. *Guns*, 16; *Men*, 100.
July 24   Commander: William Patterson.
   Bond: Continental, $10,000; State, £4000.
   Bonders: William Patterson, mariner, principal; Jona[than] Peele, jr., and George Williams, of Salem, sureties.
   Owners: Jonathan Peele, jr., and others.
   Witnesses: Jona[than] Ingersoll, Jona[than] Symonds.
     M. A., VI, 336, 337, **169**, 24.

1778 MONTGOMERY, Brigantine. *Guns*, 16; *Men*, 100.
Oct. 22   Commander: Thomas Benson.
   Bond: Continental, $10,000; State, £4000.
   Bonders: Thomas Benson, mariner, principal; Peter Lander and Joshua Ward, of Salem, sureties.
   Owners: George Williams and others, of Salem.
   Witnesses: Thomas Downing, W. Prosser.
     M. A., VI, 329, 330, **169**, 244.

1780 MONTGOMERY, Brigantine. *Guns*, 8; *Men*, 20.
Sept. 12 Commander: John Carnes, of Beverly.
   Owners: John Norris and others, of Salem.
     C. C. **196**, X, 89; M. A., **171**, 272; Felt, II, 271.

1781 MONTGOMERY, Brig.
   Commander: Samuel Hobbs.
   Boston Gazette, Sept. 10, 1781.

1782 MONTGOMERY, Schooner. *Guns*, 4; *Men*, 15.
Mar. 29   Commander: Benjamin Ashton, of Marblehead.
     C. C. **196**, X, 86; M. A., **172**, 127.

1782 MONTGOMERY, Brigantine. *Guns*, 6; *Men*, 20.
June 20   Commander: James Barr, jr., of Salem.
     C. C. **196**, X, 87; M. A., **172**, 176; *Essex Inst. Hist. Coll.*, XXVII (1890), 143.

1782 MOORE, Ship. *Guns*, 14; *Men*, 40.
Mar. 14 *Commander:* Ezekiel Burroughs, of Boston.
  C. C. **196**, x, 91; M. A., **172**, 118.

1780 MORNING STAR, Sloop. *Tons*, 80; *Guns*, 10; *Men*, 50.
Sept. 25 *Commander:* John Ravel [Revell].
    Petitioner: Elias Hasket Derby, of Salem.
      M. A., XL, 108, **171**, 280; Court Files, 103381; *Boston Gazette*, Nov. 13, 1780; *London Chronicle*, Jan. 9, 1781.

1780 MORNING STAR, Sloop. *Guns*, 8; *Men*, 12.
Dec. 18 *Commander:* Francis Roch, of Salem.
  C. C. **196**, x, 94.

1780 MURR, Brigantine.
    Commander: John Burchmore, of Salem.
      Note. The name of the vessel should perhaps have been spelled *Myrrh*.
      Mass. Soldiers and Sailors of Revolution, II, 820 (Nov. 18, 1780; Felt, II, 276.

1779 NANCY, Brig. *Guns*, 16.
    Commander: —— ——.
      Note. On the Penobscot Expedition and captured by the enemy.
      Williamson, *History of Maine*, II, 470, 476; Wheeler, *History of Castine*, 38.

1779 NANCY, Brigantine. *Guns*, 8; *Men*, 20.
Oct. 13 *Commander:* Peter Collas.
    Bond: Continental, $5000; State, £4000.
    Bonders: Peter Collis [signed Collas], mariner, principal; William Shattuck and John Shattuck, of Boston, sureties.
    Owners: William and John Shattuck.
    Witnesses: Stephen H. Gray, James Perkins.
      M. A., VI, 298, 299, **170**, 423.

1779 NANCY, Sloop. *Guns*, 8; *Men*, 12.
Nov. 25 *Commander:* David Smith.
    Bond: Continental, $5000; State, £4000.
    Bonders: David Smith, mariner, principal; Elias Hasket Derby and Nehemiah Holt, of Salem, sureties.
    Owner: Elias Hasket Derby.
    Witnesses: Mansfield Burrill, William Beckett.
      M. A., VI, 294, 297, **171**, 33.

1780 Nancy, Brigantine. *Guns*, 4; *Men*, 13.
Nov. 20   *Commander:* Thomas Parker, of Boston.
        C. C. **196**, x, 109; M. A., **171**, 305^2.

1781 Nancey, Schooner. *Guns*, 6; *Men*, 25.
Feb. 27   *Commander:* George Leach, of Salem.
        C. C. **196**, x, 100; M. A., **171**, 347.

1781 Nancy, Brig. *Guns*, 4; *Men*, 14.
June 25   *Commander:* Litchfield Luce, of Boston.
        C. C. **196**, x, 106; M. A., **171**, 416.

1779 Neashquowoite, Schooner. *Guns*, 10; *Men*, 30.
May 7   *Commander:* Ephraim Chase.
    Bond: Continental, $5000; State, £4000.
    Bonders: Ephraim Chase, mariner, principal; John Allan, of Machias, Continental Agent for Indians, Eastern Department, and Francis Shaw, of Boston, sureties.
    Owner: The United States of America.
    Witnesses: Ja[me]s Avery, Nat[haniel] Shaw.
        M. A., vii, 260, 261, **170**, 83.

1776 Necessity, Schooner. *Guns*, 12 *swivels; Men*, 30.
Oct. 3   *Commander:* William Lecraw.
    Bond: Continental, $5000.
    Bonders: William Lecraw, principal, Joshua Orne and John Selman — all of Marblehead.
    Owners: Joshua Orne and John Selman.
    Witnesses: John Bray, William Orchard.
        M. A., vi, 296, **165**, 307.

1777 Neptune. *Guns*, 14.
    Commander: Charles Thompson.
    London Chronicle, April 22, 1777. See *Black Eagle*.

1777 Neptune, Ship. *Guns*, 24; *Men*, 120.
July 17   *Commander:* William Friend, of Newburyport.
        C. C. **196**, xi, 9.

1779 Neptune, Brigantine. *Guns*, 14; *Men*, 80.
Aug. 5   *Commander:* John Ashton.
    Bond: Continental, $10,000; State, £4000.
    Bonders: John Ashton, mariner, principal; Joshua Dodge and James Laskey, of Salem and Marblehead, sureties.
    Owner: Joshua Dodge, of Salem.
    Witnesses: Jno. Dall, Samuel Russell Gerry.
        M. A., vi, 321, 322, **159**, 346, **170**, 303.

1779   NEPTUNE, Ship. *Guns*, 8; *Men*, 25.
Dec. 24   *Commander:* John Wheelwright.
   Bond: Continental, $10,000; State, £4000.
   Bonders: John Wheelwright, mariner, principal; George Dodge, jr., and Eben[eze]r Parsons, of Salem and Boston, sureties.
   Owner: George Dodge, jr., of Salem.
   Witnesses: John Tufts, John Stratton.
   M. A., VI, 319, 320, **171**, 50.

1780   NEPTUNE, Ship. *Guns*, 8; *Men*, 22.
June 12   *Commander:* William Woodbury.
   Bond: Continental, $10,000; State, £4000.
   Bonders: William Woodbury, mariner, principal; George Dodge, jr., of Salem, and Daniel Sargent, of Boston, merchants, sureties.
   Owners: George Dodge, jr., and others.
   Witnesses: John Marston, Caleb Tappan.
   Note. At different times the captain spelled his name Woodbury and Woodberry.
   M. A., VI, 313, 314, **171**, 177.

1780   NEPTUNE, Ship. *Guns*, 7; *Men*, 20.
Sept. 7   *Commander:* William Woodbury, jr.
   C. C. **196**, XI, 17; M. A., **171**, 267.

1781   NEPTUNE, Ship. *Guns*, 14; *Men*, 65.
Mar. 13   *Commander:* Hugh Smith, of Salem.
   C. C. **196**, XI, 14; M. A., **171**, 349.

1781   NEPTUNE, Brigantine. *Guns*, 4; *Men*, 12.
June 1   *Commander:* Nathaniel Harman.
   Owner: Jonathan Hamilton, of Berwick.
   C. C. **196**, XI, 10.

1781   NEPTUNE, Ship. *Guns*, 15; *Men*, 60.
Aug. 13   *Commander:* Silas Smith, of Salem.
   C. C. **196**, XI, 15; M. A., **171**, 453.

1780   NEW ADVENTURE, Ship. *Guns*, 6; *Men*, 25.
Oct. 16   *Commander:* Robert Cushing, of Boston.
   C. C. **196**, XI, 27; M. A., **171**, 292.

1781   NEW ADVENTURE, Brigantine. *Guns*, 14; *Men*, 50.
May 21   *Commander:* Jonathan Neall, of Salem.
   C. C. **196**, XI, 28; M. A., **171**, 391.

1781 NIMBLE SHILLING, Schooner. *Guns*, 6; *Men*, 15.
July 14   Commander: John Cloon, of Marblehead.
C. C. **196**, XI, 32; M. A., **171**, 429.

1781 NIMBLE SHILLING, Schooner. *Guns*, 5; *Men*, 16.
Aug. 29   Commander: Samuel Hill, of Marblehead.
C. C. **196**, XI, 33; M. A., **171**, 478^2.

1782 NONSUCH, Brig. *Guns*, 4; *Men*, 16.
Dec. 13   Commander: Edward Davis, of Boston.
C. C. **196**, XI, 38; M. A., **172**, 258.

1780 NORWICH WITCH, Schooner. *Guns*, 4; *Men*, 10.
Mar. 16   Commander: Moses Hale.
Bond: Continental, $5000; State, £4000.
Bonders: Moses Hale, of Newburyport, "master of the Letter of Marque schooner *Norwich Witch*," principal; Henry Johnson, mariner, and Francis Johonnot, distiller, of Boston, sureties.
Owners: Henry Johnson & Co.
Witnesses: John Avery, jr., Eben[eze]r Oliver.
M. A., VI, 315, 316, **171**, 99.

1780 NORWICH WITCH, Schooner. *Guns*, 4; *Men*, 10.
June 16   Commander: Enoch Pike.
Bond: Continental, $5000; State, £4000.
Bonders: Enoch Pike, mariner of Newburyport, principal; Nehemiah Soames [signed Somes] and Matthew Clark, merchants of Boston, sureties.
Owners: Nehemiah Somes and others.
Witnesses: Samuel Stimpson, Caleb Child.
M. A., VI, 317, 318, **171**, 185.

1780 NORWICH WITCH, Schooner. *Guns*, 4; *Men*, 10.
Sept. 30   Commander: Amos Minor, of Suffolk County.
Owners: Henry Johnson and others, of Boston.
Note. In *Naval Records of the Revolution* the vessel's name is spelled *Watch* and the captain's Miner, but in the petition they are spelled as above.
C. C. **196**, XI, 37; M. A., **171**, 284.

1776 OLIVER CROMWELL, Sloop. *Guns*, 10; *Men*, 60.
Oct. 15   Commander: John Tiley.
Bond: Continental, amount not stated.
Bonders: John Tiley, mariner, principal; Charles Sigourney and William Foster, sureties — all of Boston.

Owners: Charles Sigourney and others.
Witnesses: Uriah Norcross, Nathaniel Frazier.
  Note. In Emmons' list is a "ship" *Oliver Cromwell,* J. Tilley, probably an error for the above.
M. A., VI, 306, **165**, 326, **181**, 270.

1776 OLIVER CROMWELL, Ship. *Guns,* 10, and 10 *swivels; Men,* 60.
Commander: W[illiam?] Coit.
Emmons, 154.

1777 OLIVER CROMWELL, Brigantine. *Guns,* 16; *Men,* 130.
Apr. 29   *Commander:* William Coles.
Bond: Continental, $10,000.
Bonders: William Coles, principal; George Dodge, jr., and John Buffington [signed Buffinton], sureties.
Owners: John Derby & Co., of Salem.
Witnesses: Edward Gibaut, Stephen Hall, 3d.
  M. A., VI, 300; *Essex Inst. Hist. Coll.*, XLV, 247: "At 3 P.M. [Aug. 6, 1777] saw two Brigs which we bore away for. . . . Out Oars (being a small Breeze) and rowed towards them. They kept near each other and hove too and formed in a Posture of Battle to receive us. Every Thing being prepared for Battle, we advanced; one of them gave several Shot, which we took no Notice of till we came nigh enough to give her two Broad Sides, She continuing her Fire. By our well directed Fire She was compelled to strike to us and earnestly beg of us to desist our Fire on her. Our Capt. then ordered to bear away for the other Brig, which orders were immediately complied with. We then charged the other with an incessant Fire for almost three Glasses. She returned our Fire some Time with Spirit, but being disanabled, wore off. The other which fell a Stern and notwithstanding she had fairly struck to us, yet seing her Partner's Fire, she worried us with her Bow Chacers, but did us no Damage. But now our Officers began to think of the Man of War, which had been in Chace all Day and was now reasonably expected to be near up with us; therefore being dark, they rightly judged it best to give over the Assault for this Night, least falling in between three of them we must be obliged to submit, and so altered our Course."

1777 OLIVER CROMWELL, Schooner.
    Commander: Jeremiah Heydon.
    London Chronicle, July 22, 1777 (Letter from Dublin, July 12): "On Sunday last a boat with several ladies and gentlemen sailed from Tramore, in the county of Waterford, on a party of pleasure, and about four leagues to the south-west fell in with a vessel, schooner rigged, which fired a gun to bring the boat along-side. The company complied and were ordered on board the privateer; they were conducted to the cabin, when they were told by an officer that they were prisoners to Capt. Jeremiah Heydon of the *Oliver Cromwell* privateer, of Marblehead. After some conversation, in which the Captain and Officers made themselves merry, they were entertained with cold ham and some excellent Madeira and then dismissed. The privateer took leave with three cheers and stood to the south-west towards Bristol Channel."

1778 OLIVER CROMWELL, Brigantine. *Guns,* 16; *Men,* 100.
July 10   *Commander:* Thomas Simmons.
    Bond: Continental, $10,000; State, £4000.
    Bonders: Thomas Simmons, mariner, principal; George Cabot and Jona[than] Ingersoll, of Salem, sureties.
    Owners: Jonathan Ingersoll and others.
    Witness: D[aniel] Hopkins.
    M. A., VI, 301, 302, **168**, 438.

1779 OLIVER CROMWELL, Ship. *Guns,* 16; *Men,* 110.
Mar. 29   *Commander:* Thomas Simmons.
    Bond: Continental, $10,000; State, £4000.
    Bonders: Thomas Simmons, principal; John Derby and Bartholomew Putnam, sureties — all of Salem.
    Owners: John Derby and others.
    Witnesses: Samuel Flagg, Jos[hu]a Ward, jr.
    M. A., VI, 305, 308, **170**, 41.

1779 OLIVER CROMWELL, Ship. *Guns,* 18; *Men,* 110.
Aug. 11   *Commander:* James Barr.
    Bond: Continental, $10,000; State, £4000.
    Bonders: James Barr, mariner, principal; Bartholomew Putnam and B[enjamin] Goodhue, jr., of Salem, sureties.
    Owner: Bartholomew Putnam.

> *Witnesses:* James Jeffry, Joseph Moses.
> M. A., VI, 303, 304, **170**, 320; Felt, II, 270; *Essex Inst. Hist. Coll.*, XXVII (1890), 133–135, 139–143.

1781 OLIVER CROMWELL, Ship. *Guns*, 16; *Men*, 85.
Apr. 13 *Commander:* John Bray, of Beverly.
> C. C. **196**, XI, 44; M. A., **171**, 371.

> OLIVER CROMWELL, Ship. *Guns*, 16; *Men*, 100.
> *Commander:* Nathaniel West, of Salem.
> > *Note.* Benjamin Cole also commanded this ship at one time.
> Essex Institute, Miscellaneous Ship Papers.

1777 PALLAS, Brigantine. *Guns*, 14; *Men*, 35.
Nov. 21 *Commander:* James Johnston.
> *Bond:* Continental, $10,000; State, £500.
> *Bonders:* James Johnston, principal; William Erskine, of Boston, and Jonathan Jackson, of Newburyport, sureties.
> *Owners:* William Erskine and others.
> *Witnesses:* Jos[eph] Hosmer, Fitch Pool.
> > *Note.* On the Penobscot Expedition and destroyed August, 1779, to prevent capture.
> M. A., VI, 242, 243, **168**, 35.

1780 PALLAS, Brigantine. *Guns*, 16; *Men*, 45.
May 22 *Commander:* Hector McNeill.
> *Bond:* Continental, $10,000; State, £4000.
> *Bonders:* Hector McNeill, mariner, of Boston, principal; John Tracy and Bossenger Foster, merchants, sureties.
> *Owners:* John Tracy and others, of Newburyport.
> *Witnesses:* W. Molineux, Thomas Perkins.
> M. A., VI, 266, 267, **171**, 164.

1780 PALLAS, Ship. *Guns*, 10; *Men*, 20.
Dec. 15 *Commander:* Gamaliel Hodges, of Salem.
> C. C. **196**, XI, 50; M. A., **171**, 313.

1781 PALLAS, Brigantine. *Guns*, 12; *Men*, 40.
Sept. 11 *Commander:* James Johnston, of Newburyport.
> C. C. **196**, XI, 51.

1781 PANTHER, Schooner. *Guns*, 8; *Men*, 35.
May 21 *Commander:* Samuel Masury, of Salem.
> C. C. **196**, XI, 53; M. A., **171**, 393; Felt, II, 276; Hunt, II, 48.

1782   PANTHER, Brig. *Guns*, 6; *Men*, 15.
July 31   *Commander:* George Lane, of Boston.
C. C. **196**, XI, 52; M. A., **172**, 182.

1777   PATTY, Sloop. *Guns*, 4; *Men*, 16.
Aug. 13   *Commander:* Nathan Nichols, of Salem.
C. C. **196**, XI, 60; *Boston Gazette*, Nov. 10, 1777.

1778   PATTY, Sloop. *Guns*, 6; *Men*, 30.
Jan. 21   *Commander:* Samuel Hobbs.
Bond: Continental, $5000; State, £500.
Bonders: Samuel Hobbs, principal; Elias Hasket Derby and Ichabod Nichols, of Salem, sureties.
Owners: Elias Hasket Derby and Ichabod Nichols.
Witness: D[aniel] Hopkins.
M. A., VI, 230, 233, **168**, 152.

1780   PATTY, Sloop. *Tons*, 80; *Guns*, 8; *Men*, 20.
Aug. 11   *Commander:* Francis Moore.
Petitioner: Adam Babcock, of Boston.
M. A., **171**, 237.

1780   PATTY, Brigantine. *Guns*, 6; *Men*, 16.
Dec. 28   *Commander:* Jonathan Oakes, of Malden.
Owners: William Shattuck and others, of Boston.
C. C. **196**, XI, 61; M. A., **171**, 320.

1781   PATTY, Brigantine. *Guns*, 6; *Men*, 15.
July 17   *Commander:* John Bishop, of Boston.
C. C. **196**, XI, 55; M. A., **171**, 425.

1781   PATTY, Ship. *Guns*, 8; *Men*, 20.
Sept. 29   *Commander:* Simon Forrester, of Salem.
C. C. **196**, XI, 57.

1782   PATTY, Ship. *Guns*, 8; *Men*, 20.
Mar. 8   *Commander:* John Derby, of Salem.
C. C. **196**, XI, 56.

1782   PATTY, Ship. *Guns*, 8; *Men*, 20.
June 29   *Commander:* David Smith, of Salem.
C. C. **196**, XI, 64; M. A., **172**, 177; Felt, II, 273.

1782   PATTY, Brig. *Guns*, 8; *Men*, 20.
Sept. 10   *Commander:* William Haydon, of Boston.
C. C. **196**, XI, 58.

1779 PEACOCK, Schooner. *Guns*, 6; *Men*, 20.
Feb. 9   *Commander:* William Parsons.
       Bond: Continental, $5000; State, £4000.
       Bonders: William Parsons, mariner, principal; John Greenleaf and William Coombs, of Newburyport, sureties.
       Owners: Eben[ezer] Parsons and others, of Newburyport.
       Witnesses: John Peck Rathbun, Benj[amin] Loring.
       M. A., VI, 236, 239, **169**, 436.

1780 PEACOCK, Schooner. *Guns*, 4; *Men*, 16.
Sept. 22   *Commander:* Sargent Smith, of Boston.
       C. C. **196**, XI, 70; M. A., **171**, 279.

1781 PEACOCK, Schooner. *Guns*, 4; *Men*, 10.
May 4   *Commander:* Elias Davis, of Boston.
       C. C. **196**, XI, 69; M. A., **171**, 382.

1781 PEACOCK, Schooner. *Guns*, 4; *Men*, 15.
Oct. 9   *Commander:* Alexander Mackay, of Boston.
       C. C. **196**, XI, 69; M. A., **172**, 20.

1782 PEACOCK, Brig. *Guns*, 4; *Men*, 12.
Oct. 17   *Commander:* Peter Wells, of Boston.
       C. C. **196**, XI, 71; M. A., **172**, 208.

1781 PEGGY, Brigantine (letter of marque).
       Commander: William Armstrong.
       Boston Gazette, Mar. 12, 1781.

1782 PENGUIN, Schooner. *Guns*, 10; *Men*, 40.
May 7   *Commander:* Samuel Foster, of Salem.
       C. C. **196**, XI, 92; M. A., **172**, 151.

1779 PENNET, Ship. *Guns*, 12; *Men*, 45.
Jan. 9   *Commander:* James Thompson.
       Bond: Continental, $10,000; State, £4000.
       Bonders: James Thompson, mariner, principal; Job Prince and Edward Carnes, of Boston, sureties.
       Owners: Peter Pennet [Pierre Penet] and others, of Boston.
       Witnesses: Henry Johnson, William Hall.
       M. A., VI, 307, 310, **139**, 240, **169**, 409: "Petition of Peter Pennet, of the Kingdom of France, Johnson Smith, of Fredericksburg in the State of Virginia, and James Thompson, of Boston."

1776 PHENIX, Sloop. *Guns*, 10; *Men*, 60.
Sept. 24   *Commander:* Joseph Cunningham.
   Bond: Continental, $5000.
   Bonders: Joseph Cunningham, mariner, John Rowe and Elias Warner, merchants — all of Boston.
   Owner: Carter Braxton, of New Castle, Virginia.
   Witnesses: Eben[ezer] Prout, Elias Parkman.
       M. A., VI, 227, **165**, 261, 269.

1776 PHOENIX, Schooner. *Guns*, 4; *Men*, 12.
Nov. 21   *Commander:* William Card.
   Bond: Continental, $5000.
   Bonders: William Card, principal, Solomon Babsden [signed Babson] and Francis Low, sureties — all of Cape Ann.
   Owners: Solomon Babson and Francis Low.
   Witness: Daniel Jones.
       M. A., VI, 229, **166**, 59.

1777 PHOENIX, Schooner. *Guns*, 12, and 8 *swivels; Men*, not stated.
July 9   *Commander:* Joseph Cunningham.
   Bond: State, £2000.
   Bonders: John Rowe, in behalf of the owners, and Joseph Cunningham.
   Owners: Robert Morris, of Philadelphia, and Carter Braxton, of Virginia.
   Witness: Timo[thy] Austin.
       M. A., **139**, 132 (Bond to enlist no man in New England outside of Massachusetts), **183**, 89, 90 (Petition, July 8, 1777, of John Rowe and Joseph Cunningham in behalf of the owners. They wish to give bonds, according to the laws of Massachusetts, and go to sea. Petition granted).

1778 PHOENIX, Brigantine. *Tons*, 120; *Guns*, 14; *Men*, 40.
Sept. 2   *Commander:* James Babson.
   Bond: Continental, $10,000; State, £4000.
   Bonders: James Babson, mariner, principal; James Tileston and Martin Brimmer, of Newburyport and Boston, sureties.
   Owners: Nathaniel Tracy and others, of Newburyport.
   Witnesses: Adam Babcock, Rufus Greene Amory.
       M. A., VI, 256, 259, **169**, 129.

1779 PHOENIX, Sch[o]oner. *Guns,* 4; *Men,* 18.
Sept. 26 *Commander:* Levi Jenne.
Bond: Continental, $5000; State, £4000.
Bonders: Levi Jennie [signed Jenne], mariner, principal; Samuel A. Otis and Isaiah Doane, of Boston, sureties.
Owner: Samuel A[llyne] Otis.
Witnesses: Nath[anie]l Paine, Benja[min] Sumner, jr.
M. A., VI, 252, 255, **170**, 393.

1780 PHOENIX, Brigantine. *Tons,* 100; *Guns,* 8; *Men,* 16.
Feb. 16 *Commander:* [John] Allen Hallet.
Bond: Continental, $10,000; State, £4000.
Bonders: Allen Hallet, mariner, principal; Thomas Harris and David Devens, of Boston, sureties.
Owners: Thomas Harris and others.
Witnesses: And[re]w Newell, Stephen Edes.
M. A., VI, 222, 223, **153**, 337, **171**, 81, **176**, 183 (Feb. 17, 1780. Petition of Capt. Hallet for leave of absence, without loss of rank in the State Navy, in order to make a cruise to the West Indies. Granted).

1780 PHOENIX, Brig. *Guns,* 8; *Men,* 16.
June 5 *Commander:* John Adams.
Bond: Continental, $10,000; State, £4000.
Bonders: John Adams, mariner, principal; David Devens and Thomas Harris, sureties — all of Boston.
Owners: Thomas Harris and others, merchants.
Witnesses: David Townsend, Isaac Townsend.
M. A., VI, 264, 265, **171**, 171.

1780 PHOENIX, Schooner. *Guns,* 2, and 6 *swivels; Men,* 12.
June 5 *Commander:* Consider Howland.
Bond: Continental, $5000; State, £4000.
Bonders: Consider Howland, mariner, principal; Lemuel Williams and Isaiah Doane, sureties.
Owners: Lemuel Williams and others.
Witness: Hen[ry?] Williams, jr.
M. A., VI, 248, 251, **171**, 191.

1780 PHOENIX, Brigantine. *Guns,* 8; *Men,* 16.
Dec. 19 *Commander:* John Howland Rickard, of Boston.
C. C. **196**, XI, 84; M. A., **171**, 317; *Boston Gazette,* July 8, 1782 (Captured Apr. 13, 1781).

1781 PHOENIX, Brig.
    Commander: Stephen Clay.
    Salem Gazette, Dec. 6, 1781: "Last Sunday Capt. Stephen Clay, in the brig *Phoenix,* arrived here in 41 days from Cadiz. He sailed in company with the brig *George and Fanny,* Capt. Adams, for Boston, and the brig *Virginia,* Capt. Hopkins, for Philadelphia, whom he parted with in Lat. 32, Long. 30."

1780 PICKERING, Ship. *Guns,* 16; *Men,* 100.
Nov. 2   *Commander:* Jonathan Haraden, of Salem.
    Note. See the ship *General Pickering.*
    C. C. **196**, XI, 86; M. A., **171**, 296.

1778 PILGRIM, Ship. *Tons,* 200; *Guns,* 16; *Men,* 140.
Sept. 11   *Commander:* Hugh Hill.
    Bond: Continental, $10,000; State, £4000.
    Bonders: Hugh Hill, mariner, principal; Andrew Cabot and Moses Brown, of Beverly, sureties.
    Owners: Andrew Cabot and others of Salem [Beverly?].
    Witnesses: Israel Thorndike, Jos[hu]a Brackett.
    M. A., VI, 228, 231, **169**, 157; Mar. Court Rec., 17, 26.

1780 PILGRIM, Ship. *Guns,* 18; *Men,* 160.
Mar. 24   *Commander:* Joseph Robinson.
    Bond: Continental, $10,000; State, £4000.
    Bonders: Joseph Robinson, mariner, principal; Andrew Cabot and Job Prince, jr., of Beverly and Boston, sureties.
    Owner: Andrew Cabot, of Beverly.
    Witness: Samuel Colesworthy, jr.
    M. A., VI, 260, 263, **171**, 104; *Boston Gazette,* Feb. 19, 1781: "Friday 7-night arrived at Salem the privateer ship *Pilgrim,* Capt. Robinson, from a cruise in which he has captured nine valuable prizes. . . ."

1781 PILGRIM, Ship. *Guns,* 18; *Men,* 150.
Apr. 14   *Commander:* Joseph Robinson, of Salem.
    Owners: John and Andrew Cabot, of Beverly.
    C. C. **196**, XI, 88; M. A., **171**, 369; Felt, II, 271; *Boston Gazette,* May 14, 1781: "Friday last arrived at Marblehead a Prize Brig of 12 four-pounders, laden with Provisions, bound from Liverpool for New-York, taken by the *Pilgrim.* The *Pilgrim* also took a Prize Ship laden with Provisions, and leaving the

Master and two or three of her Hands on board, they rose and took Possession of the Ship and were standing with her for Halifax, when luckily a small Privateer belonging to Cape-Ann came across, retook and carried her safe into the last-mentioned Port."

1781 PILGRIM, Ship. *Tons*, 300; *Guns*, 20; *Men*, 130.
Nov. 8 Commander: Joseph Robinson, of Salem.
Owners: John Cabot and others, of Beverly.
C. C. **196**, XI, 89; M. A., **172**, 59 (Petition signed by Job Prince, jr., in behalf of William Leach and others of Beverly); *Publ. Colonial Society of Mass.* (Log of the *Pilgrim*); *Boston Gazette*, June 24, 1782: "Last Monday the Prize Brig *Neptune* . . . arrived in a safe Port. She was taken . . . by the Privateer Ship *Pilgrim*, Capt. Robinson, of Beverly." *Salem Gazette*, Oct. 10, 1782: "The *Pilgrim*, an excellent privateer ship, copper-bottomed, commanded by Capt. Robinson and bound on a cruise from Beverly, was a few days ago chased on shore at Cape-Cod by a British man of war, supposed to be the *Chatham*, of fifty guns. The men, guns, stores, etc., are saved, but it is feared the hull will be lost."

1781 PINE APPLE, Schooner. *Guns*, 6; *Men*, 30.
Commander: ——— ———.
Essex Institute, Miscellaneous Ship Papers.

1782 PINK, Schooner. *Guns*, 4; *Men*, 20.
Dec. 10 Commander: Magnes Harvey, of Boston.
C. C. **196**, XI, 93; M. A., **172**, 256.

1782 PLATO, Brig. *Guns*, 8.
Commander: ——— ———.
Essex Institute, Miscellaneous Ship Papers.

1777 PLIARNE, Ship.
Commander: Samuel Green.
Note. It is not certain that this vessel was armed.
M. A., **168**, 186, 187; Marblehead Hist. Soc. See Introduction, 56.

1777 PLUTO, Brigantine. *Guns*, 10; *Men*, 60.
May 13 Commander: Nathan Brown.
Bond: Continental, $5000.
Bonders: Nathan Brown, principal, Josiah Orne, surety, both of Salem.

Owners: Josiah Orne & Co.
Witnesses: Andrew Cabot, William Harris.
M. A., VI, 232, **166**, 401.

1777 PLUTO, Brigantine. *Guns,* 10, and 10 *swivels; Men,* 60.
Nov. 21   *Commander:* Joseph Robinson.
Bond: Continental, $5000; State, £500.
Bonders: Joseph Robinson, principal; Josiah Orne and James Homer, of Boston, sureties.
Owners: Josiah Orne and James Homer.
Witness: Fitch Pool.
M. A., VI, 240, 241, **168**, 30.

1778 PLUTO, Brig. *Guns,* 8, and 8 *swivels; Men,* 45.
June 5   *Commander:* John Hill.
Bond: Continental, $5000; State, £4000.
Bonders: John Hill, principal; Henry Williams and Samuel Ward, of Salem, sureties.
Owners: Henry Williams and Samuel Ward.
Witness: D[aniel] Hopkins.
M. A., VI, 244, 247, **168**, 352.

1781 PLUTO, Schooner. *Guns,* 2; *Men,* 20.
Aug. 14   *Commander:* Joseph Seveir, of Newburyport.
C. C. **196**, XI, 95.

1782 POLACRE, Ship. *Guns,* 8; *Men,* 75.
Commander: —— ——.
Essex Institute, Miscellaneous Ship Papers.

1776 POLLY, Sloop. *Guns,* 12, and 18 *swivels; Men,* 100.
Sept. 6   *Commander:* Nathaniel Leech.
Master: Samuel Green.
Bond: Continental, not stated.
Bonders: Nathaniel Leach [signed Leech], principal; Capt. John Grush and James Mugford, sureties.
Owners: William Blacklair and James Mugford & Co., of Marblehead.
Witnesses: Swett Hooper, Arnold Martin.
M. A., VI, 224, **165**, 227; Marblehead Hist. Soc.

1776 POLLY, Sloop.
Commander: Isaac Collyer.
Note. In the *Boston Gazette* of Jan. 13, 1777, the captain is called Isaac Collins.
Boston Gazette, Dec. 2, 1776.

1779 POLLY, Schooner. *Guns*, 4; *Men*, 12.
June 18   *Commander:* Samuel Williams.
  Bond: Continental, $5000; State, £4000.
  Bonders: Samuel Williams, mariner, principal; Bartho-[lomew] Putnam and William Orne, of Salem, sureties.
  Owner: Bartholomew Putnam.
  Witnesses: Peter Lander, Joseph Grafton.
    M. A., VI, 254, 257, **170**, 174.

1780 POLLY, Brigantine. *Guns*, 6; *Men*, 15.
Jan. 4   *Commander:* Nathaniel Goodwin.
  Bond: Continental, $10,000; State, £4000.
  Bonders: Nathaniel Goodwin, mariner, principal; Thomas Russell and Samuel Conant, jr., of Boston, sureties.
  Owner: Thomas Russell.
  Witnesses: Chambers Russell, Thomas Greene.
    M. A., VI, 268, 269, **176**, 83.

1780 POLLY, Brigantine. *Guns*, 8; *Men*, 20.
Feb. 22   *Commander:* Eliphalet Ripley.
  Bond: Continental, $10,000; State, £4000.
  Bonders: Eliphalet Ripley, principal; Isaac Sears and Paschal N[elson] Smith, of Boston, sureties.
  Owner: Isaac Sears.
  Witnesses: Elia[ki]m Raymond, Joseph Skillin.
    M. A., VI, 220, 221, **171**, 83.

1780 POLLY, Brigantine. *Guns*, 6; *Men*, 14.
Oct. 11   *Commander:* George Leacey, of Virginia.
  Bonders: William Burke and Richard Hayden, of Boston.
  Owners: George Leacey and others.
    C. C. **196**, XI, 103; M. A., **171**, 290.

1781 POLLY, Ship. *Guns*, 20; *Men*, 35.
Jan. 9   *Commander:* William Coas, of Gloucester.
    C. C. **196**, XI, 100; M. A., **171**, 326.

1781 POLLEY, Ship. *Guns*, 18; *Men*, 30.
Feb. 20   *Commander:* Joseph Foster, of Cape Ann.
    C. C. **196**, XI, 97; M. A., **171**, 345.

1782 POLLY, Ship. *Guns*, 16; *Men*, 25.
Feb. 21   *Commander:* Isaac Lee.

Owners: Winthrop Sargent and others, of Gloucester.

C. C. **196**, XI, 104; M. A., **172**, 101; *Salem Gazette*, Apr. 11, 1782: "Captain Mowat lately sent out a fourteen-gun brig, under command of one of his Midshipmen with particular orders to cruise off Cape-Ann, to take a fishing-boat and man her well, but to keep out of sight himself with the brig; the boat to proceed to Beverly, Salem, or Marblehead, to land some men, and, if opportunity presented itself, to cut out some armed vessel . . . and in case of success to make the best of his way to Bagwaduce. Accordingly they took a boat and manned her with twenty-five men, touched at Cape-Ann . . . and found that the ship *Harriot*, belonging to Capt. David Pearce was ready for sea with a very valuable cargo on board. . . . On the first instant, about half-past four o'clock in the morning they boarded and cut out the ship and proceeded to sea. There scarcely appeared any doubt of their final escape, as it was dead low water and no vessel in any situation to pursue them; the wind was off shore and a leading breeze. The only prospect we had of recovering her was to get the ship *Polly* in readiness; she is pierced for twenty guns and belongs to the same owner. She was then on the ways, had her topmasts struck, and a swept hold. They began to work on her about seven o'clock and at eleven she was compleat for sea, with guns, ammunition, etc., and a hundred volunteers on board. The zeal shewn in getting the vessel ready and the resentment which appeared in every countenance promised success. They accordingly rowed out, it being almost calm, and steered E. N. E. in hopes of meeting with the enemy about day-light, which they effected and found the brig, the ship, and boat all together, steering for Penobscot, and about 12 o'clock came up with and re-took the *Harriot* and immediately gave chase to the brig, they having separated on discovering the *Polly* in chase of them; but night coming on, our people reluctantly gave over the chase and arrived the same day with the *Harriot*, to their own honour and the satisfaction of the inhabitants." *Essex Inst. Hist. Coll.*, XLV, 236 (The *Polly* was captured July 4, 1782, near Georges Banks, by H. M. frigate *Ceres*).

1782 POLLY, Schooner. *Tons*, 50; *Guns*, 6; *Men*, 12.
Dec. 11   *Commander:* John Revell.
   Petition signed by Thomas Saunders in behalf of Josiah Orne and others of Salem.
   M. A., **172**, 257.

1779 POMONA.
   Commander: —— ——.
   London Chronicle, July 29, 1779: "Two American vessels from Amsterdam, one the *Pomona* letter of marque for Boston, . . . were taken by his Majesty's frigate *Diana*."

1780 POMONA, Sloop. *Tons*, 90; *Guns*, 10; *Men*, 12.
Apr. 6   *Commander:* Jonathan Mason, jr.
   Petitioners: Jonathan Mason and others, of Salem.
   M. A., **171**, 125.

1778 POMPEY, Schooner. *Guns*, 4, and 16 *swivels; Men*, 40.
Apr. 14   *Commander:* Silas Smith.
   Bond: Continental, $5000; State, £4000.
   Bonders: Silas Smith, principal; William West and Samuel Williams, of Salem, sureties.
   Owners: William West and Samuel Williams.
   Witness: D[aniel] Hopkins.
   M. A., VI, 246, 249, **168**, 249.

1781 POMPEY, Boat. *Guns*, small arms; *Men*, 10.
Sept. 3   *Commander:* William Thomas.
   Owners: Ebenezer May and others, of Boston.
   Note. The name Jacob Flick appears on the petition as the commander of this boat, but is crossed out and the name William Thomas substituted.
   C. C. **196**, XII, 2; M. A., **171**, 467 (Aug. 23, 1781).

1782 POOLE, Ship. *Guns*, 12; *Men*, 65.
   Commander: —— ——.
   Essex Institute, Miscellaneous Ship Papers.

1782 POPPET, Schooner. *Guns*, 4; *Men*, 10.
Mar. 11   *Commander:* Thomas Barnard, of Boston.
   C. C. **196**, XII, 3; M. A., **172**, 116.

1782 POPPET, Schooner.
   Commander: Charles Cole.
   Boston Gazette, May 27, 1782.

1779 PORCUPINE, Schooner. *Guns*, 6; *Men*, 25.
Apr. 22   *Commander:* George Andrew.
  Bond: Continental, $5000; State, £4000.
  Bonders: George Andrew, of Marblehead, principal; Samuel Williams, of Salem, and Nathaniel Lindsay, of Marblehead, sureties.
  Owners: Samuel Williams, Nathaniel Lindsay, and others.
  Witnesses: Rich[ar]d Horton [?], Thomas Doliber.
  M. A., VI, 250, 253, **170**, 65.

1779 PORCUPINE, Schooner. *Guns*, 2; *Men*, 55.
Aug. 31   *Commander:* Samuel Carlton.
  Bond: Continental, $5000; State, £4000.
  Bonders: Samuel Carlton, mariner, principal; John Fisk and John Norris, of Salem, sureties.
  Owner: John Norris.
  Witnesses: John Gardner, 3d, Samuel Waters.
  M. A., VI, 237, 238, **170**, 366.

1780 PORGA, Brigantine. *Guns*, 14; *Men*, 40.
Sept. 28   *Commander:* William Armstrong, of Newburyport.
  Owner: Nehemiah Somes, of Boston.
  C. C. **196**, XII, 4; M. A., **171**, 283.

1780 PORGEE, Brig.
  Commander: Sylvanus Lowell.
  Note. The vessel's name may be a mis-spelling of *Porga.* In *Naval Records of the Revolution* the name Lowell is spelled Loell.
  Boston Gazette, July 17, 1780.

1781 PORT PACKET, Ship. *Guns*, 14; *Men*, 50.
June 1   *Commander:* George Rapall, of Newburyport.
  C. C. **196**, XII, 9.

1781 PORT PACQUET, Ship. *Guns*, 12; *Men*, 30.
Dec. 15   *Commander:* Ebenezer Stocker, of Newburyport.
  C. C. **196**, XII, 10.

1781 PORT PACKET, Ship. *Guns*, 8; *Men*, 20.
  Commander: Simon Forrester.
  Essex Institute, Miscellaneous Ship Papers.

1781 PORUS, Ship. *Guns*, 20; *Men*, 140.
June 7   *Commander:* John Carnes, of Salem.
  C. C. **196**, XII, 15; M. A., **171**, 407.

1782 PORUS, Ship. *Guns*, 22; *Men*, 150.
Aug. 30   *Commander:* Samuel Croel, of Salem.
   C. C. 196, XII, 16; *Boston Gazette*, May 5, 1783 (Salem, May 1): "Capt. Crowel, in the ship *Porus*, one of our late privateers, was arrived at [St. Christophers] with a prize ship from Africa with upwards of 200 slaves on board, taken previous to the cessation of hostilities."

1783 PRINCE RADZIWIL, Schooner. *Guns*, 6; *Men*, 15.
Mar. 18   *Commander:* Feelix Miklaszewiez, of Boston.
   Note. The vessel's name is spelled *Radizwil* in *Naval Records of the Revolution*.
   C. C. 196, XII, 18; M. A., 172, 313.

1781 PROSPECT, Brigantine. *Guns*, 12; *Men*, 60.
June 19   *Commander:* Joseph Vesey, of Boston.
   Note. The captain's name is spelled Vezey in the petition.
   C. C. 196, XII, 21; M. A., XL, 77, 171, 414.

1781 PROSPECT, Brig. *Guns*, 12; *Men*, 50.
Oct. 3   *Commander:* Amos Potter, of Boston.
   C. C. 196, XII, 20; M. A., 172, 17.

1781 PROSPECT, Brigantine. *Tons*, 100; *Guns*, 12; *Men*, 25.
Dec. 30   *Commander:* David Porter.
   Petitioners: Isaac Sears and others, of Boston.
   M. A., 172, 90.

1780 PROSPER, Ship. *Guns*, 6; *Men*, 18.
Dec. 5   *Commander:* Joseph Atkins, of Newburyport.
   C. C. 196, XII, 22; M. A., 171, 320 (Dec. 28, 1780).

1781 PROSPER, Ship. *Guns*, 8; *Men*, 30.
June 7   *Commander:* Samuel Dunn, jr., of Boston.
   C. C. 196, XII, 23.

1777 PROSPEROUS. *Guns*, 8.
   Commander: ———— ————.
   London Chronicle, Apr. 10, 1777: "The snow *Fox*, of 12 guns, and the *Prince of Wales*, of 8 guns, fitted out by orders from Admiral Gayton to cruize against the American privateers, have taken the *Rising Sun*, of 16 guns, and the *Prosperous*, of 8 guns, after a dreadful engagement of six hours. The *Fox* had 11 men killed and almost everyone on board wounded; the

KNOW all Men by these Presents, that WE Samuel Dunn _____ of Boston in the County of Suffolk in the Commonwealth of Mass.ts Mariner as Principal and William Dennie and James Swan of Boston in the County Commonwealth aforesaid are held and firmly bound to Michael Hillegas Esquire, Treasurer of the United States of America, in the penalty of TWENTY THOUSAND SPANISH MILLED DOLLARS, or other Money equivalent thereto, to be paid to the said Michael Hillegas Esq. Treasurer, as aforesaid, or to his Successors in that Office. To which payment well and truly to be made and done, WE bind ourselves, our Heirs, Executors, and Administrators, jointly and severally, firmly by these Presents. Sealed with our Seals, and dated, the Seventh Day of June, in the Year of our Lord 1781, and in the fifth Year of the Independence of the United States.

THE Condition of this Obligation is such, That whereas the above bounden Samuel Dunn jun.r _____ Master and Commander of the Ship ___ called the Prosper _____ belonging to William Dennie and James Swan of Boston in the County of Suffolk in the Commonwealth of Mass.ts mounting Eight carriage guns, and navigated by Thirty _____ men, who hath applied for and received a Commission, bearing date with these Presents, licencing and authorizing him to fit out and set forth the said Ship ___ in a warlike manner, and by and with the said Ship ___ and the officers and crew thereof, by force of arms to attack, subdue, seize and take all ships and other vessels, goods, wares and merchandizes, belonging to the Crown of Great-Britain, or any of the subjects thereof, (excepting the ships or vessels together with their cargoes, belonging to any inhabitant or inhabitants of Bermuda, and such other ships or vessels bringing persons with intent to settle within the said United States;) and any other ships or vessels, goods, wares and merchandizes, to whomsoever belonging, which are or shall be declared to be subjects of capture, by any Resolutions of Congress, or which are so deemed by the law of Nations. If therefore the said Samuel Dunn jun.r _____ shall not exceed or transgress the powers and authorities given and granted to him, in and by the said Commission, or which are or shall be given and granted to him by any Resolutions, Acts or Instructions of Congress, but, shall in all things govern and conduct himself, as Master and Commander of the said Ship ___ and the officers and crew belonging to the same, by and according to the said Commission, Resolutions, Acts and Instructions, and any Treaties subsisting or which may subsist between the United States of America and any Prince, Power or Potentate whatever; and shall not violate the law of Nations, or the rights of neutral Powers, or, of any of their subjects; and shall make reparation for all damages sustained by any misconduct, or unwarrantable proceedings of himself, or the officers or crew, of the said Ship ___ then this Obligation to be void, otherwise to remain in full force.

Signed, sealed and delivered,
in presence of us,

A Continental Bond in the Library of Congress

See page 38

Prince of Wales had five men killed and 12 wounded. The crews of the Provincial vessels were upwards of a third of them killed and the greatest part of them very much wounded. The vessels had not long sailed from Boston and had not met with any success."

1779 PROTECTOR. *Guns*, 20; *Men*, 200.
 Commander: —— ——.
 London Chronicle, Nov. 23, 1779: "A large American privateer called the *Protector*, fitted out at Salem, is taken by some of Admiral Parker's ships and sent into Barbadoes; she carried 20 nine and twelve pounders, 200 men, and is a new built ship."

1780 PROTECTOR, Frigate. *Guns*, 26.
 Commander: John Foster Williams.
 Massachusetts State Navy.

1776 PROVIDENCE. *Guns*, 12.
 Commander: —— ——.
 London Chronicle, Nov. 28, 1776: "The *Providence* privateer of 12 guns, belonging to Boston, is taken, after a warm engagement off Cape Cod, by the *Success*, Brown, and the *Mary Ann*, Collins, two armed transports, and carried into New York."

1780 PROVIDENCE, Sloop. *Guns*, 8; *Men*, 15.
Sept. 25 Commander: Isaiah Simmons, of Boston.
 C. C. **196**, XII, 28; M. A., **171**, 281.

1779 PRUDENCE, Boat. *Guns*, 1 *swivel;* *Men*, 8.
Apr. 16 Commander: Israel Stoddard.
 Bond: Continental, $5000; State, £4000.
 Bonders: Israel Stoddard, principal; William Davis and Edw[ard?] Pope, of Dartmouth, sureties.
 Owners: William Davis and others.
 Witnesses: John Nelson, John Baxter, jr.
 M. A., VI, 234, 235, **170**, 60.

1776 PUTNAM, Sloop. *Guns*, 4, and 10 *swivels;* *Men*, 45.
Aug. 26 Commander: John Harmon.
 Bond: Continental, $5000.
 Bonders: John Harmon, of York, Ebenezer Prout, of Scarborough, County of Cumberland, and David Sewall, of York.

  Owners: Joseph Morrill, Thomas Donnell, Ebenezer Norwood, William Allen, and James Scamman, of Biddeford.
  Witnesses: John Taylor, John Avery, jr.
  M. A., VI, 226, **165**, 163.

1776 PUTNAM, Sloop. *Guns*, 2, and 16 *swivels; Men*, 45.
Sept. 27 *Commander:* Joseph Bayley, jr.
  Bond: Continental, $5000.
  Bonders: Jos[eph] Bayley, jr., mariner, Pearson Jones, merchant, both of Falmouth, County of Cumberland, and Ebenezer Parsons, merchant, of Newburyport.
  Owner: The Town of Falmouth.
  Witnesses: And[re]w Giddinge [Giddings], Michael Hodge.
  M. A., VI, 225, **165**, 298.

1777 PUTNAM, Sloop. *Guns*, 4; *Men*, 30.
Jan. 7 *Commander:* Seth Hinkley.
  Bond: Continental, $5000.
  Bonders: Seth Hinkley and Enoch Ilsley, of Falmouth, Cumberland County.
  Owners: Enoch Ilsley & Co.
  Witnesses: Jno. Fox, Thomas Saunders.
  M. A., VI, 245.

1779 PUTNAM, Ship. *Guns*, 18; *Men*, 90.
Feb. 1 *Commander:* Nathan Brown.
  Essex Institute, Miscellaneous Ship Papers; Felt, II, 269.

1779 PUTNAM, Ship. *Tons*, 400; *Guns*, 20; *Men*, 150.
Mar. 3 *Commander:* Nathaniel Saltonstall.
  Bond: Continental, $10,000.
  Bonders: Nathaniel Saltonstall, principal; Nathaniel Shaw and Thomas Shaw, sureties.
  Owner: Nathaniel Shaw, of New London, Conn.
  Witnesses: Simon Wolcott, Harris [?] Rogers.
  Note. The same vessel as the ship *General Putnam.*
  M. A., VI, 262, **170**, 2 (Petition of Josiah Waters, of Boston, in behalf of Nathaniel Shaw).

1781 QUEEN OF FRANCE, Ship. *Guns*, 12; *Men*, 40.
Feb. 24 *Commander:* John Dixey, of Newburyport.
  C. C. **196**, XII, 34.

1782 QUEEN OF FRANCE, Ship. *Guns*, 8; *Men*, 20.
Nov. 23 *Commander:* Thomas Tracy, of Newburyport.
  C. C. **196**, XII, 38.

1782 QUEEN OF SPAIN, Brigantine. *Guns*, 6; *Men*, 15.
Feb. 11   Commander: Tristram Barnard, of Boston.
C. C. **196**, XII, 39; M. A., **172**, 100.

1780 RACE HORSE, Sloop. *Guns*, 8; *Men*, 20.
June 24   Commander: Clifford Byrne.
Bond: Continental, $5000; State, £4000.
Bonders: Clifford Byrne, mariner, principal; Elias Hasket Derby and Nathaniel Silsbee, merchants of Salem, sureties.
Owners: Nathaniel Silsbee and others.
Witnesses: Stephen Webb, Edward Gibaut.
M. A., VII, 43, 44, **171**, 186; Felt, II, 271.

1781 RACE HORSE, Brigantine. *Guns*, 6; *Men*, 15.
May 29   Commander: Nathaniel Thayer, of Boston.
C. C. **196**, XII, 44; M. A., **171**, 401.

1782 RACE HORSE, Schooner. *Guns*, 4; *Men*, 20.
Mar. 25   Commander: Thomas Oliver, of Marblehead.
C. C. **196**, XII, 42; M. A., **172**, 121.

1782 RACE HORSE, Schooner. *Guns*, 8; *Men*, 25.
Aug. 30   Commander: Alexander Storey, of Salem.
C. C. **196**, XII, 43.

1779 RACHEL, Ship. *Guns*, 14; *Men*, 75.
Commander: —— ——.
Essex Institute, Miscellaneous Ship Papers.

1782 RAINBOW, Sloop. *Guns*, 10; *Men*, 40.
Apr. 5   Commander: Nathaniel Coit Webb, of Salem.
C. C. **196**, XII, 49; Felt, II, 275.

1782 RAINBOW, Schooner. *Guns*, 6; *Men*, 25.
Oct. 9   Commander: Oliver Webb, of Salem.
C. C. **196**, XII, 50; M. A., **172**, 201.

1777 RAMBLER, Schooner. *Guns*, 2; *Men*, 20.
Dec. 9   Commander: Jonathan Felt.
Bond: Continental, $5000; State, £500.
Bonders: Jonathan Felt, principal; Thomas Mason and Joshua Dodge, merchants, sureties — all of Salem.
Owners: Thomas Mason and Joshua Dodge.
Witnesses: Jona[than] Andrew, Thomas Porter.
M. A., VII, 28, 29, **168**, 85.

1778 RAMBLER, Schooner. *Guns*, 8 *swivels; Men*, 20.
Apr. 20   *Commander:* Moses Lewis.
    Bond: Continental, $5000; State, £4000.
    Bonders: Moses Lewis, principal, and William Shattuck, on both bonds; John Shattuck on Continental bond.
    Signers: Moses Lewis and William Shattuck (both bonds); John Shattuck (Continental bond), Samuel Gore (State bond).
    Owners: William Shattuck and others, of Boston.
    Witnesses: William Dall, James Perkins (Continental bond); William Dall, Elisha Cole (State bond).
    M. A., VII, 11, 12, **139**, 167, **168**, 250.

1779 RAMBLER, Brigantine.
July 5   *Commander:* George Williams, jr., [of Salem].
    M. A., **170**, 206 (Petition of William Pickman, who wishes to bring her from Newburyport to Salem, to be armed and fitted out, embargo notwithstanding. Granted).

1779 RAMBLER, Brigantine. *Guns*, 14; *Men*, 85.
Sept. 2   *Commander:* John Stevens.
    Bond: Continental, $10,000; State, £4000.
    Bonders: John Stevens, mariner, principal; Ellis Mansfield and Benja[min] Daland, of Salem, sureties.
    Owner: Sam[ue]l Williams, [of Salem].
    Witnesses: Moses Brown, Israel Thorndike.
    M. A., VII, 64, 65, **170**, 362.

1779 RAMBLER, Ship. *Guns*, 14; *Men*, 50.
Oct. 16   *Commander:* Benjamin Lovett.
    Bond: Continental, $10,000; State, £4000.
    Bonders: Benjamin Lovett, mariner, principal; Andrew and John Cabot, of Beverly, sureties.
    Owner: Andrew Cabot.
    Witnesses: Sam[uel] Cabot, Fran[ci]s Cabot, jr.
    M. A., VI, 344, 347, XL, 70 (crew list, May 27, 1780), **170**, 434; *Salem Gazette*, Jan. 16, 1781 (See ship *Defence*); *Ibid.*, Nov. 22, 1781: "Last Saturday arrived at Beverly, the letter of marque ship *Rambler*, Capt. [Lovett], in 26 days from Bilboa."

1780 RAMBLER, Schooner.
Aug. 9   *Commander:* William Maley.
    Petitioners: Thomas Jones and John Stickney, of Newburyport.

M. A., **176**, 613 (Petition that the *Rambler* may go to sea notwithstanding the embargo. Granted); *Boston Gazette*, Nov. 13, 1780.

1780 Rambler, Schooner. *Guns*, 4; *Men*, 25.
Oct. 28 Commander: Benjamin Fuller, of Newburyport.
C. C. **196**, xii, 53.

1781 Rambler, Schooner. *Guns*, 4; *Men*, 25.
Apr. 10 Commander: Joseph Seveir, of Newburyport.
C. C. **196**, xii, 56.

1781 Rambler, Brigantine. *Guns*, 18.
Commander:
London Chronicle, Aug. 23, 1781: "The *Henrietta* was chaced into Loch Swillie, by two American privateers . . . One of them is called the *Cicero*, a ship mounting 20 guns; the other is a brigantine called the *Rambler*, of 18 guns, belonging to Boston."

1782 Rambler, Ship. *Guns*, 16; *Men*, 50.
Feb. 14 Commander: Benjamin Lovett, of Beverly.
C. C. **196**, xii, 54; M. A., **172**, 114.

1776 Ranger, Schooner. *Guns*, 2; *Men*, 30.
Sept. 25 Commander: Peter Roberts.
Bond: Continental, $5000.
Bonders: Peter Roberts, mariner, Jonathan Titcomb, Tristram Dalton, Thomas Thomas, and Ebenezer Parsons, merchants, all of Newburyport.
Owners: Jonathan Titcomb & Co.
Witnesses: Isaac Johnson, jr., Thomas Roberts.
M. A., vii, 38, **165**, 290.

1779 Ranger, Brigantine. *Guns*, 12; *Men*, 20.
May 21 Commander: Henry White.
Bond: Continental, $10,000; State, £4000.
Bonders: Henry White, mariner, principal; Miles Greenwood and Joseph Miller, of Salem, sureties.
Owners: Joseph Lambert and others, of Salem.
Witness: Jno. Dall.
M. A., vii, 51, 54, **170**, 131.

1780 Ranger, Brigantine.
June 12 Commander: Robert Stone, of Salem.
M. A., xl, 93.

1780 RANGER, Brigantine. *Guns*, 10; *Men*, 20.
Oct. 19   *Commander:* Samuel Babson, of Cape Ann.
           C. C. **196**, XII, 60; M. A., **171**, 293.

1781 RANGER, Brigantine. *Guns*, 8; *Men*, 20.
July 14   *Commander:* Job Knight, of Cape Ann.
           Owners: Stephen Higginson and others, of Boston.
           C. C. **196**, XII, 70; M. A., **171**, 432.

1781 RANGER, Brigantine. *Guns*, 8; *Men*, 15.
Oct. 9   *Commander:* Thomas Simmons, of Boston.
           C. C. **196**, XII, 75; M. A., **172**, 20; *Salem Gazette*, Aug. 15, 1782: "On the 5th ult. at one A.M. Capt. Thomas Simmons, Commander of the brig *Ranger*, of this port [The bond makes Boston the home port. There may have been a later *Ranger*, from Salem and commanded by Simmons], was attacked off St. Mary's, near the mouth of the Potowmuck, by Anderson and Barret, two noted commanders of two refugee barges with thirty men each, and after an obstinate engagement of three glasses, the latter were obliged to sheer off, with the loss of fifteen men killed and thirty-eight wounded. The barges rowed off to St. George's Island with their mangled crews, where they buried five who died of their wounds, and left three mortally wounded. Capt. Simmons is wounded in one of his legs, his second mate in both arms, one man killed and one wounded. Nothing could exceed the bravery of Capt. Simmons, his officers and crew, having but one man to oppose to three of the enemy and unable to derive any advantage from their guns, as the barges were lashed, one on each side, fast to the brig. Notwithstanding the disadvantage of a sudden attack added to the darkness of the night, which enabled the enemy to grapple the *Ranger* before they received any damage, Capt. Simmons and his men began and continued the engagement with such spirit, by pushing their pikes and throwing cold shot, as to merit the highest encomiums for the gallantry of their conduct."

1782 RANGER, Boat. *Guns*, 1; *Men*, 13.
May 8   *Commander:* Lot Dimick [Dimuck], of Falmouth, Barnstable County.
           C. C. **196**, XII, 65; M. A., **172**, 150.

1782 RANGER, Schooner. *Guns*, 4; *Men*, 20.
May 27 *Commander:* Joseph Christophers, of Kennebec.
C. C. **196**, XII, 63; M. A., **172**, 166.

1782 RANGER, Schooner. *Guns*, 6; *Men*, 20.
Aug. 12 *Commander:* Joshua Burges, of Gloucester.
C. C. **196**, XII, 62.

1782 RANGER, Ship. *Guns*, 6; *Men*, 15.
Dec. 2 *Commander:* Samuel Coffin, of Newburyport.
C. C. **196**, XII, 64.

1777 RATTLESNAKE, Sloop. *Guns*, 6; *Men*, 25.
Apr. 19 *Commander:* Joshua Stone.
Bond: Continental, £1500.
Bonders: Joshua Stone, mariner, of Falmouth, Cumberland County, principal, Jno. Archer and Jno. Fox.
Owners: Joseph Noyes & Co., of Falmouth, Casco Bay.
Witnesses: William McGillan [?], Thomas Saunders.
Note. The vessel's name is written *Rattle Snake*.
M. A., VII, 24, **166**, 349.

1779 RATTLESNAKE, Schooner. *Tons*, 50; *Guns*, 8; *Men*, 40.
Sept. 6 *Commander:* Thomas Johnson.
Petitioner: John Wait, of Marblehead.
M. A., **159**, 243, **170**, 375; *Boston Gazette*, Nov. 1, 1779.

1781 RATTLESNAKE, Ship. *Guns*, 20; *Men*, 85.
June 12 *Commander:* Mark Clark, of Salem.
Note. Listed as a brig by Hunt.
C. C. **196**, XII, 80; M. A., **171**, 409.

1778 RAVEN, Schooner. *Guns*, 8 *swivels*; *Men*, 23.
Aug. 28 *Commander:* John Brown.
Bond: Continental, $5000; *State*, £4000.
Bonders: John Brown, mariner, principal; Pickering Collins [signed Collings] and James Dennis, of Marblehead, sureties.
Owners: Samuel Gale [Gail?] and others, of Marblehead.
Witness: Jno. Dall.
M. A., VII, 4, 98, **169**, 116.

1778 RAVEN, Schooner. *Guns*, 2; *Men*, 30.
Oct. 23 *Commander:* Ephraim Chambers.
Bond: Continental, $5000; State, £4000.
Bonders: Ephraim Chambers, mariner, principal; sureties omitted.

>
> *Signers:* Ephraim Chambers, John Brown, and Robert Brimblecom.
> *Owners:* John Brown and others, of Marblehead.
> *Witnesses:* Edw[ar]d Baker, Henry Alline.
> M. A., VI, 355, 356, **169**, 250.

1779 RAVEN, Schooner. *Guns*, 2, and 12 *swivels; Men,* 30.
Apr. 26 *Commander:* Joseph Salter.
> *Bond:* Continental, $5000; State, £4000.
> *Bonders:* Joseph Salter, mariner, principal; John D[evereux] Dennis and Nath[anie]l Grow, of Marblehead, sureties.
> *Owners:* Sam[ue]l Gale and others, of Marblehead.
> *Witness:* John Dall.
>> *Note.* The owner wrote his name both Gale and Gail.
>
> M. A., VI, 342, 345, **170**, 68.

1780 RAVEN, Ship. *Guns,* 12; *Men,* 40.
June 2 *Commander:* William Brown.
> *Bond:* Continental, $10,000; State, £4000.
> *Bonders:* William Brown, mariner, principal; Ebenezer Parsons and Stephen Higginson, merchants, sureties — all of Boston.
> *Owners:* Stephen Higginson and others.
> *Witnesses:* Moses Pike, Daniel Sargent, jr.
> M. A., VI, 359, 360, **171**, 168.

1780 RAVEN, Ship. *Guns,* 10; *Men,* 40.
Nov. 9 *Commander:* James Davis, of Boston.
> C. C. **196**, XII, 87; M. A., **171**, 301.

1782 RAVEN, Schooner. *Guns,* 12; *Men,* 40.
May 4 *Commander:* Daniel Needham, of Salem.
> C. C. **196**, XII, 89; M. A., **172**, 147; Felt, II, 275; *Salem Gazette,* Oct. 10, 1782 (See *Junius Brutus*).

1779 RECOVERY, Brigantine. *Guns,* 8; *Men,* 20.
Dec. 16 *Commander:* Daniel Smith.
> *Bond:* Continental, $10,000; State, £4000.
> *Bonders:* Daniel Smith, principal; John Codman and William Smith, sureties — all of Boston.
> *Owners:* George Meade & Co., of Philadelphia.
> *Witnesses:* Samuel Parkman, William Codman.
> M. A., VI, 351, 352, **171**, 45.

1782 RECOVERY, Brigantine. *Guns*, 12; *Men*, 15.
June 4   *Commander:* Samuel Ingersoll, of Salem.
   C. C. **196**, XII, 102; M. A., **172**, 171.

1782 RECOVERY, Brigantine. *Guns*, 6; *Men*, 16.
Dec. 6   *Commander:* William Dennis, of Salem.
   C. C. **196**, XII, 100; M. A., **172**, 251.

1779 RENOWN, Ship. *Guns*, 14; *Men*, 95.
Aug. 7   *Commander:* Robert Adamson.
   Bond: Continental, $10,000; State, £4000.
   Bonders: Robert Adamson, mariner, principal; John Leach, jr., and Samuel Page, of Boston and Salem, sureties.
   Owners: Samuel Page and others, of Salem.
   Witness: Walter Price Bartlet.
      Note. Convoyed transports for the Penobscot Expedition.
         M. A., VII, 57, 58, VIII, 48, XXXVII, 221, 222, 262, 290, XLIV, 441, 442, 443, **145**, 414, 415 (transports and convoys), **170**, 307.

1780 RENOWN, Ship. *Tons*, 150; *Guns*, 10; *Men*, 30.
Aug. 24   *Commander:* Jonathan Felt.
   Petitioners: Samuel Page and others, of Salem.
   M. A., **171**, 261.

1782 RENOWN, Brig. *Guns*, 14; *Men*, 65.
      Commander: ——— ———.
   Essex Institute, Miscellaneous Ship Papers.

1776 REPRISAL, Brig. *Guns*, 8; *Men*, 70.
Oct. 4   *Commander:* John Wheelwright.
   Bond: Continental, $5000.
   Bonders: John Wheelwright, of Portsmouth, N. H., Samuel White, of Marblehead, and Henry Jackson, of Boston.
   Owners: Samuel White, Job Prince, and others, of Marblehead and Boston.
   Witnesses: John Adams, Timo[thy] Foster.
      M. A., VII, 45, **165**, 313.

1776 REPRISAL, Sloop. *Tons*, 60; *Guns*, 8; *Men*, 60.
Nov. 26   *Commander:* Nathaniel Carver.
   Petitioners: John Browne, Samuel Allyne Otis, and others, merchants of Boston.
   M. A., **166**, 65.

254   MASSACHUSETTS PRIVATEERS

1777   REPRISAL, Sloop. *Tons*, 70; *Guns*, 4, and 8 *swivels;* *Men*, 16.
Mar. 25   *Commander:* Nathaniel Carver.
  Bond: Continental, amount not stated.
  Bonders: Nathaniel Carver, of Plymouth, and Samuel Phillips Savage, of Weston.
  Owner: "The State of Massachusetts Bay."
  Witnesses: Jon[athan] Loring Austin, Tho[ma]s Doten.
    M. A., VII, 63, **166**, 332 (Petition of the Board of War, to be furnished with a letter of marque for the *Reprisal*, which is bound from Plymouth to France and return).

1777   REPRISAL, Brigantine. *Guns*, 10; *Men*, 55.
July 16   *Commander:* Paul Reed, of Boston.
  Bond: State, £2000.
  Bonders: Cushing & White, of Boston, part of the owners, and Paul Reed, of Townsend, County of Lincoln, mariner.
  Witnesses: Tim[othy], Austin, Jno. Furnass.
    M. A., **139**, 133 (Bond to enlist no man in New England outside of Massachusetts); C. C. **196**, XII, 110 (July 17, 1777).

1778   REPRISAL, Brigantine. *Guns*, 10; *Men*, 60.
Jan. 28   *Commander:* James Brown.
  Bond: Continental, $5000; State, £500.
  Bonders: James Brown, principal; Charles Sigourney and Cushing & White, of Boston, sureties.
  Owners: Charles Sigourney and others.
  Witnesses: Edw[ar]d Holyoke, Samuel Giles.
    M. A., VII, 34, 35, **139**, 155, **168**, 163.

1781   REPRISAL, Schooner. *Guns*, 4; *Men*, 30.
July 31   *Commander:* John Curtis.
  Owners: John Coffin Jones and others, of Boston.
    C. C. **196**, XII, 106; M. A., **171**, 438; *Boston Gazette*, Sept. 24, 1781 (See *Resolution*, Capt. Morgan).

1781   REPRISAL, Galley. *Guns*, 4; *Men*, 25.
July 31   *Commander:* Benjamin Frizel, of Pownalborough.
  Owners: Benjamin Hichborn and others, of Boston.
    C. C. **196**, XII, 107; M. A., **171**, 437.

1782   REPRISAL, Schooner. *Guns*, 6; *Men*, 12.
Mar. 18   *Commander:* Wilson Jacobs, of Providence, R. I.
  Owners: Tristram Coffin and others, of Boston.
    C. C. **196**, XII, 108; M. A., **172**, $120\frac{1}{2}$.

To the Hon'ble the Council

The Owners of War-brig Fifter set out the sloop Aristides Mathew Caish Master, request leave to fit her out for the West Indies, mounting ten Carriage & two Swivel Guns, & apprehending it may be of Service if the Master be furnished with a Commission for a fitter of Marque to deter a Commission for him we ask —

By Ord'r of the Board
Sam'l Pleasants Pres't

The Vessels are bound to Guadeloupe &c
20 - a Load. —

In Council Jan'y 16, 1777
Read & Ordered that a Commission be Issued to William Hall, Com't of the Sp. Aristides sloop — he entering into with the Resolves of Congress

Tho. Wharton jun'r

War Office Jan'y 16, 1777

Petition for a Letter of Marque for a Vessel of the State Navy

REPRISAL — RESOLUTION 255

1782 REPRISAL, Ship. *Guns*, 4; *Men*, 14.
Apr. 2   *Commander:* William Peirce Johnson, of Newburyport.
  C. C. **196**, XII, 109.

1777 REPUBLIC, Sloop. *Guns*, 2, and 10 *swivels; Men*, 10.
Jan. 16   *Commander:* [John] Allen Hallet.
  Bond: Continental, £500.
  Bonders: Samuel Allyne Otis and Allen Hallet.
  Owners: "The Honble Board of War of the Colony of Massachusetts Bay."
  Witnesses: Jonathan Loring Austin, James Warren, jr.
    Note. The *Republic* was one of the first vessels built for the Massachusetts State Navy and was first commanded by Capt. John Foster Williams.
  M. A., XLV, 212, **166**, 195 (Petition of Samuel Phillips Savage, President of the Board of War. See Introduction, p. 45).

1777 RESOLUTION, Schooner. *Guns*, 10 *swivels; Men*, 25.
Aug. 13   *Commander:* Jeremiah O'Brien.
  Bond: Continental, $5000.
  Bonders: Jeremiah Obrian [signed Obrien], of Machias, principal; Daniel Martin and John Blake, of Boston, sureties.
  Owners: Daniel Martin and others.
  Witnesses: R. G. Cranch, Henry Alline, jr.
  M. A., VII, 25, **139**, 137, **167**, 157.

1777 RESOLUTION, Schooner. *Guns*, 8 *swivels; Men*, 16.
Oct. 31   *Commander:* John Collins.
  Bond: Continental, $5000; State, £500.
  Bonders: John Collins, principal; John Blake and Daniel Martin, of Boston, sureties.
  Owners: Daniel Martin, John Blake, and others.
  Witnesses: Joseph Jackson, Jeremiah O'Brien.
  M. A., VII, 23, 26, **139**, 149, **167**, 350.

1778 RESOLUTION, Schooner. *Guns*, 1, and 8 *swivels; Men*, 20.
Apr. 13   *Commander:* Samuel Rogers.
  Bond: Continental, $5000; State, £4000.
  Bonders: Samuel Rogers, principal; Henry Bass and William Spooner, of Boston, sureties.
  Owners: Henry Bass and William Spooner.
  Witnesses: Jno. Dall, Fitch Pool.
  M. A., VII, 1, 2, **139**, 166, **168**, 257.

1778 RESOLUTION, Schooner. *Guns*, 2, and 8 *swivels; Men*, 30.
July 20   *Commander:* Zebadiah Shepardson.
   Bond: Continental, $5000; State, £4000.
   Bonders: Zebadiah Sheppardson [signed Shepardson], mariner, principal; Henry Bass and Ebenezer Dorr, of Boston, sureties.
   Owners: Henry Bass and Ebenezer Dorr.
   Witness: Fitch Poole.
   M. A., VII, 13, 14, **139**, 202, **169**, 25.

1779 RESOLUTION, Schooner. *Guns*, 4; *Men*, 25.
Mar. 12   *Commander:* Levi Doane.
   Bond: Continental, $5000; State, £4000.
   Bonders: Levi Doane, mariner, principal; Ebenezer Woodward, Gawen Brown, and John Brown, of Boston, sureties.
   Owner: Ebenezer Woodward.
   Witnesses: George Burroughs, Nathaniel Furnass.
   M. A., VI, 338, 341, **139**, 246, **159**, 293, **170**, 10.

1779 RESOLUTION, Schooner. *Guns*, 2, and 2 *cohorns* and 8
Apr. 26   *swivels; Men*, 30.
   Commander: Abel Gore.
   Bond: Continental, $5000; State, £4000.
   Bonders: Abel Gore, mariner, principal; Thomas Adams and Dan[ie]l Martin, of Boston, sureties.
   Owners: Thomas Adams and others.
   Witnesses: John Hildreth, Zacheus Morton.
   M. A., VI, 340, 343, **139**, 248, **170**, 67.

1779 RESOLUTION, Schooner. *Guns*, 6; *Men*, 25.
Dec. 1   *Commander:* Shubael Spooner.
   Bond: Continental, $5000; State, £4000.
   Bonders: Shubael Spooner, principal; Ebenezer Woodward and Levi Doane, of Boston, sureties.
   Owners: Not stated.
   Witnesses: William Doggett, Joseph Urann.
   M. A., VII, 5, 6, **139**, 263, **171**, 37.

1780 RESOLUTION, Schooner. *Guns*, 6; *Men*, 25.
Apr. 8   *Commander:* Samuel Trusk.
   Bond: Continental, $5000; State, £4000.
   Bonders: Samuel Trusk, mariner, principal; Jonathan Nutting and Ebenezer Woodward, of Boston, sureties.

Owners: Jonathan Nutting and others.
Witnesses: William Doggett, Samuel Dillaway.
   M. A., VII, 7, 8, **171**, 123.

1780 RESOLUTION, Brigantine. *Guns*, 6; *Men*, 18.
Nov. 10   *Commander:* Zachariah Sears, of Boston.
   C. C. **196**, XIII, 6; M. A., **171**, 304².

1781 RESOLUTION, Schooner. *Guns*, 6; *Men*, 25.
Mar. 31   *Commander:* Amos Potter, of Boston.
   C. C. **196**, XIII, 4; M. A., XL, 102, **171**, 360; *Boston Gazette*, May 14, 1781: "Thursday last returned into Port the Privateer Schooner *Resolution*, Capt. Potter, late Master, having taken a Schooner laden with Dry Goods, etc. During her Cruize off Halifax Harbour she fell in with a Ship of between 4 and 500 Tons, with Twelve 4-pounders and 23 Men (three of which were Sick) laden with English Goods, bound from London for Halifax; and it being a dead Calm, she row'd up within Call of the Ship, when the Commander hail'd, Whence from? Answer, Halifax. After which the following Discourse. Is two Ships (naming them) arrived there? A. Yes. Will you come on board? My Boat is leaky, but if you will send your Boat on board, I will come. Accordingly the Capt. of the Ship sent his Boat with the second Mate and Boatswain on Board the Schooner and after taking a Glass together, the Boat returned to the Ship. After which the Captain of the Ship desired Captain Potter to come on board and spend the Evening, it being a fine Night, to which he replied he would; when the Boat was again sent and he went on board. But before he embarked, he told his Crew to lay the Schooner alongside and board her as soon as he had got on board. The Boatswain overhearing him, kept it to himself 'till they got on board the Ship and then cry'd, 'A Traitor.' On which the Ship prepar'd for Action and an Engagement ensued, when the Ship shot away the *Resolution's* Foremast and she row'd off, otherwise the Ship would have been captured. They carried off Capt. Potter with them."

1781 RESOLUTION, Schooner. *Guns*, 4; *Men*, 30.
Apr. 20   *Commander:* John Savage, of Boston.
   Owners: George Stillman and others, of Machias.
   C. C. **196**, XIII, 5; M. A., **171**, 374.

1781 RESOLUTION, Schooner. *Guns*, 6; *Men*, 25.
May 18 *Commander:* William Morgan, of Boston.
C. C. **196**, XIII, 2; M. A., **171**, 390; *Boston Gazette*, Sept. 24, 1781: "Friday last returned into port the privateer schooner *Resolution*, Capt. Morgan, from a cruize, during which he, in company with Capt. Curtiss of the schooner [*Reprisal*], went to Annapolis-Royal, landed their crews, and destroyed the fort there, which consisted of nine 18 and 9-pounders, and made the whole garrison prisoners. The Governor and Captain of the garrison, with some others, they parol'd and brought off the Standard, a Sergeant and 5 or 6 other prisoners. Capt. Potter, late of the *Resolution*, was exchanged for the Governor of Annapolis and arrived last Evening from Halifax."

1782 RESOLUTION, Ship. *Guns*, 20; *Men*, 130.
Feb. 14 *Commander:* Stephen Webb.
Owners: John and Andrew Cabot, of Beverly.
Note. In *Naval Records of the Revolution* this vessel is called *Revolution*.
C. C. **196**, XIII, 42; M. A., **172**, 114; *Boston Gazette*, Jan. 6, 1783 (See *Buccaneer*, Jesse Fearson).

1782 RESOLUTION, Brigantine. *Guns*, 4; *Men*, 11.
Aug. 13 *Commander:* John Odiorne, of Salisbury.
C. C. **196**, XIII, 3.

1782 RESOLUTION, Ship. *Guns*, 20; *Men*, 130.
Commander: Samuel West.
Essex Institute, Miscellaneous Ship Papers.

1780 RESOURCE, Ship. *Guns*, 16; *Men*, 30.
June 12 *Commander:* Israel Thorndike.
Bond: Continental, $10,000; State, £4000.
Bonders: Israel Thorndike, mariner, principal; Ebenezer Parsons and Simeon Mayo, merchants of Boston, sureties.
Owners: Ebenezer Parsons and Israel Thorndike.
Witnesses: Daniel Sargent, Nehemiah Somes.
M. A., VI, 361, 362, **171**, 176.

1780 RESOURCE, Ship. *Guns*, 10; *Men*, 24.
Sept. 7 *Commander:* Richard Ober, of Beverly.
C. C. **196**, XIII, 9; M. A., XL, 65, **171**, 266.

1776 RETALIATION, Brigantine. *Guns*, 10; *Men*, 70.
Sept. 2   *Commander:* Eleazer Giles.
   First lieutenant: Thomas Stephens.
   Bond: Continental, $5000.
   Bonders: Eleazer Giles, Larkin Thorndike, and Josiah Batchelder, jr., of Beverly.
   Owners: Josiah Batchelder, jr., & Co.
   Witnesses: William Gray, William Leech.
      M. A., VII, 37, **165**, 49, 204; Marblehead Hist. Soc.

1778 RETALIATION, Sloop. *Guns*, 10; *Men*, 50.
Mar. 18   *Commander:* John Carey.
   Bond: Continental, $5000; State, £500.
   Bonders: John Carey, principal; Philip Moore and others, of Boston, sureties.
   Signers: John Carey, Ph[ilip] Moore, Ja[me]s Lockwood.
   Owners: Philip Moore and others.
   Witnesses: Edward Payne, Will[iam] Powell.
      M. A., VII, 30, 31, **139**, 174, **168**, 217.

1780 RETALIATION, Ship. *Guns*, 12; *Men*, 30.
Nov. 4   *Commander:* Joseph Goodhue, of Newburyport.
      C. C. **196**, XIII, 13; M. A., **171**, 300.

1781 RETALIATION, Ship. *Guns*, 10; *Men*, 24.
July 3   *Commander:* Samuel Sewall, of Newburyport.
      C. C. **196**, XIII, 18.

1782 RETALIATION, Ship. *Guns*, 10; *Men*, 25.
Feb. 21   *Commander:* Samuel Rice, of Kittery.
   Owners: Stephen Cross and others, of Newburyport.
      C. C. **196**, XIII, 17.

1776 RETRIEVE, Sloop. *Guns*, 10; *Men*, 80.
Aug. 29   *Commander:* Joshua Stone.
   Bond: Continental, $5000.
   Bonders: Joshua Stone, principal; Jno. Fox, merchant of Falmouth [Cumberland Co.], and George Williams, merchant of Salem.
   Owners: Enoch Insley [Ilsley] and B[enaiah?] Titcomb, of Falmouth.
   Witnesses: Seth Cushing, Eben Prout.
      M. A., VII, 36, **165**, 174, **181**, 173.

1776 REVENGE, Sloop. *Guns,* 12, and 16 *swivels; Men,* 85.
May 14   *Commander:* Joseph White.
         Bond: Continental, $5000.
         Bonders: Joseph Lee, of Beverly, and Miles Greenwood, of Salem, merchants, and Joseph White, mariner of Salem.
         Owners: Joseph Lee, Miles Greenwood, and others.
         Witnesses: John Lowell, John Molineux.
              M. A., VI, 339, **164**, 356; Min. Sup. Court, 186.

1776 REVENGE, Sloop. *Guns,* 12; *Men,* 85.
Sept. 5   *Commander:* Benjamin Warren.
         Bond: Continental, $5000.
         Bonders: Benjamin Warren, principal; Miles Greenwood and Joseph White, sureties.
         Owners: Elias Hasket Derby, Miles Greenwood, and Joseph White, of Salem.
         Witnesses: Samuel Nutting, David Bush.
              M. A., VII, 52, **165**, 208.

1776 REVENGE, Sloop. *Guns,* 8; *Men,* 60.
Oct. 25   *Commander:* Benjamin Dean.
         Bond: Continental, $5000.
         Bonders: Benjamin Dean, Miles Greenwood, and Jonathan Ingersoll — all of Salem.
         Owners: Miles Greenwood and others.
         Witnesses: W[illia]m Patterson, Peter Egan.
              M. A., VII, 47, **159**, 63, **165**, 390.

1777 REVENGE, Sloop. *Guns,* 10; *Men,* 60.
Apr. 30   *Commander:* Isaac Freeborn.
         Bond: Continental, $5000.
         Bonders: Isaac Freeborn, principal; John Dean and Mungo Mackay, sureties.
         Owners: John Dean and Mungo Mackay, of Boston.
         Witnesses: William Smith, Jno. Brown.
              M. A., VII, 50, **166**, 376; *Boston Gazette,* Mar. 9, 1778: "About ten Days after [sailing], we fell in with a Privateer Schooner, gave her a couple of Shot and she run. About eight Days after, we fell in with and took the Ship *York,* from Glasgow bound to Barbadoes, laden with dry Goods, some Provisions, etc., which we sent into Martineco. About four Days after, fell in with a large English Ship of 18 Guns, which was

too much for us. We afterwards came across a Fleet
of about 100 Sail, to Windward of Barbadoes, but
they being convoy'd by five Frigates and it blowing
a hard Gale, we could do nothing with them. We
then bore away for Martineco, sprung our Mast and
carried away our Topmast, but luckily got in and
found our Prize safe."

1777 REVENGE, Sloop. *Guns*, 8; *Men*, 25.
Sept. 4   *Commander:* Nathaniel Coit Webb.
Bond: Continental, $5000.
Bonders: Nathaniel Coit Webb, principal; Thomas Adams
and several others of Salem, sureties.
Owners: Not stated.
Signers: Nathaniel Coit Webb, Thomas Adams, Benja-
[min] Loring.
Witnesses: Tho[mas] Chase, Jona[than] Pollard.
M. A., VII, 27, **167**, 200.

1778 REVENGE, Ship.
Commander: James Tracy.
Independent Chronicle, Feb. 12, 1778: "Certain Intelli-
gence is received by the Owners of the private armed
Ship *Revenge* James Tracy, Esq., Commander, of her
safe Arrival at Bordeaux."

1778 REVENGE, Sloop. *Guns*, 10; *Men*, 50.
May 26   *Commander:* Ezekiel Burroughs.
Bond: Continental, $5000.
Bonders: Ezekiel Burroughs, principal; Mungo Mackay
and William Shattuck, of Boston, sureties.
Owners: Mungo Mackay and William Shattuck.
Witnesses: J. Hood, Jno. Shattuck.
M. A., VII, 55, **139**, 179, 186, 231, **168**, 338.

1779 REVENGE, Brigantine. *Guns*, 14; *Men*, 80.
Aug. 30   *Commander:* James Rob.
Bond: Continental, $10,000; State, £4000.
Bonders: James Robb [signed Rob], principal; Benjamin
Jepson and James Lamb, sureties.
Owners: Benjamin Jepson, James Lamb, and others, mer-
chants of Boston.
Witnesses: Theo[dore] Barrell, Benja[min] Hichborn.
M. A., VII, 59, 60, **139**, 253, **170**, 360.

1779 REVENGE, Sloop. *Guns*, 12; *Men*, 50.
Sept. 7   *Commander:* Samuel Avery.
    Bond: Continental, $5000; State, £4000.
    Bonders: Samuel Avery, mariner, principal; Mungo
      Mackay and Samuel Dunn, jr., of Boston, sureties.
    Owner: Mungo Mackay.
    Witnesses: Thomas Amory, jr., Luther Turner.
      M. A., VII, 53, 56, **170**, 371.

1779 REVENGE, Ship. *Guns*, 12; *Men*, 40.
Oct. 14   *Commander:* Elisha Turner.
    Bond: Continental, $10,000; State, £4000.
    Bonders: Elisha Turner, mariner, principal; John Cushing and Timothy Peirce, of Boston, sureties.
    Owners: Cushing & White.
    Witnesses: Eben[eze]r Wales, Moses Titcomb.
      M. A., VII, 40, 42, **170**, 425.

1780 REVENGE, Sloop.
May 6   *Commander:* Ezekiel Burroughs.
    Bond: State, £2000.
    Bonders: Mungo Mackay, merchant, and major part of the owners, and Ezekiel Burroughs, mariner, both of Boston.
    Witnesses: John Winthrop, Henry Alline.
      M. A., **139**, 269 (Bond to enlist no man in New England outside of Massachusetts).

1780 REVENGE, Sloop. *Guns*, 4; *Men*, 14.
Nov. 21   *Commander:* Archibald Rainey, of Boston.
      C. C. **196**, XIII, 35; M. A., **171**, 308.

1781 REVENGE, Schooner. *Guns*, 8; *Men*, 40.
Apr. 16   *Commander:* Benjamin Knight, of Salem.
      C. C. **196**, XIII, 28; M. A., **171**, 373.

1781 REVENGE, Sloop. *Guns*, 4; *Men*, 14.
June 28   *Commander:* Ezekiel Burroughs, of Cape Ann.
    Owner: Joshua Blanchard, of Boston.
      C. C. **196**, XIII, 23; M. A., **171**, 419.

1781 REVENGE, Schooner. *Guns*, 8; *Men*, 35.
Aug. 6   *Commander:* Zenas Cook, of Salem.
      C. C. **196**, XIII, 25; M. A., **171**, 444.

1781 REVENGE, Schooner. *Guns*, 8; *Men*, 35.
Aug. 16   *Commander:* Samuel Foster, of Salem.
      C. C. **196**, XIII, 26.

1781 REVENGE, Sloop. *Guns*, 4; *Men*, 12.
Dec. 1   *Commander:* Robert Adamson, of Boston.
            C. C. **196**, XIII, 21; M. A., **172**, 77.

1781 REVENGE, Brigantine. *Guns*, 8; *Men*, 25.
Dec. 14   *Commander:* Nathan Poor, of Newburyport.
            C. C. **196**, XIII, 32; M. A., **172**, 83.

1782 REVENGE, Sloop. *Guns*, 4; *Men*, 10.
Aug. 31   *Commander:* Isaiah Simmons, of Boston.
            C. C. **196**, XIII, 36; *Boston Gazette*, Jan. 27, 1783: "On the 6th of November last the sloop *Revenge*, Capt. Simmons, from Port au Prince for Boston, was taken by a privateer out of St. Augustine."

1783 REVENGE, Brig. *Guns*, 8; *Men*, 30.
Feb. 8   *Commander:* Amos Potter, of Boston.
            C. C. **196**, XIII, 33; M. A., **172**, 291.

1779 REVENUE, Schooner. *Guns*, 6; *Men*, 30.
May 17   *Commander:* Samuel Masury.
            Bond: Continental, $5000; State, £4000.
            Bonders: Samuel Masury, principal; Nathaniel Silsbee and Jonathan Ingersoll, of Salem, sureties.
            Owners: Nathaniel Silsbee and Jonathan Ingersoll.
            Witnesses: Joseph Grafton, David Felt.
            M. A., VI, 346, 348, **170**, 139.

1781 REVOLT, Brig. *Guns*, 8; *Men*, 20.
Oct. 29   *Commander:* Henry Phelps, of Salem.
            C. C. **196**, XIII, 38; M. A., **172**, 56; Felt, II, 273; *Salem Gazette*, Apr. 4, 1782 (See *Exchange*, Capt. Forrester).

1782 REVOLUTION, Schooner. *Guns*, 8; *Men*, 20.
Dec. 6   *Commander:* Joseph Trask.
            Owners: Robert Leach [Leech] and others, of Salem.
            C. C. **196**, XIII, 41; M. A., **172**, 250.

1778 RHODA, Brig. *Guns*, 6; *Men*, 12.
Jan. 14   *Commander:* Samuel Dugard.
            Bond: Continental, $10,000; State, £500.
            Bonders: Samuel Dugard, mariner, principal; Mark Lafitte and Stephen Higginson, merchants, sureties — all of Salem.
            Owner: Mark Lafitte.
            Witnesses: Nathaniel Ropes, W. Prosser.
            M. A., VII, 19, 20, **168**, 144.

1780 RHODES, Ship. *Tons*, 220; *Guns*, 20; *Men*, 120.
July 21   *Commander:* Nehemiah Buffinton.
   Bond: Continental, $10,000; State, £4000.
   Bonders: Nehemiah Buffinton, mariner, principal; Aaron Wait and Benjamin Goodhue, merchants, sureties — all of Salem.
   Owners: William Shillaber and others, of Salem.
   Witnesses: George Osborn, John Simonds.
      Note. These bonds seem to have found their way from the State Archives to the Court House at Boston.
   Court Files, 102721; M. A., XL, 67, **171**, 201 (July 29, 1780. Petition of William Shillaber, Benjamin Goodhue, jr., John Tucker, and Robert Goodhue, of Salem, requesting that the ship *Rhodes* be allowed to sail, notwithstanding the embargo. Granted, on condition that the ship cruise in search of the second division of the French fleet, expected on the coast, and give the French admiral information of the strength of the British fleet off Newport); Mar. Court Rec., 35; *Boston Gazette*, Nov. 13, 1780; *ibid.*, Mar. 12, 1781: "Last Wednesday se'nnight arrived at Salem the Brigantine ——, Prize to the Privateer Ship *Rhodes* of that Port, John Buffington, Commander." (The prize list in a later issue of the *Gazette* gives the captain's name Nehemiah); *ibid.*, Sept. 10, 1781: "Friday last the *Rhodes* returned into Port with a Prize Ship of 18 Guns in Ballast. She was an empty transport bound Home in concert with another Ship of the same Force, which the *Rhodes* also engaged at the same Time, but in manning the Prize the other got off." *Ibid.*, Apr. 22, 1782 (See ship *Mohawk*).

1776 RISING EMPIRE, Brigantine.
June 22   *Commander:* Richard Whellen.
   Bond: State, £2000.
   Bonders: Richard Welden [signed Whellen], of Edgartown, Walter Spooner, of Dartmouth, and Thomas Durfee, of Freetown.
   Owners: "Belonging to the said Colony."
   Witnesses: S. Holten, John Molineux.
      Note. One of the first vessels built for the Massachusetts State Navy.
   M. A., **139**, 120.

KNOW ALL MEN BY THESE PRESENTS, THAT I _Silas Canady_ of _Salem_ in the County of _Essex_ and State of _Massachusetts Bay_ in NEW-ENGLAND, for and in Consideration of the Sum of _One hundred and fifty_ Pounds lawful Money in Hand to me paid by _Benj. Clough Sumner_ of _Salem_ in the County of _Essex_ and State of _Massachusetts Bay_ the Receipt whereof I do hereby acknowledge, and do give, grant, bargain, sell and convey unto _him_ the said _Clough Sumner_ aforesaid, _one Quarter_ — of a Seamen's Share of all the Prizes or Plunder that may be taken by the _aforesaid_ armed _Ship_ called the _Rising Star_ commanded by _Capt. Howel_ of _Salem_ for and during her intended Cruise against the Enemies of the United States of AMERICA: Said Cruise to commence from the Time of her sailing from _Salem_ until her Arrival there, and Cruise ended. To the true Performance of all and singular the Covenants contained in this Deed, I bind myself, my Heirs, Executors, and Administrators, in the penal Sum of _five thousand_ — Pounds, Lawful Money. In Witness whereof I have hereunto set my Hand and Seal this _23_ Day of _September_ in the Year of our LORD, One Thousand Seven Hundred and _80_ — And in the Year of the INDEPENDENCE of the UNITED STATES of AMERICA.

Signed, Sealed and Delivered
in Presence of
Wm. Watson
_Joseph _____

Silas X Canady
     mark

To the Agent or Agents of the _said_ armed _Ship Rising Star_

SIR,

PLEASE to pay or cause to be paid unto _Benj. Clough Sumner_ _one Quarter_ — of a Seaman's Share of all the Prizes or Plunder that may or shall be taken by the _Rising Star_ commanded by _Capt. Howel_ during her intended Cruise; I having received Full Satisfaction for the same. And You will oblige

Your Humble Servant, Silas X Canady
                          mark

Assignment of Prize Money

|1780   RISING STAR, Sloop.
         Commander: —— Rowel.
         Mass. Hist. Soc., Nathan Dane Papers, Sept. 23, 1780: Assignment of "one Quarter of a Seaman's Share of all the Prizes or Plunder that may be taken by the aforesaid armed Slupe called the *Rising Star*, commanded by Capn Rowel of Salem . . . in Consideration of the Sum of Two hundred and fifty Pounds Lawful Money."

1776   RISING STATES, Brigantine. *Tons*, 210; *Guns*, 20; *Men*, 100.
Oct. 18   *Commander:* James Thompson.
         Bond: Continental, $10,000.
         Bonders: James Thompson, principal; William Davis and Samuel Alyne [Allyne] Otis, merchants of Boston, sureties.
         Owners: William Davis, Philip Moore, and others, of Boston.
         Witnesses: Samuel Freeman, Sleur [?] Riedet [?].
         M. A., VII, 46, **165**, 365, **166**, 101; *N. E. Hist. and Gen. Reg.*, July, 1876.

1777   RISING SUN. *Guns*, 16.
         Commander: —— ——.
         London Chronicle, Apr. 10, 1777 (See *Prosperous*).

1779   RIVAL, Snow. *Guns*, 8; *Men*, 25.
Dec. 26   *Commander:* William Ross.
         Bond: Continental, $10,000; State, £4000.
         Bonders: William Ross, principal; George Dodge, r., and Stephen Bruce, of Salem and Boston, sureties.
         Owner: George Dodge, jr., of Salem.
         Witnesses: William Clough, John M. Lovell.
         M. A., VI, 357, 358, **171**, 49.

1779   ROBIN, Brigantine. *Guns*, 4; *Men*, 15.
Nov. 5   *Commander:* Edmund Davis.
         Bond: Continental, $5000; State, £4000.
         Bonders: Edmund Davis, mariner, John R. Livingston and James Swan — all of Boston.
         Owner: John R. Livingston.
         Witnesses: Edmund Dunkin, Thornton Barrett.
         M. A., VI, 270, 271, **171**, 14.

1781 ROBIN HOOD, Ship. *Guns*, 14; *Men*, 60.
May 24   *Commander:* Sargent Smith, of Cape Ann.
   Owners: Stephen Higginson and Daniel Sargent, of Boston.
   C. C. **196**, XIII, 55; M. A., **171**, 396; *Boston Gazette*, May 6, 1782: "Last evening arrived here a letter of marque brig, mounting 14 carriage guns, laden with coffee and cotton, prize to the letter of marque ship *Robbin-Hood*, Capt. Smith, of this port."

1781 ROBUST, Ship. *Guns*, 12; *Men*, 25.
Oct. 31   *Commander:* Jonathan Tucker, of Salem.
   C. C. **196**, XIII, 56; M. A., **172**, 55.

1781 ROCHAMBEAU, Ship. *Guns*, 6; *Men*, 18.
Oct. 16   *Commander:* Jonathan Parsons, of Newburyport.
   C. C. **196**, XIII, 57.

1782 ROCHESTER, Boat. *Guns*, 4; *Men*, 20.
Apr. 15   *Commander:* Stephen Morton, of Boston.
   C. C. **196**, XIII, 58; M. A., **172**, 131.

1778 ROEBUCK, Schooner. *Guns*, 10; *Men*, 50.
Oct. 26   *Commander:* William Gray.
   Bond: Continental, amount not stated; State, £4000.
   Bonders: William Gray, Elias Hasket Derby, and Nathaniel Silsbee.
   Owners: Elias Hasket Derby and others, of Salem.
   Witnesses: Bartholomew Putnam, John Gardner, 3d.
     Note. In the bond the name is written *Roe-Buck*.
   M. A., VII, 9, 10, **169**, 269.

1779 ROEBUCK, Ship. *Guns*, 12; *Men*, 80.
Aug. 3   *Commander:* Jonathan Felt.
   Bond: Continental, $10,000; State, £4000.
   Bonders: Jonathan Felt, mariner, principal; Elias Hasket Derby and Nathaniel Silsbee, of Salem, sureties.
   Owner: Elias Hasket Derby.
   Witnesses: Jo[seph] Grafton, Mansfield Burrel [Burrill].
   M. A., VI, 349, 350, **170**, 299, 448.

1780 ROEBUCK, Ship. *Guns*, 14; *Men*, 90.
Oct. 9   *Commander:* Gideon Henfield, of Salem.
   C. C. **196**, II, 52; M. A., **171**, 288; *Boston Gazette*, July 1, 1782 (Captured Oct. 16, 1780); Felt II, 269.

1781 ROEBUCK, Boat. *Guns*, small arms; *Men*, 16.
June 1   *Commander:* Philip Crandal, of Falmouth, Cumberland County.
    C. C. **196**, XIII, 59; Mar. Court Rec., 62.

1781 ROMEO, Sloop. *Guns*, 10; *Men*, 15.
Mar. 6   *Commander:* John Grimes, of Boston.
    C. C. **196**, XIII, 60.

1781 ROMULUS, Brigantine. *Guns*, 14; *Men*, 25.
Jan. 10   *Commander:* Joshua Grafton, of Salem.
    C. C. **196**, XIII, 61; M. A., **171**, 327.

1781 ROMULUS, Brigantine. *Guns*, 14; *Men*, 25.
July 12   *Commander:* Joseph Waters, of Salem.
    C. C. **196**, XIII, 63; M. A., **171**, 428.

1782 ROMULUS, Brigantine. *Guns*, 14; *Men*, 20.
Nov. 20   *Commander:* Thomas Palfrey, of Salem.
    C. C. **196**, XIII, 62; M. A., **172**, 233.

1779 ROSETTE, Brigantine. *Guns*, 10; *Men*, 40.
May 14   *Commander:* Jacob Dunnell.
    Bond: Continental, $10,000; State, £4000.
    Bonders: Jacob Doniels [signed Dunnell], mariner, principal; Shrimpton Hutchinson and Nath[anie]l Greenough, of Boston, sureties.
    Owners: William and Godfrey Hutchinson, merchants.
    Witnesses: Francis Bryant, Isaac Davis.
    M. A., VI, 353, 354, **170**, 102.

1776 ROVER, Sloop. *Guns*, 8, and 10 *swivels* and 2 *cohorns*; *Men*, 50.
July 12
    Commander: Simon Forrester.
    Bond: Continental, $5000.
    Bonders: Jacob Ashton and Joseph Sprague, merchants, and Simon Forrester, mariner — all of Salem.
    Owners: Jacob Ashton, and Joseph Sprague.
    Witnesses: D[aniel] Hopkins, Jno. Molineux.
    M. A., VII, 41, **165**, 421; Emmons, 161.

1776 ROVER, Sloop. *Guns*, 8; *Men*, 45.
Nov. 13   *Commander:* Abijah Boden.
    Bond: Continental, $5000.
    Bonders: Abijah Bowden [signed Boden], principal, and Joseph Sprague, surety.

Owners: Joseph Sprague & Co., of Salem.
Witnesses: Andrew Cabot, Joshua Dodge.
M. A., VII, 39, **159**, 80, **166**, 37.

1777 ROVER, *Sloop. Guns,* 8; *Men,* 50.
Oct. 8   *Commander:* John Mitchell.
Bond: Continental, $5000; State, £500.
Bonders: John Mitchell, principal; John Derby and Andrew Cabot, sureties.
Owners: John Derby, Andrew Cabot, and others, of Salem.
Witnesses: Joseph Sprague, Jona[than] Goodhue.
M. A., VII, 21, 22, **139**, 146, **167**, 319.

1779 ROVER, Sloop. *Guns,* 10.
Commander: —— ——.
Note. On the Penobscot Expedition and captured by the enemy.
Williamson, *History of Maine,* II, 470, 476; Wheeler, *History of Castine,* 38.

1780 ROVER, Brigantine.
June 30   *Commander:* Adam Wellman.
M. A., XL, 78.

1781 ROVER, Ship. *Guns,* 24; *Men,* 100.
May 28   *Commander:* James Barr, of Salem.
C. C. **196**, XIII, 68; M. A., **171**, 398; Almon's *Remembrancer,* XII, 158, 159 (*Rover* captured by the British frigate *Medea*); Felt, II, 272; *Essex Inst. Hist. Coll.,* XXVII (1890), 136–139; *Boston Gazette* Jan. 28, 1782: "Capt. James Barr, in a brig belonging to Salem, was taken on his homeward bound passage from the West Indies, by the British fleet which sailed from New York in November last, and carried to Barbadoes."

1781 ROVER, Schooner. *Guns,* 6; *Men,* 20.
Dec. 1   *Commander:* Elijah Ayer, of Machias.
Owners: Samuel Sharp and others, of Boston.
C. C. **196**, XIII, 67; M. A., **172**, 72.

1782 ROVER, Schooner. *Guns,* 10; *Men,* 30.
June 14   *Commander:* Thomas Mogridge, of Salem.
C. C. **196**, XIII, 70; M. A. **172**, 174.

ROVER — ROYAL LOUIS

1782 ROVER, Schooner. *Guns*, 6; *Men*, 30.
Aug. 27   *Commander:* Levi Young, of Martha's Vineyard.
   Owners: Lemuel Williams and others, of Dartmouth.
   C. C. **196**, XIII, 72.

1782 ROVER, Schooner. *Guns*, 12; *Men*, 40.
   Commander: D[aniel] Needham.
   Emmons, 161.

1783 ROVER, Schooner. *Guns*, 2; *Men*, 20.
Jan. 29   *Commander:* Nicholas Melzard, of Marblehead.
   C. C. **196**, XIII, 69; M. A., **172**, 287.

1782 ROVER GALLEY, Schooner. *Guns*, 4; *Men*, 25.
Mar. 3   *Commander:* Lemuel Carver, of Dartmouth.
   C. C. **196**, XIII, 73.

1777 ROYAL AFRICAN, Snow. *Guns*, 14.
   Commander: Miles Baker.
   London Chronicle, Apr. 22, 1777 (See *Black Eagle*).

1778 ROYAL LOUIS, Sloop. *Guns*, 10; *Men*, 35.
Oct. 9   *Commander:* John Moulton.
   Bond: Continental, $5000; State, £4000.
   Bonders: William [signed John] Moulton, mariner, principal; Philip Moore and ——, sureties.
   Owners: Philip Moore and others, of Boston.
   Witnesses: John Marston, Briggs Hallowell.
      M. A., VII, 32, 33, **139**, 134, 218, **169**, 209; *Independent Chronicle*, Dec. 3, 1778: "Monday arrived the Privateer Sloop *Royal Louis* from Nantucket, where she was drove ashore in one of the late storms. She was bound to Newport, having, with a brig which sailed from hence with the French fleet, been taken by a British ship of war. The Brig, 'tis said, has since arrived in that port."

1779 ROYAL LOUIS, Sloop. *Guns*, 8; *Men*, 20.
Jan. 18   *Commander:* John Willson.
   Bond: Continental, $5000; State, £4000.
   Bonders: John Willson, mariner, principal; William Shattuck and John Shattuck, of Boston, sureties.
   Owners: William Shattuck and others.
   Witnesses: James Perkins, Stephen H. Gray.
      Note. The sloop's name is written *Royal Lewis*.
   M. A., VII, 15, 16, **169**, 416.

1779 RUBY, Brigantine. *Tons*, 90; *Guns*, 6; *Men*, 15.
Nov. 12 *Commander:* John Babson.
  Petitioners: Ebenezer Lane and Daniel Sargent.
  M. A., **171**, 21.

1781 RUBY, Brigantine. *Guns*, 4; *Men*, 15.
Apr. 9 *Commander:* Benjamin Webber, of Boston.
  Owners: John Babson, of Newburyport, and others.
  C. C. **196**, XIII, 79; M. A., **171**, 363.

1781 RUBY, Armed Vessel.
  Commander: Jonathan Nutting.
  Boston Gazette, Apr. 30, 1781.

1781 RUBY, Brig. *Guns*, 6; *Men*, 20.
Aug. 9 *Commander:* Solomon Babson, of Newburyport.
  C. C. **196**, XIII, 77; M. A., **171**, 449.

1782 RUBY, Brig. *Guns*, 6; *Men*, 21.
Sept. 16 *Commander:* Solomon Babson, of Newburyport.
  C. C. **196**, XIII, 78.

1781 SACO BOB, Schooner. *Guns*, 3; *Men*, 35.
May 22 *Commander:* Solomon Coit, of Saco.
  C. C. **196**, XIV, 12.

1779 SAILOR'S DELIGHT, Brigantine. *Guns*, 8; *Men*, 50.
Dec. 20 *Commander:* Benjamin Bates.
  Bond: Continental, $5000; State, £4000.
  Bonders: Benjamin Bates, mariner, principal; Benj[amin] Jepson and Eben[eze]r Woodward, of Boston, sureties.
  Owner: Ebenezer Woodward.
  Witnesses: William Doggett, Thomas Phillips.
  M. A., V, 178, 181, **171**, 47.

1782 ST. MARY'S PACKET, Ship. *Guns*, 12; *Men*, 30.
Aug. 7 *Commander:* John Leach, jr., of Boston.
  C. C. **196**, XIV, 68.

1782 ST. PATRICK, Brigantine. *Guns*, 10; *Men*, 25.
Apr. 8 *Commander:* Phillip Thrash, of Newburyport.
  C. C. **196**, XIV, 71.

1778 ST. PEX, Schooner. *Tons*, 45; *Guns*, swivels.
  Commander: —— ——.
  Essex Inst. Hist. Coll., XLIX, 106 (MS. Auctioneers' Sales Books in Essex Institute): "Sept. 17, 1778. Sold by

order of Capt. Stone, viz.:— privateer schooner *St. Pex*, 45 tons, with her swivels, etc., as arrived from cruise, £7450, to J. Nichols. The owners remain the same as before, except Capt. Thorndike's 1-8, bought by Jonathan Ingersol, 2-32, John Gardner, 1-32, and Joseph Grafton, 1-32."

1780 ST. TAMANY, Ship. *Tons*, 280; *Guns*, 16; *Men*, not stated.
Aug. 1   Commander: Gilbert Ash.
     Bond: Continental, $10,000; State, £4000.
     Bonders: Gilbert Ash, mariner, principal; Paschal N[elson] Smith and Leonard Jarvis, merchants, sureties — all of Boston.
     Owners: Isaac Sears and others, of Boston.
     Witnesses: Eliakim Raymond, Geo[rge] Scott.
     M. A., VII, 92, 95, **176**, 558.

1781 SALAMANDER, Cutter. *Guns*, 8; *Men*, 50.
May 28   Commander: John O'Brien, of Newburyport.
     C. C. **196**, XIII, 81.

1782 SALAMANDER, Schooner. *Guns*, 7; *Men*, 40.
Mar. 29   Commander: Andrew Reed.
     Owners: Moses Little and others, of Newburyport.
     C. C. **196**, XIII, 82.

1780 SALEM. *Guns*, 18.
     Commander: ——
     London Chronicle, Feb. 26, 1780: "An American privateer of 18 guns, called the *Salem*, was taken off Madeira after a smart engagement, by Com. Johnstone in the *Romney* man of war, which prize he took with him for Lisbon."

1780 SALEM, Brigantine.
Oct. 29   Commander: Nehemiah Andrews, of Salem.
     M. A., XL, 96.

1780 SALEM, Brigantine. *Guns*, 12; *Men*, 20.
Dec. 20   Commander: Henry Williams, of Salem.
     C. C. **196**, XIII, 85; M. A., **171**, 318.

1782 SALEM, Schooner. *Guns*, 6; *Men*, 30.
July 27   Commander: Edward Stanly, of Salem.
     C. C. **196**, XIII, 83.

272 MASSACHUSETTS PRIVATEERS

1779 SALEM PACKET, Schooner. *Guns*, 6; *Men*, 11.
  Commander: —— ——.
  London Chronicle, July 8, 1779: Capt. Penlerick in the *Mary*, May 20, 1779, "fell in with and was taken by an American letter of marque schooner called the *Salem Packet*, from Salem to Bilboa, mounting six four pounders and 11 men."

1779 SALEM PACKET, Ship. *Guns*, 12; *Men*, 25.
Nov. 25 *Commander:* Joseph Cook.
  Bond: Continental, $10,000; State, £4,000.
  Bonders: Joseph Cook, mariner, principal; Elias Hasket Derby and Nehemiah Holt, of Salem, sureties.
  Owner: Elias Hasket Derby.
  Witnesses: Mansfield Burrill, William Beckett.
  M. A., VII, 90, 93, **171**, 33.

1781 SALEM PACKET, Ship. *Guns*, 12; *Men*, 30.
Nov. 26 *Commander:* Joseph Cook, of Salem.
  C. C. **196**, XIII, 87; M. A., **172**, 84.

1782 SALEM PACKET, Ship. *Guns*, 9; *Men*, 20.
June 29 *Commander:* John Brewer, of Salem.
  C. C. **196**, XIII, 86; M. A., **172**, 177.

1778 SALISBURY, Brig. *Tons*, 100; *Guns*, 4; *Men*, 10.
Aug. 11 *Commander:* Joshua Grafton.
  Bond: Continental, $10,000; State, £4000.
  Bonders: Joshua Grafton, mariner, principal; John Norris and Jo[seph] Grafton, of Salem, sureties.
  Owners: John Norris and others.
  Witness: D[aniel] Hopkins.
  M. A., VII, 81, 82, **169**, 70.

1779 SALLY, Brigantine. *Guns*, 6; *Men*, 16.
Oct. 22 *Commander:* Luther Turner.
  Bond: Continental, $5000; State, £4000.
  Bonders: Luther Turner, mariner, principal; Mungo Mackay and Samuel Dunn, jr., of Boston, sureties.
  Owner: Samuel Dunn, jr.
  Witnesses: Thomas Amory, jr., Thomas Porter.
  M. A., VII, 170, 171, **170**, 442.

1781 SALLY, Schooner. *Guns*, not stated; *Men*, 15.
Aug. 6   *Commander:* George Rendall, of York.
   Owners: George Rendall, Benjamin Harrod and Benjamin Balch, of Newburyport.
   C. C. **196**, XIII, 97; Court Files, 103371.

1782 SALLY, Sloop. *Guns*, 2; *Men*, 16.
Dec. 26   *Commander:* Ebenezer Crocker, of Barnstable.
   C. C. **196**, XIII, 93; M. A., **172**, 265.

1779 SALLY AND BECKY, Ship. *Guns*, 8; *Men*, 25.
June 25   *Commander:* Moses Grinnell.
   Bond: Continental, $10,000; State, £4000.
   Bonders: Moses Grinnell, mariner, principal; Isaac Sears and Paschal N[elson] Smith, of Boston, sureties.
   Owner: Isaac Sears.
   Witnesses: Anth[on]y Griffiths, Joseph Skillin.
   M. A., VII, 88, 91, **170**, 182.

1778 SARATOGA, Brig. *Guns*, 8; *Men*, 30.
July 1   *Commander:* John Tittle.
   Bond: Continental, $10,000; State, £4000.
   Bonders: John Tittle, mariner, principal; Andrew Cabot and Joseph Lee, merchants of Beverly, sureties.
   Owner: Andrew Cabot.
   Witnesses: Sam[uel] Cabot, William Leech.
   M. A., VII, 123, 134, **168**, 403.

1779 SARATOGA, Brigantine. *Guns*, 12; *Men*, 25.
Apr. 27   *Commander:* John Brooks.
   Bond: Continental, $5000; State, £4000.
   Bonders: John Brooks, principal; Nathan Nichols and Joseph Grafton, sureties — all of Salem.
   Owners: Nathan Nichols and Joseph Grafton.
   Witnesses: Ichabod Nichols, John Fisk.
   M. A., VII, 175, 178, **170**, 71.

1779 SARATOGA, Brigantine. *Guns*, 10; *Men*, 30.
Oct. 5   *Commander:* Ephraim Emerton.
   Bond: Continental, $10,000; State, £4000.
   Bonders: Ephraim Emerton, mariner, principal; Joseph Chipman and Joseph Grafton, of Salem, sureties.
   Owner: Joseph Grafton.
   Witnesses: Thomas Blanchard, John Fisk.
   M. A., VII, 181, 182, **170**, 416.

1779 SARATOGA, Brig. *Guns,* 10; *Men,* 30.
Nov. 20   *Commander:* Stephen Webb.
   Petitioner: Andrew Cabot, of Beverly.
   M. A., **171**, 28.

1780 SARATOGA, Brigantine. *Guns,* 12; *Men,* 70.
May 10   *Commander:* Mark Clark.
   Bond: Continental, $10,000; State, £4000.
   Bonders: Mark Clark, principal; Jonathan Mason and Benjamin Lovett, sureties — all of Boston.
   Owner: Samuel Williams, of Salem.
   Witnesses: Benjamin Loring, Theodore Hopkins.
   M. A., VII, 119, 120, **171**, 157.

1780 SARATOGA, Brigantine (privateer).
   Commander: Eleazar Giles, of Beverly.
   Owners: John and Andrew Cabot.
   M. A., XL, 94; Marblehead Hist. Soc.; *Publ. Colonial Society of Mass.,* XXIV, 416.

1781 SARATOGA, Brig (letter of marque).
   Commander: Andrew Thorndike.
   Salem Gazette, Apr. 17, 1781; *Publ. Colonial Society of Mass.,* XXIV, 434 (June 16, 1781).

1776 SATISFACTION, Sloop. *Guns,* 14; *Men,* 100.
Nov. 4   *Commander:* John Stevens.
   Bond: Continental, $5000.
   Bonders: John Stevens, principal; John Cushing and Sam[ue]l White, of Boston, sureties.
   Owners: John Cushing and Samuel White.
   Witnesses: Nath[anie]l Pearce, Joseph Drinkwater.
   M. A., VII, 160, **159**, 74, 77, **166**, 15.

1777 SATISFACTION, Sloop. *Guns,* 14; *Men,* 50.
May 10   *Commander:* John Wheelwright.
   Bond: Continental, $5000.
   Bonders: John Wheelwright, principal; John Cushing and Samuel White, merchants of Boston, sureties.
   Owners: John Cushing and Samuel White.
   Witnesses: Joseph Martin, Olive Cushing.
   M. A., VII, 133, **139**, 97, **166**, 399.

1778 SATISFACTION, Brigantine. *Guns,* 14; *Men,* 80.
Apr. 2   *Commander:* Nathaniel Thayer.
   Bond: Continental, $5000; State, £500.

Bonders: Nath[anie]l Thayer, principal; Joseph Barrell and Job Prince, merchants of Boston, sureties.
Owners: Job Prince and others.
Witnesses: Thomas Prince, Benjamin Homer.
M. A., VII, 94, 97, **139**, 163, **168**, 239.

1779 SATISFACTION, Schooner. *Guns,* 4, and 4 *swivels; Men,* 20.
June 2 *Commander:* Nathaniel Kinsman.
Bond: Continental, $5000; State, £4000.
Bonders: Nathaniel Kinsman, of Ipswich, principal; Thomas Burnham, of Ipswich, and Francis Rust, of Boston, sureties.
Owners: James Clinton and Robert Newman, of Ipswich.
Witness: W. Harris.
M. A., VII, 141, 144, **170**, 147.

1782 SATISFACTION, Schooner. *Guns,* 10; *Men,* 20.
Aug. 3 *Commander:* Michael Smithers, of Salem.
C. C. **196**, XIV, 7.

SATISFACTION, Schooner. *Guns,* 6; *Men,* 30.
Commander: Edward Stanly.
Paine, 459.

1780 SAUCY JACK, Schooner. *Guns,* 16.
Commander: —— ——.
Boston Gazette, June 5, 1780: "Friday last returned to Salem from a Cruise the Privateer *Saucy-Jack.* Besides the Prizes already mentioned to have been taken by her, she in Concert with a Privateer belonging to Philadelphia have captured two Vessels, in Ballast, having on board only a Number of the Feminine Gender, Passengers, who were bound from New-York to Bermuda, fearing a Visit from the Squadron of our illustrious Ally, daily expected in these Seas." *Ibid.,* Aug. 6, 1781: "Saturday last was sent into this Port [by two French frigates from Rhode Island] the Privateer *Saucy Jack,* of 16 guns, which had been out of Halifax only a few Days and had taken nothing. She formerly belonged to Salem." Felt, II, 270.

1782 SCAMMELL, Schooner. *Guns,* 16; *Men,* 60.
Apr. 13 *Commander:* Noah Stoddard, of Boston.
C. C. **196**, XIV, 13; M. A., **172**, 133; *Boston Gazette,* June 3, 1782: "Captain Stoddard, in the Privateer Schooner called the *Scammell's Revenge,* belonging to

this Port, has captured and sent in here a Sloop called the *Fox*." *Ibid.*, July 15, 1782 (At Lunenburgh, see *Hero*, Capt. Babcock).

1782 SCARBOROUGH, Ship. *Guns*, 10; *Men*, 40.
Feb. 11   *Commander:* Jonathan Jewett, of Newburyport.
C. C. **196**, XIV, 14.

1777 SCORPION, Schooner. *Guns*, 2, and 14 *swivels; Men*, 40.
Nov. 8   *Commander:* Israel Thorndike.
Bond: Continental, $5000; State, £500.
Bonders: Israel Thorndike, principal; Daniel Hopkins, of Salem, and William Baker, jr., of Boston, sureties.
Owners: Joseph White and Miles Greenwood, of Salem.
Witness: John Dall.
M. A., VII, 135, 138, **167**, 436.

1778 SCORPION, Schooner. *Guns*, 16 *swivels; Men*, 40.
Feb. 27   *Commander:* John Brooks.
Bond: Continental, $5000; State, £500.
Bonders: John Brooks, principal; Elias Hasket Derby and Ichabod Nichols, of Salem, sureties.
Owners: Elias Hasket Derby and Ichabod Nichols.
Witness: D[aniel] Hopkins.
M. A., VII, 131, 132, **168**, 191.

1778 SCORPION, Schooner. *Guns*, 2; *Men*, 40.
June 16   *Commander:* Benjamin Ives.
Bond: Continental, $5000; State, £4000.
Bonders: Benjamin Ives, mariner, principal; Josiah Batchelder, jr., and Samuel Ward, of Beverly, sureties.
Owners: Josiah Batchelder & Co., of Beverly.
Witness: Jno. Dall.
Note. In the petition the captain is called Benjamin Niles.
M. A., VII, 101, 102, **168**, 371.

1778 SCORPION, Schooner. *Guns*, 16 *swivels; Men*, 35.
July 23   *Commander:* William Gray.
Bond: Continental, $5000; State, £4000.
Bonders: William Gray, mariner, principal; Elias Hasket Derby and Miles Greenwood, merchants of Salem, sureties.
Owners: Elias Hasket Derby and Miles Greenwood.
Witness: Robert Stone.
M. A., VII, 125, 126, **169**, 33.

1779 SCORPION, Schooner. *Guns*, 2; *Men*, 20.
Mar. 18   *Commander:* Benjamin Ives.
   Bond: Continental, $5000; State, £4000.
   Bonders: Benjamin Ives, principal; Josiah Batchelder, jr., and Livermore Whittridge, of Beverly, sureties.
   Owner: Josiah Batchelder, jr.
   Witnesses: Joseph Raymond, Joanna Batchelder.
      M. A., VII, 139, 142, **170**, 25.

1779 SCORPION, Schooner. *Tons*, 70; *Guns*, 4; *Men*, 13.
Sept. 28   *Commander:* Perry Howland.
   Petitioner: Josiah Batchelder, jr., of Beverly.
      M. A., **170**, 410.

1782 SCORPION, Sloop. *Guns*, 6.
         Commander: —— ——.
   Essex Institute, Miscellaneous Ship Papers.

1782 SCOTCH TRICK, Boat. *Guns*, 2; *Men*, 12.
Sept. 5   *Commander:* Joshua Wing.
      Owner: Feelix Miklaszewiez, of Boston.
         C. C. **196**, XIV, 18.

1781 SCOURGE, Ship. *Guns*, 20; *Men*, 120.
May 24   *Commander:* Timothy Parker, of Norwich, Conn.
      Owners: Moses Brown, Israel Thorndike, and others, of Beverly.
         C. C. **196**, XIV, 19; M. A., **171**, 395; *Boston Gazette*, Apr. 22, 1782 (See *Mohawk*, Capt. Smith); Middlebrook, *Maritime Connecticut during the Revolution*, II, 217.

1782 SCULPIN, Schooner. *Guns*, 10 *swivels*.
         Commander: —— ——.
   Essex Institute, Miscellaneous Ship Papers.

1781 SEAFLOWER, Brigantine. *Guns*, 8; *Men*, 18.
July 23   *Commander:* William Willcomb, of Newburyport.
         C. C. **196**, XIV, 24.

1781 SEAFLOWER, Brigantine. *Guns*, 6; *Men*, 15.
July 27   *Commander:* William Willcomb, of Newburyport.
      Note. The captain's name is spelled Wilcomb in the petition.
         C. C. **196**, XIV, 25; M. A., **171**, 436.

1782 SEAFLOWER, Sloop. *Guns*, 6; *Men*, 40.
Apr. 16   *Commander:* David Nye, of Wareham.
   Owners: Peleg Wadsworth and others, of Boston.
   C. C. **196**, XIV, 23; M. A., **172**, 136; Mar. Court Rec., 100.

1782 SEAFLOWER, Sloop. *Guns*, 4; *Men*, 30.
May 13   *Commander:* David Hawley, of Boston.
   C. C. **196**, XIV, 21; M. A., **172**, 157.

1782 SEAFLOWER, Sloop. *Guns*, 4; *Men*, 30.
July 8   *Commander:* Robinson Jones, of Falmouth, Barnstable County.
   Owners: Peleg Wadsworth and others, of Plymouth.
   C. C. **196**, XIV, 22.

1779 SEBASTIAN, Ship. *Guns*, 10; *Men*, 30.
Feb. 18   *Commander:* Benjamin Lovett.
   Bond: Continental, $10,000; State, £4000.
   Bonders: Benjamin Lovett, mariner, principal; Andrew Cabot and Job Prince, of Boston and Salem, sureties.
   Owners: Andrew Cabot and others.
   Witnesses: Nathaniel Thayer, Samuel Prince.
   M. A., VII, 86, 89, **169**, 444.

1779 SEBASTIAN, Ship. *Tons*, 200; *Guns*, 10; *Men*, 30.
Sept. 18   *Commander:* Benjamin Ellinwood.
   Petition signed by Job Prince in behalf of Andrew and John Cabot, of Beverly.
   M. A., **170**, 403.

1780 SEBASTIAN, Ship. *Guns*, 10; *Men*, 30.
Aug. 21   *Commander:* Ichabod Groves.
   Owner: Andrew Cabot, of Beverly.
   C. C. **196**, XIV, 26; M. A., **171**, 258.

1781 SENEGAL, Schooner. *Guns*, 8; *Men*, 35.
June 4   *Commander:* Nathaniel Bently, of Newburyport.
   C. C. **196**, XIV, 29; M. A., **171**, 403.

1782 SHAKER, Galley. *Guns*, 6; *Men*, 40.
May 8   *Commander:* Samuel Stacy.
   Owners: Job Prince and others, of Boston.
   C. C. **196**, XIV, 32; M. A., **172**, 153.

1783 SHAKER, Galley. *Guns*, 6; *Men*, 40.
Feb. 26   *Commander:* James Lovett, jr., of Beverly.
   C. C. **196**, XIV, 31; M. A., **172**, 307.

1778 SHARK, Schooner. *Guns*, 14 *swivels; Men*, 20.
May 8   *Commander:* David Masury.
   Bond: Continental, $5000; State, £4000.
   Bonders: David Masury, principal; Marshal Mansfield and Abijah Northey, of Salem, sureties.
   Owners: Marshal Mansfield and others.
   Witness: D[aniel] Hopkins.
   M. A., VII, 77, 78, **168**, 293.

1779 SHARK, Schooner. *Guns*, 6; *Men*, 30.
May 3   *Commander:* William Preston.
   Bond: Continental, $5000; State, £4000.
   Bonders: William Preston, mariner, principal; Thomas Thomas and William Tidcomb [Titcomb?], of Newburyport, sureties.
   Owner: Samuel Batchelder, of Newburyport.
   Witnesses: Jo[seph] Cutler, Benaiah Titcomb.
   M. A., VII, 164, 165, **170**, 77.

1779 SHARK, Schooner. *Guns*, 2; *Men*, 20.
Oct. 19   *Commander:* Nathaniel Bently.
   Bond: Continental, $5000; State, £4000.
   Bonders: Nathaniel Bently, mariner, principal; Daniel Sargent and Joseph Billings, sureties.
   Owners: Thomas Thomas and others.
   Witnesses: S. Wall, Joseph Billings, jr.
   M. A., VII, 70, 72, **170**, 438.

1781 SHARK, Brigantine. *Guns*, 14; *Men*, 80.
Apr. 12   *Commander:* David Allen, of Boston.
   C. C. **196**, XIV, 30; M. A., **171**, 366.

1782 SHARK, Sloop. *Guns*, 10 *swivels.*
   Commander: ———— ————.
   Essex Institute, Miscellaneous Ship Papers; *London Chronicle,* Sept. 7, 1782 (See *Grampus,* Capt. Holmes).

1779 SHAVING MILL, Boat. *Guns*, 1 *swivel; Men*, 8.
May 13   *Commander:* Ebenezer Nye.
   Bond: Continental, $5000; State, £4000.
   Bonders: Ebenezer Nye, mariner, principal; Nathaniel Freeman and Joseph Dimick [signed Dimuck], sureties.
   Owner: Joseph Dimuck, [of Falmouth, Barnstable Co.].
   Witnesses: E. Nye, N. Bodfish.
   M. A., VII, 117, 118, **170**, 95.

1781 Shaving Mill.
    Commander: —— Plympton [Nathan Plimpton?].
    Boston Gazette, Aug. 13, 1781: "The *Shaving-Mill*, commanded by Captain Plympton, has taken a sloop and schooner laden with fish, both of which are in a safe port."

1781 Shaving Mill, Boat. *Guns and men;* not stated.
Aug. 20   *Commander:* Daniel Loring, of Kingston.
    C. C. **196**, xiv, 33; M. A., **171**, 460.

1782 Sherwood, Brig. *Guns*, 14; *Men*, 11.
    Commander: J[onathan?] Tucker.
      Note. Compare *Mermaid*, Capt. Jonathan Tucker. Possibly the same vessel. The name as written on the original bond might have been carelessly read *Sherwood*.
    Emmons, 163.

1781 Siren, Ship. *Guns*, 12; *Men*, 50.
June 13   *Commander:* David Stevenson, of Marblehead.
    C. C. **196**, xiv, 34; M. A., **171**, 412.

1778 Sky Rocket, Ship. *Tons*, 200; *Guns*, 16; *Men*, 90.
Dec. 17   *Commander:* Isaac Somes.
    Bond: Continental, $10,000; State, £4000.
    Bonders: Isaac Somes, mariner, principal; Ebenezer Parsons and Joseph Stanwood, of Cape Ann, sureties.
    Owners: Daniel Sargent and Ebenezer Parsons, of Cape Ann.
    Witnesses: Benj[ami]n Lunt, Eben[ezer] Lane.
    M. A., vii, 66, 67, **169**, 376.

1779 Sky Rocket, Ship. *Tons*, 220; *Guns*, 16; *Men*, 80.
June 10   *Commander:* William Burke.
    Bond: Continental, $10,000; State, £4000.
    Bonders: William Burke, mariner, of Boston, principal; Joseph Stanwood, of Newburyport, and Nehemiah Somes, of Boston, sureties.
    Owners: Joseph Stanwood and others.
    Witnesses: Adams Bailey, jr., Joseph Noyes.
      Note. On the Penobscot Expedition, and destroyed to prevent capture.
    M. A., viii, 3, 5, xxxvii, 280, **170**, 160.

1778 SNATCH CAT, Sloop. *Guns*, 6; *Men*, 25.
June 22   Commander: David Allen.
   Bond: Continental, $5000; State, £4000.
   Bonders: David Allan [signed Allen], mariner, principal; John Hinckley [signed Hinkley] and Dimond Morton, of Boston, sureties.
   Owners: John Hinkley, Dimond Morton, and others.
   Witnesses: Fitch Pool, Jno. Dall.
   M. A., VII, 129, 130, **139**, 193, **168**, 380.

1778 SNATCH CAT, Sloop. *Guns*, 8; *Men*, 25.
Aug. 17   Commander: Thomas Shuker.
   Bond: Continental, $5000; State, £4000.
   Bonders: Thomas Shuker, mariner, principal; David Allen and John Kneeland, of Boston, sureties.
   Owners: John Hinkley and Dimond Morton.
   Witness: Fitch Pool.
   M. A., VII, 149, 152, **139**, 207, **169**, 84.

1778 SNOW BIRD, Schooner. *Guns*, 8 swivels; *Men*, 23.
Mar. 19   Commander: Thomas Doliber.
   Bond: Continental, $5000; State, £500.
   Bonders: Thomas Doliber, principal; Benjamin Needham and William Andrews, of Marblehead, sureties.
   Owners: Benjamin Needham and William Andrews.
   Witness: D[aniel] Hopkins.
   M. A., VII, 147, 150, **168**, 222.

1781 SPANISH FAME, Brigantine. *Guns*, 10; *Men*, 25.
Jan. 17   Commander: Joseph Cunningham, of Boston.
   C. C. **196**, XIV, 38; M. A., **171**, 333.

1781 SPANISH FAME, Brigantine. *Guns*, 10; *Men*, 25.
Aug. 24   Commander: James Rob, of Boston.
   C. C. **196**, XIV, 39; M. A., **171**, 468.

1782 SPANISH PACKET, Ship. *Guns*, 10; *Men*, 20.
Feb. 26   Commander: Thomas Dalling, of Beverly.
   Owners: Francis Cabot, jr., and others, of Salem.
   C. C. **196**, XIV, 40; M. A., **172**, 103.

1777 SPANKER. *Guns*, 20.
   Commander: —— ——.
   London Chronicle, Aug. 12, 1777: "The *Spanker*, an American privateer of 20 guns, belonging to Boston,

is said to be taken after a long engagement off Cape Cod by two armed transports and carried into New York. The *Spanker*, when she struck, had but 19 men left alive out of above 100."

1780 SPEED, Brigantine (privateer).
June 17   *Commander:* Benjamin Cox, of Salem.
   M. A., XL, 79.

1776 SPEEDWELL, Brigantine. *Guns*, 8, and 12 *swivels; Men*, 70.
Sept. 6   *Commander:* Jonathan Greely.
   Bond: Continental, $5000.
   Bonders: Jonathan Greely, Thomas Melvill, and John Hinckley [signed Hinkley], all of Boston.
   Owners: Thomas Melvill, William Foster, John Hinkley, and others.
   Witnesses: Benja[min] Edes, Benjamin Edes, jr.
      Note. In various documents this vessel is called both brigantine and schooner.
   M. A., VII, 158, **139**, 105, 129 (Apr. 17, 1777: Bond "not to ship or receive any men on Board said Schooner *Speedwell* that are the Inhabitants of any Town within said State that have not raised their Proportion of the Continental Army"), 148, **152**, 271, **165**, 214, **181**, 215.

1776 SPEEDWELL, Schooner. *Guns*, 3; *Men*, 12.
Nov. 14   *Commander:* Philemon Haskell.
   Bond: Continental, $5000.
   Bonders: Philemon Haskell, Samuel Whittemore, and William Murphy — all of Gloucester.
   Owner: David Peirce, of Gloucester.
   Witnesses: Jona[than] Carver, Elnathan Haskell.
   M. A., VII, 161; **166**, 31.

1777 SPEEDWELL, Sloop.
Apr. 16   *Commander:* Joshua Stone.
   Petitioner: Joseph Noyes.
   M. A., Council Records.

1778 SPEEDWELL, Brigantine.
Apr. 10   *Commander:* Jonathan Greely.
   Bond: State, £2000.
   Bonders: John Hinckley [signed Hinkley], Thomas Melvill and David Bradley [signed Bradlee], major part of

the owners, and Jonathan Greely, mariner — all of Boston.
Witnesses: Joseph Dunckerley, Henry Alline, jr.
M. A., **139**, 164, 199 (Apr. 10, July 3, 1778: Bonds to enlist no man in New England outside of Massachusetts); *Independent Chronicle*, July 23, 1778: "Tuesday last arrived a Prize Sloop from Dominico bound to New York, laden with Sugar, Coffee, Cocoa, Limes, etc. She was captured by Captain Greely in the *Speedwell*, three Days after his leaving this Port."

1778 SPEEDWELL, Brigantine. *Guns,* 14; *Men,* 70.
Oct. 31 Commander: Jacob Dunnell.
Bond: Continental, $5000; State, £4000.
Bonders: Jacob Dunnell, mariner, principal; sureties omitted.
Owners: John[?] Melvill and others, of Boston.
Signers: Jacob Dunnell, Thomas Melvill, John Hinkley.
Witnesses: Nat[haniel] Barber, W. Scollay.
Note. John Melvill is an error for Thomas.
M. A., VII, 85, 87, **139**, 225, **169**, 283; *Independent Chronicle*, Nov. 27, 1778 (See *Free Mason*, William Dennis).

1779 SPEEDWELL, Brigantine. *Guns,* 8; *Men,* 20.
May 20 Commander: Jonathan Greely.
Bond: Continental, $5000; State, £4000.
Bonders: Jonathan Greely, principal; Samuel Broome and Stephen Bruce, of Boston, sureties.
Owners: Stephen Bruce and others.
Witnesses: Thomas Fosdick, Pepperrell Tyler.
M. A., VII, 79, 80, **170**, 126.

1779 SPEEDWELL, Schooner. *Guns,* 6; *Men,* 40.
Aug. 26 Commander: John Tucker.
Bond: Continental, $5000; State, £4000.
Bonders: John Tucker, mariner, principal; John Stevens and David Pearce, of Marblehead, sureties.
Owners: John Tucker and others, of Gloucester.
Witnesses: William Homan, John S. Ellery.
M. A., VII, 105, 106, **170**, 355.

1780 SPEEDWELL, Brigantine. *Guns,* 6; *Men,* 16.
May 24 Commander: John Ingersoll.
Bond: Continental, $10,000; State, £4000.

> *Bonders:* John Ingersoll, mariner, principal; Robert Stone and Joshua Ward, merchants, sureties — all of Salem.
> *Owners:* Joseph White and others, of Salem.
> *Witnesses:* Benja[min] Moses, Jona[than] Fay, jr.
>
> M. A., VII, 73, 74, **171**, 167; *Salem Gazette*, Jan. 30, 1783 (See *Astrea*).

1781 SPEEDWELL, Brigantine. *Guns*, 10; *Men*, 50.
Sept. 29
> *Commander:* John Murphy, of Salem.
>
> C. C. **196**, XIV, 45; M. A., **172**, 14; *Salem Gazette*, Feb. 28, 1782: "The privateer brig *Speedwell*, of 14 guns, commanded by Capt. Murphy, of this port, was lately taken by the enemy and carried into Barbadoes."

1782 SPEEDWELL, Boat. *Guns*, 2; *Men*, 20.
Apr. 12
> *Commander:* Levi Barlow.
> *Owners:* Michael Hamlin and others, of Barnstable County.
>
> C. C. **196**, XIV, 41; Mar. Court Rec., 76, 80, 90, 93; Sumner's Notes (Mass. Hist. Soc. MSS.), I, 243, 247; *Independent Chronicle*, July 25, 1782: "We learn from Falmouth that Capt. Levi Barlow in the armed boat called the *Speedwell*, who hath lately captured a number of those infernal south-sea illicit traders frequenting Nantucket, etc., was drove into Nantucket harbour a short time since by a privateer schooner of Superior force manned by tory refugees and sheep-stealers from New York. . . . Barlow having landed his men on the wharf, hove up a breast-work and prepared to defend his boat from the shore, but was prevented by the forceable interposition of some of the inhabitants of that island concerned in trade and drove off, by means of which his boat was taken by the privateer and destroyed. . . . Capt. Barlow with his crew made their escape to the main and Capt. Lot Dimmick, of Falmouth, and Capt. Barlow, with a part of both their crews, proceeded immediately to Nantucket in Dimmick's shaving mill and another small boat. . . . When they arrived there, they found the privateer schooner laying off; upon which they took a wood sloop, laying at anchor, and with their crew went aboard her, making

Jamaica

Basil Keith

IN Pursuance of an Act made in the Seventh and Eighth of King *William* the Third, intituled, *An Act for preventing Frauds and regulating Abuses in the Plantation-Trade,* Thomas Dolbeare of Kingston Merchant maketh Oath, that the Ship called the Anna Pink of Jamaica whereof James Rodick is at present Master, being a Square Sterned Brigantine of Ninety Tons or thereabouts, was Built in N. America a prize to His Majesty's Ship Squirrel and condemn'd at a Court of Vice Admiralty held at St. Jago de la Vega the 21 day of June last for a Breach of the ~~Within~~ Oath. And that John Dolbeare of the Parish of Kingston Merchant together with Deponent are at present Owners thereof; and that no Foreigner, directly or indirectly, hath any Share, or Part, or Interest, therein.

Dated at the Custom-house, Kingston the 6th Day of August 1776

Sworn before Us

T Dolbeare

Secretary's Office Kingston August 6. 1776
Personally appeared before me Tho. Jackson
and was duly sworn to the above Register

Ship's Register: Wm Shafto
Dep.y Secy

William Thomson
P.M. Offr

Affidavit concerning a Vessel taken by the British

19 men including the two captains and immediately bore down upon the schooner and in spight of a warm attack from their musquetry and swivels, boarded and took the privateer with Bourn and 27 other prisoners and brought them into Falmouth."

1782 SPEEDWELL, Boat. *Guns*, 2; *Men*, 15.
Sept. 18   *Commander:* Edmund Palmer, of Springfield.
C. C. **196**, XIV, 46; M. A., **172**, 196.

1780 SPITFIRE, Brig. *Guns*, 12; *Men*, 50.
Apr. 4   *Commander:* John Pattin.
Bond: Continental, $10,000; State, £4000.
Bonders: John Pattin, mariner, principal; Richard Hinckley [signed Hinckly] and John T. Linn, of Boston, sureties.
Owners: Joseph Lee & Co.
Witnesses: Joseph Bowditch, jr., O[liver] Peabody.
Note. The vessel's name is written *Spit Fire.*
M. A., VII, 177, 180, **171**, 122.

1782 SPITFIRE, Schooner. *Guns*, 11; *Men*, 20.
Sept. 5   *Commander:* William Perkins, of Salem.
C. C. **196**, XIV, 52.

1782 SPITFIRE, Boat.
Commander: Thomas Dexter.
Boston Gazette, Dec. 2, 1782.

1783 SPITFIRE, Boat. *Guns*, 6; *Men*, 20.
Mar. 19   *Commander:* Samuel Hawley, of Stratfield.
Owner: Lemuel Williams, of [New] Bedford.
C. C. **196**, XIV, 51; M. A., **172**, 314.

1778 SPRING BIRD, Schooner. *Guns*, 14 *swivels; Men*, 30.
Mar. 10   *Commander:* James Dennis.
Bond: Continental, $5000; State, £500.
Bonders: James Dennis, principal; Knott Martin, jr., and Thomas Lewis, of Marblehead, sureties.
Owners: Thomas Pedrick, John Dixey, Pickering Collins, and others, of Marblehead.
Witnesses: Jonas Farnsworth, Daniel Sullivan.
M. A., VII, 99, 100, **168**, 198.

1778 SPRING BIRD, Schooner. *Guns*, 4, and 10 *swivels; Men*, 35.
June 29   *Commander:* Nathaniel Grow.
Bond: Continental, $5000; State, £4000.

  Bonders: Nath[anie]l Legrow [signed Grow], mariner, principal; James Dennis and Pickering Collins [signed Collings], sureties.
  Owners: Thomas Pedrick, John Dixey, and others, of Marblehead.
  Witness: Jno. Dall.
   M. A., VII, 127, 128, **168**, 396.

1778 SPRING BIRD, Schooner. *Guns,* 10 *swivels; Men,* 35.
Aug. 28 *Commander:* William Dennis.
  Bond: Continental, $5000; State, £4000.
  Bonders: William Dennis, principal; James Dennis and Pickering Collins, of Marblehead, sureties.
  Owners: Thomas Pedrick and others, of Marblehead.
  Witness: Jno. Dall.
   M. A., VII, 3, 96, **169**, 114.

1778 SPRING BIRD, Schooner. *Guns,* 4; *Men,* 25.
Nov. 6 *Commander:* Thomas Elkins.
  Bond: Continental, $5000; State, £4000.
  Bonders: Thomas Elkins, mariner, principal; John Lewis and Thomas Oliver, of Marblehead, sureties.
  Owners: John Lewis and others.
  Witness: Jno. Dall.
   M. A., VII, 83, 84, **169**, 301.

1779 SPRING BIRD, Schooner. *Guns,* 4; *Men,* 35.
Mar. 30 *Commander:* John Pattin.
  Bond: Continental, $5000; State, £4000.
  Bonders: John Pattin, mariner, principal; Samuel Gale [signed Gail] and Pickering Collins [signed Collings], of Marblehead, sureties.
  Owners: Samuel Gail and others.
  Witnesses: John Pownall, John Dall.
   M. A., VII, 103, 104, **159**, 313, **170**, 46; Mar. Court Rec., 22.

1779 SPRING BIRD, Sloop. *Guns,* 12.
  Commander: —— ——.
  Note. On Penobscot expedition and destroyed to prevent capture.
  Williamson, *History of Maine,* II, 470, 476; Wheeler, *History of Castine,* 38.

1779 SPRING BIRD, Schooner. *Guns*, 6; *Men*, 10.
Nov. 15   *Commander:* Joseph Northey.
    Bond: Continental, $5000; State, £4000.
    Bonders: Joseph Northey, mariner, principal; Thomas Oliver and John Dixey, of Marblehead, sureties.
    Owner: Thomas Oliver.
    Witnesses: William Baker, jr., Jno. Dall.
    M. A., VII, 113, 114, **171**, 22.

1781 SPRING BIRD, Schooner. *Guns*, 4; *Men*, 25.
Apr. 28   *Commander:* Paul Reed, of Booth Bay.
    Owners: Moses Little, of Newburyport, and Paul Reed.
    C. C. **196**, XIV, 54.

1777 SPY, Snow. *Guns*, 12.
    Commander: —— ——.
    London Chronicle, July 3, 1777 (Boston Prison, May 13): "In my last I acquainted you of my success in taking American prizes, but my fortune now is quite reverse. On the 2d of this month, falling in with the *Spy*, an American privateer snow of 12 guns, my vessel was taken after an engagement of three glasses and brought into this port, where myself and crew are prisoners."

1777 SPY, Schooner. *Guns*, 8 *swivels; Men*, 20.
June 21   *Commander:* John Bullock.
    Bond: Continental, $5000.
    Bonders: John Bullock, principal; Aaron Waite [signed Wait], and Richard Derby, jr., sureties — all of Salem.
    Owners: Aaron Wait and others.
    Witnesses: Nat[haniel] Barber, Timothy Foster.
    M. A., VII, 148, **167**, 40.

1777 SPY, Schooner. *Guns*, 8; *Men*, 20.
Aug. 16   *Commander:* Thomas Phillips, of Salem.
    C. C. **196**, XIV, 57.

1777 SPY, Private Armed Vessel.
    Commander: Elias Smith.
    Boston Gazette, Sept. 22, 1777.

1782 SPY, Boat. *Guns*, 4; *Men*, 10.
Sept. 2   *Commander:* Ichabod Grindall, of Haverhill.
    Owners: Stephen Cross and Ralph Cross, of Newburyport.
    C. C. **196**, XIV, 55.

1782   SPY, Boat. *Guns*, small arms; *Men*, 6.
Nov. 8   *Commander:* Rufus Whitmarsh, of Dighton.
           Owners: Samuel Fales and others, of Taunton.
           C. C. 196, XIV, 58; M. A., 172, 225.

1777   STARKS, Schooner. *Guns*, 10 *swivels*; *Men*, 25.
Sept. 11   *Commander:* Littlefield Sibely.
           Bond: Continental, not stated; State, £500.
           Bonders: Littlefield Sibble [signed Sibely], of Salem, principal; Ephraim Willard, Eben[eze]r Hall, jr., and William Gowen, sureties.
           Owners: William Wyer, Isaac Hall, and others, of Medford.
           Witnesses: Kiar Tarbell [?], Joseph Goodwin (on Continental bond); William Baker, jr., Fitch Pool (on State bond).
           M. A., VII, 145, 146, 167, 181.

1777   STARKS, Brigantine. *Guns*, 10; *Men*, 45.
Sept. 12   *Commander:* John Allen Hallet.
           Bond: Continental, $5000.
           Bonders: John Allen Hallet, principal; David Devens and Jona[than] Harris, of Boston, sureties.
           Owners: David Devens and others.
           Witnesses: Eben[eze]r Frothingham, Daniel McClister.
           M. A., VII, 143, 139, 144, 167, 229.

1777   STARKES, Brigantine. *Guns*, 6; *Men*, 20.
Dec. 8   *Commander:* Richard Quatermass.
           Bond: Continental, $10,000; State, £500.
           Bonders: Richard Quartimass [signed Quatermass], principal; Andrew Cabot and Jacob Williams, merchants, sureties.
           Owners: Andrew Cabot and others, of Salem.
           Witness: Benj[amin] Vincent.
           M. A., VII, 68, 69, 168, 67.

1778   STARKS, Brig. *Guns*, 8; *Men*, 20.
Oct. 6   *Commander:* Richard Quatermass.
           Bond: Continental, $10,000; State, £4000.
           Bonders: Richard Quartimass [signed Quatermass], mariner, principal; Andrew Cabot and Samuel Cabot, of Beverly, sureties.
           Owners: Andrew and Samuel Cabot.
           Witnesses: Jos[hu]a Brackett, Rob[er]t Foster.
           M. A., VII, 151, 154, 169, 198.

1779   STARKS, Brigantine. *Guns*, 4; *Men*, 14.
June 4   *Commander:* Abraham Bartlett.
   Bond: Continental, $5000; State, £4000.
   Bonders: Abraham Bartlett, mariner, principal; David Devens and Jona[than] Harris, sureties.
   Owners: David Devens and others, of Boston.
   Witnesses: Thomas Harris, Andrew Newell.
   M. A., VII, 168, 169, 170, 153.

1779   STARKS, Brigantine. *Guns*, 10: *Men*, 30.
Oct. 16   *Commander:* Ezra Ober.
   Bond: Continental, $10,000; State, £4000.
   Bonders: Ezra Ober, mariner, principal; Andrew Cabot and John Cabot, of Beverly, sureties.
   Owner: Andrew Cabot.
   Witnesses: Samuel Cabot, Fran[ci]s Cabot, jr.
   M. A., VII, 166, 167, 170, 434.

1777   STORK, Brigantine. *Guns*, 6; *Men*, 12.
Sept. 2   *Commander:* John Coombs.
   Bond: Continental, not stated; State, £4000.
   Bonders: John Coombs, mariner, principal; William Coombs and Abel Greenleaf, merchants of Newburyport, sureties.
   Owners: William Coombs and Abel Greenleaf.
   Witnesses: B[enaiah?] Titcomb, Mich[ae]l Hodge.
   M. A., VII, 172, 174, 170, 377.

1782   STORK, Brigantine. *Guns*, 4; *Men*, 12.
Aug. 24   *Commander:* Enoch Pike, of Newburyport.
   C. C. 196, XIV, 72.

1776   STURDY BEGGAR, Schooner. *Guns*, 6; *Men*, 25.
June 13   *Commander:* Peter Lander.
   Bond: Continental, $5000.
   Bonders: Elias Hasket Derby and Richard Derby, jr., merchants, and Peter Lander, mariner, all of Salem.
   Owner: Elias Hasket Derby.
   Witnesses: Benja[min] Osgood, W. Prosser.
   M. A., VII, 159, 164, 391.

1776   STURDY BEGGAR, Schooner. *Guns*, 8; *Men*, 50.
Aug. 2   *Commander:* [John] Allen Hallet.
   Bond: Continental, $5000.

  Bonders: Allen Hallet, principal; Benjamin Goodhue and Peter Lander, of Salem, sureties.
  Owners: Benjamin Goodhue & Co.
  Witnesses: Miles Greenwood, William Baker.
  M. A., VII, 162, **165**, 24.

1776 STURDY BEGGAR, Schooner. *Guns*, 8; *Men*, 60.
Oct. 2 *Commander:* Edward Rolland.
  Bond: Continental, $5000.
  Bonders: Edward Rowlland [signed Rolland], principal; Daniel Hopkins and Benjamin Goodhue, jr., sureties — all of Salem.
  Owners: Benjamin Goodhue, jr., & Co.
  Witnesses: Timo[thy] Foster, Seth Loring.
   Note. Goodhue's signatures on this bond and the last are in the same handwriting but on the earlier one he omits "jr." from his name.
  M. A., VII, 163, **159**, 24, 42, 174, 177, **165**, 308.

1776 STURDY BEGGAR, Brig. *Guns*, 8; *Men*, 60.
  Commander: Daniel Hathorne.
  Felt, II, 268; Paine, 459.

1777 STURDY BEGGAR, Brigantine. *Guns*, 14; *Men*, 90.
July 26 *Commander:* Heman Doane.
  Bond: Continental, $10,000.
  Bonders: Heman Doane, principal; Mungo Mackay and Thomas Adams, of Boston, sureties.
  Owners: Mungo Mackay and Thomas Adams.
  Witnesses: John Wheelwright, Timothy Foster.
  M. A., VII, 136, **139**, 138, **167**, 122.

1777 STURDY BEGGAR, Brigantine. *Guns*, 8; *Men*, 65.
Aug. 20 *Commander:* Philip Lefavour.
  Bond: Continental, $5000.
  Bonders: Philip Lefavour, mariner, of Marblehead, Andrew Cabot and Benjamin Goodhue, merchants of Salem.
  Owners: Andrew Cabot and Benjamin Goodhue.
  Witnesses: Jno. Cabot, I[saac?] White.
  M. A., V, 13, **167**, 172.

1781 STURDY BEGGAR, Brig. *Tons*, 120; *Guns*, 16; *Men*, 100.
Aug. 13 *Commander:* Anthony Diver.
  Petitioners: George Williams and others, of Salem.
  M. A., **171**, 456.

1776 SUCCESS, Schooner. *Guns*, 2, and 8 *swivels; Men*, 14.
May 15   Commander: John Fletcher.
   Bond: Continental, $5000.
   Bonders: John Fletcher, mariner, and Joseph Marquand, merchant, both of Newburyport, and Martin Brimmer, merchant of Boston.
   Owner: Nathaniel Tracy, of Newburyport.
   Witnesses: Thomas Cushing, B. White.
      M. A., VII, 155.

1776 SUCCESS, Schooner. *Guns*, 4 *swivels; Men*, 15.
Aug. 15   Commander: Nathaniel Perley.
   Bond: Continental, $5000.
   Bonders: Nathaniel Perley, principal; Jona[than] Peele, jr., and Richard Derby, jr., sureties.
   Owner: Jonathan Peele, jr., [of Salem].
   Witnesses: William Baker, John Gleason.
      M. A., VII, 157, **165**, 52.

1778 SUCCESS, Schooner. *Guns*, 8; *Men*, 40.
Sept. 2   Commander: Philip Thrash.
   Bond: Continental, $5000; State, £4000.
   Bonders: Philip Trash [signed Phillip Thrash], mariner, principal; William Foster and James Tileston, of Boston and Newbury, sureties.
   Owners: Nathaniel Tracy and others, [of Newburyport].
   Witness: L. Cazneau.
      M. A., VII, 121, 124, **169**, 137; Mar. Court Rec., 20.

1778 SUCCESS, Brigantine. *Guns*, 16; *Men*, 20.
Dec. 11   Commander: Solomon Babson.
   Bond: Continental, $10,000; State, £4000.
   Bonders: Solomon Babson, mariner, principal; David Pearce and Sam[ue]l Stevens, of Cape Ann, sureties.
   Owner: David Pearce.
   Witnesses: John Marshall, Aaron Davis.
      Note. The owner's name seems sometimes to have been spelled Peirce.
      M. A., VII, 75, 76, **169**, 366.

1779 SUCCESS, Brigantine. *Guns*, 8; *Men*, 15.
Jan. 4   Commander: William Groves.
   Bond: Continental, $10,000; State, £4000.
   Bonders: William Groves, mariner, principal; Stephen Higginson and Benjamin Lovett, jr., of Salem, sureties.

Owners: Stephen Higginson and others.
Witnesses: Stephen Cleveland, Joseph Bowditch, jr.
M. A., VII, 173, 176, **169**, 398.

1779 SUCCESS, Schooner.
Commander: Richard Quatermass.
Boston Gazette, April 19, 1779.

1780 SUCCESS, Ship. *Guns,* 6; *Men,* 15.
Sept. 5 *Commander:* William White, of Boston.
C. C. **196**, XIV, 102; M. A., **177**, 53.

1781 SUCCESS, Brigantine. *Guns,* 10; *Men,* 30.
Jan. 11 *Commander:* James Brown, of Boston.
C. C. **196**, XIV, 95; M. A., **171**, 328.

1781 SUCCESS, Schooner. *Guns,* 2; *Men,* 18.
Dec. 15 *Commander:* Samuel Rogers, of Boston.
C. C. **196**, XIV, 99; M. A., **172**, 82.

1782 SUCCESS, Schooner. *Guns,* 6; *Men,* 25.
Apr. 18 *Commander:* Wyatt St. Barbe, of Newburyport.
C. C. **196**, XIV, 96.

1782 SUCCESS, Boat. *Guns,* not stated; *Men,* 10.
May 8 *Commander:* William Sanford, of Falmouth, Barnstable County.
C. C. **196**, XIV, 100; M. A., **172**, 150.

1782 SUCCESS, Brig. *Guns,* 16; *Men,* 20.
Sept. 18 *Commander:* Solomon Stanwood, of Cape Ann.
C. C. **196**, XIV, 101; M. A., **172**, 195.

1782 SUCCESS, Boat. *Guns,* 1; *Men,* 20.
Sept. 30 *Commander:* Seth Freeman, of Harwich.
Petitioner: Benjamin Jepson, [of Boston].
C. C. **196**, XIV, 97; M. A., **172**, 199.

1779 SURPRIZE, Schooner. *Guns,* 4; *Men,* 25.
May 3 *Commander:* Timothy Weston.
Bond: Continental, $5000; State, £4000.
Bonders: Timothy Wesson [signed Weston], mariner, principal; Robert Hichborn, John Hinkley, and Thomas Melvill, merchants of Boston, sureties.
Owners: John Hinkley and others.
Witnesses: Nathan Bacon, John Kneeland, jr.
M. A., VII, 111, 112, **170**, 76.

1780   SURPRIZE, Schooner. *Guns*, 10; *Men*, 65.
June 30   *Commander:* Benjamin Cole.
    Bond: Continental, $5000; State, £4000.
    Bonders: Benjamin Cole, mariner, principal; William West, jr., and David Felt, sureties — all of Salem.
    Owners: Nathaniel Silsbee and others, of Salem.
    Witnesses: Nathaniel Brown, Samuel Swasey.
        Note. The vessel's name is spelled *Supprize.*
    M. A., VII, 115, 116, **176**, 472, 474; Mar. Court Rec., 50.

1781   SURPRIZE, Schooner. *Guns*, 8; *Men*, 18.
Aug. 6   *Commander:* Nathaniel Perkins, of Salem.
    C. C. **196**, xv, 3; M. A., **171**, 451.

1781   SURPRIZE, Schooner. *Tons*, 45; *Guns*, 10; *Men*, 35.
Aug. 23   *Commander:* Samuel Foster.
    Petitioners: Nathaniel Silsbee and others, of Salem.
    M. A., **171**, 466.

1782   SURPRIZE, Schooner. *Guns*, 8; *Men*, 35.
Mar. 15   *Commander:* Germain Langevain, of Salem.
        Note. Germain Langevain and Jeremiah Lousvay were probably the same person. See *Fox*, Aug. 25, 1781.
    C. C. **196**, xv, 2; M. A., **172**, 119; Mar. Court Rec., 69; Sumner's Notes (Mass. Hist. Soc. MSS.), III, 52.

1782   SURPRIZE, Brigantine. *Guns*, 14; *Men*, 70.
Apr. 18   *Commander:* Benjamin Cole, of Salem.
    C. C. **196**, xv, 1; M. A., **172**, 139.

1777   SWALLOW.
    Commander: —— ——.
    London Chronicle, Aug. 16, 1777 (Letter of a British officer, Charleston, S. C., June 11): "The 16th ult. I was taken by an American privateer called the *Swallow*, belonging to Salem, and carried into this port."

1782   SWALLOW, Brigantine. *Guns*, 6; *Men*, 20.
June 5   *Commander:* Henry Higginson, of Salem.
    Owners: Stephen Higginson and others, of Boston.
    C. C. **196**, XIV, 76; M. A., **172**, 173.

1780   SWAN, Brigantine. *Tons*, 100; *Guns*, 6; *Men*, 12.
Oct. 6   *Commander:* Joshua Hills.
    Petition signed by Nehemiah Somes, of Boston, in behalf of William Coombs and others, of Newburyport.
    M. A., **171**, 287.

1782 SWAN, Brigantine.
    Commander: Hezekiah Goodhue.
    Independent Chronicle, Aug. 22, 1782: "The brig *Swan,* Capt. Goodhue, on the 20th ult., [was reported] off the Isle of Pines." *Boston Gazette,* Jan. 20, 1783.

1778 SWEAT, Schooner. *Guns,* 8, and 10 *swivels; Men,* 50.
Sept. 9   *Commander:* John Leach.
    Bond: Continental, $5000; State, £4000.
    Bonders: John Leach, mariner, principal; Samuel Page and Josiah Orne, of Salem, sureties.
    Owners: Samuel Page and Josiah Orne.
    Witness: D[aniel] Hopkins.
        Note. The vessel's name also appears as *Swett* and *Sweet* in various documents.
    M. A., VII, 153, 156, **159**, 351, **169**, 154.

1779 SWETT, Schooner. *Guns,* 12; *Men,* 60.
Aug. 19   *Commander:* Jesse Fearson.
    Bond: Continental, $5000; State, £4000.
    Bonders: Jesse Fearson, mariner, principal; Edw[ar]d Norris and Joseph Shed, of Salem, sureties.
    Owner: Edward Norris.
    Witnesses: Joshua Potter, James Miller.
    M. A., VII, 109, 110, **159**, 211, 286, **170**, 337.

1776 SWIFT, Sloop.
June 5   *Commander:* John Wigglesworth.
    Bond: State, £2000.
    Bonders: John Wigglesworth, Edward Wigglesworth, and James Warren.
    Owners: "Belonging to said Colony of the Massachusetts Bay and fitted out by Order of the great and general Court to cruise on the Sea Coasts of America for the Defence of American Liberty and to make Captures," etc.
    Witnesses: Eleazar Brooks, Timo[thy] Langdon.
    M. A., VII, 179, **164**, 377, 383, **195**, 8 (Letter of James Warren, May 22, 1776: He has purchased "a sloop to observe the motions of the Enemy," etc.), **209**, 262, 269. See Introduction, p. 58.

1779 SWIFT, Schooner. *Guns,* 8; *Men,* 30.
May 4   *Commander:* John Farrington.
    Bond: Continental, $5000; State, £4000.

Bonders: John Farrington, mariner, principal; Shrimpton Hutchinson and Nathaniel Greenough, of Boston, sureties.
Owners: William and Godfrey Hutchinson.
Witnesses: Joseph Dobel, Joshua Pilsberry.
M. A., VII, 71, 122, **170**, 78.

1779 SWIFT, Schooner.
Commander, Samuel Masury.
Marblehead Hist. Soc.

1781 SWIFT, Brigantine. *Guns,* 8; *Men,* 20.
Jan. 3 *Commander:* Asa Woodberry.
Owners: William Homan and others, of Beverly.
C. C. **196**, XIV, 93; M. A., **171**, 324.

1781 SWIFT, Schooner. *Guns,* 12; *Men,* 30.
May 28 *Commander:* Thomas Saunders.
Owners: Nehemiah Parsons and others of Gloucester.
C. C. **196**, XIV, 90; M. A., **171**, 399.

1781 SWIFT, Brigantine. *Guns,* 14; *Men,* 70.
June 5 *Commander:* John Tittle, of Beverly.
C. C. **196**, XIV, 91; M. A., **171**, 405.

1781 SWIFT, Brig. *Guns,* 14; *Men,* 70.
Oct. 20 *Commander:* Israel Johnson, of Salem.
C. C. **196**, XIV, 87; M. A., **172**, 36.

1782 SWIFT, Cutter. *Guns,* 6; *Men,* 16.
Feb. 17 *Commander:* John Frost, of Portsmouth, N. H.
Owners: Benjamin Guild & Co., of Boston.
C. C. **196**, XIV, 85; M. A., **172**, 295.

1779 TARTAR, Ship. *Guns,* 20; *Men,* 130.
Oct. 18 *Commander:* David Porter.
Bond: Continental, $10,000; State, £4000.
Bonders: David Porter, mariner, principal; Samuel Dunn, jr., and Mungo Mackay, of Boston, sureties.
Owner: Mungo Mackay.
Witnesses: Thomas Porter, Mungo Mackay, jr.
M. A., VII, 231, 232, **170**, 435.

1782 TARTAR, Ship.
Commander: John Cathcart.
Massachusetts State Navy.

1782 TARTAR, Schooner. *Guns,* 10; *Men,* 18.
Oct. 11   *Commander:* Thomas Dexter, of Salem.
           C. C. **196**, xv, 12; M. A., **172**, 202.

1783 TARTAR, Schooner [?]. *Guns,* 14; *Men,* 60.
Jan. 8   *Commander:* John Cathcart, of Boston.
           Note. This vessel appears as a schooner in the bond, but was undoubtedly a ship, as she is called in the petition. She was the ship *Tartar*, formerly of the State Navy under the same captain, and had been sold out of the State service.
           C. C. **196**, xv, 10; M. A., **172**, 279; *Boston Gazette,* Mar. 17, 1783: "The Letter of Marque Ship *Tartar*, Captain Cathcart, is taken by the *Bellisarius* and carried into New York."

1778 TATNIBUSH, Schooner. *Guns,* 8 *swivels; Men,* 25.
Apr. 6   *Commander:* Jeremiah Rolls.
           Bond: Continental, $5000; State, £500.
           Bonders: Jeremiah Rolls [signed Role], principal; Aaron Wait and others, of Salem, sureties.
           Owners: Aaron Wait and others.
           Witness: Fitch Pool.
           Note. This vessel is listed as a sloop by Felt and Hunt.
           M. A., VII, 235, 236, **168**, 244.

1781 TEMPEST, Ship. *Guns,* 12; *Men,* 40.
Nov. 29   *Commander:* Isaac Somes, of Gloucester.
           C. C. **196**, xv, 17; M. A., **172**, 74; Babson's *History of Gloucester,* 426 (Lost at sea).

1777 TERRIBLE, Schooner. *Guns,* 4, and 10 *swivels; Men,* 35.
Nov. 28   *Commander:* John Conway.
           Bond: Continental, $5000.
           Bonders: John Connaway [signed Conway], principal; Azor Orne and Samuel Trivett [signed Trevett], sureties — all of Marblehead.
           Owners: Thomas Gerry and Samuel Trevett, of Marblehead.
           Witnesses: John Roads, Charles Halloran.
           M. A., VII, 225, **168**, 50.

1779 TERRIBLE, Brigantine. *Guns,* 12; *Men,* 70.
May 12   *Commander:* John Conway.
           Bond: Continental, $5000; State, £4000.

Bonders: John Conway, mariner, principal; Samuel
Pote and James Laskey, of Marblehead, sureties.
Owners: Samuel Pote and others.
Witnesses: H[enr]y Sibley, Jno. Dall.
Note. Was to convoy transports on the Penobscot Expedition, but probably did not go.
M. A., VII, 204, 205, XXXVII, 221, XLIV, 440, 444, **145**, 132, **159**, 281, **170**, 94; *Boston Post,* Dec. 18, 1779.

1778 TERRIBLE CREATURE, Brigantine. *Guns,* 16, and 6 *swivels;*
Mar. 10   *Men,* 100.
Commander: Robert Richardson.
Bond: Continental, $10,000; State, £500.
Bonders: Robert Richardson, principal; George Cabot and Andrew Cabot, of Beverly, sureties.
Owners: George and Andrew Cabot and others.
Witnesses: Francis Thayer, Joseph Thomas.
M. A., VII, 233, 234, **168**, 197.

1779 THAMES, Ship. *Guns,* 10; *Men,* 30.
Oct. 29   *Commander:* Madett Engs.
Bond: Continental, $10,000; State, £4000.
Bonders: Madett Engs, mariner, principal; Thomas Russell and Samuel Conant, jr., of Boston, sureties.
Owners: Madett Engs and others, of Boston.
Witnesses: Chambers Russell, John Cogswell.
M. A., VII, 219, 220, **170**, 450.

1779 THETIS, Ship. *Guns,* 6; *Men,* 18.
Nov. 3   *Commander:* Jacob Cole.
Bond: Continental, $10,000; State, £4000.
Bonders: Jacob Cole, mariner, principal; John Stanton and John Larkin, of Boston, sureties.
Owner: John Stanton.
Witnesses: Thomas Tileston, Abel Moore.
M. A., VII, 212, 215, **171**, 10.

1779 THOMAS, Brigantine. *Guns,* 6; *Men,* 18.
Apr. 22   *Commander:* Jonathan Oakes.
Bond: Continental, $5000; State, £4000.
Bonders: Jonathan Oakes, principal; John Larkin and Thomas Harris, of Boston, sureties.
Owners: John Larkin and Thomas Harris.
Witnesses: Matt[he]w Clark, Isaac Townsend.
M. A., VII, 203, 207, **170**, 62.

1779 THOMAS, Brigantine. *Guns,* 5; *Men,* 16.
Nov. 3   *Commander:* Thomas Rider.
   Bond: Continental, $5000; State, £4000.
   Bonders: Thomas Rider, mariner, principal; John Larkin and Miller Johnston, of Boston, sureties.
   Owners: John Larkin and others.
   Witnesses: William Capin, Peleg Thatcher.
   M. A., VII, 185, 186, **171,** 9.

1780 THOMAS, Ship. *Guns,* 16; *Men,* 25.
Apr. 12   *Commander:* Samuel Ingersoll.
   Bond: Continental, $5000; State, £4000.
   Bonders: Samuel Ingersoll, principal; Joseph White and Jonathan Ingersoll, sureties — all of Salem.
   Owners: Joseph White and Jonathan Ingersoll.
   Witness: Retier [?] Whittemore.
   M. A., VII, 210, 213, **171,** 127.

1780 THOMAS, Brigantine. *Guns,* 16; *Men,* 30.
Apr. 19   *Commander:* Edward Tyler.
   Bond: Continental, $10,000; State, £4000.
   Bonders: Edward Tyler, mariner, principal; Thomas Russell and Samuel Conant, jr., of Boston, sureties.
   Owner: Thomas Russell.
   Witnesses: Lendall Pitts, Thomas Greene.
   M. A., VII, 201, 202, **171,** 131.

1780 THOMAS, Brigantine. *Guns,* 12; *Men,* 35.
Aug. 15   *Commander:* Isaac Smith.
   Petitioner: Thomas Russell, of Boston.
   M. A., **171,** 246; C. C. **196,** XV, 25.

1780 THOMAS, Ship. *Guns,* 10; *Men,* 20.
Dec. 15   *Commander:* Francis Boardman, of Salem.
   C. C. **196,** XV, 22; M. A., **171,** 313.

1781 THOMAS, Ship. *Guns,* 10; *Men,* 20.
Nov. 22   *Commander:* Francis Boardman, of Salem.
   C. C. **196,** XV, 23; M. A., **172,** 70.

1782 THOMAS, Ship.
   Commander: [Thomas?] Palfray.
   Salem Gazette, Oct. 10, 1782 (See brig *Adventure,* Capt. Tucker).

1778   THORN, Brigantine. *Guns*, 14; *Men*, 30.
Oct. 22   *Commander:* John Coombs.
   Bond: Continental, $5000; State, £4000.
   Bonders: John Coombs, principal; Ebenezer Parsons and William Coombs, of Newburyport, sureties.
   Owners: John Coombs and others.
   Witnesses: Andrew Giddings, Ebenezer Lane.
   M. A., VII, 189, 191, **169**, 245.

1779   THORN, Brigantine. *Guns*, 6; *Men*, 12.
Aug. 20   *Commander:* Moses Hale.
   Bond: Continental, $5000; State, £4000.
   Bonders: Moses Hale, mariner, principal; Ebenezer Parsons and Ebenezer Lane, sureties.
   Owners: Daniel Sargent and others, of Newburyport.
   Witnesses: Isaac Randall, Gideon Woodwell, jr.
   M. A., VII, 195, 196, **170**, 344.

1779   THORN, Ship of War.
Nov. 11   *Commander:* Daniel Waters.
   Bond: State, £2000.
   Bonders: Isaiah Doane, of Boston, merchant and major part of the owners, and Daniel Waters, of Boston, mariner.
   Witnesses: John R. Livingston, Henry Alline.
      Note. A former British sloop of war, captured by the Continental Navy.
      M. A., **139**, 259 (Bond to enlist no man in New England outside of Massachusetts), **159**, 283, 290; *Boston Gazette*, Feb. 21, 1780 (quoting the journal of the first lieutenant on the engagement of the *Thorn* with two privateers from New York, the *Governor Tryon*, 16, and *Sir William Erskine*, 18): ". . . The next morning, December 25 [1779], at 6 A.M. the two brigs were on our larboard beam about two miles distant, light breezes from the west; they, to appearance, were making preparations for engaging. At 9 A.M. the wind sprung up from the S. W.; made sail for them in as good order as circumstances would admit. At 10 A.M. came up with the sternmost, as she was the heaviest, and he hailed: From White Hall, and ask'd Capt. Waters what right he had to wear the 13 stars in his pendant. Capt. Waters answered: I'll let you know presently; then shifted our ensign and gave her

a broadside within pistol shot, which she returned, as did the other brig on our weather bow. A warm engagement commenced on both sides for about two glasses, when the largest brig laid us on board on our weather quarter, whilst the other amused us on our weather bow, who kept up a regular fire; but she upon our quarter was soon convinced of her error, receiving such a warm and well directed fire from our marines and seeing his men running about deck with pikes in their backs instead of their hands, were undoubtedly glad to get off again. But soon shot alongside again and renew'd his cannonade with surprising spirit, but after two or three broadsides was obliged to haul down what remained of his colours. There must have been great slaughter, as the blood was seen to run out of the scuppers. The other brig seeing her consort had struck, made what sail she could to make her escape, but they found us as ready to follow as she was to run, after Capt. Waters had ordered the captured brig to follow. This engagement lasted about four glasses. Capt. Waters received a wound in his right knee about one glass before the first struck. At 3 P.M. came up with the other, after firing several chace shot thro' her quarter, when with reluctance they hauled down their colours. Capt. Waters ordered me on board to send the officers on board the *Thorn* and immediately make sail for the other brig, which was making from us. Fresh breezes and cloudy weather. At 8 P.M. the *Thorn* hove to, losing sight of the chace."

1779 THORN, Brigantine. *Guns*, 6; *Men*, 15.
Dec. 7   *Commander:* William Russell.
    Bond: Continental, $10,000; State, £4000.
    Bonders: William Russell, mariner principal; Daniel Sargent and Eben[ezer] Parsons, of Newbury, sureties.
    Owners: Daniel Sargent and others.
    Witnesses: John M. Lovell, Nehemiah Somes.
    M. A., VII, 193, 194, 171, 41.

1780 THORN, Ship. *Guns*, 18; *Men*, 120.
Apr. 5   *Commander:* Richard Cowell.
    Bond: Continental, $20,000; State, £4000.

Bonders: Richard Cowell, mariner, principal; Joshua
Orne, jr., and Samuel Parkman, sureties.
Owner: Nathaniel Tracy, of Newburyport.
Witnesses: Thomas Dennis, Daniel Oliver.
M. A., VII, 190, 192, **171**, 124.

1781 THORN, Ship. *Guns,* 18; *Men,* 120.
Jan. 11   *Commander:* Samuel Tucker, of Marblehead.
Owners: John Tracy and others, of Newburyport.
C. C. **196**, xv, 26; M. A., **171**, 330; *Salem Gazette,* Mar.
27, 1781: "Last Friday arrived at a safe port a
packet from Jamaica bound to London, captured by
the ship *Thorn,* who engaged her two glasses, during
which, the packet had four men killed and fourteen
wounded. The *Thorn* had not a single man hurt."
Boston Gazette, June 11, 1781: "Since our last the
Thorn Capt. Tucker, returned into Salem, after a
short cruize of ten days, to land his prisoners, having
taken three prizes." *Salem Gazette,* Aug. 7, 1781:
"The ship *Thorn,* Capt. Tucker, . . . has been taken
by a British frigate, and since re-taken by two French
ships." *Ibid.,* Nov. 29, 1781: "We hear that the ship
Jason, formerly commanded by Capt. Manly and
lately taken from the enemy, with a valuable cargo
on board, by the *Thorn* privateer, is arrived at a safe
port." *Ibid.,* Jan. 3, 1782: "Since our last, a Cartel
arrived at Cape-Ann from Halifax. By her we have
intelligence that the ship *Jason,* lately captured by
the *Thorn,* of Newbury Port, together with two brigs,
were lately taken by the *Bellisarius* and carried to
Halifax. The privateer ship, *Harlequin* was also
taken by the same ship; but by the ignorance of the
Prize Master, was afterwards cast away and entirely
lost." *Essex Inst.,* XLV, 322 (Thorn captured Aug. 19,
1782, at sea, by H. M. frigate *Arethusa*); Felt, II, 272.

1781 THRASHER, Schooner. *Guns,* 8; *Men,* 30.
June 4   *Commander:* Benjamin Cole, of Salem.
C. C. **196**, xv, 29; M. A., **171**, 404.

1782 THRASHER, Schooner.
Commander: Nathaniel Perkins.
Salem Gazette, July 4, 1782: "Last Thursday evening
Capt. Perkins in a small schooner privateer called

the *Thresher*, arrived here from a cruise in which she has taken six prizes." (In a later issue of the same paper — October 31 — the schooner is called *Thrasher*.) *Boston Gazette*, July 8, 1782.

1782 THRASHER, Schooner. *Guns*, 6; *Men*, 20.
Dec. 31   *Commander:* William Baldwin, of Salem.
C. C. **196**, xv, 28; M. A., **172**, 269.

1779 THREE BROTHERS, Brigantine. *Guns*, 4; *Men*, 12.
May 28   *Commander:* Thomas Fossey.
Bond: Continental, $5000; State, £4000.
Bonders: Thomas Fossey, mariner, principal; Edward Gray and Ebenezer Bailey, of Boston, sureties.
Owners: Edward Gray and others.
Witnesses: Benj[amin] Gray, John Savage.
M. A., VII, 229, 230, **170**, 137.

1782 THREE FRIENDS, Schooner. *Guns*, 4; *Men*, 25.
Dec. 30   *Commander:* William Young, of Boston.
C. C. **196**, xv, 31; M. A., **172**, 268.

1779 THREE SISTERS, Ship. *Tons*, 240; *Guns*, 10; *Men*, 40.
Oct. 29   *Commander:* Nathaniel West.
Bond: Continental, $10,000; State, £4000.
Bonders: Nat[haniel] West, mariner, principal; Elias Hasket Derby and Nathaniel Silsbee, of Salem, sureties.
Owners: Elias Hasket Derby and others.
Witnesses: Eben[ezer] Winship, Nehemiah Holt.
M. A., VII, 216, 218, **170**, 449.

1779 THUNDERBOLT, *Guns*, 18.
Commander:
London Chronicle, Jan. 11, 1780 (Letter from New York, Nov. 27, 1779): "One of his Majesty's ships of 24 guns has brought in here the *Thunderbolt*, an American privateer of 18 guns, belonging to Salem; she had on different cruises taken 17 prizes."

1778 TIGER, Schooner. *Guns*, 4; *Men*, 10.
Dec. 14   *Commander:* Nathaniel Brookhouse.
Bond: Continental, $5000; State, £4000.
Bonders: Nathaniel Brookhouse, mariner, principal; Henry Rust and George Williams, jr., of Salem, sureties.

Owners: Henry Rust and George Williams, jr.
Witnesses: Benja[min] Brown, Samuel Cheever.
   Note. In this case and the four following, the name of the vessel is spelled *Tyger*.
   M. A., VII, 208, 211, **159**, 278, **169**, 364; Felt, II, 270.

1779 TIGER, Schooner. *Guns*, 4 *swivels*; *Men*, 20.
Feb. 24   Commander: Ephraim Chambers.
   Bond: Continental, $5000; State, £4000.
   Bonders: Ephraim Chambers, mariner, principal; Jona[than] Glover and Edw[ar]d Fettyplace, of Marblehead, sureties.
   Owners: Jonathan Glover and others.
   Witnesses: William Dennis, John Martin.
   M. A., VII, 245, 246, **169**, 449.

1779 TIGER, Brigantine. *Guns*, 6; *Men*, 10.
Nov. 23   Commander: William Orne.
   Bond: Continental, not stated; State, £4000.
   Bonders: John Leech and George Williams, jr., sureties, and William Orne, principal — all of Salem.
   Owner: John Leech.
   Witnesses: William West, Caleb Smith, William West, jr.
   M. A., VII, 187, 188, **171**, 36.

1780 TIGER, Brigantine. *Guns*, 12; *Men*, 40.
Apr. 5   Commander: Joseph Leach.
   Bond: Continental, $5000; State, £4000.
   Bonders: Joseph Leach, mariner, principal; Henry Williams and George Williams, jr., merchants of Salem, sureties.
   Owners: George Williams, jr., and others.
   Witnesses: William West, jr., Thomas West.
   M. A., VII, 197, 198, **171**, 121.

1781 TIGER, Brigantine. *Guns*, 14; *Men*, 70.
Apr. 16   Commander: Samuel Croel, of Salem.
   C. C. **196**, xv, 68; M. A., **171**, 375; *Salem Gazette*, Aug. 7, 1781: "Friday was sent into a safe harbour a snow, prize to the brig *Tyger*, Captain Crow."

1781 TIGER, Schooner. *Guns*, 6; *Men*, 15.
Dec. 8   Commander: Jeremiah O'Brien, of Machias.
   Owners: Billing Putnam, of Newburyport, and Jeremiah O'Brien.
   C. C. **196**, xv, 33.

1782 TIGER, Ship. *Guns*, 16; *Men*, 75.
July 11   *Commander:* John Tucker, of Gloucester.
  Note. The name is spelled *Tyger*.
  C. C. **196**, xv, 70.

1783 TITUS, Sloop. *Guns*, 4; *Men*, 11.
Feb. 8   *Commander:* John Burchmore, of Salem.
  C. C. **196**, xv, 34; M. A., **172**, 292.

1779 TOM, Brigantine. *Tons*, 120; *Guns*, 16; *Men*, 30.
Oct. 1   *Commander:* John Lee.
  Bond: Continental, not stated; State, £4000.
  Bonders: John Lee, of Newburyport, principal; Joseph Laughton and Shrimpton Hunt, jr., of Boston, sureties.
  Owners: [John Tracy and others].
  Witness: James Johnston.
   M. A., VII, 183, 184, **170**, 414½ (Petition signed by Joseph Laughton in behalf of John Tracy and others).

1780 TRACY, Ship. *Tons*, 200; *Guns*, 16; *Men*, 100.
May 19   *Commander:* John B. Hopkins.
  Bond: Continental, $10,000; State, £4000.
  Bonders: John B[urrows] Hopkins, mariner, principal; John Cushing and Samuel White, merchants of Boston, sureties.
  Owners: John Cushing and Samuel White.
  Witnesses: Edw[ar]d Holyoke, Tho[ma]s Oliver.
   M. A., VI, 34, 35, **139**, 273, **171**, 262, **176**, 366, 483; *Independent Chronicle*, July 6, 1780: "Last Sunday returned from a cruize the privateer ship *Tracy*, Capt. Hopkins, and brought in with him a prize ship mounting 14 carriage guns, four and six pounders, and about 50 seamen, from Cork bound to New York. . . . The *Tracy* mounts 18 carriage guns, four and six pounders. The prize engaged Capt. Hopkins about 20 minutes, in which time she had 5 men killed and 8 wounded. Capt. Hopkins had only 3 men wounded."

1777 TRENTON, Sloop. *Tons*, 85; *Guns*, 10, and 14 *swivels; Men*, 70.
Apr. 24   *Commander:* John Leach.
  Petitioner: Samuel Page, of Salem, for himself and company.
  M. A., **166**, 365.

KNOW all Men by these Presents, That WE *James Robb of Boston in the County of Suffolk & State of Massachusetts Bay, John Welch and Thomas Newell Junr. of Boston aforesaid* are held and firmly bound to *Honble Samuel Huntington Esqr and others Members of Congress* Esquires, and to each of them, in Trust for the United States of New-Hampshire, Massachusetts-Bay, Rhode-Island, Connecticut, New-York, New-Jersey, Pennsylvania, Delaware, Maryland, Virginia, North-Carolina, South-Carolina, and Georgia, in North-America, in the Penalty of *ten thousand Dollars* to be paid to the said *Honble Samuel Huntington Esqr & others* or to their certain Attorney, Executors, Administrators or Assigns: To which Payment, well and truly to be made and done, We do bind Ourselves, our Heirs, Executors and Administrators, jointly and severally, firmly by these Presents. Sealed with our Seals, and dated the *fifth* Day of *June* in the Year of our Lord 1780 and in the *fourth* Year of the Independence of the United States of America.

THE Condition of this Obligation is such, That if the above bounden *James Robb* who is Commander of the *Briggt* called *the Triton* belonging to *John Welch and others of Boston* mounting *Eight* Carriage Guns, and navigated by *twenty* Men, and who hath applied for a Commission or Letters of Marque and Reprisal, to arm, equip, and set forth to Sea, the said *Briggt* as a Private Ship of War, and to make Captures of Vessels and Cargoes belonging to the Crown and Subjects of Great-Britain, shall not exceed or transgress the Powers and Authorities which shall be contained in the said Commission, but shall in all Things observe and conduct himself, and govern his Crew, by and according to the same, and shall make Reparation for all damages sustained by any Misconduct or unwarrantable Proceedings of himself, or the Officers or Crew of the said *Briggt*. Then this Obligation shall be void, or else remain in Force.

Sealed and Delivered in the Presence of

John Lowell
W. Head

James Robb
John Welsh Junr

Thomas Newell

A Continental Bond

1777 TRENTON, Sloop. *Guns,* 10; *Men,* 70.
May 9   *Commander:* Thomas Colony.
   Bond: Continental, $5000.
   Bonders: Thomas Colony, principal; Samuel Page, of
      Salem, and Thomas Cartwright, of Boston.
   Owners: Samuel Page & Co.
   Witnesses: John Coulston, Benjamin Loring, jr.
   M. A., VII, 227.

1778 TRENTON, Sloop. *Guns,* 10, and 4 *swivels; Men,* 25.
Mar. 11   *Commander:* Joseph Leach.
   Bond: Continental, $5000; State, £500.
   Bonders: Joseph Leach, principal; John Dutch and Jer-
      athmeel Peirce (on State bond), Aaron Wait and John
      Dutch (on Continental bond), sureties — all of Salem.
   Owners: Aaron Wait and John Dutch.
   Witness: D[aniel] Hopkins.
   M. A., VII, 239, 240, **168**, 205.

1780 TRITON, Brigantine. *Guns,* 8; *Men,* 20.
June 5   *Commander:* James Rob.
   Bond: Continental, $10,000; State, £4000.
   Bonders: James Robb [signed Rob], principal; John
      Welch [signed John Welsh, jr.] and Thomas Newell, jr.,
      sureties — all of Boston.
   Owners: John Welch [Welsh?] and others, of Boston.
   Witnesses: John Lowell, Jos[eph] Head.
   M. A., VII, 199, 200, **171**, 172.

1780 TRITON, Brigantine. *Guns,* 4; *Men,* 12.
Dec. 9   *Commander:* Ebenezer Stocker, of Newburyport.
   C. C. **196**, XV, 41.

1781 TRITON, Ship. *Guns,* 12; *Men,* 90.
   Commander: Joseph Rati.
      Note. In Paine's list is the ship *Trenton,* 12 guns,
         Capt. Joseph Nati, doubtless the same vessel.
      Boston Gazette, June 25, 1781; *Salem Gazette,* Aug. 7,
         1781 (Prize of ship *Tryton,* Joseph Rati, advertised
         for sale); Essex Institute, Miscellaneous Ship Papers.

1781 TROOPER, Ship. *Guns,* 8; *Men,* 30.
   Commander: S[amuel?] Dunn.
      Note. Compare *Prosper,* Capt. Samuel Dunn, jr.
         Possibly the same vessel. The name as written on

the original bond might have been carelessly read *Trooper*.

Emmons, 166.

1776 TRUE AMERICAN, Schooner. *Guns*, 10; *Men*, 80.
Aug. 5   *Commander:* Daniel Hathorne.
    Bond: Continental, $5000.
    Bonders: Daniel Hathorne, mariner, principal; Benjamin Goodhue and Miles Greenwood, traders — all of Salem.
    Owners: Benjamin Goodhue and others.
    Witnesses: Ichabod Nichols, Josh[ua] Dodge.
    M. A., VII, 243, **159**, 10, **165**, 20, 38.

1776 TRUE AMERICAN, Schooner. *Guns*, 10, and 12 *swivels*; *Men*, 65.
Dec. 3   *Commander:* William Carlton.
    Bond: Continental, $5000.
    Bonders: William Carlton, principal; Joseph Sprague and Benjamin Goodhue, sureties.
    Owners: Joseph Sprague & Co., of Salem.
    Witnesses: James Jeffrey, Sam[uel] Ward.
    M. A., VII, 242, **166**, 71, 72.

1778 TRUE AMERICAN, Brig. *Tons*, 90; *Guns*, 7, and 4 *swivels;*
May 20   *Men*, 25.
    Commander: John Buffinton.
    Petitioner: Andrew Cabot, of Salem.
    M. A., **168**, 237.

1778 TRUE AMERICAN, Brigantine. *Guns*, 12, and 4 *swivels;*
Oct. 13   *Men*, 60.
    Commander: Robert Brookhouse.
    Bond: Continental, $5000; State, £4000.
    Bonders: Robert Brookhouse, mariner, principal; Josiah Orne and John Buffington [signed Buffinton], of Salem, sureties.
    Owners: Josiah Orne and John Buffinton.
    Witness: D[aniel] Hopkins.
    M. A., VII, 237, 238, **169**, 215.

1779 TRUE AMERICAN, Brigantine. *Guns*, 6; *Men*, 13.
May 5   *Commander:* Zachariah Sears.
    Bond: Continental, $10,000; State, £4000.
    Bonders: Zachariah Sears, mariner, principal; William Foster and Stephen Higginson, of Boston, sureties.
    Owner: Stephen Higginson.
    Witnesses: George Burroughs, David Spear.
    M. A., V, 44, 46, **170**, 79.

TRUE AMERICAN, Schooner. *Guns*, 6; MEN, 50.
    Commander: Israel Thorndike.
    Paine, 459.

1776   TRUE BLUE, Schooner. *Guns*, 10, and 12 *swivels; Men*, 75.
Aug. 30   *Commander:* William Coles.
    Bond: Continental, $5000.
    Bonders: William Cole [signed Coles], principal; Jonathan Glover and Thomas Gerry, merchants of Marblehead.
    Owners: Jonathan Glover & Co.
    Witnesses: John Selman, Samuel Russell Gerry.
    M. A., VII, 244, **159**, 17, **165**, 192.

1776   TRUE BLUE, Sloop. *Tons*, 55; *Guns*, 6, and 8 *swivels; Men*, 40.
Oct. 28   *Commander:* Oliver Allen.
    Bond: Continental, $5000.
    Bonders: Oliver Allen, principal, Ebenezer White, of Rochester, and Abiel Peirce, of Middleborough.
    Owners: Oliver Allen, Ed[war]d Hammond and others, of Rochester and Wareham.
    Witnesses: Edward Mitchell, Jonathan Willis.
    M. A., VII, 241, **165**, 392.

1777   TRUE BLUE, Armed vessel. *Guns*, 6; *Men*, 65.
Apr. 28   *Commander:* Richard Stiles.
    Bond: Continental, $5000.
    Bonders: Richard Stiles, principal; Azor Orne and Samuel Russell Gerry, sureties.
    Owners: Azor Orne and others, of Marblehead.
    Witnesses: Ja[me]s Mugford, Timo[thy] Foster.
    M. A., VII, 226, **166**, 370.

1777   TRUE BLUE, Schooner. *Guns*, 10; *Men*, 70.
Apr. 29   *Commander:* John Buffinton.
    Bond: Continental, $5000.
    Bonders: John Buffington [signed Buffinton], principal; George Dodge and William Coles, sureties.
    Owners: George Dodge and others, of Salem.
    Witnesses: Edward Gibaut, Stephen Hall, 3d.
    M. A., VII, 223.

1777   TRUE BLUE, Schooner. *Guns*, 10; *Men*, 65.
Dec. 16   *Commander:* Laurence Furlong.
    Bond: Continental, $5000.

Bonders: Lawrence Forlong [signed Laurence Furlong], principal; Cushing & White, of Boston, sureties.
Owners: Cushing & White [John Cushing and Samuel White].
Witnesses: Olive Cushing, Robert Cushing.
M. A., VII, 228, VIII, 1, **168**, 86.

1779 TRUE BLUE, Schooner. *Guns,* 4; *Men,* 15.
June 16   *Commander:* Jonathan Mason, jr.
Bond: Continental, $5000; State, £4000.
Bonders: Jonathan Mason, jr., principal; George Dodge, Joshua Dodge, and Nathan Goodale, of Salem, sureties.
Owner: Nathan Goodale.
Witnesses: Samuel Williams, Nathan Ward.
M. A., VII, 221, 222, **170**, 170.

1777 TRUELOVE. *Guns,* 10.
Commander:
London Chronicle, July 22, 1777: "The *Truelove,* American privateer of ten guns, from Boston, was taken the 29th of May and carried into the Grenades."

1778 TRYAL, Schooner. *Guns,* 8 *swivels; Men,* 20.
Sept. 7   *Commander:* William Munday.
Bond: Continental, $5000; State, £4000.
Bonders: William Munday, mariner, principal; Amos Mansfield and Jno. McMillan, of Salem, sureties.
Owners: Amos Mansfield and others.
Witness: D[aniel] Hopkins.
M. A., VII, 206, 209, **169**, 146.

1779 TRYAL, Boat [Schooner]. *Guns,* 4 *swivels; Men,* 18.
Mar. 30   *Commander:* Thomas Saunders.
Bond: State, £4000.
Bonders: Thomas Saunders, mariner, principal; John Fletcher and John Beach, of Newbury and Cape Ann, sureties.
Owners: Thomas Saunders and others, of Cape Ann.
Witnesses: Thomas Fleet, John Dall.
M. A., VII, 224, **170**, 44; *Boston Gazette,* July 3, 1780.

1779 TRYAL, Schooner.
Commander: John Marsh.
Boston Gazette, June 21, 1779.

1782 TRYALL, Schooner. *Tons*, 30; *Guns*, 4 *swivels; Men*, 20.
Feb. 7   *Commander:* John Andrews.
        Petitioners: Nath[anie]l Bennet and John Andrews, of Cape Ann.
        M. A., **172**, 97.

1782 TRYAL, Schooner. *Guns*, 4; *Men*, 15.
Apr. 13   *Commander:* Thomas Osier, of Kennebec.
        Owners: Ebenezer Parsons and others, of Boston.
        C. C. **196**, xv, 50; M. A., **172**, 132.

1782 TRYALL, Schooner. *Guns*, 6; *Men*, 20.
Aug. 20   *Commander:* Samuel Rogers, of Boston.
        C. C. **196**, xv, 53.

1781 TWIN SISTERS, Ship. *Guns*, 16; *Men*, 25.
Apr. 19   *Commander:* Samuel Avery, of Boston.
        C. C. **196**, xv, 56; M. A., **171**, 372.

1779 TWO BROTHERS, Ship. *Guns*, 10; *Men*, 25.
Dec. 17   *Commander:* John Rust.
        Bond: Continental, $10,000; State, £4000.
        Bonders: John Rust, mariner, principal; Henry Rust and Robert Leach [signed Leech], sureties.
        Owner: Henry Rust.
        Witnesses: Sam[uel] Ward, Zachariah Pool.
        M. A., VII, 214, 217, **171**, 46.

1780 TWO BROTHERS, Ship. *Guns*, 8; *Men*, 30.
Oct. 30   *Commander:* Daniel Sanders, of Salem.
        C. C. **196**, xv, 59; M. A., **171**, 298; Felt, II, 271.

1781 TWO BROTHERS, Ship. *Guns*, not stated; *Men*, 25.
Mar. 14   *Commander:* William Gray, of Salem.
        C. C. **196**, xv, 58; M. A., **171**, 350.

1782 TYBALT, Brigantine. *Guns*, 8; *Men*, 20.
Jan. 30   *Commander:* Philip Howland, of Dartmouth.
        Owners: Isaiah Doane and others, of Boston.
        C. C. **196**, xv, 67.

1783 TYBALT, Brig. *Tons*, 120; *Guns*, 10; *Men*, 70.
Mar. 28   *Commander:* Elias Davis.
        Petitioners: Samuel Brown and others, of Boston.
            Note. This is believed to be the last petition for a privateer commission granted during the Revolution.
        M. A., **172**, 324.

1776 TYRANNICIDE, Sloop. *Guns,* 14; *Men,* 75.
May 18   *Commander:* John Fisk.
   Bond: State, £2000.
   Bonders: John Fisk, mariner, Richard Derby, jr., and David Phippen, all of Salem.
   Owners: "Belonging to the said Colony of the Massachusetts Bay."
   Witnesses: Thomas Safford, William Gray, 3d.
      Note. This was one of the first vessels built for the Massachusetts State Navy. She was soon converted into a brigantine. The name is spelled *Tiranicide* in the bond.
   M. A., **139**, 119, **159**, 28, 69, 111, 125, 131, **164**, 392.

1780 ULYSSES, Ship. *Guns,* 10; *Men,* 40.
Oct. 6   *Commander:* Daniel McNeill, of Boston.
   C. C. **196**, xv, 71; M. A., **171**, 301.

1776 UNION, Sloop. *Guns,* 10; *Men,* 65.
Sept. 2   *Commander:* Isaac Somes.
   Bond: Continental, $5000.
   Bonders: Isaac Somes, principal; John Pitts and John Winthrop, jr., sureties.
   Owner: John Winthrop, jr., of Boston.
   Witnesses: Nathaniel Appleton, John Molineux.
      M. A., VII, 248, **159**, 14, **165**, 198, **210**, 178; British Admiralty Records, Consuls' Letters, No. 3837 (Nov. 26, 1776): A French vessel arriving at Alicante reported having met, off the Rock of Lisbon, "a North American armed vessel which forcibly put on board of her 11 Sailors, part of crews belonging to two English vessels which she had seized on 12th Nov. about 25 Leagues W. of said Rock. This Pirate is a sloop called the *Union,* belong[ing] to Cape Ann, of 10 Carriage Guns, 8 Swivels, and 40 Men. Comd. by Isaac Soams, she had capt. 3 other ships, of which 2 sent to Cape Ann, another in ballast let go."

1777 UNION, Schooner. *Guns,* 4, and 4 *swivels; Men,* 15.
June 13   *Commander:* William White.
   Bond: Continental, $5000.
   Bonders: William White, of Gloucester, principal; John Codman and William Smith, of Boston, sureties.

Owners: John Codman and William Smith.
Witnesses: Daniel Johonnot, Josiah Spear.
M. A., VII, 263, **167**, 27.

1777 UNION, Schooner. *Guns*, 8; *Men*, 25.
Aug. 19   Commander: John Blackler, of Marblehead.
Owners: Aaron Wait & Co., of Salem.
C. C. **196**, xv, 72; Andrews, *Guide to Public Record Office*, II, 339.

1779 UNION, Sloop. *Guns*, 6; *Men*, 10.
Jan. 7   Commander: Nathaniel Sargent.
Bond: Continental, $5000; State, £4000.
Bonders: Nathaniel Sargent, mariner, principal; Winthrop Sargent and Joseph Foster, merchants of Gloucester, sureties.
Owners: Winthrop Sargent and others, of Cape Ann.
Witnesses: William Pearson, Winthrop Allen.
M. A., VII, 254, 255, **169**, 406.

1779 UNION, Brigantine. *Tons*, 120; *Guns*, 6, and 4 *swivels; Men*,
Jan. 9   20.
Commander: William Langdell.
Bond: Continental, $10,000; State, £4000.
Bonders: William Langdell, mariner, principal; Joseph Sprague and Sam[uel] Ward, of Salem, sureties.
Owners: Samuel Ward and others.
Witnesses: Jos[hu]a Ward, jr., J[ohn] Burchmore.
M. A., VII, 262, 265, **169**, 399.

1779 UNION. *Guns*, 20.
Commander:
London Chronicle, May 4, 1779: "The *Union*, an American privateer of 20 guns besides swivels, bound from Bilboa to Boston, laden with arms, saltpetre and other goods, is taken by the *Lively* privateer and carried into Lisbon."

1779 UNION, Sloop. *Guns*, 4; *Men*, 30.
Sept. 3   Commander: Lot Dimuck.
Bond: Continental, $5000; State, £4000.
Bonders: Lot Dimuck, mariner, principal; Nath[anie]l Shiverick and Job Parker of Falmouth, Barnstable County, sureties.
Owners: Andrew Croawell [Croaswell] and others, of Falmouth.

>   *Witnesses:* Nath[anie]l Allen, Silas Hatch, jr.
>   M. A., VII, 256 257, 170, 370 (Petition of the "Committee of Correspondence of the Town of Falmouth").

1780 UNION, Sloop. *Tons,* 40; *Guns,* 2; *Men,* 7.
May 1   *Commander:* Thomas Studson.
>   *Petitioners:* John Gray and others, of Plymouth.
>   M. A., 171, 143.

1780 UNION, Ship. *Guns,* 4; *Men,* 18.
July 21   *Commander:* Thomas Nicolson.
>   *Bond:* Continental, $10,000; State, £4000.
>   *Bonders:* Thomas Nicolson, mariner of Plymouth, principal; Martin and Andrew Brimmer, merchants of Boston, sureties.
>   *Owner:* Martin Brimmer.
>   *Witnesses:* Daniel Sigourney, Herman Brimmer.
>   M. A., VII, 250, 251, 171, 202.

1780 UNION, Brigantine. *Guns,* 8; *Men,* 20.
Oct. 9   *Commander:* Jonathan Gardner, 3d, of Salem.
>   C. C. 196, xv, 76; M. A., XL, 86, 171, 289; Mar. Court Rec., 38.

1781 UNION, Polacre. *Guns,* 4; *Men,* 15.
Feb. 6   *Commander:* Thomas Powars, of Boston.
>   C. C. 196, xv, 79.

1781 UNION, Schooner. *Guns,* 4; *Men,* 20.
Mar. 21   *Commander:* Daniel Parsons, of Cape Ann.
>   C. C. 196, xv, 78.

1781 UNION, Brigantine. *Guns,* 10; *Men,* 18.
Aug. 13   *Commander:* Henry Butler Elwell, of Falmouth, Cumberland County.
>   C. C. 196, xv, 73; M. A., 171, 454.

1781 UNION, Ship. *Guns,* 4; *Men,* 12.
Oct. 3   *Commander:* Edward Sohier, of Boston.
>   C. C. 196, xv, 80.

1781 UNION, Brig. *Guns,* 6; *Men,* 20.
Nov. 13   *Commander:* Uriah Gardner, of Boston.
>   C. C. 196, xv, 77; M. A., 172, 61.

1782 UNION, Brig. *Guns,* 6; *Men,* 20.
July 11   *Commander:* Reuben Gage, of Falmouth, Cumberland County.
>   C. C. 196, xv, 75.

UNION — VAGRANT 313

1782 UNION, Brig. *Guns*, 6; *Men*, 17.
Dec. 31   *Commander:* Isaac Smith, of Boston.
  Owners: William Gray, jr., and others, of Salem.
  C. C. 196, xv, 81; M. A., 172, 270.

1783 UNION, Sloop. *Guns*, 6; *Men*, 30.
Feb. 2   *Commander:* John Fearson, of Salem.
  C. C. 196, xv, 74; M. A., 172, 302.

1775 UNITY, Sloop.
June 12   *Commander:* Jeremiah O'Brien.
  Note. Fitted out at Machias for immediate service. After the capture of the British schooner *Margaretta*, June 12, 1775, the sloop's name was changed from *Unity* to *Machias Liberty*.
  Coll. Maine Hist. Soc., VI, 130, 131.

1779 UNITY, Ship. *Guns*, 10; *Men*, 50.
Mar. 19   *Commander:* Nathaniel Bently.
  Bond: Continental, $10,000; State, £4000.
  Bonders: Nathaniel Bentley [signed Bently], principal; Samuel Batchelder and John Coffin Jones, of Newburyport, sureties.
  Owners: Lee & Jones and others, of Newburyport.
  Witnesses: Joseph Marquand, William Vans.
  M. A., VII, 247, 249, 170, 26.

1779 UNITY, Ship. *Guns*, 10; *Men*, 50.
June 11   *Commander:* Jeremiah Pearson.
  Bond: Continental, $10,000; State, £4000.
  Bonders: Jeremiah Pearson, mariner of Newburyport, principal; Simon Elliot and Joseph Head, of Boston, sureties.
  Owners: Lee & Jones, of Newburyport.
  Witnesses: Joseph Callender, Benj[amin] Jepson.
  M. A., VII, 252, 253.

1778 VAGRANT, Brigantine. *Guns*, 10; *Men*, 45.
Oct. 14   *Commander:* John Conway.
  Bond: Continental, $5000; State, £4000.
  Bonders: John Conway, mariner, principal; Thomas and Jonathan Harris, of Boston, sureties.
  Owners: Jonathan Harris and others.
  Witnesses: Andrew Newell, William Stimpson.
  M. A., VII, 272, 273, 139, 219, 169, 228.

1780 VALIANT, Schooner.
June 3   *Commander:* Joshua Ellingwood, of Beverly.
  M. A., XL, 103; *Publ. Colonial Society of Mass.*, XXIV, 419.

1777 VELONA, Brig. *Guns*, 14; *Men*, 90.
Apr. 29 *Commander:* Thomas Stevens.
  Bond: Continental, $5000.
  Bonders: Thomas Stevens, principal; Capt. James Mugford and Capt. Joseph Cunningham, sureties.
  Owners: James Mugford and others, of Marblehead.
  Witnesses: Timothy Foster, George Dodge, jr.
  M. A., VII, 277, **166**, 371.

1778 VENGEANCE, Brig. *Guns*, 20.
  Commander: Wingate Newman.
  Note. This vessel was sometimes called a ship.
  Boston Post, Jan. 9, 1779 (Letter of Capt. Newman, Oct. 4, 1778): "On the 17th of September, in Latt. 49 N. and Long. 20 West, fell in with the Ship *Harriot*, Packet of sixteen guns and forty-five men, ... from Falmouth bound to New York, which, after a small resistance, struck. I man'd her and ordered her for Newbury-Port. And on the 21st of the same month fell in with the Snow *Eagle*, Packet from New York bound to Falmouth, ... mounting fourteen carriage guns and sixty men including some officers of the British army, which, after an engagement of about twenty minutes, was obliged to strike to us, which I likewise ordered for Newbury-Port. Col. Howard of the 1st Regiment of Guards was killed and several other officers, and a number wounded. Lucky for me, not one man killed or wounded except myself, by a musket ball in my thigh. ... Among the passengers was four Colonels, three Majors, one Cornet of dragoons. ... I have delivered my prisoners to the British Commissary residing here [Coruna], taking his receipt for the same, obligating him to return a like number of American prisoners of equal rank." *Boston Gazette*, Jan. 11, June 14, 1779; Paullin's *Out-Letters of the Marine Committee*, II, 97.

1779 VENGEANCE, Ship. *Tons*, 350; *Guns*, 20; *Men*, 120.
June 30 *Commander:* Thomas Thomas.

Petition signed by Samuel White in behalf of Nathaniel Tracy and others, of Newburyport.
> *Note.* On the Penobscot Expedition and destroyed to prevent capture.
> M. A., xxxvii, 280, 170, 193.

1777 VENUS, Brigantine. *Guns,* 12; *Men,* 65.
July 7   *Commander:* Samuel Dunn, jr.
Bond: Continental, $10,000.
Bonders: Capt. Samuel Dunn, jr., James Swan, and William Corlis, of Boston.
Owners: Samuel Dunn and James Swan.
Witnesses: Josiah Bacon, Spencer Walker.
M. A., vii, 283, 167, 65.

1779 VENUS, Brigantine. *Guns,* 16; *Men,* 75.
Aug. 9   *Commander:* Richard Whellen.
Bond: Continental, $5000; State, £4000.
Bonders: Richard Whellen, mariner, principal; John Walker, jr., and Isaac Sears, of Boston, sureties.
Owners: John Walker, jr., and others.
Witness: Jno. Dall.
M. A., vii, 280, 281, 170, 312.

1779 VENUS, Brigantine.
Aug. 13   *Commander:* Richard Whellen.
Bond: State, £5000.
Bonders: Richard Weldon [signed Whellen], mariner, Leonard Jarvis and Joseph Russell, merchants of Boston.
Owners: Not stated.
Witnesses: William Vernon, James Warren.
> M. A., vii, 264: "The Council . . . at the Request of the Navy Board, Eastern department, have permitted the said Richard Weldon . . . to sail (the Embargo notwithstanding) to Bedford in order to Convoy the Schooner *Hannah and Molley,* now laying there loaded with flour for the use of the Navy of the United States, from said Bedford to the Harbour of Boston and then to be permitted to proceed his Cruise."

1780 VENUS, Brigantine. *Guns,* 6; *Men,* 20.
Apr. 18   *Commander:* Nathaniel Harmon.
Bond: Continental, $10,000; State, £4000.

  Bonders: Nathaniel Harmon, mariner, principal; Mungo
Mackay and Daniel McNeill, merchants of Boston,
sureties.
  Owners: Daniel McNeill and others.
  Witnesses: Not witnessed.
  M. A., VII, 278, 279, **171**, 129.

1780   VENUS, Brigantine.
Aug. 15   *Commander:* Peter Silver, of Salem.
  M. A., XL, 52.

1780   VENUS, Brigantine. *Guns*, 6; *Men*, 15.
Nov. 8   *Commander:* Michael Leslie, of Boston.
  C. C. **196**, XV, 96; M. A., **171**, 302.

1780   VENUS, Brigantine. *Guns*, 6; *Men*, 15.
Dec. 23   *Commander:* John Young, of Boston.
  C. C. **196**, XV, 100; M. A., **171**, 319.

1781   VENUS, Ship. *Guns*, 10; *Men*, 80.
June 11   *Commander:* George W[aith] Babcock, of Providence,
R. I.
  Owners: Thomas Harris and others, of Boston.
  C. C. **196**, XV, 91; M. A., **171**, 408; *Essex Inst.*, XLV,
329 (Captured, July 16, 1781, by H. M. S. *Danae*).

1781   VENUS, Brig. *Guns*, 6; *Men*, 15.
Oct. 13   *Commander:* Henry Higginson, of Salem.
  Owners: Daniel and Robert McNeill and others, of Suffolk County.
  C. C. **196**, XV, 95; M. A., **172**, 30.

1782   VENUS, Ship. *Guns*, 10; *Men*, 20.
July 3   *Commander:* Thomas Nicolson of Salem.
  C. C. **196**, XV, 98; M. A., **172**, 178; *Boston Gazette*,
Jan. 27, 1783: "Arrived a Schooner from New York,
Prize to the Ship *Venus* of Salem."

1780   VICTORY, Brigantine. *Guns*, 10; *Men*, 50.
Apr. 24   *Commander:* Jonathan Nutting.
  Bond: Continental, $5000; State, £4000.
  Bonders: Jonathan Nutting, mariner, principal; Ebenezer Woodward and Benjamin Jepson, of Boston, sureties.
  Owners: Jonathan Nutting and Ebenezer Woodward.
  Witnesses: James Lamb, jr., William Doggett.
  M. A., VII, 268, 269, **139**, 268, **171**, 135.

1779 VIGILANT, Brigantine. *Guns*, 6; *Men*, 18.
July 29   *Commander:* Nicholas Malescot.
   Bond: Continental, $10,000; State, £4000.
   Bonders: Nicholas Malescot, mariner, principal; James Macduff and P[eter] Aldoph of Boston, sureties.
   Owner: James Macduff.
   Witness: Jno. Dall.
      M. A., VII, 266, 267, **170**, 282.

1776 VIPER, Schooner. *Guns*, 6, and 8 *swivels; Men*, 50.
Sept. 9   *Commander:* Benjamin Wormell.
   Bond: Continental, $5000.
   Bonders: Benjamin Wormell, William Spooner, and Stephen Bruce — all of Boston.
   Owners: William Spooner, Stephen Bruce, and others.
   Witnesses: John Avery, jr., William Baker.
      M. A., VII, 276, **165**, 223.

1778 VIPER, Schooner. *Tons*, 33; *Guns*, 14 *swivels; Men*, 30.
Apr. 14   *Commander:* Benjamin Chapman.
   Bond: Continental, $5000; State, £4000.
   Bonders: Benjamin Chapman, principal; Henry Rust and Israel Hutchinson, of Salem, sureties.
   Owners: Henry Rust and Israel Hutchinson.
   Witness: D[aniel] Hopkins.
      M. A., VII, 282, 284, **168**, 259.

1778 VIPER, Schooner. *Guns*, 14 *swivels; Men*, 30.
Sept. 30   *Commander:* Joseph Pitman.
   Bond: Continental, $5000; State, £4000.
   Bonders: Joseph Pitman, mariner, principal; Henry Rust and John Leach, of Salem, sureties.
   Owners: Henry Rust and others.
   Witnesses: John Dutch, Robert Leech.
      M. A., VII, 274, 275, **169**, 182.

1780 VIPER, Ship. *Guns*, 16; *Men*, 120.
May 9   *Commander:* William Williams.
   Bond: Continental, $10,000; State, £4000.
   Bonders: William Williams, mariner, principal; John R. Livingston and David Dickson, merchants of Boston, sureties.
   Owners: John R. Livingston and David Dickson.
   Witnesses: Maria Sheaffe (on Continental bond), Sarah Sheaffe (on State bond), Charles Jarvis (on both).
      M. A., VII, 285, 286, **139**, 271, **171**, 155.

1782 VIPER, Ship. *Guns*, 14; *Men*, 65.
Apr. 9   *Commander:* Jonathan Neall, of Salem.
         C. C. 196, XVI, 5; *Salem Gazette*, July 4, 1782: "Capt. Neil, in the privateer ship *Viper*, now on a cruise from this port, lately took a vessel laden with salt, which, after being ordered for this place, was retaken by two letters of marque bound to Quebec. Mr. John Bailey, Capt. Neil's prize master, and three of his men, on their arrival at that place, determined on a voyage to Europe rather than suffer a long and loathsome imprisonment in Quebec. They accordingly shipped themselves on board a snow bound to London and two days after leaving the river St. Lawrence, Mr. Bailey and his three men, joined by another of the crew, attacked and subdued the Captain and the remainder of his men, five in number, and thereby rendering themselves masters of the vessel, altered her course and arrived in Marblehead harbour on Tuesday last, being nine days after she was taken." Felt, II, 274.

1782 VIPER, Schooner. *Guns*, 2; *Men*, 25.
July 23   *Commander:* Benjamin Hilton, of Salem.
         C. C. 196, XVI, 3.

1782 VIPER, Schooner. *Guns*, 8; *Men*, 25.
Sept. 30   *Commander:* Thomas Coburn, of Salem.
         C. C. 196, XVI, 1.

1779 VIRGIN, Brigantine. *Guns*, 16; *Men*, 30.
Jan. 28   *Commander:* Isaac Green Pearson.
         Bond: Continental, $5000; State, £4000.
         Bonders: Isaac Green Pearson, mariner, principal; Lee & Jones and Joseph Marquand, of Newburyport, sureties.
         Owners: Lee & Jones.
         Witness: James Tileston.
         M. A., VII, 270, 271, **169**, 425.

1780 VIRGIN, Brigantine. *Guns*, 8; *Men*, 25.
Dec. 20   *Commander:* Jonathan Coolidge, of Newburyport.
         C. C. 196, XVI, 6.

1782 VIRGINIA, Ship. *Guns*, 10; *Men*, 25.
Feb. 12   *Commander:* William Claghorn, of Bedford.
         Owners: Jonathan Nutting and others, of Boston.
         C. C. 196, XVI, 7; M. A., 172, 98.

1782 VOLUNTEER, Galley. *Guns*, 1; *Men*, 25.
May 13   *Commander:* William Hart, of Boston.
C. C. **196**, XVI, 10; M. A., **172**, 156.

1782 VOLUNTEER, Schooner. *Guns*, 8; *Men*, 20.
July 18   *Commander:* Litchfield Luce, of Boston.
C. C. **196**, XVI, 11.

1782 VULTURE, Brigantine. *Guns*, 4; *Men*, 12.
Jan. 29   *Commander:* Abraham Tappan, of Newburyport.
C. C. **196**, XVI, 13.

1782 VULTURE, Schooner. *Guns*, 4; *Men*, 18.
Oct. 19   *Commander:* William Chaloner, of Machias.
C. C. **196**, XVI, 12.

1775 WARREN, Schooner.
Nov.   *Commander:* Daniel Adams.
Note. Afterwards commanded by William Burke. Washington's Fleet.

1776 WARREN, Sloop. *Guns*, 6; *Men*, 50.
July 5   *Commander:* John Phillips.
Bond: Continental, $5000.
Bonders: John Phillips, mariner, Lemuel Williams, merchant, both of Dartmouth, and John Grannis, of Falmouth, Barnstable County.
Owners: Lemuel Williams and Leonard Jarvis, of Dartmouth.
Witnesses: Benj[amin] Edes, Jno. Furnass.
M. A., VII, 326, **165**, 414.

1776 WARREN, Schooner. *Guns*, 4; *Men*, 50.
Aug. 2   *Commander:* William Coas.
Bond: Continental, $5000.
Bonders: Joseph Foster, Winthrop Sargent and Epes Sargent — all of Gloucester, and John Winthrop, jr., of Boston, merchants, and William Coas, mariner of Gloucester.
Owners: Joseph Foster, Winthrop and Epes Sargent, and John Winthrop, jr.
Witnesses: Jacob Allen, James Prentiss, William Winthrop.
M. A., VII, 323, **165**, 19, 23; *Independent Chronicle*, Sept. 19, 1776: "Last Saturday was sent into Cape-Ann by the Schooner *Warren*, Capt. William Coas,

a Ship of 400 Tons Burthen called the *Picary* [and on Monday] a Brig ... from the Coast of Guinea ... bound for London with some Elephants Teeth and Gold Dust."

1776 WARREN, Sloop. *Guns*, 6; *Men*, 50.
Aug. 21   *Commander:* Wyatt Barlow.
   Bond: Continental, $5000.
   Bonders: Wyatt Barlow, principal; Walter Spooner and Edw[ar]d Pope, sureties.
   Owners: Lemuel Williams and Leonard Jarvis, of Dartmouth.
   Witnesses: Timothy Foster, William Hazen.
      M. A., VII, 325, **165**, 117.

1776 WARREN, Schooner. *Guns*, 8; *Men*, 60.
Oct. 21   *Commander:* John Coulston.
   Bond: Continental, $5000.
   Bonders: John Colson [signed Coulston], mariner of Gloucester, John Coffin Jones, of Newburyport, and Stephen Bruce, of Boston, merchants.
   Owners: John Coffin Jones, Stephen Bruce, and others.
   Witnesses: Perez Morton, Benj[amin] Hichborn.
      M. A., VII, 328, **165**, 374.

1776 WARREN, Schooner. *Tons*, 50; *Guns*, 6, and 10 *swivels;*
Oct. 28   *Men*, 50.
   Commander: Israel Thorndike.
   Bond: Continental, $5000.
   Bonders: Israel Thorndike, Josiah Batchelder, jr., and Nathan Leech.
   Owners: Josiah Batchelder, jr., & Co., of Beverly.
   Witnesses: Joseph Thorndike, William Leech.
      M. A., VII, 310, **165**, 396.

1777 WARREN, Schooner.
   Commander: Henry Thorndike.
   Boston Gazette, Jan. 13, 1777.

1777 WARREN, Schooner. *Guns*, 10; *Men*, 55.
Apr. 30   *Commander:* Nicholas Ogelbe.
   Bond: Continental, $5000.
   Bonders: Nicholas Ogilvie [signed Ogelbe], principal; Josiah Batchelder, jr., and Eleazer Giles, sureties.
   Owners: Josiah Batchelder, jr., & Co., of Beverly.
   Witnesses: John Cuming, Joseph Hosmer.
      M. A., VII, 332, **166**, 374.

1777   WARREN, Schooner. *Guns*, 10; *Men*, 50.
Sept. 3   *Commander:* Silas Howell.
           Bond: Continental, $5000.
           Bonders: Silas Howell and Winthrop Sargent, of Gloucester, and John Winthrop, jr., of Boston.
           Owners: Winthrop Sargent, Epes Sargent, and others, of Gloucester.
           Witnesses: Isaac Phillips, John Lowell.
               M. A., VII, 320, **167**, 198.

1777   WARREN, Schooner. *Guns*, 10; *Men*, 55.
Dec. 3   *Commander:* John Revell.
           Bond: Continental, $5000; State, £500.
           Bonders: John Revell, principal; Josiah Batchelder and Ebenezer Porter, sureties.
           Owner: Josiah Batchelder, of Beverly.
           Witness: D[aniel] Hopkins.
               M. A., VII, 329, 330, **168**, 59.

1775   WASHINGTON, Brigantine.
Nov.   *Commander:* Sion Martindale.
           Washington's Fleet.

1775   WASHINGTON, Armed vessel. *Tons*, 40.
Dec. 11   *Commander:* Offin Boardman.
           Bond: State, £5000.
           Bonders: Offin Boardman, mariner, and Abner Greenleaf, merchant, both of Newburyport.
           Owners: Not stated.
           Witnesses: William Cooper, Perez Morton.
               M. A., VII, 295.

1776   WASHINGTON, Armed vessel. *Tons*, 75.
Mar. 20   *Commander:* Joseph Stockman.
           Bond: State, £1000.
           Bonders: Joseph Stockman, Stanton Prentice, and Eliphalet Flint.
           Bound to "the Treasurer and Receiver general of the Colony."
           Owners: Not stated.
           Witnesses: Joseph Jackson, William Helme.
               M. A., VII, 298.

1776   WASHINGTON, Schooner. *Guns*, 6; *Men*, 35.
Aug. 6   *Commander:* Nathaniel Odiorne.
           Bond: Continental, $5000.

Bonders: Nathaniel Odiorne, mariner of Portsmouth, N. H., John Stickney, of Newburyport, and Ebenezer Prout, of Scarborough, merchants.
Owners: Thomas Jones, John Stickney, and Joseph Marquand, merchants of Newburyport.
Witnesses: John Avery, jr., Jno. Molineux.
M. A., VII, 292, **165**, 26.

1776 WASHINGTON, Brigantine. *Guns*, 12; *Men*, 80.
Oct. 3   *Commander:* Elias Smith.
Bond: Continental, $5000.
Bonders: Elias Smith, principal, John Dyson, of Beverly, and Thomas Farrington, of Cambridge.
Owners: John Dyson, Thomas Davis, and others, of Beverly.
Witnesses: Samuel Freeman, Abraham Gray.
M. A., VII, 288, **139**, 93, **159**, 21, 55, 58, **165**, 311; *Independent Chronicle*, Jan. 23, 1777: "Capt. Smith in the Privateer Brig *Washington*, belonging to Beverly, arrived at Plymouth a few Days ago from a Cruise, during which he took eight Prizes."

1776 WASHINGTON, Schooner. *Guns*, 6, and 10 *swivels; Men*, 35.
Oct. 10   *Commander:* Joseph Rowe.
Bond: Continental, $5000.
Bonders: Joseph Rowe, principal; Eleazer Johnson, of Newburyport, and Joseph Dennis, mariner, of Ipswich, sureties.
Owners: Thomas Jones, John Stickney, and others, of Newburyport.
Witnesses: Michael Farley, Seth Loring.
M. A., VII, 287, **165**, 332.

1777 WASHINGTON, Sloop.
Commander: Joseph Jauncey.
Note. This may have been a Connecticut vessel.
Boston Gazette, Jan. 13, 1777.

1777 WASHINGTON, Schooner. *Guns*, 6; *Men*, 30.
Apr. 22   *Commander:* Joseph Stockman.
Bond: Continental, £500.
Bonders: Joseph Stockman, mariner, of Salisbury, and Joseph Marquand, of Newburyport.

WASHINGTON 323

    Owners: Thomas Jones, John Stickney, and Joseph Marquand.
    Witnesses: Peter Barbour, Henry Alline, jr.
    M. A., VII, 297, **166**, 361.

1777   WASHINGTON, Brigantine. *Guns,* 12; *Men,* 75.
May 2   *Commander:* Elias Smith.
    Bond: Continental, $5000.
    Bonders: Elias Smith, mariner of Beverly, Samuel Thwing and Thomas Lamb, merchants of Boston.
    Owners: Samuel Thwing, Thomas Lamb, and others.
    Witnesses: R. G. Cranch, Henry Alline, jr.
    M. A., VII, 306, **159**, 58, **166**, 379.

1777   WASHINGTON, Schooner. *Guns,* 6; *Men,* 30.
June 3   *Commander:* Thomas Clough.
    Bond: Continental, $5000.
    Bonders: Thomas Clough, principal, John Cushing, and Joseph Marquand — all of Newburyport.
    Owner: Joseph Marquand.
    Witnesses: Edward Holyoke, James Delap.
    M. A., VII, 305, **167**, 6.

1777   WASHINGTON, Schooner. *Guns,* 6, and 10 *swivels; Men,* 35.
Sept. 5   *Commander:* William Preston.
    Bond: Continental, $5000; State, £500.
    Bonders: William Preston, of Newburyport, principal; Thomas Jones and John Stickney, sureties.
    Owners: Thomas Jones, John Stickney, and Joseph McWan, of Newburyport.
    Witnesses: Fitch Pool, William Baker, jr.
    M. A., VII, 289, 290, **167**, 201.

1777   WASHINGTON, Brigantine. *Guns,* 14, and 12 *swivels; Men,* 75.
Nov. 8   *Commander:* Nicholas Ogelbe.
    Bond: Continental, $10,000; State, £500.
    Bonders: Nicholas Ogleby (and Oglisbe) [signed Ogelbe], principal; Samuel Clap and Samuel Thwing, sureties.
    Owners: Samuel Clap, Samuel Thwing, and others.
    Witnesses: Edward Burbeck, David Townsend.
    M. A., VII, 301, 302, **167**, 437.

1778   WASHINGTON, Brigantine. *Guns,* 12; *Men,* 80.
May 25   *Commander:* Nathaniel Wardell.
    Bond: Continental, $10,000; State, £4000.

324   MASSACHUSETTS PRIVATEERS

  Bonders: Nathaniel Wardell, principal; William Shattuck and Samuel Thwing, of Boston, sureties.
  Owners: William Shattuck and others.
  Witnesses: Samuel Clap, Jno. Shattuck.
    M. A., VII, 299, 300, **139**, 177, **168**, 313; *Essex Inst. Hist. Coll.*, XLV, 329 (Captured May 30, 1778, south of Georges Banks, by H. M. S. *Blonde*).

1781 WASHINGTON, Ship. *Guns,* 7; *Men,* 15.
Sept. 25 *Commander:* Edmond Lewis, of Salem.
    C. C. **196**, XVI, 19; M. A., **172**, 12.

1776 WASP, Snow.
    Commander: —— Harthorne [Daniel Hathorne?].
    Emmons, 168.

1779 WASP, Schooner. *Guns,* 8; *Men,* 40.
May 7 *Commander:* John Somes.
  Bond: Continental, $5000; State, £4000.
  Bonders: John Somes, mariner, principal; Ebenezer Parsons and John Low, jr., of Newbury, sureties.
  Owner: Nehemiah Somes.
  Witnesses: Richard Phelan, Eben[ezer] Lane.
    M. A., VII, 315, 318, **170**, 84, Mar. Court Rec., 22.

1779 WASP, Schooner. *Guns,* 8; *Men,* 40.
Aug. 3 *Commander:* Isaac Somes.
  Bond: Continental, $5000; State, £4000.
  Bonders: Isaac Somes, mariner, principal; sureties omitted.
  Signers: Isaac Somes, Eben[ezer] Parsons, John Low, jr.
  Owner: Ebenezer Parsons, of Newburyport.
  Witnesses: Nicho[las] Lobdell, Uriah Oakes, John Somes.
    M. A., VII, 313, 316, **159**, 252, 256, **170**, 298.

1779 WASP, Schooner. *Tons,* 60; *Guns,* 8; *Men,* 40.
Oct. 7 *Commander:* Nathaniel Sargent.
  Petitioner: Ebenezer Parsons, of Newburyport.
    M. A., **170**, 417; Mar. Court Rec., 85; Court Files, 103256; *Boston Gazette,* May 20, 1782.

1780 WASP, Schooner. *Guns,* 4; *Men,* 16.
Sept. 22 *Commander:* Enoch Pike, of Newburyport.
  Owner: Daniel Sargent, of Boston.
    C. C. **196**, XVI, 23; M. A., **171**, 279.

State of Massachusetts-Bay.

Edmund Howes of Yarmouth in the County of Barnstable and State aforesaid, maketh Oath, that the Brigt. Allegiance whereof *Reading ————* is at present Master, being a *square* stern'd Vessel of the Burthen of *sixty* Tons, or thereabouts, was built at *Harwich* in the State of *Massachusetts Bay* ———— in the Year One Thousand Seven Hundred and *seventy five* ————

Jer: Powell
Presid of the Council

And that *the said Edmund Howes is* at present Owner thereof; and that no Subject of the King of Great-Britain, directly or indirectly hath any Share, Part or Interest therein.

Edmund Howes

John Lowry D.S.

Port of Boston

THE Oath aforesaid was administered at the Naval-Office for the said Port of *Boston* the *fifteenth* Day of *September* Anno Domini, One Thousand Seven Hundred and *seventy nine* ————

Before me, *W. B. Finney*, Naval-Officer.

Affidavit as to the American Ownership of a Vessel

1782 WASP, Boat. *Guns*, small arms; *Men*, 9.
Jan. 26   *Commander:* Thomas Thompson, of Boston.
   C. C. **196**, XVI, 24; M. A., **172**, 95.

1782 WASP, Brigantine. *Guns*, 6; *Men*, 20.
June 5   *Commander:* Daniel McNeill, of Boston.
   C. C. **196**, XVI, 22; M. A., **172**, 173.

1782 WASP, Boat. *Guns*, 1; *Men*, 18.
June 29   *Commander:* Thomas Thompson, of Boston.
   C. C. **196**, XVI, 25; M. A., **178**, 438.

1777 WEAZLE, Sloop. *Guns*, 10; *Men*, 50.
Nov. 24   *Commander:* Benjamin Parmenter.
   Bond: Continental, $5000; State, £500.
   Bonders: Benj[amin] Parmenter, principal; Arch[ibal]d Blair and John Blair, of Boston, sureties.
   Owners: Archibald and John Blair.
   Witnesses: Thomas Crafts, John Avery, jr.
      M. A., VII, 319, 322, **168**, 40.

1781 WEAZLE, Brigantine. *Guns*, 4; *Men*, 12.
Mar. 27   *Commander:* John Coombs, of Newburyport.
   C. C. **196**, XVI, 29.

1781 WEAZLE, Brigantine. *Guns*, 4; *Men*, 15.
Aug. 23   *Commander:* William Peirce Johnson, of Newburyport.
   C. C. **196**, XVI, 30.

1778 WEXFORD, Brigantine. *Guns*, 16; *Men*, 100.
Jan. 2   *Commander:* John Fletcher.
   Bond: Continental, $10,000; State, £500.
   Bonders: John Fletcher, principal; Nathaniel Tracy and John Coffin Jones, sureties — all of Newburyport.
   Owners: Nathaniel Tracy and others.
   Witness: W[illia]m Baker.
      M. A., VII, 321, 324, **168**, 127.

1781 WEXFORD, Brigantine. *Guns*, 20; *Men*, 120.
Aug. 4   *Commander:* John P[eck] Rathbun, of Boston.
      Note. In the bond the captain's name is spelled Rathburne, but he himself wrote it Rathbun.
   C. C. **196**, XVI, 31; M. A., **171**, 442.

1779 WILD CAT, Brigantine. *Tons*, 130; *Guns*, 12; *Men*, 65.
May 22   *Commander:* David Ropes.
   Bond: Continental, $10,000; State, £4000.

Bonders: David Ropes, mariner, principal; John Fisk and John Norris, of Salem, sureties.
Owners: John Fisk and others.
Witnesses: Peter Lander, Edw[ar]d Rolland.
M. A., VII, 333, 336, **170**, 133; Felt, II, 269, 270.

1777 WILKES, Brigantine. *Guns,* 14; *Men,* 100.
July 17   *Commander:* John Foster Williams.
Bond: Continental, $10,000.
Bonders: John Foster Williams, commander, Caleb Davis, Gustavus Fellows, and John Tileston, merchants and owners, all of Boston.
Owners: Caleb Davis and others.
Witness: Henry Alline, jr.
M. A., VII, 317, **139**, 135, **167**, 36.

1779 WILKES, Brigantine. *Guns,* 12; *Men,* 30.
Dec. 28   *Commander:* William Pearce.
Bond: Continental, $10,000; State, £4000.
Bonders: William Pearce, mariner, principal; Samuel A[llyne] Otis and Nehemiah Ingersoll, of Boston, sureties.
Owners: William Pearce and others.
Witnesses: David Henley, Russell Sturgis.
M. A., VII, 309, 312, **171**, 51.

1780 WILKES, Brigantine. *Guns,* 14; *Men,* 70.
Apr. 21   *Commander:* Job Knight.
Bond: Continental, $5000; State, £4000.
Bonders: Job Knight, mariner, principal; David Pearce and John Stevens, of Cape Ann, sureties.
Owners: John Stevens and others.
Witnesses: Andrew Sargent, William Pearce.
M. A., VII, 311, 314, **171**, 132.

1779 WILLIAM, Ship. *Guns,* 8; *Men,* 20.
Sept. 16   *Commander:* George Rapall.
Bond: Continental, $10,000; State, £4000.
Bonders: George Rappall [signed Rapall], mariner, principal; Samuel Newhall and Richard Hinkley [signed Hinckly], sureties.
Owners: Samuel Newhall and others, of Newburyport.
Witnesses: John Avery, John Avery, jr.
M. A., VII, 331, 334, **170**, 400.

1779   WILLIAM, Brigantine. *Guns*, 4; *Men*, 15.
Oct. 9   *Commander:* David Allen.
   Bond: Continental, $10,000; State, £4000.
   Bonders: David Allen, mariner, principal; Benjamin Thompson and Eben[ezer] Woodward, of Boston, sureties.
   Owner: Benjamin Thompson.
   Witnesses: William Raymond, Ebenezer Hancock.
      M. A., VII, 335, 338, **170**, 418.

1780   WILLIAM, Ship. *Guns*, 12; *Men*, 30.
Dec. 25   *Commander:* William Peirce Johnson, of Newburyport.
      C. C. **196**, XVI, 39.

1781   WILLIAM, Schooner.
      Commander: Solomon Coit.
      Owner: Ebenezer Norwood, of Pepperrelborough.
         Mar. Court Rec., 45 (Captured schooner *Halifax Bob* May 3, 1781, and brought her into Pepperrelborough); *Boston Gazette*, May 28, 1781.

1781   WILLIAM, Ship. *Guns*, 8; *Men*, 25.
June 21   *Commander:* Joseph Rowe, of Newburyport.
      C. C. **196**, XVI, 40; M. A., **171**, 417.

1782   WILLIAM, Ship. *Guns*, 8; *Men*, 25.
      Commander: Jesse Fearson.
      Essex Institute, Miscellaneous Ship Papers.

1782   WILLING MAID, Schooner. *Guns*, 4; *Men*, 25.
July 24   *Commander:* John Savage, of Salem.
      C. C. **196**, XVI, 45.

1782   WINTHROP, Sloop.
      Commander: George Little.
      Massachusetts State Navy.

1776   WOLFE, Sloop. *Guns*, 10, and 10 *swivels;* *Men*, 90.
Sept. 4   *Commander:* Nathaniel Freeman.
   Bond: Continental, $5000.
   Bonders: Nathaniel Freeman, Samuel Doggett, Gustavus Fellows, Nehemiah Somes, and Samuel Partridge — all of Boston.
   Owners: Samuel Doggett, Samuel Partridge, and others.
   Witnesses: Peter Edes, Benjamin Gill.
      M. A., VII, 327, **165**, 210.

1777 WOOSTER, Sloop.
    Commander: Enoch Staples.
    Note. This may have been a Connecticut vessel.
    Boston Gazette, Nov. 3, 1777.

1776 YANKEE, Sloop. *Tons,* 75.
Jan. 4   *Commander:* Corban Barnes.
    Bond: State, £5000.
    Bonders: Corban Barnes, mariner, principal, and Samuel Jackson, merchant, surety, both of Plymouth.
    Witnesses: James Warren, William Watson.
        Note. Capt. Barnes's commission is dated Dec. 17, 1775.
    M. A., **139**, 118.

1776 YANKEE, Sloop. *Guns,* 9; *Men,* 60.
May 23   *Commander:* Henry Johnson.
    Bond: Continental, £5000.
    Bonders: Paul Dudley Sargent and Henry Johnson, mariner, both of Boston, and Nathaniel Crafts, merchant of Watertown.
    Owners: P. D. Sargent & Co.
    Witnesses: Perez Morton, Benjamin Hichborn.
    M. A., VII, 342, **164**, 339; *American Gazette* (Salem), July 9, 1776: "On Wednesday last was taken and sent into Cape-Ann by the *Yankey* Privateer Sloop in the Continental Service, lately fitted out of Boston to cruise against the unnatural Enemies of America, commanded by Captain Henry Johnson, the Ship *Creighton* [and] the Ship *Zechariah Baily*." *N. E. Chronicle,* July 11, 1776; *Boston Gazette,* Dec. 9, 1776 (Quoting letter of an Englishman relating to the capture of the *Yankee*): ". . . The capture of the privateer was solely owing to the ill-judged lenity and brotherly kindness of Captain Johnson, who, not considering his English prisoners in the same light that he would Frenchmen or Spaniards, put them under no sort of confinement, but permitted them to walk the decks as freely as his own people, at all times. Taking advantage of this indulgence the prisoners one day, watching their opportunity when most of the privateer's people were below and asleep, shut down the hatches and making all fast had immediate possession of the vessel without using any force." *Am. Archives,* Fifth Series, I, 684, 754–756.

1776   YANKEE HERO, Armed Vessel. *Tons*, 120.
Jan. 13   *Commander:* Thomas Thomas.
   Bond: State, £1000.
   Bonders: Thomas Thomas, mariner, Jonathan Jackson, Nathaniel Tracy, and John Tracy, merchants—all of Newburyport.
   Witnesses: Robert Tracy, Ed[war]d Jackson.
   M. A., VII, 339.

1776   YANKEE HERO, Armed Vessel (Brig). *Tons*, 120; *Guns*,
Feb. 20   14; *Men*, 40.
   Commander: James Tracy.
   Bond: State, £1000.
   Bonders: James Tracy, mariner, Jonathan Jackson, Nathaniel Tracy and John Tracy, merchants of Newburyport, and Joseph Lee, merchant of Marblehead.
   Witnesses: Enoch Titcomb, 3d, William Ames.
      M. A., VII, 341, 165, 122; *Amer. Archives*, Fourth Series, VI, 748. (Commission, Feb. 20, 1776); *Mass. Spy*, Sept. 11, 1776 (Action with H. M. frigate *Milford*, 28, June 7, 1776): ". . . After some time the ship hauled her wind so close, which obliged the brig to do the same, that Capt. Tracy was unable to fight his lee guns; upon this he backed under her stern, but the ship, which sailed much faster and worked as quick, had the advantage and brought her broadside again upon him, which he could not evade, and in this manner they lay not an hundred feet from each other yawing to and fro for an hour and twenty minutes, the privateer's men valiantly maintaining their quarters against such a superior force. About this time the ship's foremast guns beginning to slack fire, Capt. Tracy tacked under his stern and when clear of the smoke and fire, perceived his rigging to be most shockingly cut, yards flying about without braces, some of his principal sails shot to rags and half of his men to appearance dying and wounded. . . . [The frigate] again came up and renewed the attack, which obliged Capt. Tracy to have recourse to his guns again, though he still kept some hands aloft to his rigging, but before the brig had again fired two broadsides, Captain Tracy received a wound in his right thigh and in a few minutes he could not stand;

he laid himself over the arm chest and barricadoe, determined to keep up the fire, but in a short time, from pain and loss of blood, he was unable to command, growing faint, and they helped him below. As soon as he came to, he found his firing had ceased and his people round him wounded, not having a surgeon with them, in a most distressed situation, most of them groaning and some expiring. Struck severely with such a spectacle, Capt. Tracy ordered his people to take him up in a chair upon the quarter deck and resolved again to attack the ship, which was all this time keeping up her fire; but after getting into the air, he was so faint that he was for some time unable to speak and finding no alternative but they must be taken or sunk, for the sake of the brave men that remained he ordered them to strike to the ship."

1781 YOUNG RICHARD, Brigantine. *Tons*, 110; *Guns*, 10; *Men*, 20.
Sept. 4   *Commander:* William Ropes.
    Petition signed by Elisha Sigourney in behalf of Elias Hasket Derby and others, of Salem.
    M. A., **172**, 1.

1777 ZANGA, Brigantine. *Guns*, 16; *Men*, 110.
July 10   *Commander:* Arthur Crawford.
    Bond: Continental, $5000.
    Bonders: Arthur Crawford, of Providence, R. I., Perez Morton and Benjamin Hichborn, both of Boston.
    Owners: Perez Morton, Benjamin Hichborn, and others.
    Witnesses: James Hughes, Seth Sumner.
    M. A., VII, 343, **139**, 152, **167**, 64.

1780 ZEPHYR, Brigantine. *Guns*, 4; *Men*, 15.
Nov. 8   *Commander:* George Lane, of Boston.
    C. C. **196**, XVI, 56; M. A., **171**, 304.

1775 ——, Schooner. *Guns*, small arms; *Men*, 20.
June 12   *Commander:* Benjamin Foster, of Machias.
    Note. Took part in the capture of the British schooner *Margaretta.* See sloop *Unity.*
    Coll. Maine Hist. Soc., VI, 130, 131.

1781 ——, Boat (30-foot keel). *Guns, small arms; Men*, 10.
Apr. 20   *Commander:* George Claghorn.

Bond: State, "twenty thousand Dollars in Specie or other Money equivalent thereto."
Bonders: George Claghorn, mariner of Dartmouth, principal; Walter Spooner and Edward Pope, sureties.
Bound to Henry Gardner.
Owners: George Claghorn and others.
Witnesses: Belcher Noyes, jr., W. Harris.
M. A., **139**, 277.

1781 ——, Boat. *Guns*, 4; *Men*, 20.
Apr. 20   *Commander:* William Cooke, of Dartmouth.
C. C. **196**, 1, 7.

INDEX

INDEX

Achilles, 151.
Active, 50.
Adams, Charles, 77.
Adams, Daniel, 120, 145, 210, 319.
Adams, Jacob, 220.
Adams, John, 15, 16, 18, 25, 99.
Adams, John (captain), 120, 156, 165, 184, 193, 202, 209, 236, 237, 253.
Adams, John Quincy, 99.
Adams, Samuel, 17, 152.
Adams, Thomas, 44, 53, 84, 87, 88, 89, 100, 115, 129, 149, 185, 198, 203, 204, 211, 256, 261, 290.
Adams & Dexter, 204.
Adamson, Robert, 253, 263.
Addiscott, William, 203.
Adkinson, Atkinson, *see* Adkison.
Adkison, John, 183.
Admiral Digby, 188.
Adolph, *see* Aldoph.
Adventure, 96, 298.
Alcock, Mansel, 131.
Aldolph, Peter, 88, 317.
Alecock, *see* Alcock.
Allan, John, 44, 214, 227.
Allen, David, 92, 135, 279, 281, 327.
Allen, Jacob, 201, 319.
Allen, Joseph, 201.
Allen, Nathaniel, 312.
Allen, Oliver, 307.
Allen, William, 246.
Allen, Winthrop, 153, 311.
Alley, Reuben, 162.
Alline, Henry, 198, 252, 262, 299.
Alline, Henry, jr., 52, 75, 152, 153, 183, 255, 283, 323, 326.
Almy, William, 96.
Ames, William, 329.
Amory, Rufus Greene, 235.
Amory, Thomas, jr., 68, 96, 156, 171, 220, 262, 272.
Amphion, 188.
Amphitrite, 74.
Anderson, ——, 250.
Anderson, Charles, 207.
Andrew, George, 243.
Andrew, Jonathan, 247.
Andrews, John, 309.
Andrews, Nehemiah, 271.
Andrews, William, 281.
Andromeda, 74.

Angier, Oakes, 70.
Appleton, Nathaniel, 310.
Appleton, Thomas, 128, 217.
Archbald, Francis, 204.
Archer, John, 83, 251.
Archibald, Francis, 54.
Archibald, James, 214.
Arethusa, 301.
Armed Neutrality of 1780, 38.
Armstrong, William, 208, 234, 243.
Arnold, David, 44.
Arnold, James, 92.
Arnold, Nathaniel, 189.
Ash, Gilbert, 217, 271.
Ashby, George, 210.
Ashby, George, jr., 107.
Ashton, Benjamin, 225.
Ashton, Jacob, 90, 103, 136, 193, 267.
Ashton, John, 161, 227.
Astrea, 284.
Atkins, Henry, 124.
Atkins, Joseph, 177, 244.
Atkins, Silas, 71, 89, 91.
Atkins, Silas, jr., 86, 89.
Atwood, Ebenezer, 191.
Atwood, John, 72.
Aubin, Philip, 197.
Aurora, 79.
Austin, Benjamin, 50.
Austin, John, 165.
Austin, Jonathan Loring, 254, 255.
Austin, Josiah, 160.
Austin, Timothy, 154, 235, 254.
Avery, James, 227.
Avery, John, 45, 53, 67, 71, 326.
Avery, John, jr., 66, 70, 128, 157, 169, 177, 194, 229, 246, 317, 322, 325, 326.
Avery, Samuel, 72, 73, 120, 192, 262, 309.
Ayer, Elijah, 171, 214, 268.
Ayres, John, 212.

Babbidge, Christopher, 132, 194.
Babcock, Adam, 59, 75, 127, 167, 217, 233, 235.
Babcock, George Waith, 149, 175, 180, 215, 220, 276, 316.
Babsden, *see* Babson.
Babson, James, 59, 148, 235.
Babson, John, 112, 156, 270.

Babson, Samuel, 118, 250.
Babson, Solomon, 235, 270, 291.
Babson, Zebulon, 112.
Bacon, Edward, 57, 158.
Bacon, Edward, jr., 68.
Bacon, Josiah, 217, 315.
Bacon, Nathan, 292.
Bailey, Adams, jr., 280.
Bailey, Ebenezer, 302.
Bailey, John, 318.
Bailey, *see* Bayley.
Baker, Benjamin, 119.
Baker, Edward, 208, 252.
Baker, Miles, 83, 269.
Baker, Nathaniel, 91.
Baker, W., 178.
Baker, William, 73, 76, 83, 128, 198, 208, 290, 291, 317, 325.
Baker, William, jr., 71, 157, 170, 177, 182, 203, 209, 276, 287, 288, 323.
Balch, Benjamin, 213, 273.
Baldwin, William, 185, 302.
Ballard, Elisha, 200.
Bancroft, Daniel, 162.
Barbaroux, John, 171.
Barber, Nathaniel, 46, 200, 283, 287.
Barbour, Peter, 323.
Barclay, Thomas, 156, 170.
Barker, Robert, 113.
Barlow, Levi, 284.
Barlow, Wyatt, 320.
Barnard, John, 211.
Barnard, Thomas, 242.
Barnard, Tristram, 96, 247.
Barnes, Corban, 328.
Barnes, Samuel, 173.
Barr, James, 231, 268.
Barr, James, jr., 225.
Barr, John, 111.
Barrell, Joseph, 44, 73, 80, 100, 140, 146, 203, 275.
Barrell, Theodore, 261.
Barret, ——, 250.
Barrett, Nathaniel, 155.
Barrett, Samuel, 155.
Barrett, Thornton, 105, 117, 265.
Barry, Howard, 78.
Barteman, ——, 175, 176.
Bartlet, Walter Price, 82, 208, 209, 212, 253.
Bartlet, William, 115, 173.
Bartlett, Abraham, 101, 102, 103, 126, 289.
Bartlett, Isaac, 211.
Bartlett, John, 161.
Bartlett, Josiah, 15.
Bartlett, Nicholas, 69, 145.
Bartlett, Nicholas, jr., 71, 175.
Bartlett, Samuel, 187.

Bass, Henry, 86, 103, 255, 256.
Bassett, Barakiah, 126.
Bassett, Christopher, 197.
Bassett, Edward, 127.
Bassett, Nathan, 163.
Batchelder, Joanna, 120, 276.
Batchelder, Joseph, jr., 82.
Batchelder, Josiah, 20, 120, 130, 276, 321.
Batchelder, Josiah, jr., 120, 130, 259, 276, 277, 320.
Batchelder, Samuel, 42, 131, 185, 186, 187, 224, 279, 313.
Batchelder, Sarah, 133.
Bates, Benjamin, 270.
Battan, John, 184.
Baxter, John, jr., 245.
Bayley, Joseph, jr., 246.
Bayley, Samuel, 78, 79.
Beach, John, 134, 157, 166, 308.
Becket, William, 152, 226, 272.
Beckford, Ebenezer, 152, 165.
Belcher, Sarson, 92.
Belisarius, 77, 296, 301.
Bell, Daniel, 74, 218.
Bellamy, Justus, 164.
Bennet, John, 54.
Bennet, Nathaniel, 309.
Benson, Francis, 119.
Benson, Thomas, 173, 195, 208, 225.
Bentley, *see* Bently.
Bently, Nathaniel, 42, 80, 131, 181, 195, 278, 279, 313.
Besse, Barzillai, 85.
Bethel, 12.
Betsey, 97.
Bicker, Martin, 126.
Bickford, Benjamin, 223.
Bigelow, Daniel, 97.
Biggs, ——, 74.
Billings, James, 165.
Billings, Joseph, 80, 279.
Billings, Joseph, jr., 279.
Billings, Joshua, jr., 165.
Bindon, Joshua, 79.
Bird, 104.
Birrell, Robert, 137.
Bishop, John, 81, 233.
Black Eagle, 198, 227, 269.
Blacklair, William, 239.
Blackler, John, 147, 211, 311.
Blair, Archibald, 127, 138, 325.
Blair, John, 325.
Blake, John, 89, 255.
Blanchard, Joshua, 162, 273.
Blanchard, Joshua, jr., 156.
Blanchard, Thomas, 273.
Blonde, 324.
Blyth, Benjamin, 115, 122, 123.

INDEX

Boardman, Francis, 133, 178, 298.
Boardman, Jacob, 79, 127, 154.
Boardman, Offin, 321.
Boardman, Offin, jr., 202.
Boden, Abijah, 267.
Boden, Benjamin, 139.
Bodfish, N., 110, 279.
Boies, John, 133.
Bootman, Thomas, jr., see Buttman.
Bootman, William, 78.
Boscawen, 132.
Bosson, William, 54.
Boston, 50, 53, 55, 59, 128.
Boston Revenge, 40, 116.
Bott, James, 131.
Bourn, ———, 285.
Bowden, see Boden.
Bowditch, Joseph, jr., 285, 292.
Bowdoin, James, 59.
Bowdoin, James, jr., 178, 215.
Bowen, ———, 93.
Bowers, Jerathmeel, 138.
Bowman, see Boardman.
Boyd, James, 149.
Boylston, Joshua, 54.
Brackett, Joshua, 237, 288.
Bradford, John, 86, 115, 194, 203.
Bradford, William, 115.
Bradlee, David, 83, 283.
Bradley, see Bradlee.
Braxton, Carter, 235.
Bray, David, 220.
Bray, John, 227, 232.
Breck, Samuel, 122.
Brenton, Silas, C., 170.
Brewer, David, 103.
Brewer, John, 272.
Brewster, Martin, 181.
Briant, David, 83.
Briggs, Johnson, 66, 92.
Briggs, William, 98.
Bright, William, 122.
Brimblecom, Robert, 252.
Brimmer, Andrew, 312.
Brimmer, Herman, 191, 312.
Brimmer, Martin, 78, 120, 168, 174, 235, 290, 312.
Brinley, Catherine, 105.
Brinley, Nathaniel, 105.
Brookhouse, Nathaniel, 108, 196, 210, 302.
Brookhouse, Robert, 100, 182, 209, 306.
Brooks, Eleazar, 294.
Brooks, John, 133, 196, 273, 276.
Brooks, Thomas, 142.
Broome, Samuel, 72, 73, 154, 155, 181, 187, 214, 283.
Broughton, Nicholson, 163, 212.

Brown, Benjamin, 303.
Brown, Francis, 97, 114, 187.
Brown, Gawen, 218, 256.
Brown, Gawen, jr., 221.
Brown, Gower, see Brown, Gawen.
Brown, James, 133, 254, 292.
Brown, John, 83, 211, 219, 251, 252, 256, 260.
Brown, Jonathan, 70, 86.
Brown, Moses, 110, 142, 188, 222, 237, 248, 277.
Brown, Nathan, 183, 189, 225, 238, 246.
Brown, Nathaniel, 293.
Brown, Samuel, 200, 309.
Brown, William, 53, 86, 103, 109, 219, 252.
Browne, John, 115, 185, 253.
Bruce, Stephen, 81, 100, 106, 140, 169, 209, 222, 224, 265, 283, 317, 320.
Bryant, Francis, 267.
Bryant, James, 89.
Bryant, William, 89.
Buccaneer, 99, 258.
Buckram, 210.
Buffington, see Buffinton.
Buffinton, John, 138, 216, 230, 264, 306, 307.
Buffinton, Nehemiah, 182, 222, 223, 264.
Buffum, Samuel, 206.
Bullock, John, 287.
Bunker, George, 105.
Bunker, William, 183.
Burbank, Silas, 178.
Burbeck, Edward, 323.
Burchmore, John, 226, 304, 311.
Burchmore, Zachariah, 85, 173.
Burges, Joshua, 131, 133, 251.
Burgis, see Burges.
Burke, John, 116.
Burke, William, 174, 240, 280, 319.
Burnham, Thomas, 275.
Burrel, see Burrill.
Burrill, Mansfield, 226, 266, 272.
Burroughs, Ezekiel, 180, 226, 261, 262.
Burroughs, George, 77, 134, 198, 256, 306.
Bush, David, 260.
Butler, Samuel, 178.
Buttman, Thomas, jr., 139, 194.
Byrne, Clifford, 122, 247.

Cabot, Andrew, 88, 91, 96, 99, 102, 110, 111, 137, 138, 144, 164, 196, 237, 239, 248, 258, 268, 273, 274, 278, 288, 289, 290, 297, 306.
Cabot, Francis, 136, 161.
Cabot, Francis, jr., 248, 281, 289.

INDEX

Cabot, George, 124, 137, 161, 173, 231, 297.
Cabot, John, 88, 91, 96, 111, 237, 238, 248, 258, 274, 278, 289, 290.
Cabot, Samuel, 248, 273, 288, 289.
Caldwell, Robert, 73, 77, 120, 155.
Calef, John, 170, 219.
Call, Benjamin, 109.
Call, John, 171.
Call, Richard, 152.
Call, Samuel, 109.
Callender, Joseph, 313.
Capen, William, 298.
Captain, 85.
Card, William, 235.
Carente, Andre, 178.
Carey, John, 98, 179, 259.
Carlton, Samuel, 243.
Carlton, William, 84, 144, 222, 223, 306.
Carnes, Edward, 106, 234.
Carnes, John, 147, 173, 174, 207, 223, 225, 243.
Carrick, *see* Carwick.
Carter, James, 73.
Cartwright, John, 173.
Cartwright, Thomas, 305.
Carver, John, 163.
Carver, Jonathan, 282.
Carver, Lemuel, 269.
Carver, Nathaniel, 43, 253, 254.
Carwick, John, 117.
Cathcart, John, 108, 123, 133, 295, 296.
Cazneau, L., 291.
Ceres, 241.
Chace, William, 215.
Chadbourn, B., 31, 125.
Chaloche, René, 77, 80, 208.
Chaloner, John, 70.
Chaloner, William, 319
Chambers, Ephraim, 251, 252, 303.
Champney, John, 54.
Chance, 69.
Chandler, Joseph, 167.
Channing, John, 120.
Chaple, William, 119.
Chapman, Benjamin, 317.
Chapman, John, 153.
Chapman, Joseph, jr., 111.
Charlestown, 132, 175.
Chase, Ephraim, 227.
Chase, Joseph, 69.
Chase, Moses, 91.
Chase, Thomas, 261.
Chatham, 154, 185, 238.
Cheever, James, 172.
Cheever, Nathaniel, 206.
Cheever, Samuel, 303.
Chilcott, Richard, 105, 113.
Child, Caleb, 229.

Chipman, Joseph, 273.
Choate, Joseph, 169, 179, 182.
Christophers, Joseph, 251.
Cicero, 88, 249.
Claghorn, George, 330, 331.
Claghorn, William, 318.
Clap, Samuel, 323, 324.
Clark, Daniel, 129.
Clark, David, 198.
Clark, John, 191.
Clark, Mark, 251, 274.
Clark, Matthew, 71, 153, 229, 297.
Clark, Seth, 104.
Clarke, Francis, 210.
Clarke, Ichabod, 122.
Clarke, John, 191, 221.
Clarke, Samuel, 137, 219, 221.
Clay, Stephen, 188, 212, 237.
Cleaves, Joshua, 173.
Cleaves, Putnam, 166.
Cleveland, Stephen, 115, 137, 292.
Cleveland, William, 193.
Cleves, *see* Cleaves.
Clinton, James, 275.
Cloon, John, 211, 229.
Clough, Thomas, 323.
Clough, William, 100, 169, 224, 265.
Clouston, John, 138, 185.
Clouston, Thomas, 75.
Coas, William, 56, 153, 154, 240, 319.
Coats, David, 158.
Cobb, David, 73.
Cobb, Isaac, 89,
Coburn, John, 54.
Coburn, Thomas, 141, 318.
Cockran, ——, 187.
Codding, George, 138.
Codman, John, 121, 126, 178, 201, 252, 310, 311.
Codman, John, jr., 101.
Codman, William, 252.
Codman & Smith, 87, 101, 124, 126, 218.
Coffin, Alexander, 69, 176.
Coffin, Enoch, 80, 172.
Coffin, Henry, 187.
Coffin, James, 224.
Coffin, Samuel, 127, 172, 251.
Coffin, Tristram, 254.
Coffin, William, 72.
Cogswell, John, 297.
Coit, Solomon, 270, 327.
Coit, William, 70, 166, 230.
Colburn, Jeremiah, 70.
Cole, Benjamin, 293, 301.
Cole, Charles, 188, 242.
Cole, Elisha, 248.
Cole, Jacob, 147, 222, 297.
Cole, William, *see* Coles.

INDEX

Coleman, Silvanus, 115.
Coleman, William, 71.
Coles, John, 115, 122, 123.
Coles, William, 88, 102, 230, 307.
Colesworthy, Samuel, jr., 110, 237.
Collas, Peter, 183, 226.
Collier, see Collyer.
Collings, see Collins.
Collins, Isaac, see Collyer.
Collins, James, 106.
Collins, John, 123, 167, 183, 255.
Collins, Joseph, 106.
Collins, Pickering, 251, 285, 286.
Collis, see Collas.
Collyer, Isaac, 239.
Collyer, Thomas, 76, 224.
Colony, Thomas, 305.
Colson, see Coulston.
Colven, James, 138.
Comerais, Arnold, 217.
Conant, Samuel, 101.
Conant, Samuel, jr., 95, 122, 126, 140, 156, 240, 297, 298.
Condy, James Foster, 66.
Conner, Benjamin, 185.
Connoly, Thomas, 136.
Connaway, see Conway.
Conway, John, 138, 139, 204, 296, 297, 313.
Cook, Benjamin, 183, 204.
Cook, Joseph, 204, 272.
Cook, Zenas, 108, 202, 262.
Cooke, John, 160.
Cooke, William, 331.
Coolidge, Jonathan, 318.
Coombes, Ebenezer, 140.
Coombs, John, 289, 299, 325.
Coombs, William, 125, 234, 289, 293, 299.
Cooper, William, 23, 50, 141, 185, 321.
Corlis, William, 217, 315.
Costin, Joseph, 121, 126.
Cotton, Mary, 162.
Coulchester, ——, 104.
Coulston, John, 157, 305, 320.
Cowell, Richard, 216, 300, 301.
Cowell, William, 167.
Cox, Benjamin, 282.
Crabtree, Agreen, 32, 33, 164, 165.
Crafts, Nathaniel, 106, 328.
Crafts, Thomas, 91, 92, 325.
Crafts, William, jr., 171.
Craig, James, 148.
Cranch, R. G., 255, 323.
Crandal, Philip, 267.
Crawford, Arthur, 330.
Crawford, Gideon, jr., 69.
Creed, William, 66, 123, 171, 195.
Creighton, 328.

Creighton, George, 67.
Croaswell, Andrew, 311.
Croawell, see Croaswell.
Crocker, Ebenezer, 273.
Croel, Aaron, 113, 145.
Croel, Samuel, 95, 107, 145, 159, 160, 244, 303.
Cross, Hannah, 78.
Cross, John, 89.
Cross, Ralph, 78, 287.
Cross, Ralph, jr., 78, 186.
Cross, Stephen, 142, 197, 259, 287.
Crowel, see Croel.
Crowninshield, Benjamin, 167, 205.
Crowninshield, George, 218.
Cudworth, Nathaniel, 144, 208.
Cuming, John, 320.
Cunningham, Joseph, 189, 198, 199, 200, 235, 281, 314.
Curtis, John, 254, 258.
Cushing, Caleb, 31, 48, 59.
Cushing, Charles, 138.
Cushing, Jeremiah, 104.
Cushing, John, 77, 146, 185, 221, 262, 274, 304, 308, 323.
Cushing, Joseph, 168.
Cushing, Nathan, 33, 53, 55.
Cushing, Olive, 274, 308.
Cushing, Robert, 113, 228, 308.
Cushing, Seth, 259.
Cushing, Thomas, 48, 50, 291.
Cushing & White, 46, 254, 262, 308.
Cutler, Joseph, 47, 108, 142, 186, 279.
Cutter, ——, 26.
Cutting, Nathaniel, 122.

Daccaretta, John, 213.
Daggett, see Doggett.
Daggett, Samuel, 218.
Daggin, John, see Dàguin.
Dàguin, Jean, 205.
Daland, Benjamin, 248.
Dall, John, 76, 80, 88, 98, 129, 130, 139, 144, 146, 158, 159, 161, 166, 167, 169, 170, 175, 184, 187, 194, 200, 203, 208, 227, 249, 251, 252, 255, 276, 281, 286, 287, 297, 308, 315, 317.
Dall, William, 77, 98, 142, 143, 146, 169, 170, 248.
Dallet, J. E., 80.
Dalling, Thomas, 281.
Dalton, Tristam, 50, 80, 81, 108, 125, 186, 249.
Dana, Francis, 67, 200.
Danae, 316.
Daniel, 223.
Dansel, see D'Ansel.
D'Ansel, ——, 205.
Darbey, Joseph, 178.

INDEX

Dashwood, Samuel, 73.
Davis, Aaron, 291.
Davis, Amasa, 83.
Davis, Caleb, 50, 107, 326.
Davis, Ebenezer, 162.
Davis, Edmund, 265.
Davis, Edward, 97, 100, 116, 229.
Davis, Elias, 125, 129, 234, 309.
Davis, Isaac, 171, 267.
Davis, James, 252.
Davis, Joshua, 192.
Davis, Samuel, 164.
Davis, Simon, 164.
Davis, Thomas, 50, 51, 52, 170, 322.
Davis, William, 155, 245, 265.
Davis & Benson, 164.
Davison, Oliver, 105.
Day, William, 148.
Dean, Benjamin, 260.
Dean, John, 73, 260.
Defence, 248.
Degge, James, 197, 198.
Deland, Thorndike, 113, 145.
Delap, James, 323.
De Luce, William, 119.
Demick, *see* Dimuck.
Denney, *see* Dennie.
Dennie, Thomas, 75, 83, 181.
Dennis, Francis Bowden, 165, 166.
Dennis, James, 164, 165, 175, 251, 285, 286.
Dennis, John Devereux, 252.
Dennis, Joseph, 81, 125, 322.
Dennis, Thomas, 301.
Dennis, William, 75, 139, 253, 283, 286, 303.
Derby, Elias Hasket, 94, 95, 103, 126, 136, 167, 183, 204, 205, 223, 226, 233, 247, 260, 266, 272, 276, 289, 302, 330.
Derby, John, 76, 230, 231, 233, 267.
Derby, Richard, jr., 43, 54, 55, 59, 165, 185, 287, 289, 291, 310.
Desaint Pry, *see* Pry.
Devens, David, 71, 139, 152, 153, 236, 288, 289.
Devereux, Burrill, 145.
Devol, Silas, 138.
Dexter, Samuel, 20.
Dexter, Thomas, 109, 285, 296.
Diana, 145, 242.
Dickson, David, 115, 194, 317.
Digby, 93, 188, 189.
Dike, Nicholas, 164.
Diligent, 213.
Dillaway, Samuel, 257.
Dilworth, James, 83.
Diman, James, jr., 152.
Dimick, Dimmick, *see* Dimuck.
Dimuck, Joseph, 110, 126, 279.

Dimuck, Lot, 250, 284, 311.
Dissmore, Thomas, 174, 193.
Diver, Anthony, 99, 100, 132, 290.
Divers, *see* Diver.
Dixey, John, 139, 246, 285, 286, 287.
Doane, Elisha, 81.
Doane, Heman, 290.
Doane, Isaiah, 80, 170, 187, 210, 219, 236, 299, 309.
Doane, Levi, 134, 160, 256.
Dobel, Joseph, 295.
Dodge, George, 191, 307, 308.
Dodge, George, jr., 97, 138, 161, 228, 230, 265, 314.
Dodge, Joseph, 214.
Dodge, Joshua, 116, 161, 162, 179, 191, 227, 247, 268, 306, 308.
Dogget, *see* Doggett.
Doggett, Samuel, 327.
Doggett, William, 256, 257, 270, 316.
Doliver, Thomas, 243, 281.
Dollanson, Dollenson, *see* Donaldson.
Dolphin, 33, 40, 45, 55, 56, 86.
Dombléder, Etienne, 205, 208.
Donaldson, John, 91, 135, 143.
Doniels, *see* Dunnell.
Donnaldson, John & Co., 73.
Donnell, Thomas, 246.
Donnelson, *see* Donaldson.
Dorr, Ebenezer, 103, 198, 256.
Doten, Thomas, 254.
Doul, John, 161.
Downing, Thomas, 225.
Drinkwaltor, Samuel, 213.
Drinkwater, Joseph, 274.
Dubergier, Pierre, 205.
Dugard, Samuel, 263.
Dunckerly, Joseph, 283.
Dunham, Abijah, 97.
Dunham, Benjamin, 178, 209, 210.
Dunham, Cornelius, 181.
Dunkin, Edmund, 65, 96, 98, 200, 265.
Dunn, Benjamin, 200.
Dunn, John Agusta, 201, 210.
Dunn, Samuel, 217, 305, 315.
Dunn, Samuel, jr., 96, 99, 149, 155, 156, 171, 244, 262, 272, 295, 305, 315.
Dunnell, Jacob, 131, 267, 283.
Dunton, Isaac, 143.
Dupuy, Michael, 208.
Durbergier, *see* Dubergier.
Durfee, Thomas, 264.
Dutch, John, 159, 182, 202, 209, 305, 317.
Dyar, Charles, 166.
Dyson, John, 50, 51, 52, 68, 133, 322.

Eagle, 166, 189, 314.
Edes, Benjamin, 282, 319.

INDEX

Edes, Benjamin, jr., 282.
Edes, Peter, 327.
Edes, Stephen, 236.
Edmonds, John, 104, 110.
Edwards, Abraham, 220.
Egan, Peter, 260.
Eldred, James, 220.
Eliot, Simon, 82, 313.
Elkins, Betsey, 133.
Elkins, Eliza, 95, 133.
Elkins, Thomas, 286.
Elledge, Richard, 101.
Ellery, John S., 283.
Ellet, *see* Eliot.
Ellingwood, Joshua, 217, 314.
Ellinwood, Benjamin, 66, 278.
Ellinwood, Richard, 100.
Ellinwood, William, 120.
Elliott, *see* Eliot.
Ellwell, *see* Elwell.
Elwell, Henry Butler, 312.
Elwell, Isaac, 141.
Elwell, Jonathan, 153.
Emerson, Edward, 23.
Emerton, Ephraim, 102, 103, 183, 273.
Emery, Samuel, 183.
Endeavor, 96.
Engs, Madett, 297.
Erskine, William, 78, 97, 98, 122, 143, 174, 232.
Eskridge, Thomas, 181.
Ewers, Silas, 91.
Exchange, 263.
Experiment, 196.

Fair American, 93.
Fairfield, William, 73.
Falcon, 19.
Fales, Samuel, 288.
Fanny, 58, 59.
Faris, William, 96, 219.
Farley, Michael, 31, 48, 124, 125, 322.
Farley, Nathaniel, 125.
Farnsworth, Jonas, 285.
Farrey, John, 102, 127.
Farrington, John, 294, 295.
Farrington, Thomas, 322.
Farris, *see* Faris.
Fay, Jonathan, jr., 284.
Fearing, Israel, 162.
Fearson, Jesse, 88, 92, 99, 133, 258, 294, 327.
Fearson, John, 313.
Fellowes, *see* Fellows.
Fellows, Cornelius, 104, 184.
Fellows, Gustavus, 108, 185, 326, 327.
Felt, David, 117, 263, 293.
Felt, David, jr., 118.
Felt, John, 116, 197.

Felt, Jonathan, 247, 253, 266.
Felt, Nehemiah, 167.
Fenno, John, 219.
Ferring, *see* Fearing.
Ferry, *see* Farrey.
Ferson, *see* Fearson.
Fettyplace, Edward, 75, 303.
Fettyplace, Edward, jr., 117, 139.
Fish, *see* Fisk.
Fisher, Jabez, 31, 48.
Fisher, William, 82, 142.
Fisk, John, 95, 136, 147, 150, 169, 173, 179, 206, 243, 273, 310, 326.
Fitch, John Browne, 109.
Flagg, Samuel, 84, 160, 205, 216, 231.
Fleet, Thomas, 308.
Fletcher, John, 195, 291, 308, 325.
Flick, Jacob, 242.
Flint, Eliphalet, 321.
Floyd, Stephen, 162.
Flying Fish, 58.
Forister, *see* Forrester.
Forrester, Gerald, 95.
Forrester, Simon, 85, 95, 123, 193, 233, 243, 263, 267.
Forster, *see* Foster.
Fosdick, N., 224.
Fosdick, Thomas, 283.
Fossey, Thomas, 140, 302.
Foster, Benjamin, 19, 330.
Foster, Bossenger, 232.
Foster, James, 218.
Foster, Jedediah, 31, 48.
Foster, Jonathan, 86.
Foster, Joseph, 59, 148, 154, 240, 311, 319.
Foster, Moses, 177.
Foster, Nathaniel, 218.
Foster, Robert, 161, 214, 288.
Foster, Samuel, 130, 234, 262, 293.
Foster, Timothy, 88, 89, 100, 117, 127, 148, 168, 253, 287, 290, 307, 314, 320.
Foster, William, 69, 83, 84, 111, 112, 176, 229, 282, 291, 306.
Fowle, Edmund, 65.
Fowler, Stephen, 178.
Fox, 244, 276, 293.
Fox, John, 246, 251, 259.
Franklin, 199.
Frazer, *see* Frazier.
Frazier, John, 72, 73, 172.
Frazier, John G., 199.
Frazier, Nalbro, 147, 156, 179.
Frazier, Nathaniel, 230.
Frazier, Phoenix, 97, 130, 180.
Freeborn, Isaac, 260.
Freeman, Nathaniel, 20, 75, 83, 110, 279, 327.
Freeman, Samuel, 265, 322.

Freeman, Seth, 292.
Free Mason, 283.
Friend, William, 179, 227.
Frizel, Benjamin, 254.
Frost, John, 295.
Frothingham, Ebenezer, 70, 288.
Fuller, Abraham, 129.
Fuller, Benjamin, 249.
Fulton, John, 214.
Furlong, Laurence, 307, 3 .
Furnass, John, 66, 75, 128, 152, 154, 213, 215, 217, 254, 319.
Furnass, John M., 66, 75, 128.
Furnass, Nathaniel, 215, 256.
Furnes, Anthony, 180.

Gage, Reuben, 312.
Gage, Zachariah, 96.
Gail, *see* Gale.
Gale, Samuel, 251, 252, 286.
Gallison, Henry, 96.
Gardiner, William, 75.
Gardner, Andrew, 50, 65.
Gardner, Coas, 169.
Gardner, Elisha, 54.
Gardner, Henry, 40, 43, 46, 65, 66, 104, 108, 128, 331.
Gardner, J., 68.
Gardner, John, 103, 271.
Gardner, John, jr., 144, 152, 164.
Gardner, John, 3rd, 148, 243, 266.
Gardner, Jonathan, 3rd, 312.
Gardner, Joseph, 198, 221.
Gardner, Thomas, jr., 206.
Gardner, Uriah, 312.
Gates, 47.
Gates, Thomas, 142.
Gavett, John, 132.
Gayton, Admiral, 244.
General Greene, 113.
General Mercer, 58, 59.
General Mifflin, 220.
General Pickering, 237.
General Putnam, 52, 246.
George and Fanny, 237.
Gerrish, Joseph, 31.
Gerry, Elbridge, 20, 25.
Gerry, Samuel Russell, 97, 117, 227, 307.
Gerry, Thomas, 296, 307.
Geyer, Peter, 125, 164.
Gibaut, Edward, 230, 247, 307.
Gibbs, John, 162.
Giddinge, *see* Giddings.
Giddings, Andrew, 99, 112, 125, 246, 299.
Giles, Eleazer, 91, 259, 274, 320.
Giles, Samuel, 163, 254.
Gill, Benjamin, 327.

Gill, John, 185.
Gill, Moses, 31, 48, 50, 59, 67.
Gill, Samuel, 191, 197.
Gleason, John, 291.
Glover, ———, 190.
Glover, Jonathan, 119, 303, 307.
Godfrey, James, 215.
Goldthwait, Benjamin, 68.
Goodale, Nathan, 94, 103, 108, 119, 136, 137, 193, 308.
Goodhue, Benjamin, 144, 164, 264, 290, 306.
Goodhue, Benjamin, jr., 231, 290.
Goodhue, Daniel, 125.
Goodhue, Hezekiah, 294.
Goodhue, Jonathan, 268.
Goodhue, Joseph, 259.
Goodhue, Robert, 264.
Goodnow, Jesse, 68.
Goodnow, William, 68.
Goodwin, Benjamin, 72.
Goodwin, Eunice, 95.
Goodwin, Joseph, 288.
Goodwin, Lazarus, 165.
Goodwin, Nathaniel, 112, 180, 210, 240.
Gordon, ———, 119.
Gore, Abel, 208, 256.
Gore, Samuel, 248.
Gorham, Benjamin, 210, 211.
Gorham, Nathaniel, 218.
Gorham, Shubael, 198.
Gorham, Sturgis, 211.
Gould, Nathaniel, 218.
Gould, William, 65.
Governor Tryon, 299.
Gowen, William, 140, 288.
Grafton, J., 150.
Grafton, Joseph, 117, 182, 224, 240, 263, 266, 271, 273.
Grafton, Joshua, 101, 209, 212, 218, 267, 272.
Grampus, 279.
Grand Turk, 57.
Grannis, John, 319.
Gray, Abraham, 322.
Gray, Alexander, 203.
Gray, Benjamin, 302.
Gray, Edward, 302.
Gray, John, 312.
Gray, Stephen, H., 78, 147, 195, 226, 269.
Gray, William, 108, 118, 135, 190, 218, 259, 266, 276, 309.
Gray, William, jr., 169, 313.
Gray, William, 3rd, 310.
Greely, Jonathan, 101, 282, 283.
Green, Peter, 56, 57.
Green, Samuel, 56, 57, 238, 239.
Greene, Benjamin, 121.

INDEX   343

Greene, Nathaniel, 67, 68.
Greene, Thomas, 95, 122, 140, 156, 240, 298.
Greenleaf, Abel, 289.
Greenleaf, Abner, 141, 321.
Greenleaf, B., 48.
Greenleaf, John, 234.
Greenleaf, Jonathan, 20, 179.
Greenleaf, Joseph, 109.
Greenleaf, Oliver, 181.
Greenleaf, William, 218.
Greenough, Nathaniel, 171, 179, 267, 295.
Greenough, Samuel, 179.
Greenwood, Miles, 94, 95, 133, 206, 249, 269, 276, 290, 306.
Grenell, John, 59.
Gridley, Richard, 70.
Griffin, Joseph, 147.
Griffiths, Anthony, 105, 186, 273.
Grimes, John, 73, 221, 267.
Grindall, Ichabod, 287.
Grinnell, Moses, 273.
Grinnell, William, 212.
Grooves, J., 104.
Grout, Jonathan, 23.
Groves, Ichabod, 278.
Groves, William, 82, 121, 130, 291.
Grow, Nathaniel, 252, 285, 286.
Grush, John, 79, 145, 239.
Guild, Benjamin, 295.
Guliker, John, 103, 128, 129, 198.
Guyer, *see* Geyer.

Hacker, Hoysted, 88.
Hackett, Redmond, 76.
Haggerty, *see* Hegerty.
Hale, Moses, 112, 156, 229, 299.
Halifax Bob, 327.
Hall, Ebenezer, 288.
Hall, Isaac, 288.
Hall, Moses, 169.
Hall, Stephen, 103, 114.
Hall, Stephen, 3rd, 230, 307.
Hall, William, 234.
Hallet, Allen, *see* Hallet, John Allen.
Hallet, John Allen, 45, 66, 71, 137, 152, 221, 222, 236, 255, 288, 289, 290.
Halloran, Charles, 296.
Halloway, Ichabod, 164.
Hallowell, Briggs, 212, 269.
Hambleton, *see* Hamilton.
Hamilton, Charles, 165, 193.
Hamilton, Jonathan, 127, 228.
Hamlin, Michael, 284.
Hammatt, Benjamin, jr., 89, 138.
Hammon, Micah, 52.
Hammond, Benjamin, 117, 159, 201.
Hammond, Benjamin, jr., 159.

Hammond, Edward, 307.
Hancock, 50, 59, 148.
Hancock, Ebenezer, 327.
Hancock, John, 57, 65.
Hannah, 24, 97, 115.
Hannah and Molly, 32, 46, 315.
Haraden, Jonathan, 150, 151, 195, 237.
Harding, Jesse, 81.
Harding, Nathaniel, 82, 117.
Hardy, Ishmael, 146, 157, 158, 200, 206.
Harlequin, 121, 301.
Harman, *see* Harmon.
Harmon, John, 172, 245.
Harmon, Nathaniel, 228, 315, 316.
Harriden, *see* Haraden.
Harriot, 241, 314.
Harrod, Benjamin, 172, 273.
Harris, John, 152.
Harris, John, jr., 152.
Harris, Jonathan, 71, 72, 152, 288, 289, 313.
Harris, Thomas, 70, 71, 72, 152, 153, 236, 289, 297, 313, 316.
Harris, W., 68, 97, 184, 331.
Harris, William, 165, 239.
Hart, John, 79.
Hart, William, 319.
Harthorne, *see* Hathorne.
Harvey, John, 90.
Harvey, Magnes, 238.
Haskell, Elnathan, 282.
Haskell, Philemon, 81, 282.
Haskell, Robert, 119.
Haskin, Barnett, 157.
Hastings, Jonathan, jr., 162.
Hastings, Samuel, 140.
Hatch, Naler, 200.
Hatch, Silas, jr., 110, 312.
Hatch, Walter, 179.
Hathaway, Nathaniel, 183.
Hathorne, Daniel, 161, 223, 290, 306, 324.
Hawes, *see* Haws.
Hawley, David, 278.
Hawley, Samuel, 285.
Haws, Thomas, 98, 170.
Hawthorne, *see* Hathorne.
Hayden, Richard, 240.
Haydon, William, 112, 163, 197, 233.
Hayes, *see* Hays.
Hayman, William, 156.
Hays, John, 77.
Hazard, Nathaniel, 148.
Hazen, William, 320.
Head, John, 170.
Head, Joseph, 72, 131, 172, 181, 214, 305, 313.
Heard, John, 193.
Hearn, Michael, 144, 164.

344 INDEX

Hegerty, Jeremiah, 201.
Helme, Gabriel, 167.
Helme, Hugh, 172, 222.
Helme, William, 321.
Helms, see Helme.
Hendrick Hudson, 173.
Henfield, Gideon, 95, 141, 160, 266.
Henfield, Joseph, 210.
Henley, David, 326.
Henley, Samuel, 101.
Henrietta, 249.
Henshaw, Andrew, 97.
Herbert, Thomas, 206.
Herkimer, Benjamin, 130.
Hero, 73, 85, 180, 276.
Herrick, John, 78.
Herrick, William, 113.
Heydon, Jeremiah, 231.
Hibbert, Jeremiah, 168.
Hichborn, Benjamin, 165, 254, 261, 320, 328, 330.
Hichborn, Robert, 292.
Higgerty, see Hegerty.
Higginson, Henry, 195, 293, 316.
Higginson, Stephen, 68, 90, 100, 104, 121, 124, 125, 128, 134, 137, 156, 198, 250, 252, 263, 266, 291, 292, 293, 306.
Hildreth, John, 256.
Hill, Benjamin, 78.
Hill, Hugh, 88, 99, 119, 237.
Hill, John, 239.
Hill, Samuel, 229.
Hills, Joshua, 293.
Hills, Stephen, 137, 214, 221.
Hilton, Benjamin, 318.
Hinckley, John, see Hinkley.
Hinckley, Joseph, 180.
Hinckley, Richard, 139, 285.
Hinkley, John, 103, 120, 281, 282, 283, 292.
Hinkley, Seth, 246.
Hinman, Elisha, 109.
Hobbs, Samuel, 103, 126, 150, 225, 233.
Hodge, Michael, 246, 289.
Hodges, Gamaliel, 178, 219, 232.
Holbrook, Samuel, jr., 66.
Holker, John, 59.
Holland, Stephen, 168.
Holland, William, 170.
Holmes, Alexander, 78, 98.
Holmes, Thomas, 158, 191, 279.
Holt, Nehemiah, 94, 204, 205, 226, 272, 302.
Holten, Samuel, 31, 48, 264.
Holton, see Holten.
Holyoke, Edward, 163, 221, 254, 304, 323.
Homan, William, 283, 295.
Homer, Benjamin, 84, 147, 275.

Homer, Eleazer, 117.
Homer, James, 239.
Hood, J., 261.
Hooper, Stephen, 76, 82, 108, 142, 185, 186, 216.
Hooper, Swett, 239.
Hooton, John, 54.
Hope, 175.
Hopkins, ——, 237.
Hopkins, Caleb, 89, 155, 165.
Hopkins, Daniel, 59, 82, 85, 87, 100, 109, 117, 123, 131, 134, 141, 158, 159, 160, 161, 165, 166, 173, 179, 181, 182, 202, 205, 209, 212, 225, 231, 233, 239, 242, 267, 272, 276, 279, 281, 290, 294, 305, 306, 308, 317, 321.
Hopkins, James, 204.
Hopkins, John Burrows, 304.
Hopkins, Michael, 122.
Hopkins, Theodore, 274.
Horn, John, 143.
Horton, Richard, 243.
Horton, Samuel, 145.
Hosmer, Joseph, 138, 232, 320.
Hovey, Ivory, 192.
Howard, ——, 314.
Howe, 209.
Howell, Silas, 109, 321.
Howes, Edmund, 83.
Howes, Enoch, 170.
Howland, Consider, 236.
Howland, Daniel, 134.
Howland, Perry, 277.
Howland, Philip, 309.
Hubbard, Daniel, 167.
Hubbard, Thomas, G. 167.
Hughes, James, 89, 165, 330.
Hugounene, Jean Baptiste, 207.
Humphreys, Benjamin, 194.
Humphries, see Humphreys.
Hunt, Shrimpton, 304.
Hunt, Thomas, 73, 172.
Hutchinson, Godfrey, 171, 179, 267, 295.
Hutchinson, Israel, 317.
Hutchinson, John, jr., 126.
Hutchinson, Shrimpton, 98, 105, 171, 267, 295.
Hutchinson, William, 105, 171, 179, 267, 295.
Hyer, John, 44, 45, 203.

Ilsley, Daniel, 165.
Ilsley, Enoch, 83, 246, 259.
Independence, 43, 53, 54, 55.
Industry, 131.
Ingals, Eleazar, 130.
Ingels, James, 211,
Ingersoll, David, 117, 224.
Ingersoll, John, 76, 283, 284.

INDEX

Ingersoll, Jonathan, 161, 184, 193, 204, 223, 225, 231, 260, 263, 271, 298.
Ingersoll, Nehemiah, 326.
Ingersoll, Samuel, 94, 124, 183, 223, 253, 298.
Ingraham, Joseph, 206.
Insley, *see* Ilsley.
Ives, Benjamin, 133, 276, 277.

Jack, 121.
Jackman, Timothy, 154.
Jackson, Edward, 329.
Jackson, Henry, 253.
Jackson, Jonathan, 48, 99, 123, 127, 168, 170, 202, 232, 329.
Jackson, Joseph, 255, 321.
Jackson, Samuel, 72, 328.
Jackson, Thomas, 115, 203.
Jackson & Gray, 179.
Jackson, Tracy & Tracy, 156, 168.
Jacobs, Daniel, 115.
Jacobs, Wilson, 254.
Jaggar, William, 73, 142.
James, 191.
James, Ambrose, 121.
James, William, 68, 204.
Jarvis, Benjamin, 80, 112, 163, 197.
Jarvis, Charles, 223, 317.
Jarvis, Edward, 133.
Jarvis, James, 114, 188.
Jarvis, Leonard, 74, 112, 113, 120, 163, 197, 213, 214, 271, 315, 319, 320.
Jarvis, Philip, 113, 163.
Jarvis & Russell, 90.
Jason, 301.
Jauncey, Joseph, 96, 322.
Jay, John, 39.
Jeffrey, *see* Jeffry.
Jeffries, D., 218.
Jeffry, James, 90, 103, 136, 232, 306.
Jenks, David, 85.
Jenne, Levi, 236.
Jepson, Benjamin, 177, 261, 270, 292, 313.
Jersey, 55.
Jewett, Abel, 23.
Jewett, Jonathan, 127, 276.
Johnson, Eleazar, 125, 322.
Johnson, Eleazar, jr., 108.
Johnson, Henry, 90, 131, 221, 229, 234, 328.
Johnson, Isaac, jr., 249.
Johnson, Israel, 134, 135, 295.
Johnson, James, 167.
Johnson, Nicholas, 105, 186.
Johnson, Samuel, 172.
Johnson, Thomas, 251.
Johnson, William, *see* Johnson, Nicholas
Johnson, William Peirce, 255, 325, 327.

Johnston, James, 232, 304.
Johnston, John, 69, 107.
Johnston, Miller, 207, 298.
Johnston, Nicholas, 219.
Johonnot, Daniel, 311.
Johonnot, Francis, 65, 90, 98, 131, 156, 170, 229.
Johonnot, Gabriel, 57, 70.
Johonnot, George Stewart, 90, 172.
Johonnot, Mary, 90.
Jolly, Gené, 76.
Jones, Daniel, 235.
Jones, John Coffin, 72, 82, 99, 125, 140, 174, 203, 224, 254, 313, 320, 325.
Jones, Pearson, 246.
Jones, Robinson, 278.
Jones, Silas, 119.
Jones, Thomas, 70, 248, 322, 323.
Jones, William, 23.
Junius Brutus, 88, 252.
Juno, 106.

Kean, John, 78, 174.
Kelly, Matthew, 154.
Kendrick, 173.
Kendrick, John, 59, 105, 127, 214.
Keyes, John, 115.
King Herod, 83.
Kinsman, Nathaniel, 275.
Knap, Anthony, 195.
Knapp, William, 113, 131.
Kneeland, John, 281.
Kneeland, John, jr., 292.
Knight, Benjamin, 172, 262.
Knight, Job, 250, 326.
Knowlton, Joseph, 118.
Knox, Thomas, 179.
Knox, William, 105.

Lacey, *see* Leacey.
Ladurantie, 204.
Lafitte, Mark, 104, 128, 217, 263.
Lakeman, Ebenezer, 112.
Lakeman, Richard, 113.
Lamb, James, 261.
Lamb, James, jr., 81, 316.
Lamb, John, 128.
Lamb, Thomas, 73, 323.
Lambert, John, 114, 213.
Lambert, Jonathan, 213.
Lambert, Joseph, 78, 152, 205, 249.
Lamprell, Nicholas, 126, 204.
Lander, John, 161.
Lander, Peter, 116, 160, 209, 224, 225, 240, 289, 290, 326.
Lander, William, jr., 161.
Lane, Ebenezer, 69, 112, 125, 270, 280, 299, 324.
Lane, George, 233, 330.

INDEX

Langdell, William, 94, 311.
Langdon, Timothy, 33, 294.
Langdon, William, *see* Langdell.
Langevain, Germain, 293; *see* Lousvay, Jeremiah.
Langeway, *see* Langevain.
Lansvay, *see* Lousvay.
Larkin, John, 71, 133, 297, 298.
Larreguy, John, 80, 130.
Lash, Robert, 91.
Laskey, James, 227, 297.
Lateman, *see* Lakeman.
Laughton, ——, 189.
Laughton, Joseph, 80, 96, 140, 157, 169, 179, 182, 304.
Laurens, Henry, 65.
Lawhorn, John, 207.
Lawrence, Asa, 124.
Lawrence, David, 184.
Lawrence, William, 89, 140.
Lawton, *see* Laughton.
Leacey, George, 240.
Leach, George, 227.
Leach, James, 70.
Leach, John, 116, 117, 121, 136, 165, 196, 209, 294, 304, 317.
Leach, John, jr., 136, 189, 253, 270.
Leach, Joseph, 122, 178, 303, 305.
Leach, Nathaniel, *see* Leech, Nathan.
Leach, William, 130, 238.
Leach, *see* Leech.
Lecraw, William, 84, 227.
Lee, 44.
Lee, Isaac, 240.
Lee, John, 92, 126, 127, 158, 168, 222, 304.
Lee, Joseph, 48, 123, 139, 168, 260, 273, 285, 329.
Lee, Martha, 168.
Lee, Thomas, 195.
Lee, William, 168.
Lee, William R., 139.
Lee & Jones, 224, 313, 318.
Leech, John, 155, 303.
Leech, Nathan, 130, 239, 320.
Leech, Robert, 196, 263, 309, 317.
Leech, William, 259, 273, 320.
Leech, *see* Leach.
Lefavour, Philip, 290.
Legrow, *see* Grow.
Leonard, Nathaniel, 72.
Leslie, Michael, 316.
Letters of Marque, 4, 5, 6, 14, 45, 60.
Levant, 146.
Lewis, Edmund, 139, 324.
Lewis, John, 145, 286.
Lewis, Moses, 89, 248.
Lewis, Thomas, 285.
Lincoln, Benjamin, 31, 48.

Lindsay, Nathaniel, 243.
Linn, John T., 285.
Lion, Peter Joseph, 130.
Little, Ebenezer, 154.
Little, George, 327.
Little, Moses, 79, 127, 142, 154, 271, 287.
Lively, 311.
Livingston, Abraham, 98.
Livingston, Henry, 78, 97, 174.
Livingston, John R., 96, 148, 265, 299, 317.
Lobb, George, 194.
Lobdell, Nicholas, 71, 324.
Lockwood, James, 259.
Loell, *see* Lowell.
Lombard, Ephraim, 124.
Long, William, 123.
Longeray, *see* Langevain and Lousvay.
Loring, Benjamin, 186, 234, 261, 274.
Loring, Benjamin, jr., 305.
Loring, Daniel, 280.
Loring, Seth, 72, 125, 203, 290, 322.
Lousvay, Jeremiah, 134; *see* Langevain, Germain.
Lovell, John M., 81, 265, 300.
Lovell, Solomon, 103.
Lovett, Benjamin, 110, 131, 135, 248, 249, 274, 278.
Lovett, Benjamin, jr., 134, 291.
Lovett, James, jr., 278.
Loviet, John, 113.
Low, Caleb, 166.
Low, Francis, 235.
Low, John, jr., 169, 324.
Lowell, John, 71, 89, 100, 260, 305, 321.
Lowell, Sylvanus, 243.
Luce, Elijah, 120.
Luce, Litchfield, 227, 319.
Lunt, Benjamin, 92, 280.
Lurvy, Benjamin, 81.
Lyde, Nathaniel Byfield, 221.
Lynham, George, 76.

McCarty, William, 79, 207.
McClallen, Hugh, 184, 193.
McClister, Daniel, 288.
McCobb, Samuel, 221.
McDaniell, Timothy, 164.
McDuff, James, 88, 317.
McGillan, William, 251.
Machias Liberty, 19, 113, 114, 313.
Mackay, Alexander, 75, 156, 234.
Mackay, Mungo, 53, 67, 73, 74, 77, 96, 149, 155, 156, 163, 165, 171, 173, 191, 208, 211, 220, 260, 261, 262, 272, 290, 295, 316.
Mackay, Mungo, jr., 68, 124, 155, 295.
Mackay, William, 103.

INDEX

Mackett, John, 103.
McLeod, David, 129.
McMillan, John, 152, 308.
MacMillion, *see* McMillan.
McNeill, Daniel, 70, 71, 108, 120, 121, 134, 148, 149, 162, 310, 316, 325.
McNeill, Hector, 51, 68, 96, 232.
McNeill, Robert, 316.
McWan, Joseph, 323.
Magee, James, 74, 75, 142, 143, 160, 174, 186.
Magge, *see* Magee.
Malcolm, Daniel, 199.
Malescot, Nicholas, 317.
Maley, William, 248.
Malloon, Daniel, 115.
Manete, 201.
Manley, John, 50, 51, 52, 106, 162, 191, 202, 301.
Manning, Richard, 95.
Mansfield, Amos, 308.
Mansfield, Benjamin Green, 94.
Mansfield, Ellis, 248.
Mansfield, Isaac, 55.
Mansfield, Marshal, 204, 279.
Mansir, *see* Mansis.
Mansis, Simon, 122, 140.
Marett, Philip, 142, 178.
Margaretta, 19, 213, 313, 330.
Margeson, John, 147.
Marisheete, 44.
Marony, *see* Morony.
Marquand, Jonas, 203.
Marquand, Joseph, 125, 186, 224, 291, 313, 318, 322, 323.
Marrett, *see* Marett.
Mars, 12, 43, 216.
Marsh, John, 131, 308.
Marshall, John, 291.
Marston, John, 181, 185, 222, 228, 269.
Marston, William, 117.
Martin, Arnold, 239.
Martin, Daniel, 44, 89, 203, 204, 255, 256.
Martin, Jacob, 124.
Martin, John, 102, 303.
Martin, Joseph, 274.
Martin, Knott, jr., 285.
Martin, Peter, 100.
Martindale, Sion, 321.
Mary, 272.
Mary and Fanny, 221.
Mary Ann, 245.
Mascoll, Stephen, 40, 87, 151, 152.
Mason, Jonathan, 150, 189, 207, 242, 274.
Mason, Jonathan, jr., 107, 242, 308.
Mason, Thomas, 173, 207, 247.
Masury, David, 204, 279.

Masury, Richard, 45, 116.
Masury, Samuel, 232, 263, 295.
Maxfield, Patrick, 81, 214.
May, Ebenezer, 242.
May, George, 122.
Mayhew, Jeremiah, 128.
Mayo, Samuel, 221, 222.
Mayo, Simeon, 221, 258.
Mead, Israel, 132.
Meade, George, 156, 252.
Meagher, Richard, 83.
Medea, 268.
Meigs, Jabez, 119.
Mein, William, 82.
Melvill, John, 283.
Melvill, Thomas, 282, 292.
Melzard, Nicholas, 269.
Mercer, Archibald, 148, 162.
Merchant, John, 219, 221.
Mercury, 99, 221.
Mermaid, 280.
Meserve, William, 147.
Metcalf, Jonathan, 103, 129, 214.
Mifflin, 149.
Miklaszewiez, Feelix, 244, 277.
Milford, 329.
Miller, James, 294.
Miller, Joseph, 249.
Miller, Nathan, 153.
Miller, William, 131.
Millet, John Baptist, 101, 167, 174, 201.
Milliquet, John, 96.
Miner, *see* Minor.
Minor, Amos, 229.
Minot, *see* Minor.
Mitchell, Edward, 307.
Mitchell, Henry, 65, 69, 78, 90, 122, 131, 156, 170, 174, 191, 200.
Mitchell, John, 268.
Mocketts, *see* Mackett.
Mogridge, Thomas, 268.
Mohawk, 174, 264, 277.
Molineux, John, 125, 260, 264, 267, 310, 322.
Molineux, W., 232.
Molloy, William, 132.
Monk, 101.
Montaudevert, James, 108.
Montgomery, 150.
Moore, Abel, 297.
Moore, Francis, 233.
Moore, Patrick, 128.
Moore, Philip, 80, 138, 147, 148, 155, 156, 162, 212, 220, 259, 265, 269.
Morgan, William, 92, 254, 258.
Moriarty, John, 58, 132, 201.
Moriarty, Thomas, 58.
Morony, William, 88.
Morrill, Joseph, 246.

INDEX

Morris, James, 68.
Morris, Robert, 235.
Morton, Dimond, 70, 92, 120, 281.
Morton, James, 82.
Morton, Perez, 31, 48, 70, 141, 320, 321, 328, 330.
Morton, Stephen, 266.
Morton, Zacheus, 256.
Moses, Benjamin, 136, 284.
Moses, Joseph, 84, 232.
Moulton, Enoch, 67.
Moulton, John, 155, 269,
Moulton, Joseph, Jr., 79, 127.
Moulton, William, 269.
Mountadere, see Montaudevert.
Mowatt, Henry, 241.
Mugford, James, 135, 199, 239, 307, 314.
Mulliken, John, 168.
Munday, William, 202, 368.
Mundy, see Munday.
Munro, James, 79.
Munro, Thomas, 181.
Munroe, see Munro.
Murphy, John, 284.
Murphy, William, 282.

Nancy, 110, 188.
Nati, see Rati.
Nautilus, 19.
Navy, British, 3, 14; Continental, 14, 15, 42, 50, 51; State, 14, 42, 43, 45, 53, 57, 60, 66, 111, 113, 114, 138, 171, 185, 206, 213, 217, 218, 245, 255, 264, 295, 310, 327.
Neall, Jonathan, 135, 157, 228, 318.
Neashquowoite, 44.
Needham, Benjamin, 281.
Needham, Daniel, 166, 196, 252, 269.
Needham, Isaac, 182.
Neill, see Neall.
Nelson, John, 245.
Neptune, 83, 238.
Neutrals, treatment of, 35, 36, 37, 38.
Nevins, see Nivens.
Newell, ——, 69, 101.
Newell, Andrew, 152, 153, 236, 289, 313.
Newell, Henry, see Newhall.
Newell, Thomas, jr., 305.
Newhall, Henry, 102, 127, 140.
Newhall, Samuel, 142, 326.
Newman, Henry, 137.
Newman, Joseph, 142.
Newman, Nathaniel, 120.
Newman, Paul, 186, 224.
Newman, Robert, 68, 275.
Newman, Wingate, 162, 195, 207, 211, 314.
Newson, Thomas, 202.

Nichols, Ichabod, 94, 204, 223, 233, 273, 276, 306.
Nichols, J., 271.
Nichols, Micah, 211.
Nichols, Nathan, 85, 109, 233, 273.
Nichols, Thomas, 94.
Nichols, William, 185, 186, 187, 224.
Nicholson, Samuel, 78, 174.
Nickerson, Ebenezer, 123.
Nicolson, Thomas, 70, 312, 316.
Niel, see Neall.
Niles, see Ives.
Nimble Shilling, 96.
Nivens, James, 111, 217, 218.
Norcross, Uriah, 230.
Norice, see Norris.
Norris, Edward, 82, 107, 208, 294.
Norris, John, 147, 148, 179, 182, 189, 225, 243, 272, 326.
Northey, Abijah, 279.
Northey, Joseph, 287.
Northey, William, 160.
Norton, Benjamin, 9, 10, 11.
Norwood, Ebenezer, 246, 327.
Nowell, Nathaniel, 191.
Nowell, Samuel, 108.
Noyes, Belcher, jr., 331.
Noyes, Joseph, 213, 251, 280, 282.
Noyes, William, 124.
Nutting, John, 177.
Nutting, Jonathan, 91, 140, 256, 257, 270, 316, 318.
Nutting, Samuel, 179, 260.
Nye, David, 162, 278.
Nye, E., 279.
Nye, Ebenezer, 110, 279.

Oakes, Jonathan, 129, 168, 169, 233, 297.
Oakes, Uriah, 168, 169, 324.
Obear, see Ober.
Ober, Benjamin, 138.
Ober, Ezra, 289.
Ober, Israel, 130.
Ober, Israel F., 208.
Ober, Richard, 128, 134, 258.
Obey, John, 89.
Obrian, Obrien, see O'Brien.
O'Brien, Jeremiah, 19, 113, 114, 164, 177, 213, 255, 303, 313.
O'Brien, John, 67, 107, 177, 271.
O'Brien, William, 177.
Observer, 190.
Odiorne, John, 258.
Odiorne, Nathaniel, 202, 321, 322.
Ogelbe, Nicholas, 79, 90, 320, 323.
Ogilvie, Alexander Thompson, 184.
Ogleby, Oglisbe, see Ogelbe.
Olive Branch, 145.

INDEX

Oliver, Andrew, 91, 103.
Oliver, Daniel, 301.
Oliver, Ebenezer, 229.
Oliver, Jacob, 160.
Oliver, Thomas, 163, 221, 247, 286, 287, 304.
Olney, Joseph, 171.
Orchard, William, 227.
Orne, Azor, 23, 296, 307.
Orne, Joshua, 227.
Orne, Joshua, jr., 301.
Orne, Josiah, 152, 160, 209, 216, 238, 239, 242, 294, 306.
Orne, William, 84, 197, 240, 303.
Orsborn, see Osborn.
Osborn, George, 182, 264.
Osgood, Benjamin, 289.
Osgood, John F., 203.
Osier, Thomas, 309.
Otis, James, 31.
Otis, Samuel Allyne, 72, 236, 253, 255, 265, 326.

Page, John, 107, 134.
Page, Samuel, 82, 107, 134, 155, 208, 209, 210, 212, 253, 294, 304, 305.
Paine, Nathaniel, 236.
Paine, Samuel, 92.
Palfray, see Palfrey.
Palfrey, Thomas, 69, 136, 173, 179, 267, 298.
Palmer, Edmund, 285.
Palmer, J., 48.
Palmer, John, 80, 97, 181.
Parker, Daniel, 155, 168, 169.
Parker, Job, 311.
Parker, John, 98.
Parker, Phineas, 124.
Parker, Stephen, 168.
Parker, Thomas, 54, 169, 184, 227.
Parker, Timothy, 223, 277.
Parkman, Elias, 86, 221, 235.
Parkman, Samuel, 252, 301.
Parmenter, Benjamin, 325.
Parret, Abner, 118.
Parris, see Faris.
Parsons, Daniel, 157, 312.
Parsons, Ebenezer, 97, 112, 121, 125, 154, 169, 186, 195, 198, 228, 234, 246, 249, 252, 258, 280, 299, 300, 309, 324.
Parsons, Jonathan, 111, 266.
Parsons, Nehemiah, 295.
Parsons, William, 112, 234.
Partridge, Samuel, 327.
Pasturin & Terundet, 167.
Paton, Andrew, 194.
Patten, see Pattin.
Patterson, William, 114, 129, 213, 225, 260.

Pattin, John, 66, 285, 286.
Payne, Edward, 259.
Payne, Elijah Freeman, 120.
Payne, William, 84, 111.
Peabody, Oliver, 97, 285.
Peale, see Peele.
Pearce, David, 153, 157, 283, 291, 326.
Pearce, John, 159.
Pearce, Nathaniel, 170, 274.
Pearce, William, 326.
Pearce, see Peirce and Pierce.
Pearson, Isaac Green, 318.
Pearson, James, 153, 188.
Pearson, Jeremiah, 313.
Pearson, Jeremiah, jr., 154.
Pearscn, William, 74, 311.
Pease, John, 128.
Pedrick, Thomas, 285, 286.
Peele, Jonathan, 207.
Peele, Jonathan, jr., 107, 173, 206, 207, 225, 291.
Peggy, 178.
Peirce, Abiel, 307.
Peirce, David, 201, 241, 282.
Peirce, Ebenezer, 115, 152, 205.
Peirce, Jerathmeel, 109, 159, 165, 202, 305.
Peirce, Nathan, 159, 182.
Peirce, Nathaniel, 140, 182.
Peirce, Timothy, 90, 213, 262.
Peirce, see Pearce and Pierce.
Penet, Pierre, 234.
Pennet, Peter, see Penet, Pierre.
Penny, Timothy, 204.
Penobscot Expedition, 52, 84, 97, 98, 110, 152, 163, 173, 184, 224, 226, 232, 253, 268, 280, 286, 297, 315.
Percival, John, 75.
Perkins, Benaiah, 54.
Perkins, James, 77, 78, 98, 129, 142, 143, 146, 147, 169, 170, 226, 248, 269.
Perkins, Lemuel, 108.
Perkins, Nathaniel, 293, 301.
Perkins, Samuel, 184.
Perkins, Thomas, 171, 232.
Perkins, William, 285.
Perley, Nathaniel, 291.
Perry, John, 132.
Perry, Nathaniel, 117.
Perseverance, 145.
Phelan, Richard, 324.
Phelps, Henry, 85, 123, 263.
Philips, see Phillips.
Phillips, Isaac, 218, 321.
Phillips, John, 96, 319.
Phillips, Thomas, 270, 287.
Phippen, David, 310.
Phippen, Joshua, 213.
Phoenix, 156.

Picary, 320.
Pickering, 151.
Pickering, John, 16, 20, 87.
Pickering, Timothy, 16, 33, 87, 90.
Pickman, James, 94.
Pickman, William, 84, 90, 224, 248.
Pierce, Benjamin, 153.
Pierce, Joseph, 65.
Pierce, *see* Pearce and Peirce.
Pike, Enoch, 229, 289, 324.
Pike, Moses, 121, 252.
Pilsberry, *see* Pilsbury.
Pilsbury, Joshua, 171, 295.
Pinnet, *see* Penet.
Piper, Duncan, 188.
Pitman, Joseph, 82, 95, 317.
Pitts, John, 20, 310.
Pitts, Lendall, 298.
Pitts, Samuel, 69, 117, 212.
Platt, Jeremiah, 97.
Pliarne, 56.
Plimpton, Nathan, 105, 175, 180, 280.
Plympton, *see* Plimpton.
Pole, 73.
Pollard, Jonathan, 90, 261.
Pollard, Peter, 186.
Pool, Fitch, 102, 107, 161, 165, 211, 232, 239, 255, 256, 281, 288, 296, 323.
Pool, Zachariah, 309.
Poor, Nathan, 208, 263.
Pope, Edward, 245, 320, 331.
Porter, David, 74, 76, 77, 244, 295.
Porter, Ebenezer, 321.
Porter, John, 124, 135.
Porter, Thomas, 149, 155, 247, 272, 295.
Pote, Greenfield, 135.
Pote, Samuel, 297.
Potter, Amos, 120, 244, 257, 263.
Potter, Joshua, 294.
Powars, Thomas, 109, 155, 312.
Powars, *see* Powers.
Powell, Jeremiah, 53, 60.
Powell, Will, 259.
Powers, Gregory (or Greag), 100, 118, 119.
Pownall, John, 286.
Pratt, Joseph, 67, 94, 158, 159.
Preble, Ebenezer, 83.
Preble, John, 214.
Prentice, Stanton, 321.
Prentiss, Henry, 199.
Prentiss, James, 319.
Prescott, James, 31.
Prescott, Oliver, 162.
Preston, William, 206, 279, 323.
Price, Ezekiel, 147, 148, 156.
Price, James, 207, 215.
Prince, Job, 66, 80, 84, 91, 106, 111, 123, 138, 147, 203, 234, 253, 275, 278.

Prince, Job, jr., 66, 99, 102, 110, 122. 123, 124, 147, 204, 212, 224, 237, 238,
Prince, Samuel, 278.
Prince, Thomas, 80, 84, 124, 136, 147, 196, 275.
Prince of Wales, 244, 245.
Prince William Henry, 93.
Pringle, John, 188, 197,
Prisoners, 40, 55, 56, 57, 58.
Privateering, beginnings of, 3, 4; in the 15th and 16th centuries, 5, 6, 7; in the 17th century, 9; in colonial times, 9, 10, 11, 12, 13; criticism of, 12, 15, 19, 20, 21; in the Revolution, 13; popularity of, 14; praise of, 16; conditions of, 17; vessels engaged in, 17, 18; at the beginning of the war, 18, 19, 20; first steps toward legalizing, 20, 22, 23, 24; letters advising, 21, 22; first law passed, 25-31; later legislation, 32, 33; sources of information, 38, 39, 61, 62, 63.
Privateers, early documents relating to, 4, 5, 6, 7, 10; commissions for, 5, 6, 10, 48, 49; bonds for, 7, 8, 15, 38-44, 52; agreements relating to 12, 50, 51; definition of, 13; conduct of, 15, 17; embargo on, 15, 42, 45, 46, 47; in foreign seas, 18, 60; without commissions, 19, 20, 32, 48, 49, 56; petitions for, 22, 23, 39, 40, 44, 45, 46, 47; instructions and regulations for, 33, 34, 35, 36, 37; in squadrons, 50, 51, 52; impressment of, 52; prizes of, 53; captured, 55; miscellaneous documents relating to, 58, 59; cruises of, 60; number of, 60.
Prize courts, 8, 33, 53, 54, 55.
Procter, Edward, 103.
Prosper, 305.
Prosperous, 265.
Prosser, W., 104, 128, 216, 225, 263, 289.
Protector, 57.
Prout, Ebenezer, 70, 86, 235, 245, 259, 322.
Providence, 158.
Pruddock, Michael, 149.
Pry, Bt. Merlino Desaint, 205.
Putnam, Bartholomew, 90, 103, 116, 126, 136, 137, 138, 179, 182, 183, 193, 213, 231, 240, 266.
Putnam, Billing, 303.
Pyper, *see* Piper.

Quartermass, Quartimass, *see* Quatermass.
Quatermass, Richard, 155, 288, 292.
Quebec, 85.
Queen of England, 155.

INDEX 351

Rainey, Archibald, 262.
Raleigh, 149.
Rambler, 99.
Rand, John, 195.
Rand, Silas, 174.
Randall, Isaac, 299.
Randall, *see* Rendall.
Rantoul, *see* Rentoul.
Rapall, George, 222, 243, 326.
Rathbun, John Peck, 112, 234, 325.
Rathburne, *see* Rathbun.
Rati, Joseph, 305.
Ravel, *see* Revell.
Raven, 196.
Ray, William, 214.
Raymond, Eliakim, 80, 186, 187, 191, 197, 217, 240, 271.
Raymond, Joseph, 277.
Raymond, William, 327.
Rea, C., 210.
Read, John, 178.
Read, John, jr., 178.
Read, William, 111.
Reed, Andrew, 271.
Reed, Benjamin I. 139.
Reed, Ebenezer, 216.
Reed, Oliver, 176.
Reed, Paul, 254, 287.
Reed, Paul, jr., 154.
Rendall, George, 84, 273.
Rentall, *see* Rentoul.
Rentoul, Robert, 111, 189.
Reprisal, 43, 258.
Republic, 43, 45.
Resolution, 88, 254.
Revell, John, 224, 226, 242, 321.
Revenge, 9, 10, 11.
Revolt, 123.
Revolution, 88.
Reynolds, Nathaniel, 82, 182, 214.
Rhodes, 223.
Rice, Samuel, 127, 259.
Rich, Mathias, 153.
Rich, Obadiah, 188.
Richardson, Robert, 297.
Rickard, John Howland, 236.
Rider, Thomas, 298.
Ridgway, Thomas, 184.
Riedet, Sleur, 265.
Ripley, Eliphalet, 240.
Rising Sun, 244.
Roach, *see* Roch.
Roads, John, 296.
Roale, Roals, *see* Rolls.
Rob, James, 261, 281, 305.
Robb, *see* Rob.
Roberts, Peter, 131, 141, 197, 249.
Roberts, Thomas, 186, 249.
Robins, Robert, 92, 120.

Robinson, Joseph, 136, 137, 223, 237, 238, 239.
Robinson, Samuel, 201.
Roch, Francis, 143, 226.
Roe, Zebulon, 171.
Rogers, Daniel Denison, 74, 109.
Rogers, Harris, 246.
Rogers, John, 215.
Rogers, Samuel, 255, 292, 309.
Rogers, William, 154.
Role, *see* Rolls.
Rolland, Edward, 90, 290, 326.
Rolls, Jeremiah, 107, 296.
Romney, 271.
Ropes, David, 104, 118, 189, 190, 209, 325, 326.
Ropes, Nathaniel, 104, 128, 263.
Ropes, William, 330.
Rophey, Christopher, 215.
Rose, Alexander, 98, 142.
Ross, Alexander, 224.
Ross, David, 139.
Ross, William, 66, 265.
Rounsevell, Levi, 154.
Rowe, John, 109, 235.
Rowe, Joseph, 125, 322, 327.
Rowel, ——, 265.
Rowlland, *see* Rolland.
Royal African, 83.
Royal George, 151.
Rumney, Edward, 184.
Russell, Chambers, 95, 122, 126, 140, 156, 240, 297.
Russell, Joseph, 97, 112, 113, 163, 197, 213, 315.
Russell, Thomas, 95, 100, 122, 126, 140, 156, 183, 197, 200, 240, 297, 298.
Russell, William, 78, 206, 300.
Rust, Francis, 68, 275.
Rust, Henry, 85, 116, 117, 141, 173, 196, 302, 303, 309, 317.
Rust, John, 309.
Rye, David, 85.
Ryley, Philip, jr., 198.

Safford, Thomas, 310.
St. Barbe, Wyatt, 292.
St. John, 93.
St. Mary's Packet, 93.
St. Pry, Bt. Merlino de, *see* Pry.
Salem Packet, 223.
Sally, 212.
Salter, Joseph, 252.
Salter, Richard, 106.
Saltonstall, Nathaniel, 246.
Sampson, Stephen, 72.
Sampson, *see* Samson.
Samson, Simeon, 43, 171, 179, 185.
Sanders, Daniel, 309.

Sanders, *see* Saunders.
Sands, Edward, 115.
Sanford, William, 292.
Sargeant, *see* Sargent.
Sargent, Andrew, 326.
Sargent, Daniel, 100, 112, 125, 129, 137, 206, 228, 258, 266, 270, 279, 280, 299, 300, 324.
Sargent, Daniel, jr., 121, 252.
Sargent, Epes, 319, 321.
Sargent, Ezra, 168.
Sargent, Fitzwilliam, 153.
Sargent, John Osborne, 157.
Sargent, Nathaniel, 112, 121, 129, 311, 324.
Sargent, Paul Dudley, 44, 86, 88, 106, 120, 185, 203, 328.
Sargent, Winthrop, 144, 148, 153, 169, 241, 311, 319, 321.
Saunders, Bradbury, 75, 206.
Saunders, Thomas, 83, 242, 246, 251, 295, 308.
Saunders, ——, 44.
Savage, 139.
Savage, John, 257, 302, 327.
Savage, Samuel Phillips, 45, 254, 255.
Scamman, James, 246.
Scammel, 175, 176.
Scarborough, 19.
Scollay, W., 283.
Scott, George, 271.
Scourge, 223.
Scranton, John, 119.
Scranton, John G., 118, 119, 175, 176.
Sears, Francis, 78.
Sears, Isaac, 74, 75, 80, 105, 154, 174, 186, 187, 191, 217, 240, 244, 271, 273, 315.
Sears, Stephen, 83.
Sears, Zachariah, 257, 306.
Sears & Smith, 174.
Sellars, *see* Sellers.
Sellers, James, 135, 162.
Sellers, John, 162, 181.
Selman, John, 135, 145, 227, 307.
Sergeant, *see* Sargent.
Seveir, Joseph, 239, 249.
Sewall, David, 245.
Sewall, Samuel, 259.
Seymour, William, 113, 163.
Shannon, Frederick, 217.
Shark, 158.
Sharp, Samuel, 268.
Shattuck, John, 77, 78, 79, 98, 129, 143, 144, 146, 147, 170, 171, 195, 226, 248, 261, 269, 324.
Shattuck, William, 77, 78, 79, 87, 98, 100, 127, 128, 129, 142, 143, 144, 146, 147, 168, 169, 170, 171, 181, 185, 208, 211, 226, 233, 248, 261, 269, 324.

Shaw, Francis, 213, 214, 227.
Shaw, Francis, jr., 164.
Shaw, Nathaniel, 152, 227.
Shaw, Thomas, 246.
Sheaffe, Maria, 317.
Sheaffe, Sarah, 317.
Shed, Joseph, 294.
Shepard, Jeremiah, 116, 173.
Shepardson, Zebadiah, 256.
Shillaber, Robert, 160, 161.
Shillaber, William, 165, 264.
Shirley, William, 169.
Shiverick, Nathaniel, 145, 311.
Shoemaker, Anthony, 72.
Shorey, Peter, 87.
Shougherd, George, 97.
Shuker, Thomas, 281.
Sibble, *see* Sibely.
Sibely, Littlefield, 288.
Sibley, Henry, 297.
Sigourney, Charles, 65, 66, 229, 230, 254.
Sigourney, Daniel, 312.
Sigourney, Elisha, 184, 330.
Silsbee, Nathaniel, 94, 111, 117, 118, 126, 183, 204, 205, 247, 263, 266, 293, 302.
Silsby, *see* Silsbee.
Silver, Peter, 316.
Simmons, Isaiah, 72, 145, 146, 245, 263.
Simmons, Thomas, 100, 141, 158, 208, 212, 231, 250.
Simonds, John, 264.
Simonds, *see* Symonds.
Simpkins, ——, 132.
Simpson, Thomas, 69.
Sinclair, Daniel, 196.
Sir William Erskine, 299.
Sisson, Lavis, 164.
Skillin, Joseph, 80, 186, 187, 191, 240, 273.
Skimmer, John, 135, 203.
Skinner, ——, 144.
Skinner, Henry, 75.
Skinner, Samuel, 184.
Slater, Benjamin, 90.
Sloan, John Prout, 146.
Smiley, Alexander, 188.
Smith, Barzillai, 81, 120.
Smith, Benjamin, 205.
Smith, Caleb, 303.
Smith, Daniel, 65, 98, 252.
Smith, David, 107, 226, 233.
Smith, David, jr., 205.
Smith, Edward, 191.
Smith, Edward, jr., 172, 191.
Smith, Elias, 50, 51, 52, 84, 105, 223, 277, 287, 322, 323.
Smith, Elisha, 80.

INDEX 353

Smith, Emanuel, 86.
Smith, George, 177.
Smith, Hugh, 228.
Smith, Isaac, 81, 124, 140, 298, 313.
Smith, John, 100, 201.
Smith, Johnson, 234.
Smith, Nathan, 19.
Smith, Paschal Nelson, 74, 80, 97, 105, 154, 186, 187, 191, 197, 217, 240, 271, 273.
Smith, Phineas, 166.
Smith, Richard, 141.
Smith, Samuel, 187, 195, 197, 219.
Smith, Sargent, 234, 266.
Smith, Silas, 85, 106, 108, 116, 132, 175, 228, 242.
Smith, Thomas, 141, 144.
Smith, William, 126, 222, 252, 260, 310, 311.
Smithers, Michael, 275.
Snoden, Thomas, 89, 163.
Snow, Isaac, 70.
Sobries, Isaac, *see* Somes.
Sohier, Edward, 312.
Somes, Isaac, 125, 129, 137, 280, 296, 310, 324.
Somes, John, 72, 324.
Somes, Nehemiah, 65, 229, 243, 258, 280, 293, 300, 324, 327.
Southard, James, 163.
Souther, Daniel, 218.
Southward, George, 195.
Sparling, Thomas, 157.
Spear, David, 84, 306.
Spear, David, jr., 198.
Spear, Josiah, 311.
Speedwell, 76, 139.
Spencer, ———, 187.
Spink, Nathan, jr., 100.
Spooner, Ephraim, 71.
Spooner, Shubael, 256.
Spooner, W., 31, 48.
Spooner, Walter, 264, 320, 331.
Spooner, William, 255, 317.
Sprague, Joseph, 116, 117, 267, 268, 306, 311.
Springer, William, 182, 224.
Stacy, Samuel, 278.
Stanley, Edward, 271, 275.
Stanton, John, 297.
Stanwood, Joseph, 280.
Stanwood, Solomon, 292.
Staples, Enoch, 328.
Starkweather, Ephraim, 145.
Stephens, *see* Stevens.
Stephenson, Lusitanus, 211.
Stevens, John, 87, 248, 274, 283, 326.
Stevens, Paul, 212.
Stevens, Samuel, 291.

Stevens, Thomas, 79, 87, 130, 259, 314.
Stevenson, David, 280.
Stevenson, Robert, 79, 127, 195.
Steward, William, 84, 91, 94, 149, 203, 211.
Stewart, *see* Steward.
Stickney, John, 248, 322, 323.
Stiles, Richard, 307.
Stillman, George, 257.
Stimpson, Samuel, 229.
Stimpson, William, 313.
Stockbridge, Charles, 168.
Stocker, Ebenezer, 82, 216, 243, 305.
Stockman, Joseph, 321, 322.
Stoddard, Israel, 245.
Stoddard, Noah, 70, 91, 139, 175, 275.
Stone, Joshua, 134, 251, 259, 282.
Stone, Nathan, 83.
Stone, Robert, 78, 94, 95, 249, 276, 284.
Stone, ———, 271.
Stonehouse, Robert, 178, 202, 218.
Storey, *see* Story.
Storey, Alexander, 247.
Story, Nehemiah, 210.
Story, Seth, 111.
Story, ———, 23.
Stratton, John, 228.
Strout, Joseph, 107.
Studson, Thomas, 312.
Sturgis, Russell, 326.
Stutson, *see* Studson.
Success, 245.
Sullivan, Daniel, 285.
Sullivan, James, 23, 25, 33.
Sumner, Benjamin, jr., 236.
Sumner, Seth, 330.
Surprise, 134.
Swallow, 175.
Swan, Henry, 131.
Swan, James, 71, 86, 89, 91, 105, 115, 117, 121, 215, 217, 265, 315.
Swasey, Joseph, 113, 195.
Swasey, Nathaniel, 66.
Swasey, Samuel, 293.
Swazey, Joseph, 113.
Swett, Samuel, jr., 194.
Swift, 58.
Symonds, Jonathan, 162, 225.

Tappan, Abraham, 319.
Tappan, Caleb, 67, 93, 228.
Tappan, Daniel, 67, 93.
Tappan, Joseph, 67, 93.
Tapping, *see* Tappan.
Tarbell, Kiah, 288.
Tartar, 73, 74, 220.
Tatagay, Antoine, 137.
Taylor, Eldad, 31, 48.
Taylor, John, 48, 164, 246.

INDEX

Taylor, William, 170.
Thatcher, Peleg, 298.
Thayer, Ebenezer I., 123.
Thayer, Francis, 297.
Thayer, Nathaniel, 247, 274, 275, 278.
Thomas, 69.
Thomas, John, 71.
Thomas, Joseph, 297.
Thomas, Seth, 216, 220.
Thomas, Thomas, 99, 186, 216, 249, 279, 314, 329.
Thomas, William, 242.
Thompson, Benjamin, 327.
Thompson, Charles, 83, 227.
Thompson, Cornelius, 76, 95, 157, 171.
Thompson, James, 115, 203, 204, 234, 265.
Thompson, Samuel, 23, 70.
Thompson, Thomas, 325.
Thomson, Charles, 39.
Thorn, 166, 193.
Thorndike, Andrew, 274.
Thorndike, Henry, 320.
Thorndike, Israel, 237, 248, 258, 276, 277, 307, 320.
Thorndike, Joseph, 320.
Thorndike, Larkin, 68, 84, 259.
Thorndike, ——, 271.
Thrash, Philip, 270, 291.
Thwing, James, jr., 74.
Thwing, Nathaniel, 170, 174.
Thwing, Samuel, 323, 324.
Tibbets, Henry, 123.
Tibbets, John, 175.
Tidcomb, *see* Titcomb.
Tilden, David, 129.
Tilden, Joseph, 98, 144, 169, 170, 202.
Tilden, N., 202.
Tileston, James, 235, 291, 318.
Tileston, John, 326.
Tileston, Onesiphorus, 218.
Tileston, Thomas, 297.
Tiley, John, 229.
Tilley, *see* Tiley.
Tillotson, Thomas, 70.
Titcomb, Benaiah, 197, 259, 279, 289.
Titcomb, Enoch, jr., 177.
Titcomb, Enoch, 3rd, 168, 329.
Titcomb, Jonathan, 197, 249.
Titcomb, Moses, 262.
Titcomb, William, 216, 279.
Titcomb, William, 3rd, 99, 127.
Tittle, John, 93, 216, 273, 295.
Toppan, John, 67.
Towell, Mark, 98.
Townsend, David, 152, 159, 236, 323.
Townsend, Isaac, 65, 71, 72, 159, 236, 297.
Tracey, *see* Tracy.

Tracy, 46.
Tracy, Jackson, 100.
Tracy, James, 48, 174, 261, 329, 330.
Tracy, John, 48, 80, 96, 99, 127, 157, 168, 170, 179, 181, 182, 219, 232, 301, 304, 329.
Tracy, Nathaniel, 48, 99, 111, 140, 142, 168, 170, 219, 235, 291, 301, 315, 325, 329.
Tracy, Robert, 174, 329.
Tracy, Thomas, 141, 246.
Trask, Joseph, 263.
Trask, *see* Trusk.
Treadwell, Jacob, 125.
Trevett, Samuel, 76, 139, 296.
Trevett, Samuel, R. 139.
Tripp, Joseph, 67, 124.
Trivett, *see* Trevett.
True American, 138.
Trumbull, John, 72, 99.
Trusk, Samuel, 89, 91, 180, 256.
Truxtun, Thomas, 217.
Tuck, Sewall, 68.
Tuck, William, 79, 207, 210.
Tucker, John, 137, 164, 166, 264, 283, 304.
Tucker, Jonathan, 68, 69, 220, 266, 280, 298.
Tucker, Samuel, 128, 135, 162, 166, 170, 210, 301.
Tuckerman, Edward, 108.
Tufts, John, 228.
Tukesbury, *see* Tuksbery.
Tuksbery, Jonathan, 134.
Turner, Elisha, 131, 222, 262.
Turner, John, 90.
Turner, John, jr., 137.
Turner, Luther, 156, 171, 262, 272.
Turner, William, 65.
Tyger, 85.
Tyler, Edward, 298.
Tyler, John, 162.
Tyler, Pepperrell, 283.
Tyley, William, 153.

Unity, 19, 213, 330.
Urann, Joseph, 213, 256.

Vallison, John, 169.
Van Landt, Jacobus, 148.
Vans, William, 313.
Velson, *see* Vallison.
Venus, 46.
Vernon, Fortesque, 69.
Vernon, Samuel, 200.
Vernon, William, 15, 315.
Very, Samuel, 207.
Vesey, Joseph, 244.
Vezey, *see* Vesey.

INDEX 355

Vilson, *see* Vallison.
Vincent, Benjamin, 288.
Virginia, 237.
Volante, 19.

Wadsworth, Peleg, 85, 278.
Wait, Aaron, 107, 159, 161, 166, 264, 287, 296, 305, 311.
Wait, John, 70, 145, 159, 175, 184, 193, 194, 207, 251.
Wait, Samuel, 194.
Waite, Waitt, *see* Wait.
Waldron, Jonathan, 73.
Wales, Ebenezer, 107, 262.
Walker, John, jr., 155, 315.
Walker, Spencer, 217, 315.
Wall, S., 279.
Wallace, 74.
Ward, Artemas, 115.
Ward, Benjamin, jr., 117.
Ward, Joshua, 196, 225, 284.
Ward, Joshua, jr., 116, 225, 231, 311.
Ward, Miles, 94, 108, 141.
Ward, Miles, jr., 91.
Ward, Nathan, 308.
Ward, Richard (governor), 10, 12.
Ward, Richard, 209, 224.
Ward, Samuel, 94, 107, 116, 117, 141, 152, 181, 239, 276, 306, 309, 311.
Wardell, Nathaniel, 323, 324.
Warner, Daniel, 157.
Warner, Elias, 86, 235.
Warren, 56.
Warren, Benjamin, 161, 206, 223, 260.
Warren, James, 17, 18, 20, 31, 43, 50, 70, 185, 294, 328.
Warren, James, jr., 255.
Warren, Joseph, 20, 21.
Washington, 50.
Washington, George, 23, 24, 60; his fleet, 135, 162, 163, 166, 202, 212, 319, 321.
Wasson, *see* Watson.
Water, *see* Waters.
Waters, Daniel, 141, 144, 152, 202, 203, 299.
Waters, Joseph, 267.
Waters, Josiah, 246.
Waters, Samuel, 88, 101, 116, 148, 169, 243.
Watson, Jonathan, 209.
Watson, William, 71, 328.
Watson & Spooner, 70, 179.
Weatherell, 200.
Webb, Jonathan, 101, 116, 170, 211.
Webb, Nathaniel Coit, 71, 116, 126, 172, 247, 261.
Webb, Oliver, 247.
Webb, Samuel, 152, 205.

Webb, Stephen, 88, 102, 126, 184, 247, 258, 274.
Webber, Benjamin, 270.
Webber, Ignatius, 101, 102, 218.
Webster, Luke, 189.
Weeden, Richard, 200.
Welch, H., 147.
Welch, *see* Welsh.
Welden, Weldon, *see* Whellen.
Welles, Arnold, 220.
Wellman, Adams, 167, 191, 268.
Wells, Joseph, 216.
Wells, Peter, 81, 194, 234.
Welsh, John, 133.
Welsh, John, jr., 133, 305.
Wesson, *see* Weston.
West, Benjamin, 212.
West, George, jr., 81.
West, Jabez, 103.
West, Joseph, 83.
West, Nathaniel, 84, 189, 191, 195, 215, 232, 302.
West, Samuel, 122, 258.
West, Thomas, 194, 303.
West, William, 87, 242, 303.
West, William, jr., 117, 293, 303.
Weston, Timothy, 92, 154, 292.
Wetmore, William, 54.
Whalers, 39.
Wheaton, Joseph, 204.
Wheelwright, John, 228, 253, 274, 290.
Whellen, Richard, 46, 155, 264, 315.
Wheston, *see* Weston.
Whetcomb, John, 31, 48.
Whipple, Abraham, 170.
Whipple, William, 15, 16.
Whitcomb, Whitecomb, *see* Whetcomb.
White, B., 31, 48, 291.
White, Ebenezer, 162, 307.
White, Henry, 77, 249.
White, Isaac, 158, 290.
White, Joseph, 94, 95, 133, 260, 276, 284, 298.
White, Samuel, 79, 80, 97, 127, 147, 155, 163, 181, 221, 222, 253, 274, 304, 308, 315.
White, T., 209.
White, William, 86, 200, 292, 310.
White, ——, 85.
Whiting, Joseph, 133.
Whitmarsh, Rufus, 288.
Whittemore, Retier, 298.
Whittemore, Samuel, 160, 201, 282.
Whittridge, Livermore, 120, 130, 277.
Wier, William, 188.
Wigglesworth, Edward, 140, 294.
Wigglesworth, John, 58, 294.
Wilcomb, *see* Willcomb.
Wilder, Caleb, 213.

Wilds, Jacob, 160, 171.
Willard, Ephraim, 288.
Willcomb, William, 277.
William, 222.
Williams, David, 54.
Williams, George, 72, 84, 88, 150, 172, 173, 207, 225, 259, 290.
Williams, George, jr., 77, 124, 152, 248, 302, 303.
Williams, Henry, 152, 167, 169, 181, 218, 239, 271, 303.
Williams, Henry, jr., 236.
Williams, Jacob, 65, 288.
Williams, John, 214.
Williams, John Foster, 57, 65, 66, 69, 137, 146, 185, 245, 255, 326.
Williams, Joseph, 184, 193.
Williams, Lemuel, 236, 269, 285, 319, 320.
Williams, Robert, 73.
Williams, Samuel, 87, 240, 242, 243, 248, 274, 308.
Williams, William, 117, 156, 174, 317.
Williamson, John, 76.
Willis, Benjamin, 81.
Willis, Jonathan, 307.
Willson, John, 78, 142, 146, 152, 269.
Wilson, Alexander, 121.
Wilson, *see* Wilson.
Wing, ——, 189.
Wing, Joshua, 214, 277.
Winship, Ebenezer, 100, 302.
Winslow, Joshua, 179.
Winthrop, John, 59, 100, 120, 137, 148, 262.
Winthrop, John, jr., 310, 319, 321.

Winthrop, William, 319.
Witham, *see* Withem.
Withem, Benjamin, 219.
Wolcott, Simon, 246.
Wood, Matthew, 105.
Woodberry, Asa, 295.
Woodberry, Herbert, 128, 175, 180.
Woodberry, William, *see* Woodbury.
Woodbridge, Joshua, 117.
Woodbury, William, 179, 218, 228.
Woodbury, William, jr., 228.
Woodman, Jonathan, 160, 161.
Woods, John, 54.
Woodward, Ebenezer, 256, 270, 316, 327.
Woodwell, Gideon, jr., 299.
Workman, Mark, 57.
Wormell, Benjamin, 317.
Wormsted, Robert, 180.
Wyer, Joseph, 130.
Wyer, William, 288.

Yancey, James, 69.
Yankee Hero, 48.
Yates, *see* Yeates.
Yearman, Reuben, 201.
Yeates, George I., 82.
Yeomans, *see* Yearman.
York, 260.
Young, Daniel, 207.
Young, John, 87, 105, 316.
Young, Levi, 269.
Young, William, 206, 302.

Zechariah Baily, 328.